Introduction to Cyber Politics and Policy

Introduction to Cyber Politics and Policy

Mary Manjikian

Regent University

Los Angeles | London | New Delhi
Singapore | Washington DC | Melbourne

FOR INFORMATION:

SAGE Publications, Inc.
2455 Teller Road
Thousand Oaks, California 91320
E-mail: order@sagepub.com

SAGE Publications Ltd.
1 Oliver's Yard
55 City Road
London, EC1Y 1SP
United Kingdom

SAGE Publications India Pvt. Ltd.
B 1/I 1 Mohan Cooperative Industrial Area
Mathura Road, New Delhi 110 044
India

SAGE Publications Asia-Pacific Pte. Ltd.
18 Cross Street #10-10/11/12
China Square Central
Singapore 048423

Printed in the United States of America

Library of Congress Cataloging-in-Publication Data

Names: Manjikian, Mary, author.

Title: Introduction to cyber politics and policy / Mary Manjikian, Regent University.

Description: First edition. | Thousand Oaks, Calif.: Sage, CQ Press, [2021] |

Identifiers: LCCN 2019043952 | ISBN 9781544359304 (paperback) | ISBN 9781544359311 (epub) | ISBN 9781544359328 (epub) | ISBN 9781544359335 (ebook)

Subjects: LCSH: Internet—Government policy. | Internet—Political aspects. | Internet governance.

Classification: LCC TK5105.875.I57 M36724 2021 | DDC 384.3—dc23 LC record available at https://lccn.loc.gov/2019043952

This book is printed on acid-free paper.

Acquisitions Editor: Anna Villarruel
Editorial Assistant: Lauren Younker
Production Editor: Kelle Clarke
Copy Editor: Pam Schroeder
Typesetter: Hurix Digital
Proofreader: Barbara Coster
Indexer: Amy Murphy
Cover Designer: Anupama Krishnan
Marketing Manager: Erica DeLuca

20 21 22 23 24 10 9 8 7 6 5 4 3 2 1

BRIEF CONTENTS

DETAILED CONTENTS

PREFACE

This project began as perhaps many projects do—with self-interest. I have been teaching cyber politics for approximately ten years, but every semester, I struggle with finding materials to offer to students in these courses. Social science students lack the technology background that many peer-reviewed journal articles assume they have. Before students can begin to theorize about internet governance, then, they first need to understand the specifics of how the internet is organized in terms of hardware and software and what the implications of engineering decisions are. In contrast, students with a technology background often understand these concrete specifications but are less well versed in the basic political science and international relations concepts that could help them make sense of the policy questions arising from this technology.

And because the field of cyber politics is so interdisciplinary today—including theories drawn from law, international relations, technology studies, and economics, to name a few fields—the need for a solid text that can bridge these gaps is self-evident. I hope that this text might inspire academics who haven't taught a course yet on cyber politics to feel confident in doing so and that it might prove particularly useful for those who are taking a risk in doing so, venturing a bit farther afield from their primary research interests.

ORGANIZATION OF THE BOOK

The textbook begins in **Chapter 1** with a brief overview history of the internet from its libertarian founding to its more regulated organization today. It contains a timeline of significant events in that evolution.

Chapter 2 introduces concepts drawn from the field of technology studies and paints a big picture through encouraging students to think about what a technology is for and the ways in which power is enacted in making decisions about what tools do. In this chapter, and throughout the text, students are encouraged to ask themselves: In what ways is what I am seeing in this situation unique, and in what ways can I identify other technology issues in which similar issues have arisen? International relations students may identify parallels, for example, between the military industrial complex and the cyber industrial complex and between support for conventional weapons bans and support for cyberweapons bans.

Chapters 3 through 5 present the three major international relations paradigms: realism, liberal internationalism, and constructivism. They lay out key concepts and explain how they relate to events in cyberspace.

Chapter 6 presents the two major approaches to internet governance: multistakeholderism and cyber sovereignty. The pros and cons of each approach are presented, and the realist, liberal internationalist, and constructivist paradigms are applied in evaluating them.

Chapter 7 looks specifically at the phenomena of cybercrime, again utilizing the language of uniqueness to think through how cybercrime is both different and the same as other types of criminal activities.

Chapters 8 and 9 invite the student to think specifically about the new types of actors that we can identify in the cyber environment. **Chapter 8** considers the rise of international corporations like Google and Twitter as players within the international environment and asks whether this necessarily leads to a waning of state power. It also looks at the responsibilities that such actors have taken on in the international environment and asks whether technology actors are sufficient to do the jobs that they have reluctantly inherited in this new environment. **Chapter 9** considers how states and corporations can cooperate in the provision of cybersecurity through the phenomenon of public-private partnerships.

Chapter 10 focuses specifically on ethical issues in the international cyber environment. It allows students to think about issues from equity and justice and to trust in the online environment. Here again, students should begin to identify parallels among other types of issues in international relations (such as the issue of corporate social responsibility and the responsibilities of corporations to practice stewardship in the international system) and those that exist in cyberspace.

Chapter 11 looks specifically at military issues in cyberspace, drawing parallels between cyber deterrence and nuclear deterrence, and delves into issues of arms races and arms control in the cyber environment.

We conclude in **Chapter 12** with a look into the future. We consider the politics of artificial intelligence, drones, and big data analytics to thinking about the opportunities and risks associated with tomorrow's internet.

FEATURES AND PEDAGOGY

I have included three types of additional materials in the text:

- **Building a Bridge** insets are short essays from 500 to 2,000 words that attempt to provide a rudimentary background in technology aspects. They cover basic issues, such as definitions of the types of cyberweapons currently available, to more complex issues, such as introducing quantum computing to a layperson.

- **Critical Issues** are an attempt to keep things current in an ever-changing field. They help bring contemporary developments, from China's development of a Digital Silk Road to Russia's strategies of information warfare, to life—including both academic background and descriptions of the events themselves. Several also apply the three international relations paradigms to the issues at hand.

- **People and Places** provide information about major individuals and events which have been significant in the development of the internet. In many instances, students will have heard and recognize a name but may be unsure about exactly who this person is or their significance. People and Places helps to fill in these gaps.

These materials are organized so that they can be used in a variety of different sequences. Each chapter is self-contained, as are the insets.

ONE LAST THING

Because this field changes so rapidly, I wish to apologize in advance for any situations in which the materials already feel dated or inaccurate. Readers are invited to visit my website at **marymanjikian.com,** where additional teaching materials (including PowerPoints) are available for this textbook and my textbook on cybersecurity ethics. Updated case studies will be provided on that website, and there is also an area for academics teaching with these textbooks to share ideas, insights, and encouragement with one another.

ABOUT THE AUTHOR

Dr. **Mary Manjikian** is an associate dean and professor at Regent University. A former US foreign service officer serving in the Netherlands, Russia, and Bulgaria, Manjikian was a Fulbright Scholar at the Institute for Advanced Study at Durham University. She has also served as an external research Associate at the US Army War College. She is the author of *Apocalypse and Post-Politics: The Romance of the End* (Lexington Books, 2012); *Threat Talk: Comparing the Discourse of Internet Addiction and User Protection in China and the United States* (Ashgate: 2012); *The Securitization of Property Squatting in Western Europe* (Routledge, 2013), and *Cybersecurity Ethics: An Introduction* (Routledge, 2017). Her work has also appeared in *International Studies Quarterly*, *International Feminist Journal of Politics*, *International Journal of Intelligence and Counterintelligence*, and *Intelligence and National Security*.

ACKNOWLEDGMENTS

I wish to thank the reviewers, those listed below and others, who read the first draft of this textbook. They made several valuable suggestions about materials to include, materials to remove, and alternate views that should be presented and considered. Any errors that exist are of course mine.

Ranette H. Halverson, Midwestern State University

Christopher Whyte, Virginia Commonwealth University

Adell Brooks, Hinds Community College

LeMesha Craft, Coastal Carolina University

Ronald W. Vardy, University of Houston

Alexis Wichowski, Columbia University

Holly Dragoo, Georgia Tech Research Institute

1

Learning Objectives

At the end of this chapter, students will be able to do the following:

- Describe the four major phases associated with the growth of the internet and the major technological, political, and economic developments associated with each.

- Define significant terms associated with the growth of the internet.

- Describe in basic terms the technical specifications of the internet as well as what unique facets distinguish it from other technologies.

- Describe key political issues that have arisen in the growth of the internet, and describe the ways in which technological closure has begun to occur regarding these issues.

WHAT IS THE INTERNET?

Students today probably do not remember a time when they lacked internet access. If you were born in the 1990s, you have always been able to send e-mail, access a library of resources online, and purchase products from all over the world. However, the internet has only been available to the average user since 1994, when commercial **internet service providers (ISPs)** like America Online began attracting large numbers of civilian subscribers. Thus, it is astounding to contemplate how this technology has reshaped our world and our relations with others in the space of fewer than thirty years.

Today, an estimated 4.2 billion of the world's 7 billion people have internet access. The **penetration rate** describes what percent of the population of a nation has personal access to at least some of the internet's features, either at work or in a private home. Penetration rates globally range from a high of 95 percent of North America's citizens to a low of 36 percent of Africa's citizens. If we look at the universe of internet users globally, we see that nearly half (48 percent) are in Asia, whereas 16 percent are in Europe, another 16 percent are in Latin America, and 10 percent are in Latin America. Eight percent are in North America, whereas nearly 4 percent are in the Middle East.[1]

The internet has been credited with launching or aiding in revolutions in the former Soviet Union and the Middle East. It has changed how people shop, how they search for information about whom to vote for, as well as changing how people are educated and trained worldwide. International recruitment sites like LinkedIn have aided in the recruitment and hiring of international staff, whereas e-government initiatives have changed how citizens think about and interact with their elected leaders and government agencies providing services.

E-commerce (or online shopping) has created a global marketplace. In 2016, more than half of all global internet users purchased something online, and nearly 70 percent of millennials prefer shopping online rather than in a store. In the United States, nearly half of all e-commerce sales are through Amazon.com, and this company is considered a driving force in e-commerce globally.[2] Through the wonders of e-commerce, users are as likely to buy something directly from a store in China as they are to purchase it locally.

The internet's expansion also introduced new players to the international system. Today, Amazon's annual revenue dwarfs the GNP of many smaller nations, and there are more citizens of Facebook than there are in any nation. Thus, as nations and international bodies like the United Nations and the International Telecommunications Union work to shape the rules and structures of the internet, players like Google and Twitter are gaining a seat at the table. Policies made on these platforms—such as a decision to disallow hate speech or to police news for factual content—have international effects. Thus, companies like Google are now shaping international policies in the ways that nations and international bodies did in the past.

The internet's growth also created new legal issues. From the beginning of widespread civilian use of the internet (beginning in the mid-1990s, with the e-commerce revolution taking place in 1998), states have been concerned about issues of jurisdiction in the online environment. Consider a situation in which, for example, a Canadian citizen logs onto the internet in his country, visits a Scandinavian website hosting child pornography, and downloads an image of a Brazilian child, uploaded by a user in Asia. Even if viewing, downloading, and storing child pornography is a crime in Canada, where exactly did the crime occur? Whose laws determine how the crime should be treated? Should the Canadian user be extradited to Brazil? Asia? Or Scandinavia?

In this chapter, we summarize the issues that the internet's creation poses for scholars of politics and international relations. We begin by describing the internet's origins. Initially, the internet had an "American flavor" due to the fact that American research dollars funded the internet and the fact that it developed in America. In the early years, American policy makers argued that this technology was associated with ideas like freedom of information or globalization due to the circumstances of its birth. However, today many nations dispute this contention, arguing that it is possible for Russia to have a "Russian internet," which looks quite different from the technology as it was envisioned by its American designers. Over time, the internet has become more divided, polarized, and militarized. This brief history illustrates how it got there.

A Brief History of the Internet

Barely fifty years have passed since the internet was first envisioned until today, when the internet is nearly ubiquitous—present in nearly every household in America, utilized daily by millions of people, and where at least two generations of individuals cannot even envision or conceptualize of life before the internet.

Major Policy Issues on the Internet

However, despite its ubiquity, there are still significant points of contention regarding the use and regulation of this technology today. First, some analysts see the internet as an arena for peace and cooperation, whereas others see it as a place defined by conflict. Analysts also disagree about particular aspects of cyber warfare—including what it is, how states that carry out acts of cyber warfare should be sanctioned or censored, and how acts of cyber warfare relate to the principles of traditional warfare.

Next, analysts disagree about the phenomenon of regulation. As the internet has developed, analysts disagree regarding which activities should be permitted or banned in cyberspace. Should states allow people to engage in online pornography, the deploying of viruses and cyberweapons, and identity theft? And if they do not wish to have individual citizens or groups engaged in such activities, how should they regulate the internet so that they do not occur? Indeed, the speed at which internet connectivity technologies have developed has outpaced the ability of governments to regulate them, both nationally and internationally. As a result, although states may think that they control many aspects of this "information revolution" and its ramifications, they do not actually do so. Harvard political scientist Karl Deutsch once said that "history sometimes amounts to nothing more than a litany of unintended consequences and unforeseen side effects."[3] That is, technological changes appear to be leading the policy component as well as the development of legal and other regulatory schemes.

Next, analysts and policy makers disagree about governance of the internet. They ask: Who should make rules regarding regulations on the internet—professionals, states, or the international community? Is the internet best understood as a self-regulating entity that has emerged and grown, developing its organic structures of governance through the work of those technology experts who have created it? Or is it more similar to a territory that has been discovered and that then needs to be colonized by preexisting states and integrated into their real territory? That is, should we think about Russian cyberspace and Chinese cyberspace, or should we instead think of the internet as a borderless territory and community—like outer space or the ocean—which belongs to all nations and therefore needs to be administered by an international body like the United Nations? Who governs the internet? Does anyone?

Analysts and policy makers also disagree about norms and values in cyberspace. They ask: Where do the norms governing behavior on the internet come from, and whose values should they reflect? Do these norms somehow emerge naturally or "organically" from the internet itself, or are they norms, values, and laws that already exist and apply to other areas of national and international politics that are then transferred onto the cyber realm and applied there? Should activities like censorship and surveillance (which might be forbidden or intensely regulated in a state's real territory) be allowed to occur on the internet? And if not, how might they be prevented?

Analysts and policy makers also disagree about sovereignty or control in the internet environment. They ask: How should we conceptualize the "territory" of the internet? Does it belong to a particular state (i.e., "the Russian internet"), or should it be considered some form of global commons? Is it a "world apart" from normal nation-state relations, or does it interact with existing forms of power like political, social, and economic power?

The Four Phases of the Internet's History

In this chapter, we divide the internet's history into four phases: The first, the infancy of the internet, spans the period from 1963, when plans for what was then known as ARPAnet were first articulated, until 1984, when it was released from US military control to become a utility open to civilians as well. The second phase of the growth of the internet can be termed the period of growth and early regulation. This phase proceeded from 1984 until 2000. Phase three is the securitization of cyberspace and growth of internet governance (2001–2012); Phase four is the era of surveillance and big data (2013–present).

This division is somewhat arbitrary. However, these four phases provide a useful shorthand for becoming familiar with the significant events that have occurred in cyberspace in the last 50 years. They also enable us to see a particular arc in the story of cyberspace from its infancy, in which both users and developers had almost a utopian vision of how the technology could develop as well as how it might change and shape our international system. We see how individuals have become more cynical or more realistic—aware of the harms that internet access can provide as well as good. States became aware of risks and security threats, the possibility of online crime, and the rise of events like online terrorist recruitment. The growth of hacking and computer viruses showed that cyberspace is not a world apart but rather a portal into the real world. Real-world harms can occur through the use of cyberspace.

Each era saw the emergence of new challenges and debates and had ramifications for social, political, and economic systems both nationally and internationally. The initial phase saw the creation of technological advances. Most of those who created this new technology had expertise that was technological rather than legal or policy related. They were interested in seeing how preexisting technological capabilities might be extended over the globe. Many individuals who were active in this initial phase now note that they were not completely aware of what they were creating or the role that it might come to play in today's world.

In the second phase, from 1984 until 2000, we see the development of e-commerce and the extension of the internet from a domain that mostly belonged to technology experts, scholars, and military officials to the larger civilian community. People could access a home internet, where they could read the news, participate in chat groups, and communicate globally. During this period, states began to struggle with questions like who could collect sales tax on goods sold across state borders in the United States and who should regulate international commerce on the internet. People also became aware of the internet's dark side as the US Congress convened hearings on issues like internet pornography. During this phase, the United States also sought to extend the internet reach internationally, optimistically believing that the spread of this technology would enhance values like freedom of information and democratic governance.

In the third phase, from 2001 until 2012, states became aware of the national security issues associated with this technology. In the aftermath of the 9/11 terrorist attacks, the US security community became aware that the internet could be used by extremist groups for organizing, recruiting members, and sharing information. This era also saw significant advances in the development of strategic military doctrines for "fighting in cyberspace." The US military described cyberspace as a "domain" that needed to be protected from enemies and intruders. Policy makers no longer viewed the internet as a utopian world apart that bears no connection to physical space. Analysts stopped describing cyberspace as a "global village," instead describing it as a "virtual battlefield" or arena for conflict.

The final phase that we examine in this work is the era of big data and surveillance, which dates from 2012 until the present day. In the aftermath of Edward Snowden's revelations to the international community about how US intelligence officials were collecting user data in cyberspace, individuals and states became aware of privacy issues and surveillance concerns. People became aware that they had a digital identity intimately connected to their real identity in the physical world. They became aware that users were the product that was being sold in cyberspace. Their data was being collected, analyzed, and packaged to monitor their activities, predict their actions, and manipulate their opinions and even their votes.

Later in this volume, we consider the advent of technologies like artificial intelligence to make some predictions about what the internet of the future might look like and how we as users might interact with it.

THE INFANCY OF THE INTERNET (1963–1984)

In this section, we focus on the theme of **path dependence** (defined later in this section) and built-in constraints. The internet was developed by skilled technical people who had their own values and visions of the internet. However, it was also primarily supported by US government funds, in particular, those of the military. As a result, later critics faulted the internet for being "too American" or "too Western." They stated that the United States has played an outsized role in the conduct and regulation of internet issues today due to advantages that accrued by virtue of the internet's birth in the United States. Some nations have also voiced suspicion of the internet being introduced into their societies, even going so far as to label it a "CIA plot." Here we consider how a technology's history (or birth) affects where it can go in the future and how it is understood by those inside and outside of that birth.

In a recent memoir, retired Air Force General Michael Hayden describes how the internet was built.[4] Today's internet began as a project of the Advanced Research Projects Association (ARPA, which is now the Defense Advanced Research Projects Association, or DARPA), and it was created to solve a particular technical problem. Department of Defense contractors working in the field of computer science wanted to be able to share data with one another simply and efficiently. Before the establishment of network connectivity, all of the contractors could communicate directly with the Department of Defense but not with one another. In attempting to solve this real technical problem, the Department of Defense did not have a grand vision of what would eventually emerge. They never foresaw a time when the technology would be international, available to civilians, or used as a **backbone** for the conduct of activities like e-commerce, e-governance, the dissemination of news, or the posting of social media. Even the internet's planners were unaware of how societies might someday depend on the internet for the provision of essential goods and services, nor were they aware of the vulnerabilities and threats that might surface as the result of this creation.

Hayden argues that people had no idea what they had built.[5] His story thus echoes an earlier story about the first public demonstration of the telegraph in 1844. In demonstrating his invention to members of Congress, Samuel F. B. Morse sent a message from the US Capitol in Washington, DC, to Baltimore, Maryland. The text that he chose was taken from the Bible's Old Testament (Numbers 23:23), and its text was "What hath God Wrought?"[6] Like Hayden, Morse did not foresee precisely what this technology was, how it might be used, or its eventual impact.

The technology that allowed the development of computer connectivity into a network that became the internet was something called packet switching. Packet switching refers to a process by which data is transferred over a connection (first a telephone line using a modem and later a cable). Your data (an e-mail message, a photo, or a social media post) is broken down into many parts, packaged into units called packets, and then transferred over a network that uses network switches or routers. Your data is then reassembled into its final form when it reaches its destination. Your packets are labeled with information that identifies the sender and the recipient address. The network then decides how best (most efficiently and quickly) to send your data on its journey.[7]

Funding for the creation of the network that would carry this data was allocated in 1966, and it was taken from the US Defense Department's Ballistic Missile Defense Program. Today some foreign nations, including US adversaries, believe that because the internet was born in the United States as part of a US Defense Department research project, other nations should be wary of allowing this technology into their societies because the US government may have created this technology to achieve aggressive or belligerent purposes, including destabilizing the governments of adversarial regimes. Most pointedly, in the wake of the 2013 revelations that the US National Security Agency had engaged in spying on US citizens and allies through the internet, Russia's President Vladimir Putin suggested that the US Central Intelligence Agency invented the internet for this purpose.[8]

Work on the internet connectivity project began in 1969, and the original ARPAnet connected four research facilities—the University of California at Los Angeles (UCLA), the Stanford Research Institute, the University of California at Santa Barbara, and the University of Utah School of Computing. In the 1970s, the ARPAnet was extended to the East Coast of the United States, and in 1973 it continued to grow, reaching research facilities in Norway and London. Ray Tomlinson invented the technology allowing us to send e-mails in 1971.

At the same time that the internet's physical structure was being created, advances in computing were creating much of the framework for the types of services and features that we see in today's internet. For example, in 1978, scientists developed **asymmetric cryptography** and the Rivest, Shamir, and Adelman (RSA) algorithm. This invention allowed for secure communications between two parties even over a nonsecure communications channel through the use of mathematically linked virtual keys. (This development allowed for the later growth of online services like e-commerce or filling out forms with confidential information.)

In 1984, those parts of ARPAnet that connected military facilities were broken off to create MILNET, which later became the internal Department of Defense "intranet," known as NIPRnet. In 1990, the US military turned over the bulk of the internet to civilian control. The US National Science Foundation, a government agency, became the entity administering the civilian internet that we know and utilize today.

The Birth of Hacking

Although most Americans were not even aware of the internet in the 1970s and 1980s (although many began to join the World Wide Web in the early 1990s), US government officials were already learning about threats that computer connectivity could pose. The well-known computer hacker Kevin Mitnick first achieved notoriety as a high school student in 1979, when he was able to gain unauthorized access to a California company, the Digital Equipment System. Mitnick, who served time in prison for his hacking exploits, and who went on to become an international security consultant, advising others in how to secure their computer systems and information against hacking, utilized **social engineering**, or the use of non-technical means to gain the trust of users in order to "con" them into providing confidential information[9] to convince individuals to provide him with information that allowed him to hack into computer systems without authorization.

And in 1984, the Hollywood movie *War Games* featured the story of a high school student who nearly caused a nuclear war when he accidentally hacked into the computer system belonging to NORAD, the North American Aerospace Defense Command.[10] In his memoir, General Hayden describes how US President Ronald Reagan saw the movie and immediately summoned members of the US defense community to ask them: "How much of this movie is real? Could this happen here?" As a result of events like hacking, the US government began to recognize the security threats posed by computer connectivity, eventually passing the Computer Security Act of 1987 and creating the first Computer Emergency Response Team (CERT) in 1988, to collect information and respond to unauthorized breaches of government computers.

At the same time, as computer connectivity began to grow, the US government moved to implement national standards in areas such as modem speeds so that data could be transferred quickly and efficiently among military and government facilities and academic institutions in the United States and throughout the world.

Path Dependence and the First-Mover Advantage

But why does it matter that internet connectivity technology developed in the United States and not elsewhere, and why does it matter that the initial blueprint for the technology as well as the initial impetus to govern and regulate this technology began in the United States and not elsewhere?

The term *path dependence* describes how technologies can become locked into specific pathways as the result of earlier design decisions. Those who develop new technologies may not even be aware of how their decisions at the early, developmental stages of technology affect how technology develops and looks many years later. In considering how path dependence affected the internet's development, we should remember that the United States was and is a wealthy nation with a highly developed technology sector. As a result, American telephone lines and later cables were quickly able to carry large amounts of data, and few people (except those in highly rural areas) were excluded from participation in the civilian internet as a result of technological shortcomings in America's existing communications infrastructure. In developing this technology, then, American defense planners were not cognizant or responsive to the needs of those in developing countries who might later find it difficult to connect to the internet due to communications shortfalls in their own. Also, America is a capitalist country with a highly developed private sector. As a result, the American internet grew from the bottom up as commercial ISPs were formed and as they engaged in competition with one another to sign up subscribers to the civilian internet. (In contrast, in many developing nations, the internet has grown in a top-down matter at the behest and with the support of government programs, often featuring a newly formed Ministry of Information Technology, which has taken responsibility for this effort.)

Finally, because the internet grew up in the United States, it made sense for American policy makers to set up and fund the structures, like the Internet Society and the Internet Corporation for Assigned Names and Numbers (ICANN), which sought to resolve standards and connectivity issues as the internet proliferated in the United States and later internationally.

The internet thus came to have an "American flavor," as it was associated with and arguably carried the values of the nation in which it was born. In addition, America and American corporations enjoyed what is known as a first-mover advantage. Those actors who are first movers or early entrants to a field can accrue certain advantages over time, from having a significant market share of consumers to helping set the parameters within which later entrants must operate. Here we can think of the first online bookstore, Amazon.com. Being the first in that market allowed Amazon to condition customers to expect to receive goods in a rapid timeframe. Other bookstores that did not have that same capacity eventually went bankrupt. Amazon also captured a significant share of the market for e-readers, and later entrants to that field struggled to keep up and compete with the Amazon Kindle. Thus, Amazon came to control the e-reader market as the result of its first-mover advantage.[11] Many of the corporations that operate in cyberspace today—including Google, Microsoft, eBay, and Amazon—were able to develop a strong brand and significant market share in the United States, which later translated into economic and political power on a global scale.

Today, some nations are critical of America's position as a hegemon or leading player in cyberspace, suggesting that the extension of internet technology to their nations represents a new form of American colonialism. Here it is important to remember the circumstances under which internet technology grew, and how these circumstances both limited and shaped the internet's reach and policies today. Figure 1.1 provides a brief summary of the key events associated with these circumstances.

Timeline: Key Milestones in the History of the Internet

Figure 1.1 The Birth of the Internet	
1865	International Telecommunication Union is established to regulate international dimensions of the telegraph industry.
1938	British science fiction author H. G. Wells conceptualizes of a "world brain" in a series of essays about a global encyclopedia.
1962	Central Intelligence Agency Analyst Orrin Clotworthy publishes an internal article that describes a possible future in which computers are linked and ubiquitous.

(Continued)

Figure 1.1 (Continued)

1963	Computer scientist J.C.R. Licklider produces memoranda discussing the concept of the "intergalactic computer network." That same year, Licklider comes to head a project at ARPA.
1966	The US Advanced Research Projects Agency funds a project to create a computer network to allow ARPA researchers to share information among themselves quickly.
1969	Work begins on ARPAnet, connecting four West Coast universities: UCLA, Stanford Research Institute, UC Santa Barbara, and University of Utah school of computing.
1970	ARPAnet reaches the US East Coast, at Cambridge, Massachusetts.
1971	Ray Tomlinson creates e-mail technology.
1973	Satellite links allow the US system to connect internationally to Norway and London.
1977	US Senator Abraham Ribicoff introduces the first federal legislation aimed at protecting federal computer systems and defining "computer crimes."
1978	Development of asymmetric cryptography and the RSA algorithm occurs.
1983	Teenage hackers break into several government computers, including a nonclassified computer at the Los Alamos National Lab in New Mexico.
1984	The parts of ARPAnet that connect military facilities are broken off to create MILNET (ARPAnet was decommissioned in 1990).
1985	The US National Science Foundation is tasked with creating a similar network for academic institutions (NSFNET). This later becomes the backbone of the civilian internet.
1986	The Internet Engineering Task Force (IETF) is formed by the US government to develop and promote internet standards.
1987	President Ronald Reagan signs the Computer Security Act of 1987, an attempt to protect federal agency computers.
1988	The first Computer Emergency Response Team (CERT) is created in the United States and serves as a reporting center for computer crimes and security problems.
1989	First large-scale computer "worm" infects 600,000 government computers.

THE PERIOD OF GROWTH AND EARLY REGULATION (1984–2000)

The second phase of the internet's growth is the period of growth and early regulation. This phase proceeded from 1984 until 2000. During this period, the internet spread internationally as well as penetrating households—moving beyond purely academic or think tank usage. In this period, ISPs began providing content, like news, to users—and early types of e-commerce were created. People spoke of "surfing the web" or traveling on the information superhighway.

A key development at this time was segmentation or fragmentation of the internet. Users were able to customize what they saw on the internet, subscribing to feeds about topics of interest and interacting with others with similar interests and values. MIT Media Lab Founder Nicholas Negroponte utilized the phrase "the daily me" to describe how internet users could choose which news stories and new sources they saw. At this point, customization was considered to be a positive development with no downside. Later on, however, this ability to customize one's internet experience would be blamed for the growth of political extremism and polarization, particularly in the United States.

This period also saw the advent of internet censorship and filtering, mostly on a state level. States became aware of how nongovernmental organizations could use the internet to organize and communicate with supporters. They saw how such an organization could prove detrimental to state control of the media and civil society. Thus, 1998 saw the beginning of a large-scale network of state surveillance of citizen activism on the web in Russia, implemented by the Russian FSB, the post-soviet version of the KGB. The law establishing this network of surveillance was officially accepted in Russia in July 2000.[12]

Globalization and the Internet

In considering the internet's development, we can consider the idea of technological momentum. New technologies do not develop in isolation but rather as part of a "large technical system" with both technology and social or human components. These social components may influence how technology develops.[13] In considering the internet's growth, we must consider the political and social climate in which the technology grew. Beginning in the mid-1980s, policy makers and academics began to describe a phenomenon called globalization. As Drezner writes, "Globalization is the cluster of technological, economic and political innovations that have drastically reduced the barriers to economic, political and cultural exchange."[14] As new technological innovations—such as cable television and 24-hour news—made it easier for citizens across the world to receive information about events that were happening, many analysts believed that these events would empower citizens and make it harder for authoritarian regimes to enforce top-down control of their citizens.

Also, with the collapse of the Soviet Union in 1989 and breakup of the Commonwealth of Independent States (CIS) in 1991, and the creation of fifteen new independent countries, Western politicians were euphoric. Policy makers and political analysts stated that the United States had won the Cold War against the Soviet Union and that the Soviet Union's abandonment of the economic system of communism showed that capitalism and democracy were triumphing everywhere in the world. An influential essay called "The End of History and the Last Man" by former Reagan policy adviser Francis Fukuyama, published in 1989,[15] reflected this worldview. Fukuyama argued that modernization was an inevitable process and that forces like globalization were allowing ideas to move through the world faster than ever before, leading to the breakdown of government control and the ultimate triumph of democracy, capitalism, and globalized institutions. As a result, he and others believed that modernizing nations would end up looking similar. To participate in a global economy, for example, states would find themselves adopting policies regarding monetary policy, regulation of utilities, and citizen rights that would look similar. They would also create similar structures and processes. The term *convergence* was utilized to describe this tendency.[16]

Thus, the internet's growth was embedded in larger forces like globalization, free trade, and the growth of markets, and it, therefore, seemed logical to envision the internet as an agent of that change. Both President Clinton and Vice President Al Gore spoke about the internet as a vehicle for the export of American ideas like democracy, freedom of information, and freedom of assembly. Policy makers utilized utopian language in describing how the internet could further equality between citizens and nations and further education internationally through making content available to users. They envisioned the United States playing a leading role in extending the internet's reach globally by offering both foreign aid and opportunities provided by US commercial interests internationally. The Clinton administration described how the US government would work to bridge what was termed the "digital divide," which separated developing nations from the promise of prosperity and education through a lack of the infrastructure necessary to connect to the internet.[17]

Internet enthusiasts spoke of a "global village" (or global commons) in which citizens might identify not as members of a particular nation but rather as "netizens" who lived in a world of cyberspace, which was borderless and open to all.[18] Also, at this time, most analysts believed that the norms that would exist in cyberspace would be a product of the internet environment, which was still mainly conceptualized as space apart from traditional governments and government structures. That is, people did not believe or speak of "Russian cyberspace" or "American cyberspace." They did not conceptualize of a future in which states might clash in cyberspace, and they did not imagine that states might someday differ about which nation's norms should prevail in cyberspace.

However, at the same time, states like Russia and China, which had been characterized by tight state control over media, struggled with how to grapple with new phenomena like multiple independent news sources. Although Russia, in particular, had passed a media law in 1991 that allowed for the growth and creation of new, privately owned media outlets—rather than exclusively state-owned and -run enterprises—the transition to a free press had not been problem free. Independent media outlets were credited with playing a vital role in the opposition to a KGB-backed coup attempt in 1991, which led ultimately to the downfall of the Commonwealth of Independent States (CIS) and the extension of freedom to fifteen former Soviet republics. As we will see, throughout the 2000s, Russia began implementing a series of laws aimed at regulating independent activity in the "blogosphere," including extending existing legislation regarding libel and slander of individuals and public officials to blogs and other forms of informal media. In addition, they implemented measures requiring bloggers to register as journalists and eventually began banning certain types of online media outlets on the grounds that they were contributing to the growth of extremism (both nationalist and Islamic terrorism) in Russia.[19]

Thus, we can see how the internet came to be seen not as a "world apart" but rather an extension of existing physical spaces such as the media space, the legal space, and the economic space within nations. Despite its utopian origins, over time, it came to be regarded not as a separate, independently existing entity that did not conform to the constraints of the real physical world but rather as a technology that was born into a real-world environment and that would need to conform to that environment.

The Advent of E-Commerce

One way in which the real, physical world and the virtual world of the internet came together was through the advent of e-commerce, or online shopping. Many consumers today can scarcely imagine a world without e-commerce. However, when e-commerce arrived on the scene in the late 1990s, online shopping was a fundamentally new idea. It was seen as fraught with risk. Consumers struggled with whether to trust new online entities that did not have an established reputation and with which they did not have an existing history. How could they feel that their money was safe, that they would receive the goods that they had ordered, and that they would be satisfied with these goods? Initially, many consumers were uncomfortable giving personal information to a website and also did not trust websites to recommend additional products or services to them.[20] Consumers were uniformly confused by new business models like eBay, which required them to bid on goods or services and to carry out calculations that asked them to consider the probability that they would win an auction versus the risk that they might lose through being outbid. Also, particularly in the developing world, people often had a preexisting cultural inclination to wish to do business with vendors whom they knew personally or to physically feel and hold the garments or goods that they wished to purchase.

In addition, early e-consumers encountered technological barriers to engaging in online shopping such as low bandwidth, which caused pages to load slowly, or for connections to be dropped during the transaction. At the same time, e-commerce's advent required changes in many other industries—from banking systems that needed to develop protocols for tracking and clearing large numbers of international payments to legal regimes for carrying out online dispute resolution (ODR) between consumers and companies when there was a disagreement about goods or services rendered or ordered online.[21]

Like many novel or emerging technologies, e-commerce spawned many social, political, and economic developments, many of which were unexpected. Developing e-commerce could often require less of an initial investment than starting a bricks-and-mortar business did because one did not need to buy real estate for a showroom or a warehouse, as goods could often be shipped straight from the factory to a consumer. Therefore, economists expected that it would lead to a democratization of the marketplace and the growth of entrepreneurship. However, the first-mover advantage allowed for extremely large-scale marketplaces like Amazon.com in the West and Alibaba in China to capture a significant market share through investing in and patenting online commerce technologies.[22] In addition, online commerce has in some cases helped cause the bankruptcies of established physical store chains in the United States and abroad. Also, even now, many sectors of the world—including the Caribbean and Africa—are missing out on the economic advantages of participation in e-commerce due to lagging physical infrastructure and a less-educated workforce.[23]

Finally, whereas in the West, e-commerce giants like Amazon seem to function mainly as independent retailers who are free of government regulations and ties, Alibaba, the largest e-retailer in China, actually works quite closely with the Chinese government, sharing information about consumers and purchasers and benefitting from advantages conferred to it in the economic sector.[24] Today, some analysts argue that the international and regional competition for market shares between e-commerce giants such as Amazon and Alibaba is a new type of warfare, leading to increased conflicts in the international system rather than a new era of international prosperity as first promised.[25]

The Growth of Off-Shoring

As this period drew to a close, it was clear that despite its promise as a great leveler, enabling people throughout the world to have free access to information and education, the internet was not achieving this goal. Instead, critics argued that internet technology increased inequalities in the international system. They pointed to corporate decisions in the United States and Western Europe to outsource jobs to remote contractors located in developing countries. Beginning in the late 1990s, American and international corporations like Texas Instruments, American Express, and British Airways established remote call centers that took orders, made reservations, or provided technical support.[26] These centers, which utilized modern telephone and internet technology, were in nations like India, where wages were low and worker protection laws were less developed. "Off-shoring" refers to moving an activity that is produced within the firm to another country so that the activity is still associated with the same firm but performed elsewhere.[27] Trade economists argued that corporations' ability to outsource functions over the internet made it harder for skilled workers unions in the United States and Western Europe to bargain for favorable terms. If they asked for too much, the company might decide to take its business elsewhere. Simultaneously, internet technology was making individual workers more productive, which sometimes meant that corporations decided to employ fewer workers. The internet, combined with globalization, was thus implicated in the creation of precariousness or economic instability.[28] Workers worried that they could be replaced by someone in another country and eventually by a machine.

Critics also pointed to the wealth amassed by entrepreneurs like Mark Zuckerberg, the founder of Facebook, and Bill Gates, Microsoft's founder. Critics began to worry about the outsized influence of a global super-elite, especially because these individuals had not been elected and were not accountable to citizens in the same way that elected officials were. Critics worried about agreements being made between individual entrepreneurs and global states that might have repercussions on a state's citizens in ways that were opaque and lacked transparency. Comparisons were made to the so-called robber barons, the early 19th-century capitalists like Commodore Vanderbilt, Andrew Carnegie, and J. Paul Getty, who amassed fortunes while building American infrastructure in industries like railroads and manufacturing.[29]

Privatization of the Internet

Much of the initial impetus for the internet's creation came through the aegis of the US government. However, in this second period of the internet's growth, many actors participating in creating the internet's infrastructure—both the physical infrastructure or hardware as well as the internal infrastructure, known as software or code—were private corporations. That is, individual enterpreneurs created the internet's "architecture," from the search engines that allowed users to find what they wanted on the web to the sites, like eBay and Amazon, that they most wanted to reach.

One of the significant advances at this time was the advent of commercial search engines, like Google, WebCrawler, and Yahoo.[30] Prior to their invention, users could only find pages online if they knew the **Internet Protocol (IP) address** or the specific web address of another user. But in 1996, Stanford students Larry Page and Sergei Brin created a proprietary algorithm to rank and classify web pages. In essence, a page that was linked to many other pages was seen as being more important and credible than one that few other pages linked to. Therefore, the page with the highest number of links to it would appear first in a Google search. This algorithm, known as Google, was available to internet users for free but was financed through the sale of advertising links that appeared alongside web searches. Also, companies could pay to be a sponsored link, which would appear in a list of links called up through a web search.[31]

By 2006, policy makers were raising concerns about how private companies like Google could influence what information users saw. In countries like Germany, where strict laws adopted after the rise of the Nazi Party in World War Two prevent citizens from accessing neo-Nazi propaganda and neo-Nazi websites, policy makers expressed concern about materials that their citizens could access through a Google search. Google began asking questions internally about what its corporate foreign policy should be. Should this company always seek to cooperate with the national leadership in nations where citizens used Google? Alternatively, should Google, as a company that began in America, always seek to promote freedom of speech?[32] How should Google work with leaders in nations like China, which might ask it to engage in repression of information that Chinese citizens might desire? And as Google began to develop services like Google Earth, which allowed citizens to see satellite maps of locations across the world, it began to ask questions about its responsibility as a purveyor of security. Should Google comply with US requests not to offer users printouts that might reveal the location of military bases or troops?

In the aftermath of the US 2016 presidential elections, policy makers are still grappling with these complicated issues. Congresspeople in the United States have asked whether Google is complicit in suppressing some types of news and information, and promoting other types of news and information, in instances where doing so may have altered people's votes. Similarly, some critics of private information sites like GreatSchools.net have asked if this platform's activity—making information about factors like the demographic and racial makeup of public schools in the United States—is actually leading to increased educational segregation as some families are using the information available to choose schools that are highly racially segregated. Is it enough for a website to claim that it is merely making a service available that people desire, or should it be required to buy into a particular set of social values? Should it have to consider possible social or political effects of providing a service?[33]

Finally, states are becoming aware of how they and their citizens are vulnerable when states do not control many aspects of today's internet directly themselves—from the building of physical infrastructure like data pipelines (the vast majority of which are privately owned and administered)[34] to the creation of the software that runs critical infrastructure like roads, bridges, and hospital records. To what degree should states be allowed to dictate how private businesses run their activities, mainly when these activities may have implications for a state's national security?

As noted earlier, rapid technological changes throughout the internet era mean that often legislation and the ability to regulate technologies lags far behind the technology itself. These issues, which first came to the forefront in the late 1990s, are far from resolved, even today.

The Issue of Intellectual Property

Just as the media community was struggling to integrate new types of media—like newsfeeds and blogs—into its space, and economists were struggling with how to regulate and structure e-commerce, the legal community was asking questions about how intellectual property rights apply online. Whereas initial internet "evangelists" believed that everything that resided on the internet should be free to everyone, over time, the notion that online information could be owned and sold gained strength. Media organizations erected paywalls and asked users to pay for content access, and groups like the World Intellectual Property Organization

(WIPO) worked to implement penalties for individuals and corporations trafficking online in stolen intellectual property—including movies, music, and books and manuscripts. WIPO defines **intellectual property** as "creations of the mind, such as inventions; literary and artistic works; designs; and symbols, names, and images used in commerce."

However, the fact that files (including music, videos, and text) could easily and quickly be cloned or copied online meant that it was increasingly difficult for the creators of intellectual property to retain the rights to their materials. The advent of peer-to-peer network sharing programs like Napster also made it easier for users to directly connect to one another to share copies of materials off of their home computers without having to pass the material first through a central site or clearinghouse. As a result, in 1993, the US government set up the Working Group on Intellectual Property Rights to examine how legal concepts regarding the ownership of ideas and creative materials might be applied to what they termed the *National Information Infrastructure*.[35]

By the late 1990s, the US government had labeled groups like Napster (1999–2001) as "online pirates," and US legal cases sought to shut down websites that served as clearinghouses for **online piracy** activities. The Digital Millennium Copyright Law went into force in 1998. However, even today, not all nations agree with the notion that intellectual property laws apply the same way in cyberspace as they do in real-life situations, and not all agree that there should be a universal norm against pirating intellectual property online. Instead, they argue, the prohibition on network file sharing is an American norm that US and Western corporations are attempting to impose on those in the developing world who may struggle to afford access to Western publications and ideas.

States also began to realize that their national economies were becoming dependent on the internet, with the 2000 G8 Charter on the Global Information Society describing information technology as "a vital engine of growth for the world economy." The internet thus was no longer regarded as an organic entity that could be said to be "evolving" but instead began to be perceived as an extension of a state's physical space and economic, social, and military power in the world.

Policy makers and investors also worried that governments around the world, including in the United States, might not be sufficiently well equipped to face new developing problems in cyberspace, including the growth of viruses and hacking attacks on US institutions and businesses. At the same time, they became aware of the existence of cybercrimes, including the transmission of online pornography. The United States began considering how to regulate the "dark side" of the internet with the first hearings on online pornography called by the US Congress in 1995.[36] The Clinton administration also released the first American cybersecurity strategy in 2000.

And as the internet became more international in character, with Beijing joining the internet revolution and companies like eBay and Amazon becoming established, states within the international system also began to consider whether international structures were necessary to regulate and administer the internet. Here, the United States, as the founder and creator of the internet, still played a leading role. The United States worked to establish the Internet Corporation for Assigned Names and Numbers (ICANN), which although housed in the United States and funded through the Department of Commerce, in fact managed the allocation of IP addresses for organizations and individuals throughout the world, with the monetary proceedings going to the United States.

As this period of growth and change in cyberspace draws to a close, the first issues of economic volatility in cyberspace are becoming apparent. Although investors were initially euphoric about the growth of e-commerce, by 2000, it became apparent that many internet stocks were overvalued. Many internet companies went bankrupt, leading to the end of the dot-com "bubble" in 2000.

Figure 1.2 Timeline Phase Two: The Growth of Internet Threat and Regulation	
1990	Englishman Tim Berners-Lee merges hypertext and browsing functionality to create the World Wide Web.
1992	**Governance:** • Fifty countries have access to the internet. • Ebone, a European version of the NSFNET backbone in the United States, is established. • The Internet Society (ISOC) is founded, with a mission to "assure the open development, evolution, and use of the Internet for the benefit of all people throughout the world."
1993	Mosaic, an early web browser, is created.
1994	**Cybersecurity:** • The first commercial spam is released. **E-Commerce:** • Amazon is established as an online retailer. • Beijing connects to the internet through CAINONET.
1995	**Governance:** • NSFNET ceases to be administered by the National Science Foundation and instead becomes public property. **Regulation:** • US Congress proposes first legislation aimed at regulating online pornography, including protecting children. **E-Commerce and Social Media:** • The first use of a webcam occurs. • The first item is sold on eBay. • MIT Media Lab Founder Nicholas Negroponte uses the term *the daily me* to refer to internet users' ability to receive a daily customized newsfeed tailored to their interests. **Cybersecurity:** • The US military begins to develop and define the doctrine of asymmetric warfare.

1996	**Cybersecurity:**
	• The first act of online piracy occurs (Metallica's "Until it Sleeps" becomes the first pirated track).
	• Russia opens an internet café.

1997	**Social Media:**
	The first social media (sixdegrees.com) is developed.
	The term *weblog* (later shortened to *blog*) is first used.

1998	**Censorship:**
	• China begins creating a filtering, censorship, and surveillance system that comes to be known as the Great Firewall of China.
	• Russia's internal security bureau begins establishing the system of state-run surveillance of electronic media and communications known as "SORM."
	Governance:
	• ICANN, a California nonprofit, is established by the US government and awarded a contract by the US Department of Commerce to administer the distribution of domain names in cyberspace.
	• Digital Millennium Copyright Law passes in the United States.
	Cybersecurity:
	• President Clinton introduces Presidential Directive PDD63, which defines and calls attention to critical infrastructure protection.
	• The US government creates the federal Computer Incident Response Center (US-CERT).

1999	**Intellectual Property:**
	• Napster's peer-to-peer network for file sharing begins.
	Cybersecurity:
	• Nations undertake extensive preparations for the Y2K problem, which does not materialize.
	E-Commerce:
	• China implements regulations limiting foreign capital investment in internet startups in China.

2000	**Cybersecurity:**
	• First large-scale cyberattacks: Distributed Denial of Service (DDOS) Attacks and "I love you" virus hit sites in the United States and internationally.
	• The US Congress convenes hearings about cybersecurity, and President Clinton releases cybersecurity strategy.
	Governance:
	• The United States joins Council of European Cybercrime Treaty to address issues of prosecution and jurisdiction for cybercrime and cybervandalism.
	• G8 adopts Charter on the Global Information Society.
	E-Commerce:
	• Dotcom "bubble" bursts with NASDAQ falling from 5,000 to 2,000 points.

THE SECURITIZATION AND MILITARIZATION OF CYBERSPACE (2000–2012)

The next period in the internet's development, the securitization of cyberspace and the growth of internet governance, spans the period from 2000 until 2012. At this time, states began speaking of the internet as part of their "strategic terrain," utilizing military language to speak about cyberspace as an extension of their physical territory. Policy makers also began to speak of **cyber sovereignty** as policy makers and citizens increasingly accepted the notion that one could identify American, Russian, and Chinese cyberspace. States also became aware of the vulnerabilities created by their dependence on the internet—for commerce, social communications, and military use. At the same time, international organizations developed for the governance of the internet, resolving physical problems that occurred such as how new undersea cables would be built and regulated and how new domain names would be assigned.

Following the terrorist attacks on the United States on September 11, 2001, a sea change took place as a sense of pessimism and threat replaced much of the initial optimism generated by the internet's founders. Many of the internet's features that had initially been seen as exciting and liberating—such as the ability to browse and participate in forums anonymously, the speed at which activities occur on the internet, and the ability of the internet to carry large volumes of information of uncertain or unregulated quality—came instead to be seen as liabilities.

The term **attribution problem** describes the difficulties that cybersecurity experts encountered in trying to trace a virus, worm, or another weapon back to its source to identify and sanction the hacker. The advent in 2002 of TOR, a program that internet users could use to disguise their IP addresses so that they could not be traced back to their online postings, activities, or attacks, made attribution particularly tricky.

Policy makers became aware of the many different types of vulnerabilities that our national computer systems were threatened by. Although some of these attacks might be regarded as merely nuisance behavior, the most significant attacks have the ability to paralyze a nation's economy (through an attack on the financial sector); to destabilize the transportation routes that carry food to, from, and throughout a nation; or to cause mass casualties through scenarios like an attack on a hospital that forbids health-care workers to access patient data or an attack on a nuclear power facility or hydroelectric dam. A report by the White House Council of Economic Advisors notes that currently, cyberattacks cost the US economy somewhere between $57 billion to $109 billion a year.[37] At the same time, they can have grave political effects—leading to rising tensions among the United States, its adversaries, and even its allies.

Beginning with 9/11, policy makers in the United States and abroad became aware of the ways in which national security systems were vulnerable as well as the fact that so many activities of daily life were now dependent upon access to internet technology. The term *critical infrastructure* was coined to describe all of the structures within a nation—from the agricultural sector to the carrying out of water and sewage treatment, to the running of transportation activities within a nation—that citizens count on their nation to be able to provide. And as a result of the 9/11 attacks on the United States, the first domestic attacks within the United States since Pearl Harbor in 1941, planners and policy makers within the United States became aware of the possibility that an adversary could attack these structures, causing significant damage and perhaps widespread panic to the US political, social, and economic systems.

Thus, the result of widespread internet penetration into nearly every sector of society has resulted in a paradoxical situation: Using the internet has made nations more productive and prosperous and has created unprecedented opportunities for citizens. However, the fact that individuals, corporations, and nations now rely on the internet to support so many of their traditional functions—from law enforcement to education to military warfighting—means that everyone now is also dependent on this technology and therefore vulnerable if the technology should fail.

On an international level, the international system is more connected than ever before—which presents opportunities for increased cooperation between states—but our international system is also more vulnerable due to the numbers of ways in which states and their people now interact both formally and informally. In many Western nations, citizens have become concerned about what they perceived as an increased amount of government surveillance of their activities and their lives. They have begun to voice concerns about actions by groups like the US National Security Agency, which has been capturing and storing data about American citizens' web searches, posts, and online activities to combat terrorism both domestically and abroad. In recent years, we have also seen data breaches in which state-sponsored and individual hackers have electronically broken into the computers of corporations and government agencies, releasing people's highly personal data. In some instances, individuals have been merely embarrassed, whereas in other instances they have experienced long-range financial hardships as the result of identity thefts. Law enforcement agencies have expressed concern about the so-called dark web, untraceable and hidden computer networks that harbor "black markets" where users can purchase illegal drugs and computer viruses or even order a service like an assassination. National security professionals also warn that unsavory groups, from white nationalists to neo-Nazis to terrorists, have mastered techniques to utilize the internet to organize, share information, and even recruit new members.

Militarizing the Internet

Particularly in the wake of the 9/11 terrorist attacks on the United States, optimism about the potential of the internet to create world peace and prosperity was replaced by cynicism. As Manjikian writes, "Realists saw cyberspace as an avenue for insurgents and national enemies to penetrate 'real' defenses. It was viewed as a frontier or border requiring protection and vigilance in contrast to less strategically significant territory."[38]

Indeed, as early as 1976, Boeing engineer Thomas Rona coined the phrase **information warfare,** describing the dangers presented by US dependency on information capabilities as a function of logistics in the conduct of warfare.[39] In this view, the internet is merely an extension of existing spaces (like radio waves) in which military personnel carry out electronic warfare or information warfare. The term *electronic warfare* refers here to all types of warfare in which one side targets the communications systems of others—whether by jamming or scrambling a radio signal, attempting to disrupt a satellite signal, or targeting another side's ability to access or utilize the internet.[40]

Moreover, in the aftermath of terrorist attacks against the United States, counterterrorism experts began to consider how terrorist groups could utilize the internet to organize or to launch attacks against developed nations that were increasingly coming to rely on the internet to carry out activities in political, economic, and social spheres. In 2004, terrorist analyst Marc Sageman described how terrorist groups were using cyberspace to organize. In his work, he described the internet not as space that was free and common to all but rather as a "failed space" that was anarchic, lacking a strong governing and regulating structure that was necessary to keep it safe.[41] The phrase "Cyber Pearl Harbor" was coined to describe the possibility that the United States might be taken by surprise by a large-scale cyberattack for which they were unprepared.

Features previously associated with media democratization and the growth of civil society—such as the ability of anyone to access the internet and to set up a site where they could share their ideas and perspectives cheaply and easily—began to be viewed differently. Analysts warned of asymmetric warfare, referring to "engagement between dissimilar forces" characterized often by the use of unconventional means of warfare and the element of surprise. US military doctrine experts had begun speaking of asymmetric warfare as early as 1995.[42] However, in the aftermath of 9/11, the concept received renewed attention, with particular reference to how terrorists engaged in asymmetric warfare, including through the use of social media and internet communications.

The US Cyber Command

As a result, beginning in 2002, the US military began to develop doctrines or plans for fighting in cyberspace, including the conduct of offensive cyber operations. Here, it was acknowledged that each state should seek "information dominance," or the ability to be the most technologically advanced, with the best ability to understand the cyberspace environment and to respond quickly to events occurring there. In 2006, the US government took the first steps toward the establishment of the US Cyber Command, which would be tasked explicitly with defending the "cyber domain."

The newest command, USCYBERCOM, was established in 2009. Its mission is to defend the Department of Defense's information networks (sometimes referred to as the DODIN) and to carry out both offensive (active) and defensive (passive) cyber operations. It also sets policies regarding US cyberspace strategy and has legal experts who work to reconcile existing legal understandings (including International Humanitarian Law and the Law of Armed Conflict) with the specific issues that may arise in an online environment. Finally, it plans for the creation of new cyberweapons and works to integrate cyberweapons policies with defense policies in other areas, including the use and deployment of conventional forces. USCYBERCOM is headquartered at Ft. Meade, Maryland, adjacent to the US National Security Agency.

Figure 1.3	Timeline Phase Three: Securitization of Cyberspace and the Growth of Internet Governance
2001	• President George Bush creates President's Critical Infrastructure Protection Board, to develop a national cybersecurity strategy. • First White House cybersecurity adviser is appointed. • Phrase "Cyber Pearl Harbor" is first used. • Internet Telecommunication Union proposes to United Nations the first World Summit on the Information Society (to be held in 2003 and 2005). • The Shanghai Cooperation Organization, a Eurasian political, economic, and security alliance that includes China, Kazakhstan, Kyrgyzstan, Russia, Tajikistan, and Uzbekistan, is created.
2002	**Cybersecurity and Cybercrime:** • BitTorrent, a tool used for pirating video and other types of media, is created. • President Bush publishes National Security Presidential Directive (NSPD) 16 on offensive cyber operations. **Social Media and E-Commerce:** • Wikipedia, the world's first online encyclopedia, which can be written and edited by anyone, is created. • iTunes is created. **Governance:** • The International Telecommunication Union, now part of the United Nations, proposes holding the first World Summit on the Information Society, leading to summits in 2003 and 2005. • Researcher Tim Wu coins term *net neutrality*. • Google's subsidiary in Hong Kong provides information about online activities by two Chinese political dissidents to the Chinese government.
2003	**Cybersecurity and Cybercrime:** • White House issues its first cybersecurity plan. • The United States houses many cybersecurity functions in the newly created Department of Homeland Security. • The public release of TOR, anonymizing software, occurs.

(Continued)

Figure 1.3 (Continued)

2004	**Social Media:** • Facebook is created. **Cybersecurity and Cybercrime:** • The Budapest Convention on Cybercrime is the first international treaty to address internet and computer crime by harmonizing national laws, improving investigative techniques, and increasing cooperation among nations. Participants include the Council of Europe members as well as observer states Canada, Japan, Philippines, South Africa, and the United States.
2005	**Governance:** • The United Nations of Internet Governance Forum, a dialogue group for stakeholders in internet governance, is created to establish terms and concepts.
2006	**Social Media:** • WikiLeaks is established as an international space for governmental whistle-blowing. • Twitter is created. **Governance:** • The US State Department establishes the Global Internet Freedom Task Force to monitor internet freedom worldwide, to respond to challenges on the internet, and to advance internet freedom through financial and technology support. **Censorship:** • Russia adopts a law that broadens the definition of extremist activity to include criticism of public officials, including in social media or online platforms. • Google establishes Google.cn—a filtered search engine for users in China.
2007	**Cybersecurity:** • Russia conducts international cyberwar against Estonia. • The *US Army and Marine Corps Counterinsurgency Manual* describes cyberspace as a "virtual sanctuary" for terrorists and criminals. **E-Commerce:** • Amazon invents the Kindle e-reader.
2008	**Governance:** • The first cloud computing technology is released. • Representatives from Google, Yahoo, Microsoft, and Cisco are asked to testify before the Senate Committee on the Judiciary. They are accused of helping China's government violate its citizens' human rights. **Cybersecurity:** • Russia conducts international cyberwar against Georgia.

2009	**E-Commerce and Cryptocurrency:**
	• The first Bitcoins are mined.
	Cybersecurity:
	• The US Cyber Command is created as a US military entity charged with conducting offensive and defensive cyber operations.
2010	**Governance:**
	• The first Cyrillic domain is created, ending the monopoly of Latin characters on the internet.
	Cybersecurity:
	• Evidence is uncovered that US intelligence agencies have deployed the Stuxnet virus against Iran to damage its nuclear program.
	• The US government crafts the National Cyber Incident Response Plan.
	Social Media:
	• The Arab Spring begins throughout the Middle East and North Africa. Many analysts credit social media as a driving force behind the events that destabilize and replace governments throughout the region.
2011	**Cybersecurity:**
	• The North Atlantic Treaty Organization (NATO) defines the concept of "hybrid warfare."
2012	**Cybersecurity:**
	• The Shamoon virus wipes out the computer system of Saudi Aramco, a major oil company located in Saudi Arabia. The virus is traced back to Iran.
	Governance:
	• Russian President Putin is reelected and puts into place a blacklist of banned websites in Russia.
	• The International Telecommunication Union facilitates the World Conference on International Telecommunications 2012 (WCIT-12) in Dubai. WCIT-12 is a treaty-level conference to address international telecommunications regulations and international rules for telecommunications, including international tariffs.
	• The US government drafts legislation opposing US participation in the WCIT treaty.

THE ERA OF SURVEILLANCE AND BIG DATA (2008–PRESENT)

In this final phase, we focus on developments from 2013, when the Snowden revelations about National Security Agency spying on the internet became public, until the present day. Some of the major issues that have emerged during this last period include issues of privacy and data sovereignty or data governance. In short, many internet users became aware that they themselves were the product being produced and sold on the internet because each user creates a profile of himself or herself as he or she uploads information, creates information, and searches for information online. In the aftermath of the 2016 US presidential election, citizens also became aware that websites and search engines had begun selling access to that data, including selling targeted ads that only some subsets of users would see based on user characteristics.

During this period, then, many states, including the European Union, took steps in the aftermath of the Snowden revelations to safeguard their citizens' data online. This often meant passing legislation mandating that data produced by European citizens within Europe be housed and stored within Europe and not shared with those outside of Europe without the knowledge and permission of the users themselves.

In considering how citizens themselves had become the product, states and citizens also became aware of the large role that private corporations like Google, Facebook, and WikiLeaks had come to play in politics, both on a national and a global level. Thus, many nations, including the United States, convened congressional and parliamentary hearings aimed at better understanding and regulating the role played by private actors in national and international affairs. During these hearings, observers also became aware that a private person like Mark Zuckerberg, the founder of Facebook, is not as accountable to American citizens as an elected official might be. His actions may be less transparent, and he may not conceptualize his personal role or the role of his corporation in relation to goals like preserving American democracy in the same way that an elected official might.

During this period, pundits and analysts also began asking some variant of the question "Can the internet be saved?" Here, they were asking if those who use the internet could still be said to have a role in steering the internet or weighing in on what this technology should and should not be used for. In 2014, one of the internet's original founders, Tim Berners-Lee, proposed the adoption of a Magna Carta for the internet, echoing earlier rhetoric about a Declaration of Independence for the internet.[43] Although these issues are far from resolved, it is important to consider the events of this last period to understand how we have arrived at the present moment.

At the same time, new technological developments—such as the advent of social media like Facebook and Twitter—were also drawing the world closer together. Here social media is defined as "any electronic medium where users may create, share or view user-generated content which can include videos, photographs, speech or sound."[44] The state began to seem like a porous entity that national governments could not completely control. Analysts pointed to the role that these technologies played in the so-called Arab Spring in 2010 as well as in protests in Iran and Moldova in 2009 and in the United States during the 2009 G-20 summit and Occupy movements.[45] In response to mounting protests, some governments, like the government of Egypt, have ordered cell phone providers in their nations to shut down service so that people can no longer access social media.[46]

However, at this time, analysts were also starting to voice concerns about the ways in which internet media was being used by consumers who were learning to "curate" their own news and information. By the mid-2000s, blogging was a feature of American life, with individuals subscribing to and visiting blogs about issues of importance to them from lifestyles (like dating or having children) to politics and economics. The growth of services like the AdSense advertising platform enabled individuals to make money through selling access to their readers to advertisers who placed ads on their blog platforms.[47] Although consumers appreciated the ability to hone in on the information most important to them, academic Cass Sunstein began voicing concerns about the ways in which individuals now had the ability to "consume only content which aligns with our beliefs."[48] He warned that individuals were now able to "isolate ourselves in ideological and partisan enclaves" in which we were not challenged to understand others' perspectives or indeed to even encounter facts that might conflict with pre-established worldviews. In this way, he argued, online media tended not to change individuals' minds as they learned more about the topic but rather to reinforce their preexisting prejudices and subjective biases that they might bring to their exploration of a topic online. Here, he noted that search engines like Google were implicated in this process through a mechanism by which Google's artificial intelligence programs learned which types of news you liked and then proceeded to show you more of it. In this way, search engines engaged in a type of censorship, shielding readers from ideas that they might find to be harmful or distressing rather than exposing them to a full range of views on a subject.[49]

Political scientists noted a polarization of the American electorate, describing the fact that individuals often did not interact with others who had different ideological views online or that when they did interact, interactions sometimes became hostile or abusive. Political scientists note that the degree of distance between the attitudes of Democratic and Republican voters on a variety of social issues became significantly larger beginning in 2002 or 2003, at the same time that social media and social media segmentation became common among internet users.[50]

The End of American Hegemony?

The sense of animosity that many nations felt toward the United States in particular—due to its behaving as a sort of internet hegemon with a preponderance of power and rule-making ability within the international community—was exacerbated with the revelations by Edward Snowden in 2013. (A hegemon is an actor that exercises a preponderance of power within a system, with the result that this actor acts as a leader, influencing other actors as well as the structure of the system itself.)[51]

Edward Snowden, an American computer scientist working on contracts with the US National Security Agency and the US Central Intelligence Agency, became aware that in the aftermath of 9/11, the US government had begun engaging in large-scale surveillance and data collection. In particular, these agencies were utilizing computer programs that allowed them to scan and store users' e-mails as well as information about the people and organizations with which they were interacting in cyberspace. The National Security Agency was accused of having spied on American citizens both at home and abroad as well as on both private citizens and public figures internationally. They were found to have hacked into phone records and conversations as well as electronic communications of individuals working at the United Nations and individuals like German Chancellor Angela Merkel.

Although the US government claimed that these types of surveillance were a necessary part of its counterterrorism activities and that it was necessary to monitor suspected terrorists to keep America safe, other nations reacted by accusing the United States of hypocrisy in its foreign policy and cybersecurity policies. Although America had claimed to be an avid supporter of internet freedom, they claimed, in reality it had engaged in the sorts of activities typically undertaken by authoritarian regimes. Snowden, who sought and received political asylum in Russia, has remained a firm critic of US surveillance policies.

At this point, many of the related international policy arguments about the internet were not focused so much on the specifics of how the international cyberspace architecture might look and function. Rather, they focused on the newly emerging idea that data (both individual data and large-scale data sets that showed how people behaved in cyberspace) was a vital resource. Most internet users did not understand the economics behind the internet, nor had they thought much about how it was that services like Twitter or Facebook were available to them for free. They were also unaware of the ways in which their online activities could be tracked or the types of data that they were producing by browsing, shopping online, or logging activities like going for a run. That is, they were unaware that they were producing a digital footprint, which is defined as "a combination of activities and behavior when the entity under consideration (a person or something else) is acting in the digital environment." These may be log-on or -off records, addresses of visited web pages, open or developed files, e-mail, or chat records.[52]

At this point, computer users were only starting to become aware of the phenomenon of ubiquitous computing, which is defined as "the practice of embedding technology within everyday objects so that they can store and collect data, sharing it with other objects within the Internet of Things to which they are connected."[53] That is, users didn't always realize that they were producing data streams due to signals being emitted and stored from objects like cell phones that they carried while driving, shopping, or engaging in physical activity.

If users didn't know they were producing all of this information, they were also unaware that companies like Facebook were collecting this information, storing it, and selling it to other entities—like companies that might decide to target you with advertising for a specific product based on your digital footprint. Advertisers began to state that "data is the new oil" because it was a resource produced by users that once unearthed, had value. It could be exploited, stored, or traded to others for a price.

In this way, the Snowden revelations showed computer users just how little online privacy they actually had. They also showed how the internet had changed since its inception. Whereas in the 1990s users may have had a reasonable expectation of anonymity and privacy when they went online to participate in conversations or to search for information, the advent of more sophisticated ways of collecting and tracking data (including the use of facial recognition software in social media sites like Facebook), as well as aggregating data from multiple data streams, meant that corporations and advertisers as well as the government often knew a great deal more about individual users than they might have suspected.[54] Writing in 2012, philosopher Danah Boyd described the advent of **big data**, or the ways in which researchers were able to search, aggregate, and cross-reference large data sets (such as all of the messages sent on a particular topic on Twitter during a particular day).[55]

Users were similarly unaware of the extent to which artificial intelligence was used to analyze data about citizens and to make decisions that affected them as a result. Corporations and state entities were able to deploy artificially intelligent agents or bots to run programs—called **algorithms**—which sought to analyze and identify patterns in user data and as a result to arrive at statistical generalizations about groups of users. For example, a bank might use an artificially intelligent agent to decide whether or not you were a good credit risk, affecting your ability to purchase a home or automobile. An employer might also use intelligent agents to sort through résumés and decide which individuals should be interviewed for a job opening.[56]

By the mid-2010s, analysts and policy makers were beginning to query the extent to which algorithms had begun to govern citizens' daily lives. Professional groups like the Association for Computing Machinery (ACM) acknowledged that such algorithms often reflected the inherent, even unconscious, biases of their creators—or biases that existed within society.[57] (For example, an artificially intelligent program might conclude that only women can be secretaries or nurses because most images found in Google Images of secretaries and nurses are female.) Thus, they called for greater transparency and accountability in how algorithms were utilized and deployed. At this point, new regulations began to be passed regarding the preservation of user privacy. In particular, the Council of Europe passed the Directive on Privacy and Electronic Communications (E-Privacy Directive), which required that citizens be informed of situations in which their data was being collected (such as browsing a website) and that they confirmed their agreement with the conditions of that data collection. (This principle is known as informed consent.)

Figure 1.4 Timeline Phase Four: Rise of Big Data and Social Media Analytics

2013 **Cybersecurity:**
- US citizen and Central Intelligence Agency contractor Edward Snowden utilizes internet technology and social media to publicize his claims that the US National Security Agency has engaged in unauthorized surveillance of US and other citizens.
- The NATO-supported *Tallinn Manual*, a document spelling out the applicability of international law in the area of warfare to the conduct of cyber warfare, is published.

(Continued)

Figure 1.4 (Continued)

2014 **Cybersecurity:**
- US Office of Personnel Management networks that contain information on thousands of applicants for top secret clearances are breached.
- Russia conducts cyber warfare against Ukraine.

Governance:
- Tim Berners-Lee, one of the internet's original founders, proposes a "magna carta" to protect the internet as a neutral system free from government and corporate manipulation.
- European Court of Justice rules that "Right to Be Forgotten" is valid within the European Union, allowing European Union citizens to request the removal of personal information from search results.

2015 **Cybersecurity:**
- A US teenage hacker successfully uses phishing and social engineering to gain access to the personal e-mail account of US CIA Director John Brennan.

2016 **Cybersecurity:**
- Russia is accused of having carried out social media hacking to affect the outcome of US presidential elections including hacking into the files of the US Democratic National Committee and releasing e-mails on WikiLeaks.
- Computer hackers believed to be linked to North Korea carry out the Bangladesh Bank Heist through hacking into the financial transfer system (SWIFT). Bangladesh's Central Bank loses $100 million.

Governance:
- The General Data Protection Regulation establishes data protection and privacy rights for European Union citizens.

2017
- Google launches first fully autonomous (self-driving) car, utilizing advances in the internet of things (IoT) and artificial intelligence.

2018 **Cybersecurity:**
- The Cambridge Analytica scandal breaks—Facebook is accused of having knowingly sold advertising space and user data analytics to Russian agents seeking to affect the outcome of US presidential elections.
- The Department of Homeland Security confirms that Russian hackers have broken into voter registration files in several US states prior to 2016 elections.

CONCLUSION

As this whirlwind history of the internet has shown, some facets of internet technology are still the same as they were when the technology first began, back in the 1980s. The internet is still fast and borderless, with information traveling quickly and cheaply all over the world.

At the same time, we have seen vast changes in this environment. The original domination of this space by state actors, including those associated with the military, has given way to a new environment where private corporations today play a leading role in affecting events that happen in cyberspace.

And the United States has, arguably, lost its privileged position as the leader in cyberspace. Today, the term *race* is often invoked to describe the competitive interactions between other states that seek to take a lead in defining and administering events in the online environment, including China and Russia.

And we have seen how the internet—which began as a world apart from traditional political dealings, including interstate conflicts and legal understandings of issues like private property—has instead become part of that same world. The borders of cyberspace have become leaky, with events occurring online having real-world repercussions—from the theft of classified and proprietary information by adversary nation spies to the ability of adversaries to affect events like the outcome of elections.

Today, providing cybersecurity for a nation's critical infrastructure is a multi-billion-dollar industry, with states devoting vast resources to keeping their citizens and information safe online. Yet citizens today may trust the online environment less than they did in the past, and they may also doubt the ability of their governments to keep them safe online. They may also doubt the intentions of those corporations that provide goods and services online.

In the following chapters, we begin to ask what the internet means and who decides where that meaning is derived from. We also ask what it means to "misuse" the internet and whether states can be said to be violating the spirit of the internet somehow as they develop sophisticated policies for cyber espionage, cyber defense, and critical infrastructure protection.

QUESTIONS FOR DISCUSSION

1. How does America's place in the history of the internet's development influence current international cyber-related debates?
   a. Does the internet "boost" US hegemony, and if so, then how exactly?
   b. Is the internet inherently democratic or liberal?

2. How has the privatization of the internet changed or altered its development?
   a. Would Twitter, Facebook, or other popular social media platforms, e-commerce, and so on have been possible without a privatized internet?

b. How does a privatized internet affect states as actors in the international system?

3. Is there something inherent about the progress of technology that made the internet the logical next step to communication?

4. Is there something inherent about democracy (especially in America—consider its size) that implied or required a means for mass communication and interconnectivity?

KEY TERMS

Algorithm   29
Asymmetric cryptography   7
Attribution problem   20
Backbone   6
Big data   29
Cyber sovereignty   20
Information warfare   22

Intellectual property   17
Internet Protocol (IP) address   15
Internet service provider (ISP)   1
Online piracy   17
Path dependence   5
Penetration rate   1
Social engineering   7

FOR FURTHER READING

Ems, Lindsay. "Twitter's Place in the Tussle: How Old Power Struggles Play Out on a New Stage." *Media, Culture and Society* 36, no. 5 (2014): 720–731.

Kwak, J., Zhang, Y., and Yu, J. "Legitimacy Building and E-Commerce Platform Development in China: The Experience of Alibaba." *Technological Forecasting and Social Change* (2018): 1–10. Accessed June 20, 2019. https://doi.org/10.1016/j.techfore.2018.06.038.

Leiner, Barry, Vinton Cerf, David Clark, Robert Kahn, Leonard Kleinrock, Daniel Lynch, Jon Postel, Larry Roberts, and Stephen Wolff. "A Brief History of the Internet." Last modified 1997. Accessed June 20, 2019. https://www.internetsociety.org/internet/history-internet/brief-history-internet/.

Manjikian, M. "From Global Village to Virtual Battlespace: The Colonizing of the Internet and the Extension of Realpolitik." *International Studies Quarterly* 54, no. 2 (2010): 381–401.

Shah, R. C., and J. F. Kezan. "The Privatization of the Internet's Backbone Network." *Journal of Broadcasting & Electronic Media* 51 (2007): 93–109.

2

THE INTERNET, TECHNOLOGY STUDIES, AND INTERNATIONAL RELATIONS

Learning Objectives

At the end of this chapter students will be able to do the following:

1. Compare and contrast three positions regarding the sources of a tool's meaning: technological determinism, designer's intent, and social construction of technology

2. Define terms: *dual use technology*, *export regime*, *affordances*, and *net neutrality*.

3. Describe the uniqueness debate and the three positions related to how norms and rules should be designed for the internet: the adoption of unique rules, grafting of old rules, and borrowing from other fields.

We know that many of the internet's original architects believed that the internet would inevitably be used for the extension of traditional freedoms such as freedom of information, freedom of assembly, and freedom of the press. Indeed, the international nongovernmental organization Reporters without Borders was established in 1985, and it has subsequently published an annual "internet enemies list," which calls attention to countries that are said to be violating the spirit of the internet through engaging in surveillance or censorship.[1]

In this chapter we consider two questions: How do new technologies in particular acquire meaning and who or what exactly determines what a technology should and should not be used for? That is, when one state accuses another of improperly or unlawfully deploying a technology, what is the basis for this understanding?

WHO DECIDES WHAT A TECHNOLOGY IS FOR?

Philosophers of technology have long struggled with the question of what a technology means and who is responsible for imbuing a technology with a specific meaning. Many of the political, social, and legal debates today about establishing norms for the use of the internet and its associated technologies (like social media, artificial intelligence, and big data analytics) are part of a broader conversation that takes place every time a new technology is introduced. Users often fear new technologies and tend to imbue them with certain types of power—to shape a society and its citizens. They may also create narratives about the threats and dangers inherent in new technologies. Think, for example, about the ways in which citizens were wary when a nuclear power plant was built in their community or even about current fears related to vaccines, which have led some people to choose not to vaccinate their children.

In thinking about what a technology means and how it acts, there are three major approaches or narratives to explain how technologies come about, how they function in society, and the threats they pose to society.

Technological Determinism

In the technological determinism narrative, agency—or the ability to exercise choice—can be said to belong to the technology itself. Here, technology is said to be "driving the train" because it appears to be capable of shaping and reshaping societies. These analysts argue that a new technology contains its own ideology or values—as well as built-in immutable characteristics—and that as a result, it evolves organically of its own volition, achieving an end point as it moves toward what it is meant to be.

In describing the internet's growth, philosophers like Luciana Floridi describe the evolution of our world—from the time in which humans invented writing until today—into a **mature information society** in which everyone and everything will be connected and there will be a constant source of good connectivity available in society in the same way that modern societies now can expect that there will be safe drinking water and food.

The technological determinism narrative suggests that humans themselves (including politicians) play only a limited role in steering the evolution of new technologies because control belongs to the technologies themselves. Indeed, the speed at which the internet penetrated our societies creates a sense of inexorability or inevitability. As early internet activists like Stewart Brand first stated in 1984, "Information wants to be free."[2] Therefore, they argued, information and the internet itself actually seek their own ends, moving toward transparency, freedom of speech, bottom-up organizing, and the overthrowing of autocracy.

They believed that the internet's development would cause real-world effects like the growth of freedom internationally. They thought that the internet architecture would drive political events, thereby causing real-world effects on physical architecture or structures in the terrestrial world. Some internet optimists believed that the internet's growth would inevitably strengthen capitalism and free trade internationally. Some believed that the availability of connectivity would lead to unprecedented opportunities for individuals in the developing world. They would have more interaction with the developed world, better opportunities for education and employment, and if the digital divide could be overcome, surely states would then succeed in overcoming other divides, creating a more peaceful and stable world as a result.[3]

Technological determinists emphasize the internet's immutable characteristics because these characteristics (like openness, transparency, and interconnectivity) are seen to reside in the technology itself rather than what designers want or what users do with these technologies.[4]

However, analysts differ in their evaluations of these characteristics. Whereas one person regards the technology's emphasis on mobilizing users toward action as positive—noting its ability to create democracy through mobilizing users to vote or contribute to a political cause—others view this same capability as negative, pointing out that it also allows the coming together of like-minded individuals (like Nazis or white supremacists) to organize against democratic institutions.

Thus, analysts differed in their evaluations of what they saw as the inevitable effects of increased connectivity and internet penetration. Some analysts worried about the speed at which these changes were taking place because they seemed to be moving faster than states could create regulations and laws to affect the structures and practices that were emerging.[5]

Military analysts in particular argued that these new developments were creating new threats. Greater connectivity was said to lead to an "expansion of the threat surface." Others worried about the "weaponization of social media." These analysts argue that the internet is a technology that is not inherently democratic, open, or free. That is, they argued that it should be regarded as merely a tool. Just as a tool like a hammer could be used either for building a house or for bludgeoning someone to death, a tool like the internet could be either a tool of repression or one of emancipation depending upon whose hands it ends up in. Here Klimburg writes,

> Ultimately, we face the small but real prospect that in the not too distant future of the internet, a fabulous artifice of human civilization largely perceived today as a domain for advancing freedom and prosperity, could become instead a dark web of subjugation.[6]

Other analysts also voiced fears about the growth of a surveillance society in which individuals will have little privacy, with the waning of privacy seen as inevitable due to facets of the technology itself.[7]

The technological determinism argument regarding the internet's growth also led to the adoption in some societies of draconian measures to limit people's access to the internet. If one believes that the internet inevitably reshapes societies in a democratic fashion, then it is not surprising that an authoritarian society like North Korea would seek to establish what is in essence an intranet, which functions only within the self-contained environment of North Korea while eschewing ties to the larger outside world through the internet. If technology is viewed as fundamentally uncontrollable, then the most logical reaction to that technology seems to be forbidding or controlling access to that technology. However, whereas a purely technological deterministic argument suggests that regulating technological access and use is best done from above, many individuals and groups believe that education and limits can enable individuals to speak back to technology.

The Role of the Designer

Not all internet architects were technological determinists, however. Instead, architects and analysts like Professor Lawrence Lessig emphasized the roles that designers or inventors themselves play in determining what a technology becomes.

In this narrative, the meaning of a technology or tool comes from the person who creates it. The designer therefore has some agency or free will as he or she makes design decisions that can then structure and limit the ways in which a technology may be used. Thus, the designer helps determine what a technology becomes and what it means through the decisions that he or she makes.

This stance assumes that technologies are introduced into a world that already has politics and power distribution within it. Thus, designers may seek to uphold social, gender, or racial divisions through making decisions about who a technology is for and who may access it, or they may introduce a technology with the explicit intent of changing these power distributions. (For example, if we think about reading as a technology, then we can consider people denied the gift of literacy historically—from women, to slaves, to African Americans in the American South during the twentieth century. The decision by teachers and even printers to present reading as "not for you" had nothing to do with the technology and everything to do with the world into which the technology was introduced.) Bruno Latour has famously summarized this understanding with the phrase "artifacts have politics."[8]

The design perspective suggests that a tool's inventor clearly knows how people should and should not use a technology. This perspective posits that societies, organizations, and groups can determine objectively whether someone is misusing a technology and restrict technology use. In recent history we can identify examples of situations in which societies sanctioned those who are thought to be "misusing" a technology through ethical regimes like professional licensing requirements to legal, economic, and political sanctions. For example, many European pharmaceutical companies would not sell certain medications to American prisons when they knew these drugs would be used to carry out death sentences.[9] Here there is a legal, political, and ethical understanding in many nations and internationally regarding the right and wrong use of anesthetics and other pharmaceuticals in which using them for pain relief is sanctioned whereas using them for execution is not.

In his work, Lessig argues that the internet is a built environment, built by humans through the technology of writing code. The internet looks and behaves in particular ways because humans make programming decisions. Here the designer is seen to have the ability to build norms and values into a technology, which he or she may do either consciously or unconsciously. A designer can discourage certain types of behaviors while encouraging others. Technology scholars refer to **affordances** to describe particular facets of technology that are interwoven in technology, affecting how people use it. For example, many social media and communications technologies (like Twitter) are designed in such a way that users must use transparency in their communications because they offer only limited faculties for communicating privately rather than publicly.[10]

In thinking about the internet, we see that ARPAnet's designers had clear ideas about how it should be used and the values by which it should be governed and organized. Computer scientists who invented tools for networking, messaging, and establishing connections believed that the internet should be international rather than national in character, that it should be as free of regulation by states and other entities as possible (libertarian in character), and that users should share information freely, without cost and without barriers for sharing and use. This philosophy is summed up in "A Declaration of the Independence of Cyberspace" by Paul Barlow, written in 1996. Barlow wrote,

> Governments of the Industrial World, you weary giants of flesh and steel, I come from Cyberspace, the new home of the Mind. On behalf of the future I ask you of the past to leave us alone. You are not welcome among us. You have no sovereignty where we gather.[11]

In this story, designers created an architecture with certain features associated with specific values. The resulting product was nonhierarchical, with information moving between nodes and hubs rather than up and down to a central location at the top of a hierarchy. Within this structure anyone could join the internet from anywhere. In the language of economics, the internet was a **free good**.

In addition, the internet was envisioned as a space without borders that would not belong to any particular nation and where no nation would have jurisdiction over the activities that occurred there. The designers believed that internet users would not be citizens of a particular nation. Instead they would be "netizens." They would not be governed by the rules and norms of their physical territorial residence but would rather be governed by rules and norms that resided in the technology itself (either because they were placed there by designers or because they spontaneously emerged either from the technology itself or from the interaction of people within that technology).

Next, no information was more important than other information. All information moved at the same speed, and no source (at least initially) stood above any other source. This principle is referred to as **net neutrality**.[12] Additionally, people could join without revealing their real names or any personal information and could thus browse and participate in conversations and other activities anonymously. Finally, it was initially regarded as largely "American" because it was invented in the United States. It was associated with freedom of information, freedom of association, and freedom of speech.

The notion that the internet thus meant freedom—of information and of access—either because of some inherent attribute of the technology or because of the designer's values, was prevalent during the first two phases of internet development. Indeed, in 2006 Reporters without Borders began publishing a list of what they term *enemies of the internet*, nations that they perceived to be using internet technology incorrectly through erecting "structures" like firewalls or filters that limited citizen access to the internet and information or by requiring citizens to register their identities online or to abide by national restrictions on freedom of speech and freedom of association.[13] Furthermore, the United Nations issued a resolution in 2012 that called upon states to recognize those international human rights granted in the real world as applying to the virtual world as well. This resolution asked states to "promote and facilitate access to the Internet and international cooperation aimed at the development of media and information and communications facilities in all countries."[14] There is thus a legal precedent for accusing those who violate established ideas like freedom of the press of abusing or misusing internet technology.

Cindy Cohn, director of the Electronic Frontier Foundation, takes this understanding further, arguing that "how we build our tools will determine our rights." She argues that "our digital world can be fair or unfair. Empowering or disempowering. Utopian or dystopian depending on the choices we make along the way."[15] Thus, she worries that companies like Google and Twitter have a disproportionate amount of power to determine the future of the internet and thus of human society. She writes,

> For the last decade . . . we've seen governments and companies take negative advantage of their positions in building and running the networks, architectures and tools that the rest of us rely on. They treat us as unimportant serfs in their mass spying systems, fodder for machine learning algorithms and treat our world like a cybersecurity battleground where our private lives are mere collateral.[16]

Similarly, Brooking and Singer reference the designer's role in describing social media, arguing that

> the engineers behind social media had specifically designed their platforms to be addictive. The brain fires off a tiny burst of dopamine as a user posts a message and it receives reactions from others, trapping the brain in a cycle of posts, "likes," retweets and "shares."[17]

Today, some critics worry that if design decisions constrain our individual behaviors, then users will have fewer opportunities to practice regulating our own behaviors. For example, designers could design a cell phone that can determine if it is inside a moving car and disable its texting feature in this situation. Instead of deciding not to text and drive, we would be robbed of the ability to do so. In the social media environment, we can ask whether it is better for people to learn to identify and avoid racist ideas and speech in their own lives than for an algorithm to simply be deployed to identify and delete racist content once it is posted.

The design perspective does not, however, posit that an environment is static. Instead, we can conceptualize of a dynamic environment in which the internet's architecture and properties can change over time, depending on who has the power to design the environment. Here we can consider encryption technology. At first programmers worked to keep us and our identities and our information secret. (Anonymity was considered a nonnegotiable attribute of the internet, which was built into the environment.) Today, however, those same programmers work to make us traceable online.[18] Here, Lessig points to the 1994 Communications Assistance for Law Enforcement Act in the United States that required that networks be designed to preserve the ability of law enforcement to conduct electronic surveillance. This means that in the area of surveillance, the US Federal Communications Commission (FCC) gets to have a say in the types of systems that are designed and the types of uses to which they may be put—just as they have done previously with telephone networks.

In the same way, many analysts have queried the claim that the internet is inherently a borderless international place where concepts like nationality do not apply. They claim that the principle of nonterritoriality of the internet came about because of designers' choices and that it can be undone. Although programmers initially set up the internet without links to physical territory and territorial sovereignty, this does not mean that it has to be this way or that it cannot change.

However, as we saw with the technological determinism view of the internet, there are those who have critiqued and questioned the design view as well. One of the strongest critics of the design view of the internet was Evgeny Morozov, a journalist who grew up in Belarus, one of the most autocratic nations of the former Soviet Union. In the book *The Net Delusion: The Dark Side of Internet Freedom*, Morozov argued there is nothing inherently democratizing about the internet. Instead, he argues that internet technology is actually **dual use.** He believes that features like photo and voice recognition, in particular, could easily become instruments of surveillance and social control, depending on who deployed the technology. Morozov's ideas were later realized when participants in anti-state demonstrations in Ukraine received text messages from the government noting that their identities had been determined through facial recognition and that they would be punished if they engaged in further demonstrations. And the German company Lench IT was criticized by human rights organizations for selling its Finfisher surveillance software (intended to be used by democratic regimes for carrying out counterterrorism activities) to nations like North Korea and Belarus, who deployed it against their own citizens.

Critics like Morozov thus ask us to think about whether there is an entity such as "the design community." Back in the early days when most of the internet's architects were Western and US-based, these designers were a monolithic group who shared values, including a commitment to democratization. For most of the 1970–1990 period, the design community was unified in its support and vision of an open and largely unregulated internet, the goal of growth of the internet, and the extension of it to all who desired to participate. Here, the Internet Engineering Standards Task Force (IETF), with its philosophy of making decisions by "rough consensus," played a leading role. This body worked to make design decisions about the internet's architectural forms and its growth in as transparent a fashion as possible.[19]

However, today, there are actually multiple design communities: There are the neoliberal academic designers of the internet; there are also members of the defense community, like the US military, which paid for the creation of the internet and had different aims in its creation, including the ability to create redundant capabilities for military command and control functions. And some argue that the role of internet architecture developers is arguably "owned" by the international corporations that administer the major online platforms. In addition, we can point to designers in Saudi Arabia, North Korea, and China, all of whom are working to create user experiences for their citizens reflecting the characteristics and values of their societies.

Currently, we can identify a multiplicity of players within the design community—democratic states, autocratic states, business interests, and technology experts. These individuals and groups do not always agree on what the internet should look like, who it should serve, or what it is for. Thus, analysts sometimes refer to a **standards war,** in which different factions within the design community have attempted to put into practice different or competing visions of what the internet's architecture will ultimately look like.

Case Study: Is China "Misusing" Internet Technology?

Here we pause briefly to consider at greater length the argument that a state is "misusing" internet technology by designing an experience for its own domestic users that differs from the internet experience as originally conceptualized by designers like Barlow and Cerf. Here we can think particularly of the creation by China's government of what has come to be known as the Great Firewall of China. Beginning in the 1980s, Chinese authorities began utilizing filters to control all internet traffic that travels to and from—as well as within—China. This firewall allows the state to filter out and make unavailable content based on the inclusion of keywords.

The US-based nongovernment organization Freedom House has reported on what it sees as the Chinese government's techniques to impose "information control" and censorship as well as their crackdowns on the use of social media to prevent citizens from organizing in anti-state demonstrations or activities online.[20] At times, China has blocked citizens' access to Google and Gmail and has also utilized cyber warfare to carry out attacks on the websites attached to Microsoft, Yahoo, and Apple. Because nearly a third of the world's internet users reside in Asia, including China, groups like Freedom House worry that the internet could lose its character as an international territory without borders where information flows freely if one or two big players like China were to adopt different sets of norms and rules for how information should be treated in their territories. For this reason, they have sought to shame and sanction states whose orientations to the internet do not reflect this understanding of the internet as an international body.

Rather than denying censorship, China's government admitted to taking these actions and defended its right to do so. In April 2013, China's Communist Party issued "Document Nine," which listed seven perils presented to China by the growth of internet technology within their society. This list included threats created by exposure to Western constitutional democracy and the claim that there were "universal values" that all internet users should be in favor of. China's Ministry of Industry and Information Technology has similarly admitted to engaging in censorship and content blocking, arguing that doing so was necessary for the "healthy and lawful development of the internet."[21]

At the same time, the Chinese government used social media access to construct what many have described as a vast surveillance state. China is actively engaged in setting up a national video-surveillance network named xueliang, or "sharp eyes." This system will use facial recognition and other technologies to monitor the activities of China's citizens in schools, in public facilities, and while they are on city streets. Citizens also have monitoring software automatically installed on their smartphones. At the same time, China has created a **social credit system** that assigns citizens a score based on their past behavior, including whether they have committed actions like traffic offenses. This score can affect their credit ratings, including their ability to borrow money to take out a student loan or a mortgage.

The issue for international relations specialists is whether every country should have the right to utilize internet technologies—including new advances in artificial intelligence—to monitor their citizens in this way or whether actions like monitoring and filtering constitute a "misuse" of the internet technology as it was designed and envisioned. Within the international system, whose vision of the internet should prevail, and how much leeway do states have to decide how they will utilize these technologies internally within their own countries and perhaps against their own people?

As we will see later in the textbook when we take up the subject of internet governance, not all states within the international system agree with the US and European positions that the internet contains its own values—including a commitment to openness and free speech—and that all states should attempt to comply with these values. As we will see, Russia in particular has sided with China, espousing the position that the United States is acting unfairly in stating that the internet must reflect American norms and values. Here Russia argues that it has a right to treat the internet as part of Russia's real territory, and therefore it has the ability to create its own Russian internet reflecting Russian norms and values. Other analysts have suggested that the internet is international, rather than American, in character and that if there is a prevailing set of norms and values attached to the internet, these values and norms should be created as the result of an international consensus rather than dictated by the United States simply because the United States "invented" the internet.

WHAT ARE DIGITAL HUMAN RIGHTS?

Early internet developers described the online environment as "a world apart" from regular, terrestrial space. They hoped that people would have complete freedom online to express their ideas, to interact with others from across the globe, and to share information freely. However, what they took for granted—the idea that people would have the same rights online that they had in real space—is actually a subject of contention among states today.

Analysts make three arguments regarding the sources of human rights. The United Nations, in the Universal Declaration of Human Rights, states that there are certain basic rights that everyone has by virtue of the fact that they are human. Such rights can be positive (the right to do something) and negative (the right to be protected from something). The Universal Declaration of Human Rights states that everyone everywhere has the right, for example, to live free from violence, to not be enslaved, and to be provided with basic living requirements like food and shelter.

Today, some activists suggest modifying the Universal Declaration of Human Rights to include an additional article. Article 19 would clarify that all humans have "digital human rights" by virtue of their humanity. If this codicil passed, then a state like North Korea or China could not deprive their citizens of internet access. Doing so would constitute a human rights violation, affecting their eligibility for international foreign aid and trade preferences. In severe cases, human rights violators can even be tried by an organization like the International Criminal Court.

Digital human rights are said to include positive rights: the freedom to express opinions, to "gather" digitally in groups, and to share information. They also contain negative rights like freedom from the possibility of government surveillance. Thus, just as people have a human right to own property, these activists suggest that people should have the right to own their own data that they produce, to determine how that data is used and shared, and to be made aware of situations in which others are accessing or utilizing their data.

However, Yakupitiyage and other analysts from the developing world have questioned whether any international body truly has the power to enforce the understanding, or norm, that digital rights are an important subset of human rights—particularly because there is not currently a global consensus regarding this issue. Traditionally, the United States has argued this position, advocating for the extension of internet access globally, particularly in the developing world, because it can be seen as part of a larger "package" of human rights. However, in 2018, the United States withdrew as a member of the UN Human Rights Council, arguing that the body was both biased and heavily politicized in its aims. As a result, some policy makers in the developing world worry that in the absence of America's strong participation and advocacy of the digital human rights position, nations like Russia and China, which do not accept this position, will come to play a larger role globally, leading to a situation in which digital rights are seen as detached from broader human rights claims.[22]

However, others argue that individuals have rights not because of their basic humanity but because these rights are conferred upon them by the state. Such rights are conditional. A state can confer rights, or rescind them, and can also determine who receives such rights (e.g., stating that only men may vote).

Finally, the internet's architects claimed that people's rights derived from their positions within a certain environment (i.e., online). Tim Berners-Lee, an early internet developer, first argued for a separate Digital Bill of Rights in 2014.[23] He believes that there are universally right and wrong ways to use the internet and that states denying their citizens full access to cyberspace are misusing the internet. In addition, in the wake of the revelations by American whistle-blower Edward Snowden in 2015, activists have voiced concerns about government surveillance as well as the collection and analysis of user data. A digital Bill of Rights could thus help citizens protect their rights online through spelling out what those rights are (i.e., the ability to own your data and to protect your reputation online).

The Digital Freedom Fund has provided an extensive list of the rights that they feel users should have online. The schematic in Figure 2.1 outlines these rights

Figure 2.1 Digital Human Rights

Right	Examples
Right not to be profiled	Right to access information about your own data Right to keep your personal data protected Right to opt out of profiling Right to anonymous access and participation
Right not to be judged by a machine	Right to request a human override to algorithmic justice Right to delete the digital self

(Continued)

(Continued)

Figure 2.1 (Continued)

Right	Examples
Right to (digital) self-determination	Right to control your own data Right to object to the use of personal data Freedom to move providers Right to challenge or opt out of standard terms and conditions
Right to disconnect	Right to unplug from time to time Right to non-digital access to governmental services
Right to participate in the cultural life of one's community	Right to participate in digital expression Freedom to share and receive information Right to participate in online communities
Right not to be discriminated against	Freedom from discrimination
Right to personal safety and security	Right to digital security Right to bodily integrity Freedom from cyberbullying, trolling, and abuse
Right to political participation	Freedom from online manipulation Right to take part in political decision-making online
Right to privacy	Freedom form profiling Freedom from bulk surveillance Right to use strong encryption Right to private digital communications
Right to challenge the algorithm	Right to algorithmic transparency
Right to education and literacy	Right to digital literacy Right to understand the implications of technology

Sources

Article19.org. "#InternetofRights: Creating the Universal Declaration of Digital Rights." Last modified March 24, 2017, https://www.article19.org/blog/resources/internetofrights-creating-the-universal-declaration-of-digital-rights/.

Kaltenbach, L., and O. Le Guay. "Desperately Looking for a Data Ethic: The Importance of a Universal Declaration on Digital Human Rights." Digiworld Economic Journal 97 (2014): 102–105. https://www.thefreelibrary.com/Desperately+looking+for+a+data+ethic%3a+the+importance+of+a+Universal...-a0414693455.

Ojekunle, A. "African Governments Are Using Laws to Stifle Internet Freedom—Report." Pulse.ng. Last modified November 13, 2018, https://www.pulse.ng/bi/tech/tech-african-governments-are-using-laws-to-stifle-internet-freedom-report/prg88d6.

UN Office of the High Commissioner on Human Rights. "The Right to Privacy in the Digital Age." Last modified 2018, https://pp-international.net/2018/07/the-right-to-privacy-in-the-digital-age-for-the-report-of-the-high-commissioner-for-human-rights/.

Social Construction of Technology

Today, while many Western organizations still support either technological determinism or the design view to advance the claim that there are universal norms and values associated with internet technology that all states should comply with—unless they wish to risk being labeled "internet enemies"—there are many other states in the world who disagree.

These states often make a third argument for the source of a technology's values. This argument most closely aligns with the arguments set forth by proponents of the **social construction of technology** (SCOT) school, who argue that new technologies do not develop in a vacuum, nor do they necessarily have only one set of values and norms attached to them automatically. Rather, SCOT adherents argue, a technology's meaning is negotiated within a specific socioeconomic, political, and economic context. When a new technology is developed, its meaning may be contested. Different technology users may have conflicting visions of what the technology is for and who it is for, who may use it, and how. Over time, they argue, the debate may be settled with a specific version and meaning described as acceptable for the technology. (This process is referred to as **technological closure**.)

In this model, a technology may change from the period when it is invented, often assuming a new and unanticipated, novel form. In this model, even a designer may be surprised by what a technology eventually becomes because it may not be what even he or she anticipated.

Function creep describes how technology invented for one reason is found to be useful for other reasons as well, creating a situation in which it is used for other than the designer's intended purpose. In the United Kingdom, the 1939 National Registration Act led to the issuing of national identity cards for the purposes of rationing food during the war. By 1950, however, thirty different government agencies were using these cards for a variety of purposes—asking citizens to show such cards to pick up packages from the post office, to collect social welfare benefits, or to provide identification to police.[24]

Function creep explains why the internet has come to play such a vital role in the lives of citizens and the state today. Although initially envisioned largely as a way of sharing instant communications among citizens internationally, today the internet's function has "crept" so that it is now a news purveyor, a means of voting, a way of tracking pedophiles in a society, an advertising platform, and an engine of commerce. Here we can again consider the story we encountered earlier in this volume, where General Michael Hayden stated that the ARPAnet designers actually had no grand vision of the internet's future. They had no idea how people would use this creation—how they might use it in creative ways, some of which were normative or condoned, while others were nonnormative or sanctioned.

More than any other explanation, the SCOT school illustrates the quirky and creative ways in which new technologies can be deployed and the inability of analysts and designers to predict what a technology becomes. In recent years, social theorists have pointed to the issues associated with so-called emerging technologies. An **emerging technology** is one characterized by a high degree of uncertainty regarding its potential, which also has a network effect. (That is, the technology's existence and deployment have the ability to affect developments in a variety of other fields and also have the ability to influence a society politically, economically, and socially.) Emerging technologies often come with (or create) unseen social and ethical concerns because they are so new or unexpected that there is little preexisting research about them and their effects. When we think about the internet's creation, we see that no one ever predicted that ARPAnet's existence would later lead to the creation of social problems like the existence of Pornhub, or legal issues related to intellectual property being created on sites like YouTube, or political issues like the online radicalization of teenagers toward terrorist groups.[25] It is often difficult to predict how such a technology will develop over a period of ten or fifteen years, and as a result, these types of technologies have been particularly difficult to regulate and oversee.

PEOPLE AND PLACES

The Great Firewall of China

The term *Great Wall of China* refers to a series of fortifications that runs in an East-to-West direction across much of China. They were built beginning in 700 BC to keep out foreign invaders and protect China's people and resources.

The Great Firewall of China is more recent. This term refers to a series of measures undertaken by China's national leaders to prevent Chinese citizens from accessing certain types of information on the internet. As a one-party state, China's leaders are concerned about domestic activism that might end in calls for the end of that one-party ruling arrangement and the establishment of democratic elections. Thus China's leaders have worked to censor information about previous attempts at democratization, such as the 1989 Tiananmen Square protests, in which up to 1 million Chinese students called for an end to one-party rule and the implementation of full freedom of speech and information in China. Fang Binxing, a former president of the Beijing University of Posts and Telecommunications, is seen as the "father" of China's

Great Firewall. He argues that online controls are necessary to "prevent chaos" domestically within China.[26]

The Great Firewall is not completely impenetrable, however. Currently, many users now use tools like **virtual private networks (VPNs)** to gain access to sites overseas. A VPN, which can be set up on a cell phone, can be configured to make it look as though a user is located somewhere else, outside of China. Between 2008 and 2012, the US Department of State spent nearly $100 million on the development of tools like VPNs to be used by dissidents and activists in repressive regimes to circumvent internet censorship in their countries.[27] China has reacted to US efforts in this arena, labeling such activities as a violation of China's sovereignty and their right to control what happens in their internet. The United States, in response, has listed China's internet controls to a list of barriers that they see as impeding trade between the United States and China.[28]

In recent years, Western-based internet service companies—like Google and GitHub—have clashed with Chinese authorities, who have required that companies comply with Chinese laws regarding censorship to do business in the region. Google, in particular, was criticized by American and international bodies when it established google.cn despite requests by Chinese authorities to, for example, provide them with data on what Chinese citizens were searching for online. (In particular, the Chinese government was interested in who was searching for information about the banned religious group Falun Gong.)[29] In 2010, Google shut down the google.cn search engine. Although they claimed that they were doing so because of their strong commitment to human rights internationally, some Chinese economists have suggested that Google was actually unable to compete with the domestic Chinese search engine Baidu and that their real motivation was economic.[30]

China's leadership argues that despite the existence of the Great Firewall of China, most citizens have benefited in numerous ways from the introduction of the internet in their nation. They point in particular to the ways in which citizens in rural areas now have access to a much wider range of consumer goods from clothing and baby items to entertainment.[31] Here, China's leadership demonstrates that they have a different idea regarding the utility and ideology that they attach to the internet. They see it largely as a vehicle for commerce and the extension of education through the establishment of online learning rather than as a vehicle of democratization and free speech. The fact that Western companies are now competing less in that market, and the fact that many of the sites that Chinese users rely on are now domestic Chinese companies, helps bolster the leadership's understanding that China should have a Chinese internet rather than seeking to join the international community online.

As we think about attempts by actors like the European Union or the United Nations to regulate and oversee internet technology, we should remember that today's internet may also not reflect the internet of tomorrow. Measures like the internet of things and wearable technologies and the development of artificial intelligence mean that the threats that nations face will look different in the future—and the internet may change in rapid and unpredictable ways.

As we examine policy developments regarding regulating and governing the internet's structures, as well as policies related to cyber warfare and cyber conflict, we see how all three discourses are present. In some instances, analysts argue that cyber arms control is necessary because the internet's existence will inevitably create new conflicts (echoing here the technological determinist viewpoint). In other instances, states argue about whether states can work together or whether international bodies can be created to shape the internet's architecture in ways that encourage cooperation and sharing rather than conflict (echoing the design viewpoint). And in other instances, states have contested the meaning of internet technology. Here it is likely that we have not yet achieved technological closure or arrived at a consensus about what the internet means. However, there is evidence already that the internet has not been deployed or constructed in the same way in all states and all societies.

Figure 2.2 summarizes the differences between the three schools of thought and their implications. We turn next to the uniqueness debate, again borrowing from technology studies, to consider whether internet policy issues differ fundamentally from policy issues in real space.

Figure 2.2 Three Schools of Thought and Their Implications

	Agency Belongs To	Norms Derive From	Threats	State Response
Technological Determinism	Technology	Technology itself (i.e., information wants to be free)	Technology changes human behavior and values	Limit access to technology —censorship, registration, and filtering
Role of Designer	Designer	Aims, values of designers (i.e., designing for security and privacy)	User abuse of technology; malignant designers who create bad code or destroy environment	Build in measures to preempt threats; punish those who violate the ethos of technology
Social Construction of Technology	Users	User community, preexisting rules and norms (state)	Unanticipated uses	Introduce surveillance, rules governing use

THE UNIQUENESS DEBATE

With the internet's advent, we saw an explosion of new words to describe phenomena occurring online. Analysts referenced cybercrime, cyberstalking, cybertheft, cybertrespass and cyberwar. Military analysts warned that the United States was not sufficiently armed with the latest cutting-edge cyberweapons and that as a result, the United States faced the possibility of a Cyber Pearl Harbor or a Cyber 911 situation in which the United States could be surprised by a large-scale attack for which they are insufficiently cognizant of the dangers that they face and as a result are unprepared to respond.

Here, an important question for academics—from social scientists who study conflict to philosophers who study ethics—revolves around the uniqueness debate. How do we understand these new phenomena that have emerged as the result of the internet's development? Are they best understood as variants of existing, often age-old problems (like bullying, violence, and conflict), or are they better understood as fundamentally new issues that have emerged in this new environment?[32]

The Internet as a Unique Environment

We can identify characteristics of cyberspace that are unique in comparison to terrestrial space, including the speed at which interactions occur and the "radical connectivity" that allows information and ideas to traverse physical borders, making it difficult if not impossible for states to exercise border control in cyberspace. This radical connectivity also presents issues of legal jurisdiction related to border control, whereas the international character of the space itself presents issues related to an absence of sovereignty. On the military front, conflict in cyberspace can look different from other types of terrestrial conflicts due to the fact that cyberweapons are virtual rather than material. They can thus be developed more cheaply and more quickly and can be much harder to track than material weapons such as a missile housed permanently in one location in a missile silo. We have also considered the ways in which anonymity may be a characteristic of cyberspace, although analysts disagree as to whether this is indeed an immutable characteristic. Finally, we have considered the ways in which the internet as a highly technical built environment—differs from terrestrial space—because the state alone has neither "discovered" it, built it, nor controlled it alone. Rather, states are particularly dependent on the roles played by international organizations, technical specialists, and the business community in creating, policing, and monitoring cyberspace.

As a result of these unique characteristics, then, many internet designers claimed that digital space differed fundamentally from terrestrial space. Terrestrial space had borders inside of which states had sovereign authority, and property and ideas could be owned in terrestrial space. However, they felt that the internet was radically different and governed by its own rules and norms.

Initially, internet pioneers claimed that all content available on the internet should be free of charge and able to be freely shared. **Open source software** was thought to be the model for how individuals could work together to create new programs and content on the internet, which would then be freely available to all users. (That is, because the internet itself was a free good, some users argued that everything contained within that environment should likewise be a free good.) These same utopian idealists also argued that one of the internet's greatest virtues was that it provided a space of radical transparency where information could be freely and infinitely shared. It was therefore

Figure 2.3 Comparing Terrestrial and Digital Space

Characteristic	Manifested in Real Space	Manifested in Digital Space
Speed	Interactions formalized or slow (i.e., treaties or alliances)	Interactions (including alliances) may be fleeting or temporary
Jurisdiction	Real borders in which states have sovereignty	Borderless space across which data and ideas migrate freely and unregulated
Private property, including intellectual property	Recognized as existing on national and international levels through treaties; with penalties for violating norms	Not always recognized; norms may favor sharing or open source solutions to problems
Anonymity	Actions are carried out by real people who can be disciplined by the state for violations	Actions not always traced to an individual or group due to attribution problem
Weapons	• Tangible • Can be tracked and governed by international community	• Intangible cyberweapons • Cheap
	• Understandings regarding use and tech specifications change slowly • Utility of weapons remains over the long term	• Difficult to track and govern • Strategies, tactics, doctrines, and tech specifications change quickly • Utility of weapons decays quickly

considered to be unique and a world apart from terrestrial space. (We see some of this sentiment still existing today in the manifestos of groups like the non-profit organization WikiLeaks, which argues that internet users should not recognize legal understandings related to the dissemination of classified information, for example, but rather that people should strive to make government as transparent as possible, even if doing so involves making stolen and classified documents available.)[33]

Figure 2.3 illustrates the differences between real space and digital space with reference to the unique characteristics referenced earlier in this chapter.

A WORLD APART OR AN EXTENSION OF TERRESTRIAL SPACE?

Whereas designers described the internet as detached from physical territory, social theorists identified similarities between social phenomena occurring in the real world and those occurring in cyberspace. That is, initially, social theorists tended to describe cybercrime, cyberstalking, and other "cyber" problems as variations of those social problems that occurred in the terrestrial world. And in the beginning, something that occurred "in cyber" (from cyberbullying to cyber infidelity) was often viewed as a lighter or less serious, less real version of its real-world counterpart. In writing about criminology and sentencing guidelines, there was initially an assumption that cyber offenses were perhaps lesser offenses and that their treatment—including the penalties imposed—should be less because the severity of events did not rise to the same level as events that occurred in the terrestrial world.

At the same time, in the internet's early days, analysts assumed that events which occurred in cyberspace were confined only to cyberspace. However, by 2010, social analysts were aware that cyberbullying could in fact lead bullied teens to commit suicide in the real world. They began arguing that online behaviors—from participating in a pro-anorexia discussion board to discussing radical Islamic jihad online—had real-world repercussions.[34] In addition, the wall between people's online or digital identities and their real-world identities broke down. As individuals applied for jobs online, posted their résumés and creative work online, and paid taxes and bills online, it became clear that online activities could easily be traced back to real-world identities. In addition, with social media's emergence, platforms like Twitter and Facebook were being asked to police interactions among users, creating fewer and fewer places where anonymity was the rule for online interactions.

Today the idea that online information and activities are governed by different, unique rules is a minority position. By 2003, American courts established the understanding that the internet could be subject to proprietary control and that information and space on the internet could be privatized.[35] And analysts accepted that cyberspace and real space are intimately and deeply connected. Cyberspace is said to have "leaky borders," and analysts note that cyberspace can be used as a vector or platform for launching attacks on physical targets, such as telecommunications and electrical grids. It can also be used to meddle in real-world events, like national elections. At the same time, analysts have developed an understanding that cyberwarfare and cybercrime are not lesser variants of real warfare or real crime but rather again that they are serious events.

What Is the Dark Web?

Today, the web is commonly described as having three layers: the surface web, the deep web, and the dark web. The **surface web** encompasses all publicly identifiable and searchable sites (i.e., everything that comes up when you perform a Google search). However, the surface web is only the tip of the iceberg in terms of all of the information and activity that takes place on the web. **Deep web** refers to sites that may be "hidden" within either a legitimate or an illegitimate site and that do not come up during a standard search. Here you may need a password or to type the web address for this page directly into a server. (For example, the content you access when you use an online content management system like Desire 2 Learn or Blackboard is part of the deep web, as is information you encounter on your university's website after you log in as a student. We can also place the "Clearnet," a network of secure or encrypted channels through which individuals and corporations may make purchases using e-commerce, within the deep web.)

Dark web refers to material that is hidden intentionally and is inaccessible through a standard web browser. (The dark web is thus a subset of the deep web.) To access materials within the deep web, users have to have access to an anonymizing web browser like Tor, which encrypts the addresses from which information is sent or received as well as the pathways by which the information travels. In this way, the sites cannot be traced back to a particular user or even a particular computer. Readers may be familiar with the Silk Road, which was described as the world's largest marketplace for illegal drugs. This site was shut down by US law enforcement personnel in 2013.

Using an anonymizing browser is not always illegal. Someone might use Tor or a similar browser to engage in activities like whistle-blowing (i.e., reporting a violation of rules or protocol that has occurred at one's workplace in a situation where one fears retaliatory actions, like being fired, as a result of reporting the information) or engaging in social activism under a repressive regime. Such an instance would constitute a legitimate use of the dark web. In addition the dark web itself constitutes less than 1 percent of the web's overall geography with perhaps as few as 45,000 sites contained within it.

However, law enforcement personnel on local, state, and federal levels wish to enforce laws within the dark web—preventing activities like trafficking in illegal drugs, weapons, or human beings. Current law is unclear both in the United States and internationally regarding the methods that law enforcement can use in tracking and preventing criminal activity on the dark web or the laws that apply for indicting and sentencing those who engage in illegal activity on the dark web. Currently law enforcement personnel may use tools like adopting false identities to infiltrate such sites and may make purchases to gather evidence against those trading in illegal substances. Some lawyers believe that such activities constitute entrapment and that the rights of those who engage in dark web trafficking are therefore not being sufficiently respected. Others argue that such measures are necessary given the difficulty of pursuing criminals across the dark web.

Currently, China and Russia have both introduced regulatory measures within the international community aimed at eliminating citizen access to Tor. However, there is not a great deal of international support for this solution to the problem of how best to regulate the dark web.

Sources

Chertoff, Michael. "A Public Policy Perspective of the Dark Web." *Journal of Cyber Policy* 2, no. 1 (2017), 26–38.

Davis, C. "Addressing the Challenges of Enforcing the Law on the Dark Web." *Global Justice* (blog). Last modified December 11, 2017, https://www.law.utah.edu/addressing-the-challenges-of-enforcing-the-law-on-the-dark-web/.

Patterson, D. "How the Dark Web Works." Zdnet.com. Last modified September 1, 2016, https://www.zdnet.com/article/how-the-dark-web-works/.

How to Regulate the Internet

Although many internet characteristics have proved to be mutable, rather than immutable or unchanging characteristics, there are still certain facets of online interactions that are unusual and that present unusual challenges to policy makers and analysts today. For example, online interactions in the international community tend not to occur from a purely state-centric perspective. Rather, from the beginning, the technology community has played a major role in the development and evolution of the internet environment.

Thus, a major issue for policy analysts today is this: Do the differences between real and virtual space mean that the internet requires fundamentally different and unique structures and rules for governing and regulating it? Or can the governance and regulation of state and individual activity in online interactions—including cyber warfare—be carried out through widening existing regulations and organizations to include the cybersphere? Here we can ask: Is there something so fundamentally unique about cyberwarfare, in comparison to traditional warfare, that we need to create brand-new doctrines and institutions to regulate and control it? And is cyberterrorism fundamentally different from terrorism, or are they related? Similarly, as we think about the internet as a venue for international relations among states, we may also wish to ask: Is every encounter between states online uniquely different from activities that occur in the real world?

In considering internet regulation, we can identify three approaches where each understands the uniqueness debate somewhat differently. First, some analysts believe that cyberspace is so different from terrestrial space that states and the international community need new organizations and institutions to govern it. These analysts describe the evolution of a new type of multistakeholder governance or regulation featuring a unique constellation of actors—including technology specialists (and specialized technology organizations like the Internet Society), states, multinational corporations, and international organizations.

The second set of analysts argues that what needs to occur is **grafting**. In this scenario, some existing regulations and organizations can successfully broaden their mission to absorb new, related missions and goals for regulating the online environment. We can identify grafting in the push to widen our understanding of international law—particularly in the areas of war or conflict—such that key international law principles can also be used to explain and regulate conflicts in the cyber arena. The publication of the *Tallinn Manual* in 2012 represents an attempt to do just that. This manual, created by an international team of experts and created at the NATO Center for Excellence in Tallinn, Estonia, asked whether, for example, NATO's Article 1, which requires a NATO member to interpret an act of aggression against a fellow member state as an act of aggression against itself, could be widened such that a cyberattack against a member state would also require a response by all other NATO member states.

We can also point to the decision in 2013 to broaden the provisions of the international **Wassenaar Arrangement**, which prevails upon signatory states to consider how dual-use technologies in biology and chemistry might be used before granting export licenses to developers wishing to sell them abroad. (Here, for example, we would consider whether a laboratory that creates cultures used to test vaccines might be considered responsible if these cultures are instead used by an adversary nation to create a biological or chemical weapon.) In 2013 signatory members agreed to broaden the agreement so that states would also be asked to police and regulate the export of computer code that might be used to create cyberweapons or instruments of state surveillance.[36]

Finally, we can point to discussions regarding whether the United Nations Declaration of Human Rights should be expanded to include an Article 19, which would focus specifically on the role of the United Nations in safeguarding so-called digital human rights, including freedoms like freedom to assemble, freedom of speech, and freedom from surveillance online.[37]

A third approach to regulating the online environment is borrowing. These analysts believe that the internet is a unique strategic environment—borderless, international, and amorphous. However, there are other existing terrestrial environments that share some of these characteristics. Garett suggests viewing the online environment as similar to the ocean, arguing that "laws that have succeeded in the ocean take into account the unique characteristics of the ocean. The result is maritime law."[38] In addition, there are other areas of international governance and rule making that are highly specialized and that involve a number of players, including business interests and international corporations.[39] For example, firms may play a leading role in crafting legislation and creating structures of governance in sectors like environmental law, public health law, and even in the area of product liability.

CONCLUSION

In this chapter we have considered several vital questions that are the subject of fierce debate within the international community. We have asked where the use rules and meanings attached to a technology derive from and whether technologies should be seen as having a universal meaning and set of use rules or whether each state should feel free to steer and define a technology's role within their own society in accordance with their own values and history.

We have considered whether technology has a life of its own or whether technologies can ultimately force changes in individuals or societies. Here, we have asked how effective it is ultimately for states to attempt to create use rules and place constraints upon the use of this technology.

Finally, we have attempted to integrate the story of the internet within a larger set of issues. In the last section of this chapter, we have considered the degree to which policy making in regard to the internet should be considered as a unique set of questions that will require unique policy solutions or whether many policy issues related to the internet can be either grafted onto existing rules and structures. We have also considered the ways in which many of the qualities that allow us to describe the internet's evolution as unique—including the fact that this "territory" is unowned and global in scope as well as the fact that technical specialists and business interests have been highly involved in its creation—can actually be found to parallel developments in other areas of policy making from the fields of maritime and securities law.

As this chapter has shown, cyber policy making is rapidly evolving and highly conflictual. Compared to other sectors in which states make policies (such as working together to overcome a pandemic disease), it appears that states do not share a consensus regarding how to regulate cyberspace, what a good or healthy cyberspace might look like, or whose responsibility it is to create that space. We take up this issue again in Chapter 6 on internet governance.

QUESTIONS FOR DISCUSSION

1. Visit this site to download a copy of the 2018 United States National Cyber Strategy: https://www.whitehouse.gov/wp-content/uploads/2018/09/National-Cyber-Strategy.pdf.

   Respond to the following questions after reading through the document:

   a. How does the US vision of cybersecurity describe the relationship between security in real space and security in the online environment?

   b. What are some values that the US national cybersecurity strategy ascribes to the online environment (i.e., free and open)? Do you think that other nations would agree with this US vision? Why or why not?

   c. Can you find any phrases in the document that suggest that the United States is laying claim to the internet as belonging to or controlled by the United States? Write them down. Do you agree with these ideas? Why or why not?

2. Consider China's example as it struggles with how and when to use surveillance tools. In an article published in the *Financial Times* called "Inside China's Surveillance State," the authors quote a German minister who suggests that any nation would wish to keep its citizens safe, and therefore, it would be foolish for a nation to refuse to use facial recognition technology if it were available.

   a. What do you think? Can we have a strong state that acts internationally in the online environment that won't feel compelled to turn these same technologies inward to monitor and police their own citizens?

   b. Should there be an international norm against using the internet to spy on your nation's citizens? And how easy or difficult would it be for the international community to enforce that norm?

3. Read the essay "Can the Internet Be Saved?" found at this website: https://mondediplo.com/outsidein/can-the-internet-be-saved.

   a. Does this article reproduce the technological determinist view? Do you agree with it?

   b. Can states change the internet's meaning and parameters, or must it exist in its present form?

   c. What types of measures might you come up with to reform this technology, and what facets of its current form might you eliminate—anonymity, net neutrality?

KEY TERMS

Affordances 37
Dark web 52
Deep web 52
Dual use 39
Emerging technology 46
Free good 37
Function creep 45
Grafting 54
Mature information society 34

Net neutrality 37
Open source software 50
Social construction of technology 45
Social credit system 41
Standards war 40
Surface web 52
Technological closure 45
Virtual private network (VPN) 47
Wassenaar Arrangement 54

FOR FURTHER READING

Klimburg, A. *The Darkening Web: The War for Cyberspace* (New York, NY: Penguin, 2017).

Morozov, E. *The Net Delusion: The Dark Side of Internet Freedom* (New York, NY: Public Affairs, 2016).

Schmitt, M, ed. *Tallinn Manual 2.0 on the International Law Applicable to Cyber Operations* (New York, NY: Cambridge University Press, 2017).

Singer, P. W., and E. Brooking. *Likewar: The Weaponization of Social Media* (New York, NY: Houghton Mifflin, 2018), 3.

3

A REALIST VIEW OF CYBERSPACE

Learning Objectives

At the end of this chapter, students will be able to do the following:

1. Describe significant concepts associated with realism.

2. Apply the realist lens to describing issues of cybersecurity and cyber power.

3. Define cyber capabilities and their relation to both hard and soft power.

4. Define information warfare, asymmetric warfare, and security dilemma.

In this chapter, we introduce the first of the three paradigms that we will apply to understand the international relations of cyberspace. Here we introduce the realist lens, which presents the international system (including cyberspace) as anarchic. Because there is no natural hegemon to rule the international system and establish order, states are instead forced to engage in a self-help system where they must arm themselves to secure the imperative of state survival. The state that has the most power (here including cyber power) within the international system is thus likely to prevail. However, a security dilemma means that as states arm themselves, even if they are doing so for defensive purposes, their actions may appear to others as offensive in nature, leading to a spiral of conflict. The realist lens posits that conflict in the natural state of the international system and that it is unlikely that states will succeed in escaping the conflict spiral because it is an inherent part of the international system. Here, we consider why other states might feel threatened by what they see as a preponderance of American power in cyberspace and the actions that they might take as a result.

In this view, we consider the internet as a theater of war and conflict as states are forced to compete against one another in cyberspace due to facets of the international system and facets of the internet itself. That is, in the realist view, there is something inherently threatening about state activity in cyberspace. States are seen as locked in a spiral of conflict and misperception both in the real world and in cyberspace. In this view, states are seen as having no choice but to compete and arm in cyberspace.

In this chapter, we also ask, what does it mean to be cyber powerful, and how does cyber power work both within cyberspace and within the real world? Can cyber power be deployed outside of cyberspace, and what is the relationship between achieving hegemony or a preponderance of power in cyberspace and achieving hegemony in the international system as a whole?

THE FOUNDATIONS OF THE INTERSTATE SYSTEM: A QUICK REVIEW

To apply traditional international relations understandings to thinking about cyberspace, we begin with a quick review of some basic international relations concepts, including the role of the state and the state's relation to the international system.

What Is a State?

In international relations the state is the principal unit of analysis and primary unit of organization within the international system. What you might think of as a country or nation is referred to as a state. A state is a defined territory held together by institutions of governance, including some form of executive or ruler and a system of courts and other institutions. A state provides infrastructure to citizens, including roads and other utilities. It has a system of extracting citizen resources through taxation or the use of a military levy or conscription. It has a professionalized military that represents the state (rather than merely being a roving band of individuals) and that has the legitimate authority to act on behalf of the state. That is, it does not represent merely the wishes of a particular leader but the will of the state as a whole, no matter who is elected to the office of state leadership.

We can trace the notion of a city-state back to ancient Rome and Greece through considering territories like Athens or Sparta. Each of these city-states had a defined territory, its political institutions (which did not have to be democratic), and was capable of mobilizing its citizens to engage in specific actions. A nation refers to a group of people, all of whom identify as a nation, through sharing certain features like an ethnicity as well as a shared history and language. Not every nation is a state (e.g., a nationality might make up an ethnic minority within a state), and not every state is also a nation (e.g., a state might be multiethnic, with citizens of various nationalities within it).

What Is Sovereignty?

A state is said to be composed of a sovereign territory. Sovereignty, in simple terms, means that each state has the exclusive authority to determine what happens within the territorial borders of their state, free from outside interference by other states or actors. Other states are prohibited from interfering and from usurping that state's inherently governmental powers.

Here, it is essential to bear in mind that what we think of today as the state system (in physical space) was an entity that arose throughout several hundred years. Agricultural societies grew into unitary states with functioning legislatures and judicial systems incrementally beginning in the 1500s. The Peace of Westphalia, which ended the Thirty Years' War in 1648, is widely credited as the document that established the principle of state sovereignty, a crucial building block of our international system today. The signatories of this document agreed to respect one another's borders and to allow each state and its rules to determine what laws and rules applied within its territory.

Also, customary international law, which forms the legal basis for the resolution of many disputes among states in the international system, is a system of legal understandings that has evolved over hundreds of years. States may accept that a legal obligation—or a legal prohibition—exists regarding carrying out a specific action in the international community because doing so has become a custom and there thus exists an expectation that an issue will be handled in a particular fashion. Such customs evolve as legal suits are undertaken, legal rulings take place, and issues are resolved. The Universal Declaration of Human Rights is an example of customary international law—because it serves as a codification of an international consensus about the meaning and place of human rights in the international system—that has evolved gradually over time.[1]

For this reason, many of the issues that states resolved gradually through legal cases, tried over hundreds of years, culminating in a body of understandings known as customary international law, are not yet resolved when it comes to issues of cyberspace. Today, there are competing understandings over how to apply concepts like sovereignty and noninterference, and scholars and policy makers do not all agree on which concepts fit best or how best to apply them. In this chapter, we will also explore some of these controversies.

A REALIST VIEW OF CYBERTHREAT

As noted in Chapter 1, early internet developers had a utopian view in which the internet would be an unregulated, nonhierarchical space in which relations among actors were egalitarian and often anonymous. By 2001, however, this vision seems outdated as new actors began wielding influence in cyberspace, from corporations to states to entities like Google. Here, realists suggest that the environment itself changed in fundamental ways.

Realists believe that cyberspace is a dangerous place characterized by conflict that is inevitable and unavoidable. They view the international system itself as an anarchic space, without order, because there is no overarching authority within the international system, such as a world government. Realist thinking rests on the work of English political theorist Thomas Hobbes (1588–1679), the author of *Leviathan* (1651). Hobbes argues that human beings are not inherently peaceful and that without structures of authority (like government), we would live in a state of nature where life would be "solitary, poor, nasty, brutish and short." Therefore, Hobbes argued that people needed a sovereign to keep order so that people would not fight and kill each other over resources.[2]

Realists like Hans Morgenthau (1904–1980) built upon Hobbes's insights, arguing that the international system itself is a self-help system in which each state's greatest obligation is to protect and defend its territory so that their state would continue to survive rather than being wiped out by a neighbor.[3] Realists believe that states do not inherently trust one another, nor do they have natural shared interests, although they can form alliances or structures of cooperation for specific purposes, such as to repel a larger state. States are thus driven to balance against one another to maintain equilibrium in the international system.

In this view, conflict is inevitable because states' interests are configured by the international system itself. Their preferences (for survival, through conflict if necessary) will not alter over time, nor will they learn to cooperate or figure out how to build structures of peace. Realists see conflict as a zero-sum game in which there can only be one winner, the stronger state which prevails. That international system thus creates a security dilemma: In an anarchic system where states are concerned with survival, they will likely interpret all activities along their borders by their neighbors as offensive in nature, even if their neighbors are engaged in defensive activities. Realists thus argue that escalation of conflict (or the conflict spiral), along with arms races (in which each state competes to have a more technologically advanced and more extensive arsenal of weapons than its neighbors), are an inherent feature of the international system, even if, for example, the leader of a state might have different preferences for these relations.

Cyber Realism, Cyberterritory, and Cyber Capabilities

How does the lens of realism apply to cyberspace? Can we describe ideas like a security dilemma in cyberspace or an arms race in cyberspace?

As early as 2001, analyst Gregory Rattray argued that "cyberspace ... is actually a physical domain resulting from the creation of information systems and networks that enable electronic interaction to take place." That is, he argued that cyberspace is an electronic extension of physical, real-world territory. Here, he noted that "digital attacks on information systems take place within the physical world" because data resides on physical equipment in physical locations.[4]

Barry Posen built upon Rattray's insights in 2003, suggesting that the US military could acquire "command of the commons" of cyberspace. His work established an understanding that cyberspace was a militarized domain (not a global village) and that it could be viewed as "strategic terrain." Posen argued that nations could own and administer "their cyberspace" and that indeed, states had a duty to do so to protect their digital and real, physical assets located in both cyberspace and physical space.[5]

Realists also believe that states are compelled (by the international system) to compete for control of cyberspace—and that traditional rivalries (such as that between the United States and China or the United States and Russia) will be reproduced in cyberspace. They view the quest for cybersecurity as **zero sum,** meaning that in other words, realists believe that one state's attempts at producing cybersecurity will necessarily be viewed as threatening by its neighbors, who will then arm themselves. In such a situation, then, realists believe, if cooperation does occur, it will be temporary, and the prospects for a long-lasting peace in cyberspace are nil.[6]

In describing why cyberspace is not an ideal world apart, but rather part of existing space, analysts point to the physicality of the infrastructure of cyberspace's hardware or backbone. That is, although the internet's activity allows ideas and commerce to circulate or flow "through the ether" free of the strictures of national borders, the internet is also composed of physical structures like trunk cables and server farms. These are tangible physical assets located within the concrete, geophysical borders of specific states. Cyberspace's physical infrastructure includes the following:

- Land and undersea cables that produce connections among people, organizations, and states

- Communication satellites that orbit the Earth, passing through and above the physical space of specific states

- Server farms, routers, and other essential hardware

- Physical facilities belonging to groups that administer cyberspace, such as national computer emergency response teams

Realists therefore reject the idea that there is an information commons or that the internet is predominantly a good that states should share and administer together. Instead, states should construe their role as that of guarding "their cyberspace" and "their cyber infrastructure."[7] In this view, the security concerns that planners face in cyber are not different or unique to cyberspace. And cyber threats are described as existential threats that have the potential to destroy a state—just as surely as a conventional or nuclear strike might.

What Is the Fifth Domain of Warfare?

Beginning in 2009, the US National Security Agency, along with the Department of Defense, established the United States Cyber Command. In 2018, USCYBERCOM achieved the status of a full independent combatant command. There are currently ten unified commands within the US Department of Defense, with most associated with specific geographic areas (e.g., PACOM focuses on the coordination of military activities in the Pacific Region, whereas NORTHCOM focuses on coordinating military activity in North America). Each command is led by a combatant commander who is a senior military officer from one of the armed services.

Just as there are specific branches of the armed services assigned to defend each of the other four domains—land, sea, air, and space—the cyber command is tasked with defending "US cyberspace," which is the fifth domain. The cyber command defends the Department of Defense's internal network (the DoDIN) as well as supports many of the types of conventional and unconventional military operations that depend on access to computer resources. For example, those individuals and groups that operate and utilize nuclear weapons are dependent on digital sensors that detect incoming attacks and prepare to respond, and naval aircraft carriers are highly dependent on geographic positioning systems and other types of data sensors and data management operations. US military command, control, communications, and intelligence functions are highly dependent on access to functioning information systems, as are many types of electronic warfare (which include intercepting enemy intelligence and making sure that others are not intercepting one's communications).

Also, the US Cyber Command protects critical infrastructure within the United States as well as working with traditional US allies, like other NATO members, to make sure that all members are prepared to fight in cyberspace. Increasingly, working in this fifth domain has meant not only defending and preparing to defend US and allied assets in cyberspace; it has also meant developing offensive cyberweapons and preparing to take offensive measures in cyberspace. The US Cyber Command also trains those individuals who work in cyberspace defense.

Many times during warfare, a conflict might be fought on multiple fronts or in multiple domains. For example, during World War Two, Allied ground forces fought alongside members of US and Allied air and naval forces. In a conflict that occurs today or in the future, the cyber command will fight alongside members of other domains because all aspects of warfare are intimately linked. As new technologies are developed, members of the army are learning to work together or alongside types of machines. Snipers might

(Continued)

PEOPLE AND PLACES

rely on electronic targeting systems, infantry members might use wearable exoskeletons to augment their ability to travel long distances or carry heavy loads, and units might be better able to communicate with each other during wartime through wearing helmets equipped with Blue Force tracking technology, which shows soldiers and their leaders where all members of the unit are at all times. Cyber command plays a vital role in supporting the systems utilized by those flying unarmed autonomous vehicles, or drones. Also, cyber command is likely to play a growing role in those aspects of warfare that are dependent on artificial intelligence in the future.

Sources

Department of Defense. "Department of Defense Cyber Strategy." Accessed November 28, 2018. https://media.defense.gov/2018/Sep/18/2002041659/-1/-1/1/Factsheet_for_Strategy_and_CPR_FINAL.pdf

United States Cyber Command. "Mission and Vision." Accessed November 28, 2018. https://www.cybercom.mil/About/Mission-and-Vision/.

What Is Cyber Capability?

If states have similar security concerns in the real world and online, then how does the power accrued in one venue transfer to the other realm? In 1957, Robert Dahl noted that A could be said to have power over B if "he can get B to do something he would not otherwise do."[8] That is, in his mind, states were powerful when they could force or coerce others into doing things at their behest.

Later analysts distinguished between the hard power of military might, which allows one state to coerce another state into carrying out a specific action, and soft power, or the power of ideas. A state could use soft power to attract adherents to a particular policy position and can also persuade others through the power of ideas. That is, one could either compel other states to carry out key ideas, or one could influence them into changing their preferences through the deployment of soft power.

How can we apply these understandings to cyberspace? Nye describes **cyber power** as the ability to use the cyber domain to compel and coerce other actors. He defines four key components of cyber power. Capital strength refers to a state's physical cyber resources. This includes hardware like cables that form the internet's backbone, along with technological competencies like a well-developed infrastructure of ISPs and a robust and stable source of electricity. The second component is cyber workforce technical skills—the ability to create new types of products (such as the highly customized weapons known as advanced persistent threats) and to respond defensively and offensively to system attacks. The third component is intelligence—the ability to collect information on what one's adversaries are doing and the ability to affect the information other states are receiving, including information about your activities and capabilities. The final component is strategy—the ability to think long term about activities in cyberspace, establishing the necessary physical capabilities, training a workforce, and developing offensive and defensive cyberweapons.[9]

MEASURING CYBER CAPABILITY

But which state has the highest level of cyber capability, and how do the states of the world rank on a list of world cyber capabilities? There is little consensus regarding this question because there is at present not one universally accepted way of measuring a state's cyber power. Instead, analysts consider several different indicators.

Resilience preparedness describes a state's ability to survive an enemy cyberattack by another state or by a nonstate actor. Analysts who study cyber preparedness and emergency management stress this indicator's importance. They argue that although two states might have similar amounts of cyber infrastructure and levels of development, they may nonetheless differ in their commitment and ability to guard against system risk or cyber vulnerabilities. The International Telecommunications Union has begun preparing cyber wellness profiles of states. These profiles rely on the Cyber Readiness Index, which looks at a state's legal, technical, and organizational capacities—that is, whether it has laws in place to regulate its cyber industries and whether it has sufficient technical personnel and developed organizations in the cyber field. This index also considers how a country is doing in the field of capacity building and cooperation with other states. We might also consider whether states have a national cybersecurity strategy, whether they have a computer emergency response team (CERT), whether they have mechanisms for sharing information between the public and private sector, whether they are investing in cybersecurity research, and whether there is funding for cybersecurity initiatives.[10]

Still other analysts focus on the size of a state's weaknesses and the vulnerabilities that exist in their systems. They rank states from most to least mature based on how well they have done in identifying their weaknesses and working to put systems into place to address these weaknesses.[11]

Some analysts consider cybersecurity capability as both a technical and a political concept. Thus, they also consider whether a state has a clear and well-defined cyber strategy as well as clear military doctrines regarding the conditions for cyberweapon use.[12]

(Continued)

A state's possession of cyber capabilities, as well as the rankings of states based on their cyber capabilities, may be dynamic. Although we can easily identify and rank states in terms of conventional military capabilities, and although those rankings stay relatively constant, a ranking of cyber capabilities can shift quickly because cyberweapons are not produced on the same timeframe as conventional weapons. (For example, it might take years to produce an aircraft carrier, whereas a cyberweapon could be "assembled" overnight.) And although currently states with a **first-mover advantage** are at the top of the cyber capability hierarchy, these advantages may wane over time, upsetting the existing rankings.

Finally, given the ability of cyber materials—and cyber experts and their expertise—to move quickly across national borders, it may be difficult to know definitively which expertise and which weapons reside within which geographic borders. Some indexes address this problem through considering whether a state has strong information-sharing arrangements with other states, for example. However, there are reasons to be pessimistic about our ability to develop a universally valid and accurate cyber capability ranking over the long term.

Analysts identify four cyberspace layers—an infrastructure layer (which includes elements like the internet's backbone), a physical hardware layer (which includes elements like the electromagnetic spectrum), a syntactic layer (which includes software and network routing algorithms), and a semantic layer (which includes components that allow users to make sense of information). Here they note that having "command" over one layer does not necessarily translate to having command over other layers and that power is not necessarily fungible between layers. (That is, a state that has a highly developed infrastructure but that simultaneously has a weak semantic layer—because its citizens do not believe the information they access on social media, and much of that information is of poor or unregulated quality—might still struggle to become a major cyber power.)

We can include cyber capabilities within the US military's DIME model, which identifies four components of state power—diplomatic, informational, military, and economic. Cyber capabilities can affect diplomatic and informational elements: States can influence others in cyberspace through propaganda, psychological operations, and information warfare. Cyber capabilities are also part of military and economic power because information technology can be used to administer a complex infrastructure and deploy trained personnel throughout cyberspace. The term *force multiplier* is thus used to describe cyber power because it can be deployed along with other more traditional components of both soft and hard power to magnify their impact. That is, both Russian and American military planners have argued that information warfare can be used to "prepare the battlefield" for a conventional war. A traditional armed invasion can be much more successful if cyber warfare has first been applied to ensure that the country being invaded has no working electricity, lights, or ability to communicate with citizens or soldiers. [13]

In addition, **resilience** is a component of cyber power. Resilience is defined as "the ability of a system to resist, absorb, recover from or successfully adapt to a change in environment or conditions."[14] Resilience is important because cyberspace is a dynamic and unstable domain that is particularly vulnerable to "natural disasters, accidents, human error and malicious acts" that could cause internet connectivity, for example, to go offline.

Strategic doctrine refers to the articulation of the conditions under which cyber power might be used and how it might be deployed as well as how it might be deployed in concert with other elements of state power, including conventional forces.[15] Here, strategic doctrines describe how it is possible for a state to utilize cyber power to overcome other types of constraints that they might face, including being a small state or one with a low population density.[16]

In thinking about what makes a state powerful, we often assume that democracy is a key component of state power. Democracies are able to implement policies with strong citizen support because democratic citizens regard their government as legitimate and believe that their values are worth fighting for. However, many analysts today argue that democratic states do not have an advantage in terms of creating cyber capabilities. Analysts like Klimburg demonstrate how authoritarian states can compel even private ISPs in their nations to implement policies in the areas of surveillance and cybersecurity.[17] In contrast, democratic nations can often only suggest or request that private ISPs take steps in these areas.

Hacks, Spoofs, and Computer Network Exploitation (CNE)

As long as humans have had access to computers, talented individuals have tested the limits of these machines in all areas. In some cases, specialists have simply been curious to see what these computers could do: Could they detect intruders? Could a savvy user get around firewalls and other protections put in place to protect the data used by the computer? Could a smart person crack the codes used to encrypt messages and other data? Computer hacking—or attempting to enter a system without authorization—is an age-old practice that will likely never be entirely eliminated.

However, in other cases, computer specialists have had more harmful aims as they sought to understand, penetrate, and utilize these computers—often to enrich themselves and their organizations. In the process, these hackers (or crackers) may violate local and national laws and may often seek to actively damage the systems that they have penetrated. Terrorist organizations may seek to alter records of financial transactions, to siphon off money

(Continued)

TOOLS OF THE TRADE

(Continued)

for illegal pursuits, or to harm a nation's critical infrastructure. Enemy states may employ teams of professional hackers, often associated with their military forces, who may hack with the intent of slowing or disabling a nation's defensive systems. State-sponsored hackers may also engage in information warfare, sometimes using a state's own computers to send out false information in an attempt to stir up domestic unrest in an enemy state or even to sow domestic chaos through depriving citizens of vital resources (which may depend on a computer infrastructure to be manufactured and distributed), such as clean water or safe food.

Although the motives of the **white hat hackers** (who will invade a computer system just to see if they can do it and then alert the proper authorities of the breach discovered) and the black hat hackers (who will invade a system to see if they can destroy it or steal material or harm society) may differ, the tools used are often the same. Here we pause to briefly consider the tools used by hackers.

Types of Malware

Malware refers to any type of computer program that is intended to harm a user's computer. Malware is a general term that encompasses viruses, Trojans, and spyware.

A **virus** is a piece of malicious code that attaches itself to an existing file or program. As this file or program is exchanged by computers within or outside a network, the virus spreads, embedding itself within a number of host computers, where it can then be triggered to carry out actions including destroying data and files or collecting information about a system that it invades.

A **worm** refers to a computer program that self-replicates, making copies of itself and then spreading from computer to computer. Unlike a virus, a worm can spread independently without being attached to a specific file or program.

A **rootkit** is a collection of files that, once installed upon a host computer, allows the rootkit's deployer to carry out a variety of different types of activities on the host computer. In essence, it provides the deployer with all of the privileges that a system administrator for a network would have. The deployer can change passwords, update and change programs and configuration files for the computer, as well as engaging in activities (such as turning on a microphone or camera) for spying or intelligence gathering purposes. A rootkit is a specific type of malware that is again hidden from the host computer's administrators.[18]

Ransomware refers to programs that, once installed on a host computer system, may carry out instructions to encrypt or "lock" the user's access to data files on the computer. Computer owners may then receive an e-mail or phone call instructing them to pay a ransom to receive a key to unlock their files, which are being held hostage by the attacker. If the victim does not pay in time, the attack may threaten to destroy all of the data. A variety of targets in the United States and abroad have been subject to ransomware attacks, including city governments and hospitals.

Spyware refers to programs that aim to collect data from a targeting computer rather than to disrupt and destroy the system. Spyware may exist in an adversary's computer for a prolonged period of time without the host being aware that it is there. Types of spyware include keystroke loggers as well as cookies that can be installed on a system to monitor where users go on the web and what they do. Spyware is illegal in many countries and regions because it violates user privacy as it collects their information without their permission. Spyware may be deployed for military, espionage, or commercial purposes.

All of the weapons described here may be deployed as they are written, or they can be customized to work in specific environments. (In this way, they are similar to biological or chemical weapons, where a trained worker might alter a type of bacteria to make it airborne or waterborne or more or less virulent.) The code for a computer weapon of this sort then can be repackaged and resold by its original creator through auction and transaction sites found on the dark web. The same weapon might be deployed in a variety of times, then, in a variety of settings—with slight variations in the code used to make the original weapon.

Advanced persistent threats (APTs) are highly specialized weapons aimed at specific targets that can be developed only by sophisticated weapons teams, such as those working in a state military facility. The United States has accused both Russia and China of deploying weapons that are APTs.

Modes of Deployment

A Trojan horse attack refers to the practice of placing a specific piece of malicious code that runs within an existing file or program (rather than being attached, as a virus is). A Trojan attack may be triggered by the fulfillment of a specific set of conditions, and when these conditions are met, it may begin its work of destroying programs or data or sharing information from the targeted system with other computers or the public.

Zero day exploits (ZDEs) refer to activities in which an attacker may enter a computer system for the purposes of installing malware or spyware that can then be deployed at a later date. A ZDE can be deployed manually by the attacker or configured to turn itself on automatically in response to a specific event. (In other words, the code installed on a system might include an "if, then" clause stating, "If the stock market's Dow Jones Industrial Average falls

(Continued)

(Continued)

below this value, then begin carrying out these instructions"—such as wiping out all records of financial transactions and assets.) ZDEs are regarded as particularly dangerous because the computer system's owner may not even know that this malware has been installed upon the system until it later detonates. Although programs exist to scan both state and commercial network systems for devices like this, they are not always successful in identifying them. ZDEs are said to hide within a system until they are detonated or deployed.

The weapons described here—viruses and worms—are types of cyberweapons. Trojan horse attacks and ZDEs refer to the method of deployment or method of attack for these weapons. In this way, a virus can be said to be a Trojan horse virus because it hides within an existing program, or a ZDE may involve creating code that instructs a worm to begin replicating on a certain date.

Phishing is a practice in which an individual, state, or corporation may masquerade as someone else, through, for example, utilizing an e-mail address that is almost the same as a real address, which the recipient may be familiar with and trust. (For example, an individual might receive an e-mail from bankoamerica.com rather than bankofamerica.com and click on it, not noticing the one-letter difference from the safe address.) The individual recipient is thus tricked into clicking on a link that contains malware or even clicking on a link taking them to a replica site that looks like their bank but is in fact not. The individual might thus upload or send vital security information, such as a password or social security number, to the false address, believing it to be the real one.

Spoofing refers to practices in which replica sites and replica addresses are set up to fool targets into believing that they are the real addresses. In recent years, US naval ships have been the target of spoofing attacks. In 2018, the Russian government created false sites that replicated the addresses of GPS satellites, which ships have utilized for navigation. The US ships connected to the false sites and found themselves in locations different from the ones that they believed they were in because Russian hackers altered the GPS data being sent to the ships.

Goals of Computer Attacks

Just as computer weapons can be deployed in a variety of settings in a variety of ways, they can also be deployed toward a variety of different ends. They can thus form part of a strategy of political, technological, or economic warfare—either by a nation-state or by a non-nation-state attacker.

Computer network exploitation (CNE) is a subset of computer hacking activities, specifically those activities related to espionage and reconnaissance. Individuals engaged in CNE activities seek to gather information from a target's computers. They may be interested in collecting commercial intelligence about a rival company's technological advances, or they may be a state interested in collecting military or commercial intelligence about a rival state. CNE operations may be ongoing. That is, a hacker might visit a computer system to look around and to see how information is organized. (This is referred to as engaging in reconnaissance.) Once an enemy has a map of your state's computer systems, then, it can develop more precise weapons targeted at your state's specific vulnerabilities.[19]

Some of the most well-known CNE activities include the deployment of the Flame spy tool, which was discovered in May 2012 by Iran's National CERT. This type of spyware can spread quickly among computers that interface with one another—and once installed, the program can take screen shots of a targeted computer and record audio and video through the computer's own capabilities. It also includes a keystroke logger that can record all of the typing that takes place on a computer, allowing an enemy to eavesdrop on the user, even when he or she is producing classified information. Flame also records Skype conversations, allows broadcasting from the targeted computer to other nearby computers and devices using Bluetooth, and can record and share records of network traffic between the targeted computer and other computers. Flame spyware has been found on more than one thousand computers in nations including Iran, Israel, Palestine, Sudan, Syria, Lebanon, Saudi Arabia, and Egypt, as well as in the United States and North America.[20] The computing community disagrees about who created Flame and when and for what purpose. Some analysts argue that it shares similarities with other programs created by Kaspersky Laboratory, a Russian company that manufactures and sells computer security packages. Others believe that it may have been created by the US National Security Agency or the US Central Intelligence Agency, working in concert with Israel's Department of Defense. The malware has also been referred to as "Wiper," although some analysts believe that Wiper is a related but separate program.[21]

Experts in **computer forensic investigation** concentrate on conducting detective work that allows them to identify the creators of specific pieces of malware, often through searching for a signature that may indicate the nationality or background of the software's developer. (For example, programmers might write comments next to certain steps in a computer program in their native language. In addition, certain programmers may favor certain sequences of steps in solving a problem, which can then be identified as belonging to a particular programmer or lab.) Computer forensics thus shares common ground with other scientific practices, such as medicine and biology, where analysts may scan sequences of DNA to identify patterns and better classify diseases, aiding in diagnoses. Looking for the "signature" of a particular programmer is also in some ways similar to what musicians or literary analysts do in seeking to identify the work of a particular composer or author based on knowledge of that person's previous works.

(Continued)

(Continued)

Computer Network Attack (CNA)

Computer network attacks (CNAs) are classified as active rather than passive operations. Those who engage in CNAs are not interested merely in gathering information or preparing for future operations. Rather, they wish to achieve three actions: damaging, destroying, or disrupting computer operations or related actions (like military actions) that depend on computers for their operations.

One of the best-known CNA actions was the deployment of the Stuxnet worm, first identified in 2010. This worm is believed to have been built by the United States, working in collaboration in Israel. The worm was deployed against nuclear energy facilities in Iran, which the United States believed was in the process of creating nuclear weapons. The worm sent instructions to command and control systems within Iranian plants, which led to the gradual degradation of their equipment and served to significantly slow down their development of nuclear capability.

Others include attacks upon Ukraine's power distribution centers by Russia in 2015. These attacks were seen as coordinated by Russia's military, aimed at increasing the likelihood of success of Russia's armed invasion of Crimea in that year.

Here, both CNA and CNE can be seen as stages within military activity aimed at "preparing the battlefield" for later, ongoing conventional operations. For example, computer network exploitation might be utilized to peer into an enemy's computers to see where forces are deployed to utilize the element of surprise in carrying out an attack. (CNE would thus aid in "intelligence preparation of the battlefield.") CNA might be used to disable an enemy state's ability to communicate with its forces, who might be deployed throughout a region, thereby conferring an advantage upon the invading army if defending troops could not communicate with one another. (CNE and CNA activities might also be combined as part of the prelude to a conventional attack, gathering intelligence capabilities first and then deploying attacks against specific targets identified as the result of CNE activities.)[22]

Currently, there is not an international consensus regarding whether and under what conditions CNAs should be illegal according to international law as well as whether a CNA constitutes an act of war under existing international law. We delve into these questions more in Chapter 11 on cyberwarfare.

Today, other controversies include the question of whether election hacking could be considered a CNA and whether this too should be prohibited under international law. Finally, states do not all agree regarding what types of responses should be appropriate and legal when a CNA occurs. For example, can one state attack another with conventional military weapons if a CNA is viewed as the first stage in a conventional war, for example?

Cyber-Enabled Economic Warfare (CEEW)

The term **cyber-enabled economic warfare** (CEEW) refers to actions carried out using computers that aim to harm an adversary state's economy to adversely affect its political and military strength. The notion of attempting to adversely affect an adversary state's economy is not new. Indeed, states have long used tools like sanctions to exclude an adversary from participating in global import and export flows and the freezing of an adversary's assets, which might be deposited in foreign banks, to harm a nation economically. However, as Kuo points out, today, computers have made it easier and less expensive for an adversary nation to undertake economic attacks, and these attacks have become more ubiquitous.[23] Thus, CEEWs can be carried out as a type of **asymmetric warfare,** in which the costs of defending from an attack are significantly greater than the costs of carrying out an attack—enabling a smaller enemy to do extreme damage to a larger, better-resourced enemy.

In recent years, North Korea has utilized CEEW to carry out targeted attacks upon the economy of its neighbor, South Korea. The aim is to disrupt South Korea's economy, leading to repercussions in international financial markets as well as negative effects upon South Korea's military preparedness due to shortfalls in its military budget.[24] Other significant CEEW attacks include Iran's attack on the computer network of the Saudi Aramco oil corporation in 2012 and China's economic espionage against the United States, resulting in the theft of intellectual property.

Today, authors distinguish between CEEW and other types of attacks, such as cyber financial warfare and cybercrime.[25] CEEW attacks are thus distinguished from, for example, an attack carried out by a terrorist organization upon a bank aimed at securing financing for additional terrorist activities.

Doxing

Doxing refers to the public release of potentially embarrassing personal information about a person or organization. Doxing attacks often rely upon the use of spyware or phishing attacks in which an individual or group gains privileged access to a system to search for potentially embarrassing information that can then be publicly released or used to blackmail an individual who does not want his or her secrets to be known. One of the most well-known doxing acts was a public release in 2015 of the lists of users of AshleyMadison.com, an online site for people wishing to have extramarital affairs. Among those named as clients of the site were individuals with .gov and .mil e-mail addresses, suggesting that the US government and military employees were utilizing the site, possibly during their workdays.

In addition, in 2014, the US motion picture company Sony Pictures was hacked, most likely by North Korea's government. The North Korean government

(Continued)

(Continued)

was angry about Sony's release of a movie that portrayed their leader in an unflattering light. In retaliation, the hackers released a large cache of internal e-mails in which Sony executives discussed well-known actors and actresses in Hollywood. The release of these e-mails also counts as a form of doxing.

Figure 3.1 helps distinguish among those terms that refer to weapons, those that refer to modes of deployment, and those that refer to the goals of an attack.

Figure 3.1   Types of Cyber Weapons

Types of Weapons	Virus Worm Spyware Ransomware
Modes of Deployment	Trojan Horse Zero Day Exploit (ZDE) Phishing Spoofing
Goals of Attack	Cyber-Enabled Economic Warfare (CEEW) Computer Network Exploitation (CNE) Computer Network Attack (CNA) Intelligence Preparation of Battlefield Preparation of Battlefield Embarrass a Target

A Balance of Power in Cyberspace?

The realist view of international relations describes the international system as tending toward stable and predictable behavior. Here, state actions focused on self-preservation are seen as crucial factors in preserving that stability. In particular, we can point to the act of balancing, in which states can form new alliances or add new members to an existing alliance to preserve the balance of power between two or more players. Here, analysts point to the Cold War between Russia and the United States, which occurred from 1947 until 1989. Here, they argue that the bipolar configuration of the international system, in which the United States and the Soviet Union engaged in activities—military, political, and economic—designed to preserve the balance of power between the two states, helped preserve international system stability.

We can also identify emerging cyber power configurations (including alliances) in cyberspace. Initially, we saw a unipolar system in which the United States was a hegemon with the preponderance of power. Indeed, the United States is still considered the preeminent cyber power, but much of its power is based upon historical factors, such as the fact that the technology developed initially in the United States. (That is, the United States enjoys advantages related to path dependency and first-mover advantage.) Furthermore, it has thus far been easier for the United States to wield soft power throughout the internet because so many of the communications on the internet occur in English and because many individuals possess a common language for discussing ideas through the influence of media like Hollywood movies and American television. However, over time, the United States may see that first-mover advantage become less significant as new players move into the cyber conflict space.[26]

In describing the current situation, Sanger points to the "seven sisters" of cyber conflict—United States, Russia, China, Britain, Iran, Israel, and North Korea. These are nations with established cyber capabilities that have carried out significant events in the cyber arena. However, he notes that there are other nations—from Vietnam to Mexico—who are closing in as players in this arena.[27]

But many analysts view the international system of cyberspace as less stable than the terrestrial international system for several reasons: First, it is difficult to predict how many states currently have a fully developed cyber capability and how many might soon achieve one. The term *power gap* refers to the differences among states that are major cyber powers and those that are not. This gap is narrowing quickly, and just as significantly, the power gap between states and other types of actors (like terrorist organizations and other types of nonstate actors) is narrowing. This is because although it may take several years for a state to build up the sort of military (conventional or nuclear) forces that would cause it to be a major player in the international system, a country could quickly become a cyber power. In addition, because it is cheaper and faster to develop cyber weapons—and the major constraint upon a state's ability to do so lies in their ability to field a significant number of highly educated cyber warriors—we may in the future see even nations that did not have a significant conventional defense force but nonetheless wielding influence in cyberspace.[28]

CONSTRUCTING ALLIANCES IN CYBERSPACE

As noted, states frequently form alliances to preserve the balance of power. Alliance formation is an ancient idea that can be traced back to the Greek city-states. More recently, we can point to alliances like the Allied Powers, who fought together in World War Two against Nazi aggression, or the twelve founding members of NATO, which emerged as a defensive pact against Soviet aggression after World War Two.

We can define an alliance as "a formal agreement between two or more nations to collaborate on national security issues." For something to count as an alliance (rather than simply an informal type of friendship or an ad-hoc arrangement), three elements need to be present: There must be a formal treaty, directly concerned with national security issues, between partners who are nation-states.[29]

Bergmann points to eight elements that need to be present for an agreement to be considered an alliance: Arrangements must be between states; agreements must be explicit; they must deal with specific behavior for a particular contingency in the future; the future contingency must be uncertain; cooperation must be promised; states must agree to provide assistance in response to the event (usually an attack by a specific party) including the use of one's resources for defense; the promise must be mutual; and the agreement must be in the realm of national security.[30]

Both definitions allow for the possibility of a broad-ranging treaty or agreement that might cover a variety of types of cooperation from the provision of maritime security to air security to cybersecurity. Recently, many existing alliances—like NATO—have broadened their mandate to include cybersecurity cooperation. New alliances have also been created, like the Shanghai Cooperation Organization, which prioritizes cybersecurity cooperation, although it also contains other elements, including economic cooperation. Therefore, it does not make sense to speak of a separate balance of power or separate series of alliances in cyberspace. Instead, we might speak of "cybered alliances," as elements of cybersecurity are grafted onto existing alliances.

We can also distinguish between traditional military alliances—and structures for cooperation—such as the United Nations, the Council of Europe, and Association of South East Asian Nations (ASEAN). Structures for cooperation are better understood as regimes, utilizing the lens of liberal internationalism, rather than as military alliances. We consider their role in providing cybersecurity and cyber cooperation in more depth in Chapter 4.

Expanding the **NATO** Alliance

In 2008, NATO held the Bucharest Summit to address questions regarding the carrying out of cyberattacks formally. In the 1949 founding documents of the NATO Alliance, Article 5 stated that an attack on any one member would be treated as an attack on all members, with all members committed to the principle of collective defense. In 2008, they began to consider whether Article 5 should mean that all states should respond to defend a member who was the subject of a cyberattack rather than a conventional or nuclear attack. As a result of that meeting, NATO created two new structures: the Cyber Defense Management Authority, which works to strengthen interoperability among all member nations' resources in the area of cyber defense as well as to share information among members regarding cyberattacks, and the Cooperative Cyber Defense Center of Excellence, which works to create long-term strategy and doctrine related to the deployment of cyberweapons for defensive purposes. NATO decided that Article 5 does not apply to cyberattacks but that members should "consult together" (as required in Article 4) if a member is the subject of a cyberattack.[31]

The Shanghai Cooperation Organization (SCO)

The Shanghai Cooperation Organization (SCO) was founded in 2001, with Russia playing a leading role in establishing the structure. It currently has eight members—China, Russia, Kazakhstan, Kyrgyzstan, Tajikistan, Uzbekistan, Pakist___, and India. It describes itself as "a Eurasian political, economic and military organization," which exists to address six different types of issues: security concerns, border issues, military cooperation, intelligence sharing, counterterrorism, and countering American influence in Central Asia. Although it is widely regarded as an Eastern counterbalance to NATO, the organization is not only a military alliance.[32] Analysts note that most members (with the exception of India) are highly authoritarian, and these members also desired to shield their nations from what they regarded as corrupting Western influences that they saw existing in cyberspace. Deibert describes how Central Asian states have learned from Russia, in particular, within the organization and, as a result, have implemented legislation that would require ISPs and telecommunications companies operating in their states to automatically store information and share it with state authorities. Also, states within the SCO have designed and shared information controls, including commercial platforms for mass surveillance.

Deibert thus argues that the group functions more like a regime (or regional cooperation forum) than an alliance because its existence rests on a shared normative project of combating "three evils": terrorism, separatism, and extremism. Thus, the states of the SCO share norms and values regarding how they believe the internet should be structured and how it should develop in the future. Here, all nations support a position of cyber sovereignty, in which space could be construed as "belonging" to Russia, or China and India, and where states would have full and free authority to implement information controls within their virtual "borders."[33]

Also, as we will see later in this text, the term *cyberattack* itself is subject to a variety of interpretations. Although an alliance like NATO or an organization like the US Cyber Command regards a cyberattack as a military action that requires a military response, other organizations—like the Council of Europe, ASEAN, and the Organization of American States—actually regard cyberattacks as a type of crime rather than a military act.[34] Thus, they have utilized other types of agreements, including cooperative agreements aimed at allowing states to work together to combat crime in response to cyberattacks.

Cyber Pessimists versus Cyber Optimists

Not all analysts agree about the relationship between traditional components of power within the international system (such as nuclear or conventional military capabilities) and cyber power. Here, we distinguish between policy makers who are cyber pessimists and those who are cyber optimists.

Cyber optimists believe that even in situations when states (and other actors) develop significant cyber capabilities, this development is unlikely to destabilize the (conventional, territorial) international system. They believe that cyberweapons will serve mainly as a new type of deterrent; that is, states will be unlikely to unleash significant cyberattacks but that they will make it publicly known that they have the capability to do so to lessen the likelihood that other nations will take actions against them—from territorial attacks to taking economic reprisals against them through utilizing a weapon like sanctions.

Cyber pessimists, however, take a somewhat broader view of the utility that states will derive from becoming cyber powers. They describe the advent of cyber power as a revolutionary development that has the power to reshape global power distributions.[35] Cyber pessimists also worry that the advent of cyberweapons and cyber power can destabilize the international order and make conflict more likely.

Whether one is a cyber pessimist or a cyber optimist, what is clear is that a great deal of the utility that cyberweapons pose to their owners and wielders relates to their ability to achieve non-cyber-related aims. Here, we can consider how Russia utilized cyberattacks—including the weaponization of social media— to influence the 2016 presidential elections in the United States. In addition, China has utilized cyber espionage to steal commercial and military secrets from US vendors in particular. As a result, China has been able to create new conventional military weapons (including aircraft and aircraft carriers) utilizing the stolen technology information obtained through cyber espionage.[36]

In considering the relationship between cyber power and other measures of power, we also see that states may have different goals related to state survival within the international system and, as a result, may have different requirements for what it means for their particular nation to be "cyber powerful." Democracies with open and free medias face different threats than do more closed authoritarian systems. Well-developed consumer societies face greater dangers because citizens may conduct more and more of their financial lives online and because they may possess multiple devices that connected to the internet, therefore providing a larger "attack surface" for adversaries. Moreover, as cyberweapons themselves change, definitions and understandings of cyber power will likely change as well.

THE BEGINNING OF CYBERWAR

In Chapter 1, we presented a timeline of the key events that characterize the "history of cyberspace" to this point. However, for a realist, some of these events are more salient or significant than others. In the realist lens, the important story that one tells about the history of the internet might actually be one that focuses on the advent and continuation of cyber conflict or cyberwar within the international system. For this reason, we present a short history of cyberwar in this section.

As we see in Chapter 7, on cyber conflict, however, not all analysts agree about the existence of cyberwar as a concept, nor do all analysts classify all altercations that have occurred among states in cyberspace as war. Thus, analysts disagree about what event actually constituted the first cyberwar in cyberspace.

For our purposes, however, we begin our history with a cyber conflict that began in in 2007, when Russia was accused of conducting cyberwarfare against Estonia through defacing and shutting down government websites and shutting off electricity to the region.

The following year, a cyber conflict occurred between Russia and Georgia in 2008. In August 2008, Russia and the former Soviet republic of Georgia were engaged in an ongoing conventional war, which had begun in 2003, precipitated by a territorial dispute. Although Georgia had become an independent state, separate from Russia, in 1991, Georgia and Russia were still disputing ownership of two territories—South Ossetia and Abkhazia—which were ethnically Georgian but located within the territory of Russia.

The Russo-Georgian cyberwar of August 2008 is the first time in which cyber warfare had been used as part of an ongoing conventional war. Specifically, Russian cyber forces carried out acts of vandalism and destruction against Georgia's government. They defaced Georgian state websites, uploading pictures of Georgia's leader posing with Hitler, for example. They also engaged in **distributed denial of device (DDOS) attacks** against Georgian government sites, in essence contacting the sites so many times that they eventually were inaccessible to those who wished to reach them to gain information about events that were taking place. Here, as Deibert et al. point out, researchers know that these attacks originated within Russia, but it is unclear if Moscow ordered them, if Moscow sponsored them, or if they were merely tolerated by Moscow. This, as Deibert et al. note, is a new hallmark of information warfare. It is often impossible for researchers to trace responsibility for an attack back to a specific state or structure within a state, and this makes responding to attacks or punishing those who carry them out particularly challenging.

The cyberattack was carried out using both software and hardware attacks. In particular, Russian forces were able to sever the main cable that carries the internet signal into Tbilisi, Georgia's capital, thus affecting its physical infrastructure. In this way, Georgia was also cut off from the internet at times during the conflict.

THE FIRST CYBER ATTACK—STUXNET

In considering the historical development of cyber warfare, analysts often reference the 2010 Stuxnet attack against Iran's nuclear program. This attack was significant for several reasons. First, it was an attack launched by a state (the United States and perhaps Israel as well) aimed specifically at another state to alter or halt a state's policies (in this case, Iran's attempt at launching a nuclear weapons program). The attack was successful, resulting in a slowdown of Iran's ability to achieve the manufacture of a nuclear weapon.

The use of the Stuxnet virus was thus one of the first times where a state used a cyberattack and a cyberweapon as a substitute for a conventional attack. And because Stuxnet is considered to have been a successful attack, it increased the likelihood that states would increasingly choose to develop

(Continued)

PEOPLE AND PLACES

(Continued)

and deploy cyberweapons in addition to or instead of conventional weapons and attacks.

The attack was sophisticated technologically. Because US military and civilian intelligence operatives were unable to access the physical facility directly, they instead unleashed the Stuxnet virus utilizing a worm that spread across Microsoft Windows systems worldwide.

However, the software virus that was deployed was specifically targeted for this particular plant. Its "payload" was designed to detonate only when it encountered a particular target, specifically an industrial control system that matched specific characteristics. It was a precision-targeted weapon, and it was capable of creating real-world physical damage through the use of code. When it encountered the target, it tricked the system into running code that controlled the centrifuges at the Natanz uranium enrichment plant, which then corrupted these parts as well as sabotaging the operations at the plant in general.

Some analysts argue that the Stuxnet attack is better understood as an intelligence operation, or a type of covert activity, than it is as an act of cyber warfare. Others, however, argue that it is understood as a "use of force" under the Law of Armed Conflict (LOAC), a set of international norms governing how states should behave during wartime.[37]

As a result of the successful Stuxnet attack, many states became aware of their vulnerabilities to cyberattacks. The Stuxnet virus was an asymmetric weapon or an indicator of how both nonstate and state actors can engage in acts of cyberwar. In comparison to the costs of an armed invasion in a conventional war, the costs of developing and deploying the Stuxnet cyberweapon were relatively cheap. As a result of this attack, policy makers were convinced that terrorists could easily use cyberweapons to wreak large-scale havoc in the United States through attacking industrial control systems. Thus, in the United States, the Stuxnet attack is credited with pushing lawmakers to establish the US military Cyber Command to carry out both offensive and defensive acts of cyber warfare.

Sources

Denning, D. "Stuxnet: What Has Changed?" *Future Internet* 4 (2012): 672–687.

Lindsay, J. "Stuxnet and the Limits of Cyberwarfare." *Security Studies* 22 (2013): 365–404.

CONCLUSION

As we have seen, a cyberattack can either function on its own as a type of warfare, or it can be combined with conventional warfare attacks. By making it difficult for a nation's leaders to communicate with each other, with their troops, or with their citizens, information warfare can be used as a type of force multiplier. Conventional attacks may be more effective if an adversary's communication system is first degraded because doing so can severely handicap their ability to respond to either a conventional or a cyberattack.[38]

A Georgian analyst has suggested that nations that are poor often have an information infrastructure that lags behind that of more developed countries. Thus, she suggests, they are particularly vulnerable to cyberattacks, especially from nations, like Russia, which are more technologically sophisticated. She suggests that developing nations thus need to band together to resist cyberattacks from actors like Russia, forming alliances with other regional players, or seeking the protection of a superpower like the United States, to build up their infrastructure and capabilities so that they can defend themselves and respond to attacks.[39]

Today, many analysts point to the Russo-Georgian information war as a critical learning experience for Russia, which has gone on to carry out sophisticated cyberattacks in Ukraine and elsewhere in the former Soviet Union. We consider the concept of cyberwar more thoroughly in Chapters 9 and 11.

QUESTIONS FOR DISCUSSION

1. Compare and contrast conventional power and cyber power. Read this short article about Estonia, sometimes referred to as a tiny nation but a mighty cyber power: http://estonianworld.com/security/estonia-became-global-heavyweight-cyber-security/.

   a. What does the existence of a nation like Estonia tell us about cyber power in contrast to conventional military power?

2. In his article on China as a rising superpower, analyst Nigel Inkster suggests that China faces a unique dilemma: It is rapidly expanding its internet profile internationally—including the arena of cyber warfare—and is on its way to becoming a cyber superpower. At the same time, however, China's leadership is threatened internally by the fact that its citizens could use the internet to mobilize against a one-party state. Do you think that a nation can be both a cyber superpower internally and a state that tightly controls its own citizens' access to information? Are these two policies—domestic and international cyber policies—interrelated or separate?

   For more information, see Inkster, Nigal. "China in Cyberspace." *Survival* 52, no. 4 (2010): 55–66.

KEY TERMS

Advanced persistent threat (APT) 69
Asymmetric warfare 73
Computer forensic investigation 71
Computer network attack (CNA) 72
Computer network exploitation 70
Cyber-enabled economic warfare
  (CEEW) 73
Cyber power 64
Distributed denial of service (DDOS)
  attack 79
Doxing 73
First-mover advantage 66

Malware 68
Ransomware 68
Resilience 67
Rootkit 68
Spoofing 70
Trojan horse 69
Virus 68
White hat hackers 68
Worm 68
Zero day exploit (ZDE) 69
Zero sum 62

FOR FURTHER READING

Cho, Y., and J. Chung. "Bring the State Back In: Conflict and Cooperation among States in Cybersecurity." *Pacific Focus* 32 (2017). https://onlinelibrary-wiley-com.ezproxy.regent.edu/doi/full/10.1111/pafo.12096.

Deibert, R. "Cyberspace under Siege." *Journal of Democracy* 26, no. 3 (2015): 64–78.

Deibert, R. J., R. Rohozinski, and M. Crete-Nishihata. "Cyclones in Cyberspace: Information Shaping and Denial in the 2008 Russia-Georgia War." *Security Dialogue* 43, no. 1 (2012): 3–24.

Klimburg, A. "The Whole of Nation in Cyberpower." *Georgetown Journal of International Affairs* (2011): 171–179.

Sanger, D. E. *The Perfect Weapon: War, Sabotage, and Fear in the Cyber Age* (New York, NY: Crown, 2018).

4

LIBERAL INTERNATIONALISM, COOPERATION, AND REGIMES

Learning Objectives

At the end of this chapter, students will be able to do the following:

1. Define key terms related to the liberal internationalism paradigm, including *regime*, *norm*, and *public good*.

2. Define *digital superpower*, and describe the role of the firm in cyberspace.

3. Compare and contrast the realist view of cyber power with the liberal internationalist view of global digital superpowers.

4. Articulate criticisms of liberal internationalist narrative of internet development.

5. Describe challenges to the establishment of regimes in cyberspace.

In this chapter, we apply the liberal internationalist lens to consider the internet as a venue for global interactions. In contrast to the realist paradigm, liberal internationalists view the international system not as a battlefield but as a market. The battlefield metaphor emphasizes competition among the world's players, whereas the market metaphor emphasizes the ways in which markets create order, predictability, and stability. The market analogy also emphasizes how firms (or states) are interdependent—with their ability to achieve goals occurring not only as a result of their actions but also as a result of actions taken by competitors or cooperating firms and as the result of activities that they might participate in collectively. States can thus cooperate to share in rewards as well as to share in the risks that might arise within a market system.

In this chapter, we also consider political economy critiques of this paradigm for explaining the growth of the internet as a vehicle of commerce and trade.

WHAT IS LIBERAL INTERNATIONALISM?

Liberal internationalists, in contrast to realists, believe that peace is possible within the international system—even without an overarching authority. In this view, states are not seen as threatened by the rise of another powerful nation because power is not regarded as zero sum, where one state's rise in power necessarily threatens another's position within the international system. Thus, liberal internationalists are more optimistic than realists are about states' ability to resolve conflicts. In this paradigm, conflict is seen not as an inevitable product of an anarchic international system characterized by competition among states. Instead, it is seen as emerging due to shortage or scarcity; therefore, liberal internationalists believe, conflict can often be avoided through supporting the establishment of markets and bargaining agreements among states and other players.

Liberal internationalists draw upon the work of Immanuel Kant (1724–1804), who espoused the notion of perpetual peace. This view regards the international system as characterized by mutual interdependence among states; that is, one state's actions can affect everyone in the international system. This approach assumes that due to the nature of complex interdependence both in real life and in the cyber environment, a state cannot ultimately control the risks that it is subject to independently but only through cooperation with other states. Therefore, liberal internationalists believe, aware of their shared vulnerabilities, states will learn to cooperate to solve specific problems.

And although realists argue that states always seek to increase their power (in relation to their neighbors or the international system), liberal internationalists point to situations in which states might concede some aspect of power or decision-making authority (sovereignty) to engage in policy making or the achievement of a goal in concert with other states. Here, we can consider problems like climate change, which no state can solve on its own, because the environment is a collective good, not belonging to one state, but rather shared among states with no ability to exclude any state from this resource. All states share the rewards and the risks associated with the provision of these collective goods. In working together, these analysts believe, states will build trust in one another, enabling them to avoid conflict in the future.

Liberal internationalists also emphasize ideas like free trade because the international financial system requires the cooperation of all states to function effectively to create greater wealth for all states. Here, they assume that markets are the most effective way to create order and that therefore firms or states should not try to impede the free flow of goods, information, and services that are hallmarks of that market system. One of the most significant impediments to a liberal internationalist order, then, is a state that decides to erect barriers that interfere with the actions of a market for ideas, goods, or services. A state may refuse to participate in a market system through withdrawing entirely from the market (i.e., adopting a posture of isolationism or seeking autarky) or may attempt to actively damage existing markets through erecting barriers like tariffs.

Liberal internationalists are also optimistic about the ability of capitalism itself as a set of practices and beliefs to change nations. Some analysts thus speak of convergence, noting that if states need to adopt some form of capitalism to compete in the international system successfully, then over time, states will start to resemble one another through their dependence upon market mechanisms, openness to foreign investment, and other markers of their commitment to capitalist ideology.

LIBERAL INTERNATIONALISM IN CYBERSPACE

How does thinking about the internet as a market, not a battlefield, change our perspective on state action within cyberspace? First, it lets us ask: How might states cooperate to create order within the seemingly chaotic environment of the internet? As we saw in Chapter 3, the realist lens led states to refer to "American cyberspace" or "Russian cyberspace"—rejecting the claim that states need to cooperate to secure the internet as a common good.

But in this chapter, we assume that the internet is a public good or shared international space. States, therefore, need to cooperate to preserve this shared space—because a public good is one that no one can be prevented from partaking in and also one that can be produced only collectively. Furthermore, one user's enjoyment of the good does not diminish others' enjoyment or use of it. We often use the term *public good* to refer to utilities provided by one's city or local providers, such as water and sewage, or emergency services like the fire department. Free goods are those objects, like air, from which no users are excluded, and where again cooperation is necessary to preserve them.[1]

In his work, philosopher Luciano Floridi suggests viewing the **infosphere** in much the same way that we think about nature and our obligations as global citizens to preserve nature.[2] He suggests that internet users—including states and corporations—should work to maintain the infosphere as a space where information can flow freely and unimpeded, without the "pollution" created through wasteful information practices like the creation of spam or the barriers created by filters and firewalls. The internet is thus presented as a public good or a utility.

Other analysts use the term digital economy. The **digital economy** is "all of those economic processes, transactions, interactions, and activities that are based on digital technologies."[3] The digital economy is thus conceptualized of as a collective good that is both national and transnational with resources moving among states seamlessly. No state can regulate its digital economy alone, and each state is vulnerable to disruptions and risks appearing in the digital economy. The digital economy is vulnerable to risks associated with the overall international economy because it is seamlessly interwoven into so many aspects of global commerce today.

Some analysts distinguish between the digital economy and the internet economy. The digital economy is different from the internet economy in that the internet economy is based on internet connectivity, whereas the digital economy rests on the creation and maintenance of tools like e-banking, e-commerce, and e-trade.[4]

The Electronic Market Space

As we know, the engineers who developed the internet initially thought it should be as free of regulation and state interference as possible. Similarly, e-commerce structure designers (or architects) wanted the digital economy to be largely unregulated and free of state interference. They hoped that the digital economy would become a "pure market" that was self-regulating through the actions of market forces with little government interference in the areas of taxation and regulation.

Indeed, to a large degree, state regulatory mechanisms have been slow to develop in the digital economy due to the speed at which the digital economy expanded (outpacing the ability of states to regulate it). Moreover, the digital economy developed chaotically, and over time, private organizations, including industry organizations (like the banking industry) have stepped in to establish sector-specific governance structures and procedures.[5] Global organizations have also stepped up to support these private sector efforts, including the World Trade Organization and the Organization for Economic Cooperation and Development (OECD).

Cooperating to Reduce Risks in Cyberspace

What risks does the global digital economy face? We can identify two types of risks: threats to the internet's physical infrastructure (i.e., attacks on the physical pipelines carrying data and information) and threats in which the internet itself could be utilized as a vector. That is, the internet could be weaponized to carry viruses or materials that could harm their recipients—from corporations to individuals to states. Both attacks on the infrastructure of the internet itself, as well as attacks on secondary targets carried through the internet, could cause massive political, social, and economic disruptions to the global digital economy. Thus, states have cooperated to develop regulations and norms governing how states and nonstate actors react to, prepare for, and mitigate financial risks brought about by cyberthreats, including issues like identity theft or hacking into critical infrastructure in the banking industry.

But although we might expect states to band together to secure the functioning of the internet and to confront threats to the structure, such cooperation does not always occur for two reasons: First, many of the attacks in which the internet is used as a vector target not states but rather private actors (such as banks that work to protect their customers' data from identity theft). Private corporations own and operate many critical networks, and they have built and administered the backbone of the telecommunications infrastructure. Thus, states often must work together with private sector actors who may not agree about the severity of the threat that they are facing or who may not be equally committed to responding to these threats.

In addition, although some of these vectored threats (like the threat of identity theft) are considered universally threatening, other types of threats may be understood differently in different cultures, and states may not all agree about the severity of these threats or the necessity of a global response. For example, nations today disagree about how severe a threat is posed to the global digital economy by practices like intellectual property theft or economic cyber espionage.

Issue Areas in Cyberspace

For this reason, it is not helpful to think of cyberspace risk as a whole. Instead, we can speak of issue areas, such as risks to the international financial system, risks to international shipping and transportation, or risks to the e-commerce sector. Depending on the issue area, different types of actors are involved in making policy, including nonstate actors with specialized expertise, like international legal or banking professionals. And policy makers face different constraints when making policy across different issue areas.[6] In addition, cooperation may be of a more limited or a more long-term duration among states, depending on the specific issue area that states are trying to resolve.

If we think about states cooperating to pool their resources as mutual "insurance" against possible future losses, we see that this strategy may be more effective in some issue areas than others. That is, states will be more likely to cooperate to insure themselves against losses when there is a great deal of uncertainty about the risks states face as well as the possibility that the gains and losses will be distributed inequitably.[7] Thus, states may be inclined to cooperate to regulate the distribution of losses in relation to threats to critical infrastructure or the stock market because the threats that states are facing are so new and novel that it will be difficult for states to predict what the likely outcome will be or how these losses will be distributed. Thus, states have thus far been willing to band together to engage in specific cooperative programs, such as ensuring that wire transfers between banks internationally are secure. In addition, it is likely that democratic states might come together to form an organization dedicated to protecting the integrity of national elections from foreign interference—given how new, novel, and unpredictable this threat is.[8] States have also come together to create both bilateral and multilateral mutual legal assistance treaties (MLATs) for tackling issues like crime when jurisdictional issues are a significant obstacle or barrier to cooperation in gathering information about terrorism internationally.

Cyber Risks as Part of Security Risks

Just as cyber capabilities are entwined with other types of state capabilities, cyber risks are intertwined with other types of risk categories. Today, vectored attacks conducted through cyberspace often target a nation's **supervisory control and data acquisition (SCADA)** systems. These systems, which are computerized and online, serve to administer the supply of many goods that households depend on, like water and electricity. In addition, military command and control systems—that carry information about military operations among military officials and between officials and the equipment that they use—are highly dependent upon the internet to carry this information. The global financial system depends on access to a resilient internet that carries information about transactions and responds to events in real time. Disruption or interference with global internet connectivity in any one sector thus affects the entire global political and economic system. Thus, using the language of issue areas, we can see that rather than speaking about cyber policy as a whole—or about cyber risk as a whole—it is useful to think about cyber policy and cyber risk in specific issue areas.

HOW DO STATES COOPERATE TO REGULATE CYBERSPACE?

Thus far, our discussion of state cooperation has been rather abstract. But how specifically do states form agreements, and what is the basis of these cooperation agreements? We can identify three specific mechanisms used by states to create collective agreements in a situation where they must cooperate to produce a shared good. First, regimes can allow states to cooperate. Next, states can utilize pooled sovereignty, in giving up a measure of individual autonomy, to cooperate with others in administering a good. Finally, states can create a stewardship model in which a third party administers the good.

Regimes

In addition to comparing cyberspace to a market, analysts often compare the risks that states face in cyberspace to global health risks. Today, no state can individually ensure its citizens' health because germs can easily cross borders carried by people and goods (just as "viruses" can in cyberspace). Therefore, states have created both formal and informal regimes of cooperation to secure public health. Regimes are "sets of implicit or explicit principles, norms, rules and decision-making procedures in a given issue area" that states adopt collectively.[9] For example, if a global pandemic is declared, states have agreed to work together to share information and to engage in necessary life-saving measures like shutting down borders and erecting quarantines.

Today, states have established regimes to regulate maritime commerce, international air travel, and the exporting and importing of natural resources like oil. A regime may be formally codified in a treaty, such as the Geneva Convention, which specifies how states are to treat prisoners during wars, or the Law of Armed Conflict, which defines the rules that states should respect during warfare. A regime might also be informal and more temporary in duration.

Liberal internationalists argue for the creation of cybersecurity regimes due to the high level of interdependence among states in many different sectors of cyberspace.[10] Thus, liberal internationalists argue that there are market incentives for actors to work together to confront cybersecurity challenges as well as to share information.

ASEAN's Cybersecurity Regime

ASEAN is a group of ten nations that cooperate in the areas of politics, economics, and now cybersecurity. ASEAN views cybersecurity as a collective good, believing that the ASEAN states are interdependent, with one's fortunes and security depending on another's fortunes and security. Thus, those states within ASEAN that are technology leaders—like Singapore—are not threatened by the attempts of less developed states (like Burma) to join the technological revolution. Instead, states like Singapore and China are helping developing states create technological hardware like an ASEAN broadband corridor and are also working to help them create resilient technological infrastructure, including in essential areas like banking and the financial sector, because a threat that enters through a poorly guarded portal in a developing country can quickly spread to a developed country in a shared information space like ASEAN. The more developed states are concerned about problems like miscommunication and misattribution, specifically the fear that one ASEAN state might launch a cyberattack, but that another state might be blamed.[11]

The ASEAN nations are also creating a shared CERT, deepening their defense cooperation and working to secure the supply chain throughout the region. The ASEAN states are also working to draw up a common framework for the application of international law to disputes in cyberspace as well as to agree on shared values and norms governing state relations in cyberspace.

Analysts described ASEAN as a territory that is characterized by bounded or limited sovereignty and a high degree of regional pooled sovereignty before the advent of their efforts in the field of cybersecurity. That is, ASEAN member states have had a track record of working together in loose associations ever since the organization was founded in 1967. Here analysts

(Continued)

PEOPLE AND PLACES

(Continued)

sometimes distinguish between positive integration and negative integration, where negative integration refers to states' practices of lowering regulatory and legislative barriers to better work with their neighbors, whereas positive integration refers to states' practices of working together to implement specific policies and carry out initiatives.

Here, Hund suggests that ASEAN has failed to move beyond negative integration toward positive integration in many fields, including economic and political initiatives.[12] Thus, one might expect to see limited efforts in terms of regional integration for cybersecurity. It might be easier to achieve objectives like the reaction of an ASEAN broadband corridor while formulating a common policy, like the European Data Privacy Initiative, might be more difficult because that would require ASEAN signatories to agree on values such as what constitutes the proper amount of surveillance of citizens by the government. That second type of agreement would be more difficult to achieve, given that ASEAN includes both more democratic and more repressive regimes among its members.

Sources

Heinl, C. "Moving toward a Resilient ASEAN Cybersecurity Regime." *Asia Policy* 18 (2014). https://www.nbr.org/publication/regional-cybersecurity-moving-toward-a-resilient-asean-cybersecurity-regime/.

Hund, M. "From 'Neighborhood Watch Group' to Community?" *Australian Journal of International Affairs* 56, no. 1 (2002): 99–122.

Pooled Sovereignty

As noted earlier, states may cede some of their independent authority (or autonomy) to work together with others to solve global problems. Pooled sovereignty refers to situations in which states choose to give up autonomy to cooperate with neighboring states, particularly in cases where a resource (such as a natural resource) is shared among members in a region. States can give up some measure of state authority to craft bilateral or multilateral agreements, including changing national legislation within their states so that it conforms to a regional set of standards.[13]

Here, sovereignty may be understood not as an absolute concept (a state is either wholly sovereign, or it is not), but rather, a state may engage in what is known as bounded sovereignty. States may have complete sovereignty over some practices within their states, whereas in other areas they may cede some degree of sovereignty to a regional or international body. And the pendulum may swing back and forth between situations in which states maintain a high degree of sovereignty or control in making treaties and agreements governing a resource and cases in which states are more willing to cede authority to governmental or intergovernmental bodies.

This arc occurs because not all attempts at creating pooled sovereignty work, as the example of Britain's decision to withdraw from the European Union (known as Brexit) indicates. Citizens within a state may resent the notion that their state is not entirely independent but that their lives instead depend on a bureaucracy located far away that does not always seem responsive to their situations. They may resent the commitment of their tax dollars to regional projects that do not develop them directly (e.g., citizens of wealthier Western European nations have objected to financing the economic development of countries in Eastern Europe that have joined the European Union more recently). Also, pooled regional sovereignty may develop slowly just as statehood often grows only over a period of a hundred years or more. Thus, pooled sovereignty in relation to internet governance might not emerge for another thirty or forty years.

Stewardship

In other instances, states have created national and international trusts whose job it is to make sure that historic and natural resources within a state or global system are preserved for the current generation and for the generations to come. In allowing a national or international trust to administer a resource, or to engage in stewardship of the resource, states again cede sovereignty to this trust or foundation.[14] In considering who might engage in stewardship of the internet as a global resource that should be preserved for future generations, we can consider the role currently being played in internet governance by actors like the Internet Society, or the International Telecommunications Union, which can be seen as acting in the role of steward or trustee of the internet, speaking on its behalf, and acting to make sure that it is preserved for future generations.

OPPOSING THE LIBERAL INTERNATIONALIST VIEW

States can gain much from cooperating with other states to secure a resource like the international internet. But not all states are on board with the liberal internationalist view of the internet as a collective good. Today, some states do not accept the notion that the internet is, in fact, a collective good. Other states accept this contention but do not trust other players within the cyberspace arena enough to depend on them for the provision of their security as a collective good. Finally, some analysts argue that traditional theorizing about how states cooperate to produce collective goods is not relevant to thinking about the development of today's internet because firms—not states—have come to play an outsized role in creating, administering, and growing this entity.

Is the Internet a Collective Good?

Not all analysts agree that the internet and internet security are collective goods. The United States has always played an outsized role in its creation, its growth, and its protection and safety. Therefore, some analysts suggest that the United States will always serve as a primary guarantor of internet stability, with other states playing supporting roles. And they argue that although resources on the internet are shared, they are not shared equally. More powerful states benefit more from internet connectivity, and therefore, they argue, these states should play a greater role in securing the internet and paying the costs of doing so. (That is, in the language of realism, the United States will always serve as a hegemon.)[15]

Other states don't believe that the internet has to be international at all. They feel that the best way to preserve a nation's cybersecurity is through adopting a policy of autarky or isolation—seeking to, for example, protect critical infrastructure by lessening dependence on cyberspace and reducing connectivity.[16] Both Russian and Chinese cyberspace policies increasingly emphasize reliance upon local ISPs and hardware engineers and the localization of data within their sovereign borders. In 2018, Russia released its program for creating "the digital economy of the Russian Federation." Russia plans to spend approximately $53 million in building up key sectors of its digital economy, including sectors devoted to search capabilities, e-commerce, content, social media, and devices and interfaces. In this realist view, then, a state's digital economy is an essential component of its overall state power—both in terms of cyber power and traditional power capabilities. There is no global digital economy but only individual state economies that are components of state power.[17]

CRITICAL ISSUES

CRYPTOCURRENCY AND THE INTERNATIONAL ECONOMY

If you follow the news regularly, chances are that you have heard of something called Bitcoin. Most likely you have heard that some individuals have become Bitcoin millionaires as the result of smart investing. But what is Bitcoin—and cryptocurrency—and why does it matter in international relations?

First, we begin with some definitions. Then, we explore the relationships among traditional currencies, cryptocurrencies, and the state. Finally, we consider the ethical, military, and political implications of the advent of cryptocurrencies in national and international economies.

Defining Our Terms

What is a **cryptocurrency**? A cryptocurrency is first a digital or **virtual currency**. That is, in contrast to national and regional currencies like the US dollar or the Euro, cryptocurrency does not appear as paper money and is not printed in a conventional sense. Instead, individuals can use their computers to "mine" cryptocurrencies, like Bitcoin, through solving advanced mathematical problems for which they are paid sums of currency.

Here, one should note that although Bitcoin is the most well-known of existing cryptocurrencies, it is not the only one. Any currency scheme that relies on decentralized ledger technology, encryption, and mining is referred to as cryptocurrency. Different cryptocurrencies have different features, and users may find one type of cryptocurrency more useful than another, depending on the functions they are planning on carrying out using the currency. For example, Monero's Privacy coin is useful for those who wish to conduct transactions with a high degree of anonymity because the coin hides the addresses of both the senders and receivers as well as the total transaction value.[18]

A defining feature of cryptocurrency is its reliance on **cryptography** for security. Cryptocurrencies thus rely upon encryption to safely carry digitized financial information between participants in a financial transaction.

Cryptocurrencies also commonly rely on **blockchain** technology to track and settle financial transactions. Blockchain refers to a system whereby a record or ledger of financial transfers is kept, and it relies on **distributed ledger technology (DLT)**. In a DLT system, the computers that are transferring funds interact directly with one another, transferring funds and checking to make sure that sufficient funds are held by a participant to pay for a transaction occurring. (That is, they engage in **peer-to-peer networking**, rather than carrying out their activities through a central node to which all computers would be connected.) Each participant in a transaction keeps its own records of the transactions that occur, and computers also interface with one another to update records of transactions. Thus, rather than there being one centralized record of transactions (as there might be in a conventional bank), there are instead multiple, identical records of transactions that occur, held on multiple sites.

As Frankenfield writes, "A defining feature of a cryptocurrency, and arguably its biggest allure, is its organic nature; it is not issued by any central authority, rendering it theoretically immune to government interference or manipulation."[19]

That is, cryptocurrencies allow for a decentralization of economic power. Because cryptocurrencies are "self-governing," they remove the role that has historically been played by states and central banks. Radical proponents of the use of cryptocurrency thus argue that it may represent a way out of the capitalist-based world order that has formed the basis of our political system.[20]

(Continued)

(Continued)

The Role of the Central Bank

To understand the implications of cryptocurrency, one needs to understand how traditional banks work and how states make fiscal policy. Historically, states have controlled how much currency is issued and what interest rates are charged to borrowers. In the United States, a government agency, the US Federal Reserve (the Fed) makes these decisions. The Fed is governed by a board of governors of the Federal Reserve Board. There are twelve governors who are appointed by the president.

The Federal Reserve Board (created in 1908) allows the country to control its currency's value on the world market and to act to stem issues like inflation (simply defined here as too much money chasing too few goods). A central bank can adopt a tighter or a looser fiscal policy to encourage consumers and businesses to engage in saving or spending. A central bank also acts an insurer; it can step in to cover emergency situations like a shortfall in currency, out-of-control inflation, or a bank that fails due to making bad loans.

In addition, the value of government-issued assets resides in the fact that they are tied to a state's gold reserves in some instances as well as to a state's tax revenue streams and the value of government-owned assets. That is, people trust that their money will retain its value because they trust the country that issued it, and when people don't trust their nation's currency (due to destabilizing events like a civil war or a coup), then they are likely to move their assets elsewhere, including abroad or into alternate currencies.

Finally, in the United States—and in most nations—founding documents like the Constitution give the country the exclusive right to create money. In the US Constitution, Article 1, Section 8(5) grants the power to coin money and to regulate its value specifically to the federal government. The Constitution also forbids the use of "unauthorized instruments," although this statute has historically been interpreted to mean that individuals should not create counterfeit money rather than being applied to cryptocurrency and other forms of virtual payment.[21] In China, the Law on People's Bank of China designates this organization as having the sole authority to issue and manage currency and its circulation. Individuals and corporations are forbidden to issue or print tokens or tickets that could replace China's official currency, the renminbi.[22]

"A New Type of Asset"

In 2018, Lael Brainard, a member of the US Federal Reserve board of governors, described cryptocurrency is a "new type of asset." But what is the significance of these assets and how can its emergence in the previous decade affect today's international economy?

Today, analysts are divided about the threats and opportunities that the advent of digital or cryptocurrencies represents. Brainard points out that the new currency is not a liability of any individual or institution. Thus, he notes, "There is no trusted institution standing behind it."

Because cryptocurrencies do not have a defined relationship with a particular state or state-backed institution, they are therefore currently not **legal tender** and thus could not be utilized for certain types of financial transactions. They are also considered to be virtual currencies because they do not exist in physical means and owners do not physically own anything; rather, their claim to own the assets is validated through the blockchain.[23]

In addition, traditional financial transactions are cleared by a bank that makes sure that there is enough money in the check writer's account, for example, to allow the recipient to cash a check that has been written. In contrast, this clearing function takes place independently between computers using cryptocurrencies, with no central figure, like a bank, exercising control over these financial transactions.

And when traditional currencies are used, the state works to track financial activities by individuals and corporations. Particularly in the period since 9/11, US and international banks have developed systems for flagging suspicious transactions (such as regular recurring large cash transactions between nations associated with terrorist activity) and sharing this information with the proper authorities. Individuals and corporations must furnish proof of their identities before engaging in activities such as taking out a loan or establishing a bank account, and information is shared with the relevant authorities. Thus, the state is able to exercise its state power through extracting the relevant taxes from financial actors as well as ensuring that the proper rules and procedures for engaging in financial transactions are followed. In contrast, cryptocurrencies are considered to be borderless, international currencies—and there is not a strong state mechanism in any state for regulating international financial transfers conducted using cryptocurrency.

Cryptocurrencies thus present new challenges in areas as diverse as payments policy, supervision and regulation, financial stability, monetary policy, and the provision of financial services.[24]

Despite these concerns, however, in 2018, the global cryptocurrency market was valued at greater than $795 billion. A significant amount of the world's economy is thus being conducted in cryptocurrency.[25]

(Continued)

(Continued)

Identified Problems with Cryptocurrency

Analysts have identified several issues with the new cryptocurrencies, which are significant for international relations.

First, like paper money, the value of Bitcoin is not fixed but can fluctuate. In a conventional financial system, an event like inflation might cause a dollar, for example, to be worth less in the sense that it buys less because prices are higher—even though its denomination is the same. In the same way, Bitcoin's value may fluctuate, depending on demand for it as a good. Its value stems from its use as a means of purchasing other things and carrying out other financial transactions.[26]

The value of cryptocurrency is related to its use, its scarcity, and its perceived value. Currently, only a finite amount of currency exists, making it rare and valuable. Indeed, in 2018, Bitcoin was the highest-valued currency in the entire world. In some ways, then, cryptocurrency has similar characteristics to shares of stock rather than currency. One is said to "hold" a specific cryptocurrency, and doing so confers privileges upon the holder, allowing him or her to have a voice in the activities that occur within a currency community. In this way, someone who holds a specific cryptocurrency is similar to a shareholder in a stock corporation.

In addition, policy makers are concerned about the anonymous nature of cryptocurrency transactions. The DLT system creates ledgers that do not contain information about the currency owners' identity, although they do contain a chain of custody showing which assets have been transferred between which addresses, the amounts, and when. Because of this anonymity, as well as the fact that the currency system operates outside of state fiscal policy, the state cannot track illegal economic transactions. Cryptocurrencies are thus widely used on the dark web, where someone might, for example, pay for drugs or human trafficking with Bitcoin. And criminal groups might use Bitcoin to violate laws, whereas rogue states could use cryptocurrency to violate sanctions imposed by the international community. Cryptocurrencies can be used for money laundering and in ransomware attacks as well as physical kidnappings.

Attempts at Regulating Cryptocurrency Transactions by States

Is a competition taking place between conventional and cryptocurrencies? Can both exist side by side, or will cryptocurrency put existing banks and financial services providers out of business?

Political economists suggest that a showdown between the financial systems is inevitable. They worry about crypto-secession, as key actors withdraw from the existing international economic system. If enough actors secede in this way, states, state-backed banks, and other financial entities lose the privileged position they have thus far enjoyed.[27]

As a result of states' wishes to more tightly regulate these "anarchic" financial transactions, which seem to be occurring largely free of state interference, states have responded in two ways: States seek to more tightly regulate financial transactions involving cryptocurrencies. Next, states and international organizations may create their own cryptocurrencies, which would utilize DLT and the blockchain but which might still be the subject of fiscal and regulatory policy.

Many states have already passed rudimentary legislation recognizing cryptocurrency as a form of exchange, including Japan and Belarus. National banking authorities in both the United States and the UK now recognize a limited number of cryptocurrencies. The Federal Reserve Bank of St. Louis recognizes Bitcoin, Litecoin, Bitcoin Cash, and Ethereum. Daily prices on these currencies can now be obtained from the Federal Reserve Economic Database (FRED).[28] And in September 2017, International Monetary Fund President Christine Lagarde asked international bankers to pay more attention to cryptocurrency. Her statement can be read as a recognition of cryptocurrency as a legitimate means of exchange.[29] And the European Court of Justice ruled in 2015 that Bitcoin transactions should be exempt from value-added taxes (VAT).[30]

Facebook's Own Cryptocurrency

Recently, social media giants like Google and Facebook have discussed developing their own cryptocurrencies. These cryptocurrencies differ from projects like Bitcoin because they are asset backed. (That is, they are tied to specific items of monetary value, such as shares of Facebook stock.) Thus, they might be viewed more as private currencies, issued by corporations, rather than states. However, they will rely upon DLT to keep records of assets.

Facebook is reportedly developing a **stablecoin**—a new type of cryptocurrency that is easier to settle transactions between parties and with less price volatility.[31] Facebook employees would have the option of being paid in this currency. The new coin places a high emphasis on guaranteeing the privacy of individual's financial transactions.[32]

Here, policy makers are concerned about corporations like Amazon and Facebook achieving the status of monopoly corporations as they acquire a leading market share in more and more industries from book sales (Amazon) to advertising sales (Facebook) to banking.[33]

(Continued)

(Continued)

Applying the Paradigms

Depending on one's overall stance toward the international system—including how one defines power and influence within that system—an analyst might view the rise of cryptocurrencies differently.

Realism

Realists have four concerns in response to the rise of cryptocurrencies. They worry that the United States may lose its power within the international system if its central role as an arbiter of international fiscal policy is threatened by the rise and popularity of cryptocurrencies. Next, realists are concerned about the threats to international system stability presented as adversary nations harness the power of cryptocurrency for their own ends. Third, analysts are concerned about security risks as states move toward a "cashless society" in which individual citizens and corporations depend on cryptocurrency and other cashless mechanisms like e-wallets for the majority of financial transactions. Finally, nations may see the move toward an international currency as a threat to state power.[34]

If nations and citizens begin looking to cryptocurrencies as places to invest, and ways to preserve the value of their assets, or perhaps turn predominantly to cryptocurrencies rather than the US dollar as a medium of exchange, then the United States may lose its leading role in the world economy. It will be less able to dictate fiscal and political terms to other nations as a result of the rising role of cryptocurrency.[35]

Central Bank Digital Currencies

Due to concerns about digital currency volatility and states' inability to regulate their issuance, many states are considering creating central bank digital currencies (CBDCs) that would function as national digital currencies. A CBDC would likely still be administered through a DLT through the blockchain. But this new currency would be a liability of a central bank. In this way, the state could also monitor and regulate the transfer mechanism of digital currencies. However, a CBDC would not have to provide the anonymity that is currently associated with other forms of cryptocurrency.[36]

Some analysts are concerned that such a digital currency would be a new target for criminal actors. In addition, the use of strong centralized digital currency might also drive traditional banks and traditional currencies out of business.

In addition, Hall writes of a "potential nightmare scenario" in which Russia's economy moves toward a digital-only economy. He argues that the requirement that all financial transactions be conducted in a transparent manner in which a ledger is kept to track the movement of money could be a first step toward the construction of a vast and all-encompassing surveillance state. In such a scenario, a security threat—like a terrorist attack—could provide the pretext for allowing the state to take tighter control over the economy. In the future, DLT might even be paired with biometric identity technologies to tie people explicitly to all of their financial transactions over their lifetimes. Hall therefore concludes that "a DLT-based currency issued by the Russian Central Bank would allow the administration to wield a significant level of access to personal information in addition to economic control."[37]

The Problem with Cashless Economies

Finally, security analysts have voiced concerns about the fact that so many citizens are now dependent on cashless economic transaction mechanisms (like PayPal or Venmo) and upon the functioning of the technologies that underlie these mechanisms.[38] Because electronic payment systems cannot function without a working communications infrastructure, functioning software and functioning electricity and servers, attacks (either physical, i.e., kinetic, or cyber enabled) on any one of these components could potentially lead to social chaos if individuals were unable to access funds to purchase groceries, for example. An attack that was able to erase financial transactions (either temporarily or permanently) could sow even more chaos if, for example, financial records were destroyed and people were unable to prove that they should be receiving social benefits or a pension.

In addition, if electronic payment systems and decentralized currencies become the norm in the future, it may be increasingly difficult for states to mount a response (including a military response) aimed at securing a state's financial system if that financial system is increasingly decentralized and maintained by actors other than the state.

Liberal Internationalism

Liberal internationalists worry that relying on cryptocurrency might affect activities such as free trade or even massively disrupt the existing international economic system. Devries[39] notes that "if cryptocurrencies became the global norm for transactions, long standing systems for trade would need to be completely reformed to deal with this type of competition."

(*Continued*)

(Continued)

This new system could be more volatile than our current system. Here we can consider the increased demand in Britain for Bitcoin when investors became worried about how Britain's withdrawal from the European Union (Brexit) in 2019 would affect their investments. Brainard suggests that investors might flee what they see as "sinking global markets" through instead turning to cryptocurrencies. In such a scenario, states would play a less significant role in protecting markets from volatility and even collapse. In addition, reliance on Bitcoin is likely to be particularly high in countries where the state is seen as not being sufficiently responsive in its fiscal policy to threats like inflation. For example, in a nation like Argentina, where high inflation is the norm, citizens used to keep their money in dollars but are now more likely to keep it in Bitcoin.

Cryptocurrencies themselves are volatile because of the speed at which transactions occur; they don't need to be cleared through a central financial institution, which slows down transaction speeds. Governments might therefore be tempted to embrace cryptocurrencies because it would be mean that governments could quickly shift money in response to a national disaster, for example. However, states might also find it harder to intervene in a situation where cryptocurrencies markets are threatening to fail due to the speed at which transactions occur.

In addition, different nations might adopt different cryptocurrencies, in this way creating new types of trading blocs. For this reason, some analysts argue that states within the international system should come together cooperatively to establish rules—or even a global regime—aimed at regulating how states will treat cryptocurrencies. That is, whereas realists envision a system in which each state might issue its own cryptocurrency, with the strength of competing cryptocurrencies thus serving as a proxy for state power, liberal internationalists see a system in which states might cooperate to bolster the value and utility of a single or diverse set of cryptocurrencies that would be accepted by all states.[40]

In this way, the debate about global financial governance is closely related to the debate about global internet governance (described in Chapter 6). Some states may have a realist, national sovereignty view in which each state might attempt to issue and administer its own national cryptocurrency, acting in a competitive manner. But other actors may instead advocate for a multistakeholder approach toward the global governance of international economic matters, including the issuing, administering, and support for cryptocurrency. In a multistakeholder approach, actors as diverse as global banks, national treasuries, and international technology actors, like Facebook, might work together to create and steer the regulation of cryptocurrencies.[41]

Constructivism

Finally, a constructivist approach allows us to consider the language being used to describe cryptocurrencies at the moment as well as to think about the ideas that underlie debates about cryptocurrencies.

Here, we can consider the ways in which states have acted to either legitimize or delegitimize these newly emerging institutions and cryptocurrencies like Bitcoin themselves as well as the ways in which leaders and citizens have spoken about the issue of trust in these institutions and these currencies. How governments speak of cryptocurrency will affect these issues: Do they themselves regard it as part of their official banking sector or as something else—like an anarchic space where illegal transactions occur?

Language can also be used to paint cryptocurrency either as a niche market or as part of a larger, more mainstream shift within the international economic system. Here, the use of words like "risky" or "volatile" in particular by state officials could affect user perceptions of the currency.

Using language, states might attempt to "capture" the cryptocurrency market through painting it as existing either within or outside traditional economic relations. Cryptocurrency markets can thus be described either as an adjunct or complementary sector for traditional markets or as a competitor to these markets.

China's Constructivist Approach to Regulating Cryptocurrencies

As the world's largest economy, China has the potential to be a major actor in the field of cryptocurrency. In addition, China's citizens are already heavily dependent on cashless means of transferring money, utilizing electronic wallets for many of their day-to-day economic transactions. In addition, a majority of the activity involved in mining cryptocurrency has historically taken place in China because the power and resources necessary to carry out this activity are relatively cheap relative to other sites worldwide.

Therefore, in theory, one would expect China to be highly supportive of the development of cryptocurrencies as part of this cashless economy. However,

(Continued)

(Continued)

China has adopted a cautious approach to allowing cryptocurrencies within its borders. There are several reasons for this:

First, China has proven to be the epicenter of cryptocurrency speculation. Several scandals have broken out in China in which investors and purchasers claim that they were defrauded. In 2013, Global Bond Limited, a trading platform for Bitcoin in China, suddenly shut down. The company is said to have vanished with $5 million worth of Bitcoin. And the lack of clear legal guidelines governing cryptocurrency transactions made this case nearly impossible to prosecute. (Indeed, China's law enforcement personnel were "confused about what exactly was stolen.")[42] In some ways, cryptocurrency speculation appears to operate as a Ponzi or pyramid scheme, in which the initial investors are able to enrich themselves and then exit the system, leaving the next generation of "investors" to pay the price of the fraudulent scheme.

As a result of these concerns, China has enacted progressively stricter legislation spelling out the limits of what citizens may and may not do with cryptocurrency. In 2013, China passed legislation declaring that cryptocurrency could not be used as payment for goods or services, although it could be used as a vehicle for investment, and in 2017, China banned the exchange of funds between cryptocurrency and conventional economic means. In addition, China has designated initial coin offerings (ICOs) as "unauthorized illegal public financing."[43] It has also forbidden official state or private banks from engaging in financial activities involving cryptocurrency. The existence of a volatile currency that encourages speculation has been painted as simply too risky for a nation whose economic progress is still a relatively new phenomenon. The question has thus been whether it is worth jeopardizing China's economic miracle to participate in the international cryptocurrency market.[44]

Sources

Investopedia. "Cryptocurrency." https://www.investopedia.com/terms/c/cryptocurrency.asp.

Kall, J. "Blockchain Control." *Law Critique* 29 (2018): 133–140.

Reuters. "Privacy Coin Monero Offers Near Total Anonymity." *New York Times* (June 11, 2019). https://www.nytimes.com/reuters/2019/06/11/business/11reuters-crypto-currencies-altcoins-explainer.html.

XIe, R. "Why China Had to 'Ban' Cryptocurrency but the US Did Not: A Comparative Analysis of Regulations on Crypto-Markets between the US and China." *Washington University Global Studies Law Review* 18, no. 2 (2019): 467.

The Free Rider Problem in Cyberspace

Some states don't trust their neighbors to help secure cyberspace because of the problem of free riding. A free rider is an entity (like a state or individual) who reaps the benefits of a collective good (like clean air, clean water, or a stable internet) without actually paying into the costs of creating that collective good. Because the good established is public, no one can be excluded from its enjoyment, even if they have not paid into its creation.

In thinking about cybersecurity, some analysts argue that when one state decides not to engage in protocols aimed at guaranteeing cybersecurity, it does not merely "steal" a collective good that it did not have a hand in creating; rather, it actively undermines efforts to produce that collective good. Thinking back to the analogy of public health, we can consider how a state refusing to cooperate with international public health rules and regulations endangers everyone. Similarly, when one state decides not to act to preserve cybersecurity, this renders the whole system less stable and safe, and in this way, the costs of not acting to preserve cybersecurity are passed on to others.[45] Today, particularly in developing countries, nations may not have optimal levels of cybersecurity provisions. State and commercial entities may run outdated software that is not updated periodically. Pirated or illegal copies of software may also be used. As a result, these nations risk creating cybersecurity vulnerabilities that will then be passed on to other parts of the global internet.[46]

The 2016 Attack on the Central Bank of Bangladesh

When we think of a bank robbery, we might picture a masked man with guns ordering customers to lie on the floor of a bank as they make off with paper bags full of cash. However, the largest bank robbery in the world occurred in February 2016, and it was a virtual bank robbery.

Throughout the world, customers—from individuals to multinational corporations—rely on **SWIFT codes** to instruct their banks how to route their money to make a payment. SWIFT refers to the Society for the Worldwide Interbank Financial Telecommunication, a cooperative of nearly 3,000 organizations that work together to maintain a messaging system used to move funds internationally. The organization, founded in 1973, is headquartered in Belgium. Data resides in Belgium and the United States.[47]

Schwartz describes the risks associated with relying on SWIFT codes, noting that "any attack . . . is a concern because attackers could literally transfer money from a victim's account into their own."[48] (Not all analysts agree, however, about the flaws in the SWIFT transaction system. Others feel that the SWIFT system is safer than other electronic payment systems because it

(Continued)

PEOPLE AND PLACES

(Continued)

is a closed system whereby payments travel within a predefined space with a recipient at either end who must identify him- or herself.)[49]

In February 2016, hackers gained unauthorized access into the Bangladesh Central Bank. They then sent thirty-five fraudulent orders, requesting that money be withdrawn from the bank and sent to addresses in the Philippines and Sri Lanka. The orders totaled nearly $1 billion! Even though there were numerous errors in the requesting documents, and even though there were several red flags raised by the intermediary and receiving organizations, nearly $80 million was transferred, and most of it will never be recovered.

This story illustrates a new type of risk in international monetary systems. It involves a great many players: the governments of Bangladesh, Sri Lanka, Belgium, the United States, and the Philippines; the US Federal Reserve Bank of New York; numerous law enforcement agencies; and nonstate actors like corporations, which often administer cybersecurity. Some analysts also believe that North Korean state-sponsored hackers participated in the heist and that some of the money ultimately wound up in North Korea.

In the aftermath of the theft, numerous investigations were carried out in Bangladesh, in the US Senate, and in the infected financial institutions. These investigations reached different conclusions about who was responsible for the errors. The New York Fed blamed Bangladesh, pointing to possible involvement by insiders within Bangladesh Bank who might have provided their credentials to hackers. In addition, the bank's system had no firewall and had used secondhand equipment in building out its system. But Bangladesh blamed the SWIFT cooperative for carrying out the transactions even when there were mistakes in the orders and when no one responded to their queries. They are suing the US Federal Reserve for damages related to the incident.[50] Meanwhile, the US Federal Bureau of Investigation believes that the North Korea-based Lazarus Group, a state-sponsored hacking collective, may have been involved. Some of the code used resembled that used in the 2014 Sony Pictures hack, which was attributed to North Korea. Indeed, a US National Security Agency official has stated that in this new financial world, "nation-states may be robbing banks."[51]

Also, we can see how international actors may have made mistakes in creating procedures due to insufficient cultural knowledge. In retrospect, we can see that even though the New York Fed queried the SWIFT orders due to certain improprieties in the way they were formatted, the director of Bangladesh Bank did not receive the queries. This was because his office computer had been infected with malware that caused his printer to malfunction. However, it's also important to note that the hackers were aware that Bangladesh was an Islamic country that closed for business on Friday. In contrast, New York's offices were closed on the American weekend, for Saturday and

Sunday. As a result, the hackers had nearly four days until the heist was discovered. By that point, the money had been moved several times and was almost impossible to trace or recover.

From a liberal internationalist perspective, we can see how this incident depicts interdependence among states and how financial cybersecurity is a vitally important collective good.

Sources

Das, K., and J. Spicer. "The SWIFT Hack: How the New York Fed Fumbled over the Bangladesh Bank Cyber-Heist." *Reuters* (July 21, 2016). https://www.reuters.com.

Gilderdale, S. "SWIFT's Customer Security Programme: Preventing, Detecting and Responding to the Growing Cyber Threat." *Journal of Securities Operations and Custody* 9, no. 1 (2017): 198–205.

Groll, E. "NSA Official Suggests North Korea Was the Culprit in Bangladesh Bank Heist." *Foreign Policy* (March 21, 2017). https://foreignpolicy.com/2017/03/21/nsa-official-suggests-north-korea-was-culprit-in-bangladesh-bank-heist/.

Schwartz, M. "Bangladesh Bank Attackers Hacked SWIFT Software." Bank Info Security. Last modified April 25, 2016. http://www.bankinfosecurity.com.

Techtarget.com. "SWIFT (Society for the Worldwide Interbank Financial Telecommunication)." https://searchcio.techtarget.com/definition/SWIFT.

Critiquing Liberal Internationalism

Throughout these chapters, we have described each international relations lens as a way of seeing the international system. Each lens highlights certain facets of the international system while downplaying the influence of other factors within that system. And each lens rests on different assumptions about the international system itself.

Those who reject the liberal internationalist view of the international system, including the liberal internationalist view of cyberspace, build their critique by querying some of the assumptions that liberal internationalists take for granted. In particular, those who are critical theorists have faulted the liberal internationalist lens for the ways in which it presents the "evolution" of the international economy as organic and natural and, in their minds, neglecting the role of agency and power politics. That is, throughout this chapter, we have assumed that there are natural shared interests that states become aware of (such as a need to provide maritime security for boats traveling in international waters), and as a result, they move to create agreements to guarantee these shared interests.

Critical theorists, in contrast, believe that the international arrangements for security, including economic security, which have evolved within the international system have not merely "grown" naturally. Instead, they argue that some actors, including corporations, have consciously steered states toward adopting these cooperative arrangements that do not just benefit the international system but that also enrich corporations that are better able to conduct economic activities in a system with few tariffs, few borders, and less conflict. They argue that our present international system did not evolve organically or naturally and that its present shape is not inevitable, although liberal internationalists may present it as such.

The notion that businesses have always played a role in a state's foreign policy and a state's power—particularly its economic power—has, at least in a capitalist society, always depended on the fortunes of its businesses, including how they fare in the international sphere, is not a new idea. Indeed, state power is—in the liberal internationalist view—tied to its gross national product, which is a function of manufacturing and the production of goods and services within a state, as well as to the existence of a highly educated and trained workforce. Manufacturing, thus, depends on a state's foreign policy to keep markets open internationally so that domestic companies have international markets to buy their goods as well as to access inputs into manufacturing that are not available domestically. Free trade is thus critical for the growth of state power. Historically, this relationship has sometimes been summed up in the shorthand phrase: "What's good for General Motors is good for America."

Critiquing the Liberal Internationalist View of Cyberspace

However, the relationship between businesses and the state in the area of cyber policy and cybersecurity is somewhat different from these historical relationships. This is because firms are creating the architecture or system that makes up e-commerce themselves, and states are thus in a weaker position in terms of attempting to regulate policies in this arena because firms have gotten there first and, in creating the architecture, begun to establish terms. Here, one can argue that technologies (including the technologies of e-commerce) are driving the train forward in developing new understandings for rules and regulations in the cyber arena, with states playing catchup and following behind firms as they seek to assert control over events occurring in this arena.

In one of the best critiques of the liberal internationalist view of the internet, analyst Micky Lee calls our attention to the fact that much of the early rhetoric about the internet, particularly in the United States, used the language of technological determinism. US policy makers and corporate leaders presented it as inevitable that the internet would represent democracy and that it would gradually extend throughout the world, carrying with it certain values.[52] However, she argues that the internet's growth was far from organic and inevitable. Rather, she suggests that we consider how corporations are complicit in creating the internet in its present form.

In Lee's retelling of the history of the internet's birth, she asks us to consider the power that corporations and technological corporations in particular have in political life as well as the role that corporations have had in lobbying for and supporting government economic policies that supported the international expansion of the internet. She writes that "technology is developed within a political and economic context," and "laws are drafted to consolidate the dominant groups."

In particular, Lee argues that the extending of the internet into China and the creation of billions of internet-enabled citizens in China did not merely "happen." Rather, she argues that corporations like Google in particular lobbied the Clinton administration to be allowed to do business with China despite its identified human rights violations.[53] As a result, the Clinton administration aided and encouraged corporations to enter the Chinese market by approving the permanent normal trading status and by lobbying the World Trade Organization to admit China as a member.

These companies, she argues, actually had a vested interest in doing business with international countries, even when these countries were not democratic and did not evince a commitment to democratic values. The major aim of these corporations was to extend the global reach of their businesses, which was at odds with the publicly stated goals of countries like the United States, to extend democracy to all. She argues that these corporations were actually interested in building a stable system of global internet commerce. They were not interested in the economic, moral, or ethical import of their decisions. Such firms, one can argue, are less concerned with preserving the internet as a global common and more concerned with creating a profitable market for their goods and services. Indeed, some analysts have suggested that in relation to the internet, state policy making has often been merely a formalization of the practices already adopted by firms and professional organizations. This is because firms have lobbied democratic states specifically, in this way tailoring the regulations that would later be used to regulate the corporations themselves.

Digital Superpowers in the Global Economy

The critique of liberal internationalism, therefore, also suggests that those corporations that became **digital superpowers** did not merely evolve to occupy this position. Rather, they consciously engaged in monopolistic practices, driving competitors out of the marketplace and securing advantages for themselves that would enable them to play a commanding role in building the internet architecture as it presently exists.

Economists Iansiti and Lakhani describe the digital economy as a collection of wheels or hubs, arguing that the best way to measure an entity's digital power is through considering the size of the hub which it commands—or the number of other entities whose economic fortunes are tied to the primary entity. That is, the more connected an entity is, and the more dependent other entities are upon it, the more powerful an entity is. (Here, we can think of the firms that possess the largest market share of digital resources and users.) When they map out these connections, however, something unusual emerges. Their list of the digital superpowers thus consists of a list not of states but instead of economic entities. They write:

> The global economy is coalescing around a few digital superpowers. We see unmistakable evidence that a winner-take-all world is emerging in which a small number of "hub firms"—including Alibaba, Alphabet/Google, Amazon, Apple, Baidu, Facebook, Microsoft, and Tencent—occupy central positions. While creating real values for users, these companies are also capturing a disproportionate and expanding share of value, and that's shaping our collective economic futures.[54]

In considering these new digital superpowers, we can distinguish between those platforms that host the infrastructure to carry out services like e-commerce (i.e., eBay and Amazon) as well as those platforms or hosts that grant users access to other types of goods and services (i.e., Facebook and YouTube) including content that users create themselves.

Here we can ask: Do these digital superpowers have the same "buy-in" that a state might have in terms of feeling compelled to maintain the international digital environment (or ecosystem) as a safe and stable place? Should content and

Figure 4.1   Digital Superpowers versus States

State or Firm	Number of Citizens, Users, or Members	Annual Revenues (or GNP) in USD	Size of the Workforce
United States	270 million	8.445 trillion	163 million[55]
Facebook	2.5 billion[56]	51 billion[57]	25,000[58]
Google	1.58 billion[59]	100 billion[60]	98,771[61]
Belgium	10 million	374 billion	5 million[62]
France	65 million	2.647 trillion	23 million[63]
Russia	143 million	1.538 trillion	75 million[64]
Alibaba	552 million[65]	39.3 billion[66]	101,958[67]
Baidu	800 million[68]	Unknown[69]	42,000[70]
Amazon	100 million prime members, 203 million regular users[71]	70 billion[72]	647,500[73]

Source: Statista

infrastructure platforms be forced to spend their resources on policing these structures to guard against cybercrime, child trafficking, or terrorism? Are these issues better confronted by states rather than private firms?

Digital Superpowers as Reluctant Global Hegemons

Many commercial interests claim that this role (as "guardian of the digital infosphere") has been thrust upon them, and it is not a role that they have either desired or sought out, nor is it one that they want. Here, most citizens and policy makers believe that corporations should have an ethical or normative concern about the impact of their products as well as an interest for those in their communities. However, some critics have argued that corporations are not predominantly driven by ethics and that the carrying out of corporate social responsibility activities may be driven as much by public relations concerns or the desire for a tax incentive for charitable giving as it is by a corporation's actual ethical goals. Thus, they argue it is insufficient for citizens and policy makers to expect corporations to police themselves and instead argue for regulations that might, for example, require companies (including internet platforms) to undertake and issue environmental impact statements or to consider matters such as whether a technology like artificial intelligence will decrease the availability of jobs for humans and how such a situation might be addressed. (We discuss this question further in our chapter on artificial intelligence.)

CONCLUSION

We have now considered two lenses of international relations as they relate to cybersecurity. As we saw in Chapter 3, realism helps us understand the sources of conflict among states through the assumption that cyberspace is an extension of the anarchic international system and that conflicts in cyberspace are an extension of territorial disputes that states have traditionally fought in real space. Realism helps us understand the formation of alliances like the Shanghai Cooperation Organization, how states can engage in balancing within cyberspace, and why a conflict spiral and cyber arms race may be inevitable.

In contrast, liberal internationalism helps us understand the phenomenon of technological, social, political, and economic interdependence among states and how cybersecurity can be recognized as a collective good that requires cooperation for its preservation. This lens illuminates how globalization has caused economic and financial systems to become more intertwined as well as how phenomena like global outsourcing have led to the breakdown of state barriers in favor of greater international trade.

Each of these lenses will be relevant as we continue to examine the debates about internet governance in Chapter 6.

QUESTIONS FOR DISCUSSION

1. Compare and contrast the pros and cons associated with the use of cryptocurrencies, like Bitcoin, for individual investors, corporations, and state actors. Should states attempt to get on board with the rise of cryptocurrencies, or should they leave this sector of the economy to develop independently?

2. Do you regard the internet as a public good, like a utility? Or do you see it as a private good that should belong to each nation individually?

3. What are some collective problems that exist online that states might cooperate to regulate and overcome?

KEY TERMS

Blockchain 93
Cryptocurrency 92
Cryptography 93
Digital economy 85
Digital superpower 107
Distributed ledger technology (DLT) 93
Infosphere 85
Legal tender 95

Peer-to-peer network 93
Stablecoin 97
Supervisory control and data acquisition (SCADA) 88
SWIFT (Society for Worldwide Interbank Financial Telecommunication) code 103
Virtual currency 92

FOR FURTHER READING

Ezrachi, A., and M. Stucke. *Virtual Competition: The Promise and Perils of the Algorithm-Driven Economy* (Cambridge, MA: Harvard University Press, 2016).

Gavil, A., and H. First. *The Microsoft Antitrust Cases: Competition Policy for the Twenty-First Century* (Cambridge, MA: MIT Press, 2014).

Madrigal, A. "Are Facebook, Twitter and Google American Companies?" *Atlantic* (November 1, 2017). https://www.theatlantic.com/technology/archive/2017/11/are-facebook-twitter-and-google-american-companies/544670/.

Students may also wish to watch the congressional hearings held in November 2018 on the matter of corporate social responsibility in internet governance found on YouTube.

5

CONSTRUCTIVISM AND THE CREATION OF CYBERSECURITY THREAT

Learning Objectives

At the end of this chapter, students will be able to do the following:

1. Define the major ideas associated with constructivism—including intersubjective understandings, agency, and discourse or language.

2. List four analogies or metaphors used to describe the internet and their significance.

3. List key military terms associated with the internet—including *critical infrastructure*, *resiliency*, and *domain*.

4. Define *critical infrastructure*, *resiliency*, and other key terms.

Does language matter? How important are the words that we choose, consciously or unconsciously, to describe an event? How does our choice of words or images affect the ways in which we understand an event? In this chapter, we consider the constructivist lens in international relations. The constructivist lens assumes that the international system itself is a product of how people (individuals, groups, and nations) perceive it. That is, constructivists do not believe that the international system has a set of fixed characteristics. It is neither inherently without order and prone to violent conflict (as realists perceive it) nor inherently oriented toward peaceful and cooperative interactions (as liberal internationalists perceive it). Instead, constructivists argue that states and policy makers can alter how states perceive the international system and as a result can alter how states act within the international system. That is, they argue that states—and individuals—"build" the international system through the use of tools, including language. How we deploy language, including words and metaphors, to talk about a subject thus affects how we think about that subject.

WHAT IS CONSTRUCTIVISM?

Constructivists thus argue that the internet is not inherently either a battlefield or a marketplace. Instead, they believe that many of the concepts that we point to in the international system are not ontologically real physical realities. Instead, they argue, concepts like race or nationality are products of our intersubjective understandings. Constructivists believe that as humans, we frequently choose to act as if a particular idea or concept is real, structuring our actions as a result of that understanding. For example, constructivists argue that when we speak of who "owns" a piece of territory, or that land "belongs" to a particular entity, we are doing so not because of physical barriers between land but rather because everyone in society has agreed to abide by certain decisions that may be reflected on a map. That is, they argue, there is no physical barrier separating the state of Texas from its neighboring states. Rather, those who live along the borders between states accept the notion that some highway exits are in Texas, whereas others are in a neighboring state, because they may have passed a sign saying "Welcome to Texas." The distinction between states, they argue, is not ontologically real but is instead accepted as a matter of consensus among citizens. If, at some point, citizens decide to regard this territory differently and to speak differently about it as a result, the understandings that we have about the territory—and the rules we adopt to structure how we behave in regard to this territory—could be different. Thus, they argue that the construct of Russian cyberspace is no different from the construct of states within the United States.[17]

CRITICAL ISSUES

POLITICS OF THE DIGITAL SILK ROAD

What is the Silk Road? The term originally referred to a trade route used since 200 BC, which connected Western traders to goods found in China and Asia, including spices and silk. The Silk Road, which ran through Southern Europe, Central Asia, and China and into East Africa, is credited for carrying not only physical goods but also allowing for the exchange of ideas and technologies among many ancient civilizations.

Today, however, analysts have begun to speak of a Digital Silk Road, which is one component of China's massive development project, begun in 2013, known as the One Belt, One Road (OBOR) Initiative. Like the original Silk Road, the Digital Silk Road will allow for an increased exchange of goods, services, and ideas among the nations of Asia, Africa, and even Europe.

The OBOR Initiative has three components: a Maritime Silk Road, the Silk Road Economic Belt, and the Digital Silk Road. (It has thus been referred to as "internet plus" because the project will develop infrastructure, cross-border e-commerce, and other types of digital economic cooperation including the integration of financial markets.) The Maritime Silk Road will ultimately link Southeast China with Southeast Asia through Bangladesh, India, the Persian Gulf, and the Mediterranean. Development projects undertaken as part of the OBOR Initiative include upgrading railway links, ports, and energy pipelines as well as laying new undersea data cables (as well as cables across Pakistan) to carry increased internet traffic in developing countries in Asia and Africa. The Digital Silk Road will include more than six thousand kilometers of underwater cables between Asia and Africa, connecting China with the Arab world and Africa. Although the strategy is led by China's government, many of the business undertakings are actually being carried out by private Chinese-owned businesses including telecommunications giants Baidu and Hua Wei.

In addition to these three components, the OBOR project also includes the development of a so-called Space Silk Road, with China's Baidu corporation taking the lead in creating its own global position satellites and making these resources available to others in the region. The Space Silk Road will ultimately increase opportunities for cross-border data sharing as well as new cooperative efforts in the field of artificial intelligence. Countries will work together to identify research opportunities and create an open platform to share data, codes, and algorithms.

The project may potentially affect up to sixty countries, with a population of more than 4 billion people.[1] The OBOR project represents an aggressive move by China to take on a more activist role in international affairs through investing more than $1 trillion in the development of physical and digital infrastructure in the region.[2]

The project has the potential to create new sources of wealth in the countries that will be integrated into the Digital Silk Road and to create new scientific innovations and new types of cooperation in fields as diverse as banking, education, and communications. In some ways, the OBOR Initiative seems similar to efforts that the United States in particular made in the 1990s when it attempted to bridge the so-called digital divide between rich and poor nations, giving internet access to everyone. So why are politicians in Europe and the United States worried about the implications of the Digital Silk Road today, and are these objections valid?

(Continued)

(Continued)

To understand this question, it is useful to apply the three lenses of international relations—realism, liberal internationalism, and constructivism.

Applying the Lenses

Realism

Realists, who think of the international system as prone to conflict, and who worry about the distribution of power within the international system, view the OBOR Initiative as capable of creating new power configurations within the international system. These analysts describe the Digital Silk Road as one part of a larger strategy that China has undertaken, aimed at building a position as a regional hegemon in Asia. The Digital Silk Road is thus seen as related to other Chinese projects, including the formation of the New Development Bank, the BRICS Contingent Reserve Arrangement, and the formation of the Shanghai Cooperation Organization.[3]

These analysts believe that China is using the OBOR Initiative to establish Chinese dominance in land warfare and naval power[4] because the agreement will allow China to acquire ports in key strategic locations through providing port security and port connectivity services.

The scale of the project has led to its being compared to the Marshall Plan, a massive infrastructure project that the United States undertook, aimed at rebuilding the nations of Western Europe in the aftermath of World War Two. Although the United States described its involvement in the Marshall Plan as a benevolent act aimed at helping nations decimated by World War Two, in fact, the Marshall Plan was an important step in establishing Western Europe as a region influenced by the United States through the Cold War with the Soviet Union. Here, the United States utilized its presence in Western Europe—including its military presence—to act as a balance against Soviet domination of Eastern Europe in the same time period.

The United States, in particular, has described China as a rising power. Thus, the United States has sought to act as a balance against what they see as undue Chinese influence in Asia in particular, through making financial cooperation agreements with Japan and South Korea in particular. (This strategy is referred to as the "pivot to Asia.")

Chinese realists, however, point to what they view as undue American influence in the Asian region, pointing to attempts at establishing a Trans-Pacific Partnership—a trade agreement that would include Australia, Brunei, Canada, Chile,

Japan, Malaysia, Mexico, New Zealand, Peru, Singapore, and Vietnam. (This agreement, proposed in 2016, is no longer slated to go forward as the United States withdrew in 2018.) China's leadership, therefore, has responded to US initiatives in the region, utilizing the infrastructure initiative both to project their influence and to compete with the United States as a sponsor to developing nations. Here, we can point to China's overtures to Pakistan to sponsor digital development initiatives there, which may serve to wrest it away from the American orbit, where it has been since 9/11.[5] Here, some analysts compare OBOR not to the Marshall Plan but rather to attempts prior to World War One, whereby the Great Powers competed for power and influence in Asia and Africa. (This contest is sometimes referred to as "the great game.")

Meanwhile, Arvind Virmani, an Indian scholar of international relations, describes the OBOR Initiative as an attempt to build China's influence in the region through the acquisition of strategic assets. He suggests that the benefits to China may be great, but he wonders if the benefits to other nations, which would essentially "host" Chinese assets (while supplying land for free), will be as great.[6] Along these same lines, American Vice President Mike Pence has argued that China is trying to create debt traps. He argues that China will offer these high-speed technology services to newly industrializing countries who will, in turn, find themselves in debt to the People's Republic of China and therefore not in a position to bargain but rather be subject to their dictates.[7]

Realists View OBOR as a Security Threat

Realists in America and Europe view China's OBOR Initiative as a security threat for two reasons: First, they worry about undue Chinese geostrategic influence in Asia. In addition, they worry about military applications of many of the new technologies being introduced into the region, particularly in the area of space. Here, Abi describes the deal that China has made with Pakistan with regard to extending the Digital Silk Road in that nation. She notes that this deal also includes the establishment of an exclusive relationship between Pakistan and China in regard to the expansion of China's Baidu Satellite System. Abi notes that through this agreement, Pakistan has exclusive access to Baidu's military services, allowing for better targeting and guidance for missiles, ships, and aircraft. Thus, the extension of technology services may well lead to the closer integration of the nations of Asia in particular into the Chinese military sphere because their nation's militaries will now share technology that is interoperable among themselves and with China.[8]

(Continued)

(Continued)

Second, military and political analysts point to specific actions that the OBOR Initiative might allow China to carry out, including espionage and surveillance. If the world's data is traveling over cables and equipment that are now Chinese owned, rather than American owned, then America worries that China will have the ability to tap into this equipment to "listen in" on Western communications, mining them for intelligence, including commercial intelligence. In addition, America worries that Chinese forces could carry out attacks on American-owned undersea cables under the guise of building and repairing their own cables. Thus, the OBOR Initiative has led to calls for the international community to adopt a resolution declaring that undersea data cables are protected resources that cannot be attacked during wartime. They would thus be off limits to targeting in the same way that hospitals are.[9]

Realists Respond to OBOR

As a result of the OBOR Initiative, some Western nations are attempting to increase their own investments in creating digital infrastructure in Asia. Doing so would, they feel, allow the West to serve as a counterbalance to China in offering states in the region a choice of providers. (Currently, internet users have no say over which cables transmit their data internationally.)

These analysts are also concerned about the fact that China is still an authoritarian regime and worry that in projecting its influence in the region, China is likely to influence other nations to develop along authoritarian lines.[10] Siddiqui writes that "once these countries are totally dependent on Beijing for their Internet freedom and defense operations, they will have to manage their issues with China only, as it will run and maintain their undersea Internet cables and satellite navigation."

Realists also worry that as a regional hegemon, China could someday dominate the global communications market and dictate the future of cyberspace. In addition, it is possible that China will find itself more involved in regional conflicts as a result of its more activist policy. China might even find itself in competition with Russia for power and influence in the region.[11]

Liberal Internationalism: The Value of Connectivity

Although the realist lens thus views the Digital Silk Road as an attempt by China to establish regional hegemony and geostrategic power, the liberal internationalist lens instead focuses on the Digital Silk Road as an attempt to create new markets as well as to create connections and cooperation among members. This is not to say, however, the realists view China's attempt to create the OBOR as mostly malevolent, whereas liberal internationalists view it as wholly benevolent.

Rather, liberal internationalists emphasize China's economic goals in the region. Shen argues that China has a problem with "overcapacity." China has created so much economic productivity so quickly that it is struggling to utilize all of the resources that it has created and thus needs to find new markets. A large-scale project could lead to economic growth in Asia, producing a boom there that would require China's excess industrial products as they undertake their own building projects.[12]

In addition, liberal internationalists see China as aiming to increase its soft power or capacity for influencing others in the region. President XI Jinping is engaged in a global form of connectivity politics—reaching out to institutions globally through the creation of cooperation in spheres as diverse as banking and international lending, research, and international media and playing a leading role in developing technical and regulatory standards.[13] (However, these analysts also acknowledge that hard and soft power are two sides of the same coin and that connectivity can also be viewed through a realist lens. Thinking back to Chapter 2, we can consider the phenomenon of path dependency, or the notion that purely technological decisions that are made in the initial stages of a technology's history may have long-term effects on how a technology comes to be used and by whom. In considering the advance of the Digital Silk Road, Kohlenberg and Godehardt describe the phenomenon of strategic docking. They argue that whichever nation is able to steer the development of connectivity hubs, by shaping the network, will be powerful. The network's developers can decide who will connect to whom, who will be the center of a hub, and who must go through another node to reach their end point. Thus far, only the United States has had the power to shape networks in this way, and as a result, the United States has had unique powers to engage in activities like surveillance and intelligence sharing. The United States and other Western policy makers may, therefore, be concerned if it appears that China is developing these same capacities in Asia, in Africa, and perhaps eventually internationally.

In addition, Zeng argues that China is using the OBOR Initiative to move from a position where it was a norm taker in cyber affairs to instead become a norm shaper.[14] The OBOR Initiative is aimed at creating structures of cooperation among nations in the region in the areas of artificial intelligence, nanotechnology, quantum computing, and smart cities. If a significant number of nations come

(Continued)

(Continued)
together to cooperate in these areas, then they may develop regulatory mechanisms that could later become the standard in these fields. In this way, China could steer and shape the international order in many fields.

Constructivism

Finally, we can deploy the constructivist lens to think about the ideas and beliefs that can help shape our world. In their analysis of the Digital Silk Road, Kohlenberg and Godehardt suggest that China is aiming to create what they call "discourse power." Here, they note that the OBOR Initiative includes features like educational exchanges. In addition, China is investing in media houses and channels as well as funding the establishment of think tanks and research projects.

Discourse power means that China will have the ability to shape how others think about and talk about Chinese influence in the region, including the building of the Digital Silk Road. China's authorities currently refer to the OBOR project and its participants as "a community of common destiny in cyberspace."[15] In addition, they have begun to speak of what they term "inclusive globalization"—meaning a process of internationalization that is not US led. Thus, China may use strategic language and communications to attempt to combat what they see as the US preference for multistakeholder governance and instead to advocate for national sovereignty in internet governance, recruiting allies through the OBOR to take the Chinese side in this debate.

Future Issues

As the application of the three lenses shows, the same event can be read differently depending on the ways in which one views the international system. The OBOR can be seen as a benevolent act by a nation that genuinely wants to help others industrialize and join the digital revolution. It can be read as a threat to regional stability or as a veiled military strategy. It is a project that is in its early stages, and therefore it is not clear how it will develop. But as we saw in Chapter 2, the circumstances under which a technological initiative emerges can have long-term effects on what the technology becomes and what it means.

It is even possible that the OBOR may be the first stage in some form of international splitting of the internet into a more liberal Western bloc and a more authoritarian Asian bloc. As Nadege Rolland, a former adviser to the French government has noted, many semi-authoritarian nations may be predisposed to support an authoritarian approach toward administering their national internets, and they may, therefore, be drawn to the Chinese approach as the Digital Silk Road moves toward their regions. And it is entirely possible that a Chinese-led internet may have a distinctly Chinese flavor and feel in comparison to the Western internet.[16]

Sources

Abi, M. "China's 'Belt and Road' Plan in Pakistan Takes a Military Turn." *The Toronto Star* (December 19, 2018). Accessed June 3, 2019. https://www.thestar.com/?redirect=true.

Barker, P. "Undersea Cables and the Challenges of Protecting Seabed Lines of Communication." Fortunascorner. Last updated March 15, 2018. https://fortunascorner.com/2018/03/19/undersea-cables-challenge-protecting-seabed-lines-communication/

Deutsche Welt. "Belt and Road Forum: Will China's 'Digital Silk Road' Lead to an Authoritarian Future?" Accessed May 29, 2019. https://www.dw.com/en/belt-and-road-forum-will-chinas-digital-silk-road-lead-to-an-authoritarian-future/a-48497082.

Ferdinand, P. "Westward Ho—the China Dream and 'One Belt, One Toad': Chinese Foreign Policy under XI Jinping." *International Affairs* 92, no. 4 (2016): 949–950.

Kohlenberg, P., and N. Godehardt. "China's Global Connectivity Politics: On Confidently Dealing with Chinese Initiatives." *Center for Security Studies* (blog), last modified April 2018. Zurich, Switzerland: Center for Security Studies. https://isnblog.ethz.ch/international-relations/chinas-global-connectivity-politics-on-confidently-dealing-with-chinese-initiatives

Shen, H. "Building the Digital Silk Road? Situating the Internet in China's Belt and Road Initiative." *International Journal of Communication* 12 (2018): 2683–2701.

Virmani, A. "OBOR: Economic, Diplomatic and Strategic Directions." *Dialogue with Virmani* (blog), last modified June 5, 2016. https://dravirmani.blogspot.com/2016/06/obor-economic-diplomatic-and-strategic.html.

Wolf, S. " 'New Silk Road' and China's Hegemonic Ambitions." Deutsche Welt. https://www.dw.com/en/new-silk-road-and-chinas-hegemonic-ambitions/a-38843212.

Wong, E., L. Chi, S. Tsui, and W. Tiejun. "One Belt, One Road: China's Strategy for a New Global Financial Order." *Monthly Review* (January 1, 2017), https://monthlyreview.org/2017/01/01/one-belt-one-road/.

Zeng, J. "Does Europe Matter? The Role of Europe in Chinese Narratives of 'One Belt, One Road' and 'New Type of Great Power Relations.'" *Journal of Common Market Studies* 55, no. 5 (2017): 1162–1176.

In this way, constructivists argue, some of the knowledge that we take for granted is actually not discovered (as one might discover gravity or a new planet) but is instead produced by humans on the basis on decisions that they make about how to view the world. In the words of Alexander Wendt, an academic credited with laying out the framework of constructivism, "It's all ideas all the way down." In other words, he argues, ideas—like citizenship, nationalism, and identity—are the building blocks on which our understandings of the international system are built. Although an idea, like the Nazi ideology of the Third Reich, can lead to a particular political, social, and economic configuration at one point in world history, an idea can also become discredited and cease to play that organizing function.[18]

Analysts like Fierke argue that politicians and citizens can thus "do things with language." She gives the example of how one can christen a ship by stating publicly that the ship now has a particular name and breaking a bottle of champagne over its bow. Nothing has fundamentally changed. However, the understanding has now been created that this ship has a specific name. Similarly, a president can use a phrase like "Axis of Evil," or "Great Satan," to speak about another nation and, as a result, can destroy a long-standing relationship between two nations, moving it from friendship to enmity. Words or labels can also be used to establish a state or group as legitimate or illegitimate within the world of international relations. In this way, she argues, language is powerful.[19]

BUILDING A BRIDGE

Internet Naming and Routing Protocols

From the internet's inception, users have been impressed by the fact that information can be carried so quickly throughout the world, traversing borders and geographical distances with ease. But when you type an address into the internet, how does the internet know where to take you? When you send an e-mail, how does the internet know where to send it?

We can think of the internet as a type of virtual territory, and we can think of internet addresses as points on the map of the internet. Here, it may be helpful to think of each address that you type (e.g., www.amazon.com) as a set of GPS coordinates in cyberspace. When you type an address into the internet, a **domain name system** (DNS) acts as a sort of telephone book, translating the address that you have typed into a specific **Internet Protocol (IP) address**, which looks like a string of numbers (i.e., 70.41.251.42). This is referred to as DNS name resolution. Your ISP, like Verizon, FIOS, or your university, has specific DNS servers that it is configured to connect to.

Your computer also has an IP address that is attached to messages that you send, queries you carry out, and messages you post online (even if you think you are acting anonymously). Your IP address may change from time to time and is assigned by a Dynamic Host Configuration Protocol (DNCP) server on your network.

You may be familiar with some common domain names, like amazon .com or MIT.edu. Domains that exist outside of the United States may also have a specific suffix attached to them, like .uk, which lets you know that the server is located in the United Kingdom, or .ru, which indicates that the server is located or hosted in Russia. Domains exist in multiple levels. The .com or .edu or country-specific suffix is a top-level domain, whereas the rest of the address is located lower down on another level.

For your DNS to find the specific address associated with the website or e-mail address that you have put in, there needs to be a central authority that maintains the list (or phone book) for all of these addresses. The Internet Corporation for Assigned Names and Numbers (ICANN) is the organization responsible for carrying out this coordinating function. Founded in 1998, ICANN was a nonprofit organization located in the United States that was funded through the US Department of Commerce and associated with the US National Telecommunications and Information Administration (NTIA). In the early years, ICANN was directed by technical specialists, most of whom were American. Many of these individuals served as registrars with responsibility for administering and monitoring addresses associated with specific domains.

However, as the internet became more international, citizens and leaders in other countries objected to the fact that so many of their nation's vital functions were dependent on this organization to administer the infrastructure of the internet. They pointed out that registrars had a great deal of power. A registrar located in the United States who was in charge of administering the .ru domain, which was attached to all Russian internet addresses, could theoretically alter the internet's map so that mail and information were no longer routed to these addresses. States worried that the United States could use internet routing to punish or coerce states into taking political and economic actions in the international system through, for example, threatening to cut off internet access if they did not comply.

Thus, other organizations have jockeyed with ICANN to take over these functions. A United Nations organization, the International Telecommunication Union (ITU), also wants to be responsible for appointing registrars and administering the internet phone book. The pressure to give this job to an international organization was strengthened after the 2013 revelations by former Central Intelligence Agency contractor Edward Snowden, showing that the US National Security Agency had engaged in the monitoring of internet communications both within the United States and internationally. Today, many countries support a multistakeholder governance model that would include private corporations, multiple states, and international organizations in the administration of internet addresses and routing protocols.

Most participants in this debate about internet governance and the assignment and administration of domain names agree that the most important thing is to establish a stable and resilient mechanism for carrying out this telephone lookup function so that the internet continues to function effectively, regardless of the outcome of issues like elections or conflicts among states.

(Continued)

(Continued)

Sources

Farrell, M. "Quietly, Symbolically, US Control of the Internet Was Just Ended." *The Guardian* (March 14, 2016). https://www.theguardian.com/technology/2016/mar/14/icann-internet-control-domain-names-iana.

Malcic, S. "Proteus Online: Digital Identity and the Internet Governance Industry." *Convergence* 24, no. 2 (2018): 205–225.

Marshall, B., and S. Crawford. "How Domain Name Servers Work." Accessed October 9, 2018. http://www.howstuffworks.com.

Tyson, J. "How Internet Infrastructure Works." Accessed October 9, 2018. http://www.howstuffworks.com.

That is, constructivists believe that although our nations have historically fought wars about ideas like religion or nationality, it is not inevitable that states do so. Today, we can point to ideas like political Islam or European integration as playing crucial roles in the organization of our international system. However, tomorrow we might find these ideas less compelling and point to others instead. It is possible for states to evolve, through the use of language and concepts and the actions of leaders, to a place where such national differences might not be a source of conflict. Constructivists thus argue that states, like the United States and the United Kingdom, may behave as though they have a unique relationship of trust—but that this relationship exists because both players agree to behave as though it does. (It thus represents a sort of game in which all of the players know the rules and obey them.) Because humans make the rules, they argue, it is also possible for humans to change the rules.

This school of thought is a relatively recent addition to the field of international relations theory, and its proponents were seeking to explain the sources of some monumental changes in the international system, such as the end of the Cold War between the United States and the Soviet Union. How was it possible for states to so radically reorient their values and foreign policies, they asked? They concluded that leaders are more responsible for their environments than we had previously thought. That is, leaders and citizens have the agency to shape the international system rather than being shaped by that system and forced to behave in certain ways (i.e., belligerently).

NEITHER A BATTLEFIELD NOR A VILLAGE: LANGUAGE "CONSTRUCTS" THE INTERNET

Constructivism contributes to our understanding of cyber politics by allowing us to trace the genesis of key ideas regarding what the internet represented, the possibilities that it contained, and the rights and responsibilities that states had toward its maintenance and growth. It also helps us understand why policy makers and citizens may feel so differently about the internet today than they did in the mid-1990s.

The constructivist lens thus shares common ground with the social construction of technology approach in that it suggests that internet technology and the accompanying technologies of platforms, surveillance software, and the internet of things did not merely evolve along technological determinist lines. That is, when we look at changes in these technologies today, as constructivists we can examine how humans—including states, corporations, and technology developers—have acted to shape these technologies and our understandings of these phenomena.

Constructivists believe that individuals make decisions about how to describe and treat the internet and the functions that individuals and groups played within that environment. They chose to describe it as either part of the real world or as a world apart that was governed by different rules. They chose to describe it as a place characterized by cooperation or as one characterized by hostility. They chose to describe it as international in character or as national in character with fixed "borders," and "territory." They chose to describe it as libertarian and not subject to existing laws within the international system or as a system that was in need of regulation. They chose to think of anonymity as threatening or liberating and to describe the speed at which information traveled as a positive or a negative quality.

In the same way, individual leaders—within government and within industry—also deployed language that emphasized the ways in which the internet was either different from or similar to existing technologies. New terms like *blogger* and *platform* were created to emphasize the fact that bloggers had different rights and responsibilities than other types of journalists, whereas platforms had different responsibilities than newspapers, for example. Other policy makers deployed new language that sought to describe cyberspace as a militarized domain, coining terms like *cyberwarfare*, *cyberweapon*, *cyber warrior*, and *cybersecurity*. They began to describe cyberspace as a military domain, and they coined terms like *critical infrastructure* to describe and organize this new system.

Because cyberspace was such a fundamentally new concept to users who first went online in the mid-1990s, analysts often used metaphors or analogies to describe what it was like. But an analogy can also serve to frame how people think about an issue. As Betz and Stephens argue:

> An analogy is a linguistic device for transferring meaning from one subject to another. With, say, a "digital 9/11" the intent is to transfer various meanings related to 9/11 (i.e., global catastrophe, invasion of the homeland, violation of the previously inviolate).[20]

Moreover, different metaphors for describing cyberspace emphasized different facets of this technology. Metaphors also set up limits regarding what could and could not be done in the space and what sorts of rights and responsibilities users might have. Initially, analysts spoke of surfing the web or joining the Global Village. And in 1994, then Vice President Al Gore famously referred to the internet as the "information superhighway."[21] The choice to describe the internet as like a highway allowed policy makers to then begin to talk about how best to regulate who could travel this highway, what sorts of licenses and fees might be appropriate for travelers on the highway, and what sorts of rules of the road might be best applied to this new space.

Later, analysts chose biological analogies to emphasize the threats that cyberspace presented. Here, we can consider the adoption of the word "computer virus" to describe attacks on computer systems by cyberweapons. Betz and Stephens note that a computer virus was said to "infect" other systems. The choice of a biological metaphor, they note, gave agency to these weapons by describing them in terms similar to those of self-replicating biological organisms that had internal logic rather than being controlled by an outside operator. [22]

The Language of Cyber Risk and Cyberthreat

In thinking about the development of language associated with the cyber environment, we can examine the conditions under which terms like *cybersecurity* and *critical infrastructure* were coined and introduced into policy discussions. The term **cybersecurity** was also first used in the 1990s by computer scientists to refer to how networked computers (vs. free-standing, self-contained computers) created new kinds of technological threats (such as the possibility of downloading a virus from another computer). Cybersecurity was understood as a multifaceted problem that required action by many different actors: Individuals were asked to take individual responsibility by practicing good "cyber hygiene," installing patches and changing passwords frequently. Cybersecurity was also understood to mean that those procuring new technologies should think about who was a trusted provider of this technology and that organizations should begin to formulate plans that spelled out how they could prevent attack, and mitigate the damages from those that did occur.

Here, it is important to note that *cybersecurity* is a term that has two meanings. Professional computer scientists use the term to denote "the practice of defending computers, servers, mobile devices, electronic systems, networks, and data from malicious attacks."[26] The International Telecommunications Union defines cybersecurity as "the collection of tools, policies, security concepts, security safeguards, guidelines, risk management approaches, actions, training, best practices, assurance and technologies that can be used to protect the cyber environment and organization and user's assets."[27]

For these professionals, cybersecurity is focused on keeping networks safe from threats, making sure that data is kept private and secure, and implementing good practices for handling data and keeping software and hardware free from threats.[28]

In contrast, national security analysts and policy makers, including those in the military, use the term *cybersecurity* in relation to the provision of other types of national security. For these analysts—and indeed for most political scientists— cybersecurity relates to the provision of strategies and tactics to be implemented on a national or international level, through military or civilian means, to defend a state's critical infrastructure and citizens from malicious adversaries. The US military thus began in the early 2000s to speak of cyberspace as the **fifth domain,**

The Physical Structure of the Internet

Often people think of the internet as an abstract force, like electricity. We know that when things are stored "in the cloud," it is not a physical cloud up in the sky but rather a data cloud, which is a more abstract concept. However, although we cannot see electricity, we can see the wires that run through our neighborhood, which carry the electricity, and we can see the utility companies that create electricity and store it for our use.

The internet also depends on physical structures. The internet's physical infrastructure includes more than 350 fiber-optic cables that carry 99 percent of the world's internet traffic. The FASTER cable connects Oregon with Japan and Taiwan, running a span of 5,600 miles underneath the sea. These cables are owned and maintained by private ISP companies as well as larger companies like Google.

The cable networks carrying internet traffic are referred to as the internet's backbone. This physical infrastructure of the internet is vulnerable to physical attacks, just as an electric company would be. In recent years, analysts have expressed concerns about the possibility that an adversary could cut a cable, leading to a shutdown of international internet traffic. There are also concerns that an adversary could tap into a cable undersea to steal intelligence information. It is even possible that a shark could bite through a cable or that a ship could drop an anchor on one—bringing down our whole internet![23]

Also, the data that we generate when we log on and visit places on the internet has to be stored somewhere. Our data resides on server farms in places like Frankfurt, Amsterdam, Hong Kong, and Singapore. Server farms are usually located in places with a cool climate, a developed internet infrastructure, and a highly educated population to work with the data. For many nations, the storage of data can be a vital source of income, boosting gross domestic product and creating jobs.[24]

Today, many nations are concerned about the fact that their citizens' data is being stored elsewhere—in an international cloud, where the host nation's government might have access to it without citizens' permission. Therefore, many states are adopting laws regarding data sovereignty, which would require a company, like Google, wishing to do business in their nation to comply with local laws regarding the hosting of data within that nation.

Here again, the question of internet geography and jurisdiction appears. Burrington describes an ongoing legal conflict involving the American company Microsoft. She writes:

> At the heart of the case is whether the US government has jurisdiction to request data located in a data center in Ireland if that data belongs to an American Microsoft user. The (US) government

(Continued)

(Continued)

argues that where Microsoft stores the data is immaterial—they're an American company. . . . Microsoft challenged the warrant on the grounds that a search doesn't happen at the point of access to the data. But where is the data stored?

A recent case in the Netherlands revolved around the fact that the Netherlands serves as the endpoint (or **landing station**) for a cable that carries internet traffic between the United States and Europe. As part of an intelligence-sharing agreement, the Dutch government allowed the American government access to messages that traveled through the Netherlands. The US government was able to gather information that resulted in a drone strike on a suspected terrorist in Somalia. The citizens of the Netherlands, who strongly oppose the use of drones in warfare, criticized their government for allowing US intelligence agents access to that information.[25]

Other nations, however, profit from these international jurisdiction disputes. Here, we can consider the practice of **bulletproof hosting**, in which nations with weak laws regulating internet content might host sites for citizens of nations where such content would be illegal. For example, many neo-Nazi websites are hosted in Estonia, although their main users may be in North America and Western Europe. Nations with weak penalties and enforcement mechanisms for cybercrime might also host websites for activities such as child pornography or drug trafficking. For this reason, many nations are working to create structures of cooperation so that laws can be enforced globally.

Sources

Burrington, I. "The Strange Geopolitics of the International Cloud." *The Atlantic* (2015, November 17). https://www.theatlantic.com/technology/archive/2015/11/the-strange-geopolitics-of-the-international-cloud/416370/.

Gray, A. "This Map Shows How Undersea Cables Move Internet Traffic around the World." *World Economic Forum* (November 24, 2016). https://www.weforum.org/agenda/2016/11/this-map-shows-how-undersea-cables-move-internet-traffic-around-the-world/.

Manjikian, M. "But My Hands Are Clean: The Ethics of Intelligence Sharing and the Problem of Complicity." *International Journal of Intelligence and Counter Intelligence* 28 (2015): 692–709. https://doi.org/10.1080/08850607.2015.1051411.

which US armed forces were to train in and seek to defend both in wartime and peacetime. Traditionally, the Army and Marines defend the land domain, the Navy and the Coast Guard defend the sea or maritime domain, the Air Force defends the air domain and the space domain.

In considering cybersecurity as a facet of national security, analysts often began by describing how cyberthreats were significantly different from other types of threats that states had faced in the past. First, they pointed to the fact that cyber conflict and cybercrime were activities with low barriers to entry. That is, one did not need a great many resources, either material or financial, to launch a dangerous threat in cyberspace. An individual could craft a cyberweapon by writing malicious code utilizing only a laptop computer. Thus, groups like terrorists were as capable of engaging in cyber warfare as were states with a full conventional military arsenal. Analysts warned of the possibility of hacks or threats on the financial infrastructure of Wall Street and described cyberspace as an environment that facilitated the carrying out of asymmetric threats—that is, attacks that cost significantly more to defend against than they do to launch. Today, authoritarian regimes may also use the language of security to describe the threats that they perceive as arising in the social media environment due to how groups can now organize online.

THE BIRTH OF CRITICAL INFRASTRUCTURE

Next, they pointed to how states were particularly vulnerable to cyberattack, given states' increasingly heavy reliance on computerized systems to run many parts of the state infrastructure. Analysts began to use the term **critical infrastructure**, beginning in 1996, when the Clinton administration established the Commission on Critical Infrastructure Protection to describe those aspects of a state's infrastructure that citizens expected to have available and counted on the state to provide—including transportation infrastructure, clean water, and a safe food supply. At the same time, business interests in the United States became concerned about cybersecurity threats after the publication of a 1996 Rand Corporation study titled "The Day After . . . in Cyberspace."[29] In that analysis, the authors showed how a cascade could work through the vector of cyber, resulting in attacks on the financial sector, transportation sector (through causing plane or train crashes), the military sector (through attacks on the electrical grid that take out power at military bases), the communications sector (through shutting down or hacking into broadcasting), and the economic sector (Wall Street).

In 2002, critical infrastructure appeared in the Department of Defense Dictionary of Critical Terms, where it was defined as "the infrastructure and assets vital to a nation's security, governance, public health and safety, economy, and public confidence."[30] Here agencies throughout the US government began to consider how they might secure their organizations and infrastructure. Organizations began to speak of cyber resiliency in considering how their organizations might continue to function during a cyberattack and afterward. In 2003, the administration of President George Bush drafted a National Strategy to Secure Cyberspace and created a cybersecurity branch within the brand-new Department of Homeland Security.[31]

It was in this atmosphere of threat and uncertainty that many people in government began to suggest that the United States was not significantly well prepared to respond to cyberattacks by other actors as well as to take the necessary steps to provide for its cyber defense. Policy makers warned of a Cyber Pearl Harbor, describing a situation in which, for example, the United States might be unprepared for an attack and sustain significant casualties as a result. They also borrowed the language of nuclear war, substituting the phrase **weapons of mass disruption** to refer to a cyberwar—instead of weapons of mass destruction to refer to a nuclear war.[32] Cyber issues also became intertwined with rhetoric about terrorism after 9/11 as analysts warned about how terrorist groups were organizing in cyberspace.[33] In the aftermath of 9/11, cyberspace was described by analysts like Sageman as "failed space" that could not be sufficiently well administered and monitored and that therefore provided an "electronic safe haven" for groups like terrorists who wished to organize online.[34] We also see the use of securitized language about cyberspace in statements by Jared Cohen, the director of Google Ideas. In explaining how Google will now alter search results so that those who might be searching online for information about ISIS to engage in self-radicalization will now be redirected to anti-jihadist websites, Cohen referred to "recapturing digital territory" from extremist groups. He has also referred to shutting down of accounts linked to terrorists as "pushing them back" from the web, utilizing the language of the military—echoing ideas like opening up a front or launching a digital counterinsurgency.[35]

What Is Critical Infrastructure?

In the aftermath of the 9/11 terrorist attacks upon the United States, the US government established the Department of Homeland Security, which was tasked with providing for the protection and safety of US citizens and strategic assets located within the United States. The USA PATRIOT Act, a landmark piece of legislation that was passed in the wake of these attacks, established the Department of Homeland Security and also defined a new term for Americans: critical infrastructure.

The PATRIOT Act defines critical infrastructure as

systems and assets, whether physical or virtual, so vital to the United States that the incapacity or destruction of such systems and assets would have a debilitating impact on security, national economic security, national public health or safety, or any combination of those matters.[36]

The 2003 report by the Department of Homeland Security explains that critical infrastructures provide goods and services that Americans tend to take for granted, including things like clean water, working phones, and electricity. Without those things, America would be a different place, and what we think of as the modern "American way of life" might cease to exist.[37]

Today, the Department of Homeland Security recognizes critical infrastructure as including agriculture and food, water, public health, emergency services, defense industrial base, telecommunications, energy, transportation, banking and finance, chemicals and hazardous materials, and postal and shipping infrastructure. Because these areas are so important to Americans, the US government (including the Department of Homeland Security and the Department of Defense) pays particular attention to thinking about how such sectors might be attacked either physically or through the internet by adversary nations and domestic threats like terrorists as well as how they might defend these sectors.

For those concerned with protecting critical infrastructure from cyberattacks, there are two key issues to be aware of: First, many functions carried out in critical infrastructure sectors—from monitoring the quality of water to mapping out shipping routes to overseeing financial transactions—are automated functions that are carried out in real time, sometimes from remote locations that are not located contiguously with the factories or installations themselves. The term *SCADA* (supervisory control and data acquisition) refers to the software and hardware that controls industrial processes, including monitoring and gathering data. A SCADA system also records events that occur (logs them) and interacts with other parts of a system, including valves, pumps, and motors.[38] A hacker who enters a facility's SCADA system could potentially cause a nuclear power plant to overheat, delete or corrupt vital data like hospital records, or poison people through sending bad data back to controllers after adulterating a food or water supply. All critical infrastructure sectors are highly dependent on SCADA systems, and thus cybersecurity experts work hard to protect them.[39]

The second issue for cybersecurity experts is the fact that most of America's critical infrastructure is privately owned and administered rather than being administered and controlled by the government itself. Private companies own and run water and sewage companies, telephone and wireless companies, and hospitals. Thus, it is essential for the private and public sector actors to work together to protect and defend America's critical infrastructure.

Sources

Department of Homeland Security. "The Physical Protection of Critical Infrastructures and Key Assets." Last modified 2003. http://www.dhs.gov/xlibrary/assets/Physical_Strategy.pdf.

Inductive Automation. "What Is SCADA?" Accessed November 29, 2018. https://inductiveautomation.com/what-is-scada.

PC Magazine. "Critical Infrastructure." Accessed November 29, 2018. https://www.pcmag.com/encyclopedia/term/40480/critical-infrastructure.

US Department of Justice. "USA PATRIOT Act: Preserving Life and Liberty." https://www.justice.gov/archive/ll/highlights.htm.

Finally, analysts noted that cyberspace was uniquely threatening because there were a diverse number of malicious actors in cyberspace who could not be easily tracked, and the sophistication of cyberattack tools was proliferating, perhaps more quickly than large bureaucratic states could expand and adapt. Here, we can consider a statement by President Barack Obama in 2009, when he wrote that cyberthreats are "one of the most serious economic and national security challenges we face as a nation. . . . It is also clear that we are not as prepared as we should be, as a government or as a country."[40]

In considering the newly emerging classes of threats, analysts and policy makers began to speak of cyber risk. In 2015, the Global Zero Commission on Nuclear Risk Reduction published a report in which they emphasized how cyber exploits like unauthorized hacking could increase the likelihood that nuclear weapons could be launched. They invoked a doomsday scenario in writing:

> Questions abound: could unauthorized actors—state or non-state— spoof early warning networks into reporting attack indications that precipitate overreactions? Could such hackers breach the firewalls, the air gaps and transmit launch orders to launch crews or even to the weapons themselves? What if an insider colluded with them to provide access and passwords to the launch circuitry? Might they acquire critical codes by hacking?[41]

Authors in the field of nuclear security wrote about how the availability of cyberweapons and the increasing reliance on the internet in all aspects of national security was creating a climate of instability in which all types of conflict, both cyber and conventional, were more likely.

THE MILITARIZATION OF CYBERSPACE

As we saw in the establishment of the US Cyber Command, states were increasingly referring to "American cyberspace" or "German cyberspace," setting up military units called cyber commands and running military exercises aimed at training cyber warriors to defend their "territories" in cyberspace. States issued documents like the US National Cyberstrategy, and politicians prepared to respond to questions about how they will defend the nation's cyber resources, including critical infrastructure, software, and data.

However, not everyone agreed with this view that something had changed in cyberspace that now made it a fundamentally more dangerous environment than it had been in the past. Here, social constructivists suggest that what changed was not the environment but rather our intersubjective understanding of the cyberspace environment. They argue that through inventing a new language and new concepts like the cyberthreat and cybersecurity, analysts began to perceive this cyber "territory" differently and to behave differently on national and international levels as a result.

Opponents of "Cyber Risk" Language

Here, Quigley et al. argue that people tend to overemphasize the riskiness and the probability of harm associated with things that are unfamiliar or new things that are highly technological or things that they have little firsthand experience with. Thus, they suggest that analysts may have either misunderstood or misinterpreted how reliance upon the internet exposed individuals, groups, and societies to risk. They write that "there is evidence to suggest that the threat is exaggerated and oversimplified for some. Many note the lack of empirical evidence to support the widespread fear of cyber-terrorism and cyber warfare."[42]

Emerson has accused the "cyber gurus" who work as defense contractors, selling suites of cyberdefense tools to the US government, and the vendors of commercially available cybersecurity defense software, of preying upon people's fears of unknown internet risks to create a large-scale cyberdefense industry. He describes the cyberthreat as "amorphous." He writes that like terrorism, the threat of cyberattacks and cybercrimes is something that could ostensibly happen at any time, anywhere. It is difficult to measure the size or severity of cyberthreats accurately because they are less tangible than, for example, the threat that an enemy might launch a conventional armed invasion against our borders. He argues that given their "nonmaterial basis," states have played a crucial role in defining and raising awareness of these threats. Also, as noted in the nuclear example, cyberthreat is often presented not in isolation but rather as part of a larger scenario in which hacking or cyberwarfare leads to a more widespread societal breakdown. Emerson suggests that the vagueness of the cyberthreat may have helped create a climate of "hyper securitization" in which the threat is exaggerated, and as a result, excessive countermeasures are taken.[43]

What Are States Defending in Cyberspace?

In a related critique, Halbert suggests that the major threats that the United States faced in cyberspace by the late 1990s were actually economic: The United States and its American businesses stood to lose significant amounts of money if the internet continued to be a lawless or anarchic place in which rules regarding property and ownership (including the ownership of intellectual property) were not respected. Also, she argues that the American government was concerned about practices like cyber espionage in which actors from China, in particular, were using practices like cyber trespassing and cyber breaking and entering to steal trade secrets and proprietary information from American companies. This, she argues, was the primary reason why the United States began to speak of the operational domain of cyberspace. In her work, she traces the language of cybersecurity back to a National Security Decision Directive issued in 1984 by then-president Ronald Reagan in which he stated, "Government systems, as well as those which process the private or proprietary information of US persons and business, can become targets of foreign exploitation."[44]

In this way, Halbert asks us to consider what exactly is being secured and defended in cyberspace—is it critical infrastructure, information, commercial products, or something else? Here, constructivists argue that when states use security language to describe a threat, they may not all agree about who or what precisely is being threatened. The object being protected is referred to as the **referent object of security**. They ask who or what is being protected in cyberspace when states talk about cybersecurity. Here, we can consider how Russia, for example, describes the internet as threatening to the "spiritual purity" of the Russian people. Russia's leaders worry that citizens might lose their Russian language because so much of the internet is in English. They also worry that exposure to Hollywood and other influences might weaken institutions like the nuclear family and the Russian Orthodox Church.[45]

That is, there is not always a clear consensus among every nation that participates in cyber activities about how cyberspace should be administered to make it a safe and stable environment for individuals, groups, and states to participate in—because not all players may agree on what it means for this environment to be safe, stable, or secure. This constructivist view relies on the assumption that genuine threats to the internet did not emerge throughout the 1990s or beyond. Instead, new threats were narrated into being. Cybersecurity, along with cyberthreat, was a politically powerful concept that was invented and propagated by individuals, corporations, and states that had a vested interest in spending large amounts of government funding on cybersecurity.

However, although constructivists ask us to consider whether cyberthreat and cyber risk are real or invented and whether we understand such factors accurately rather than exaggerating them due to other political and social considerations, there are other lenses that we can also use to look at this problem.

QUESTIONS FOR DISCUSSION

1. In their work on policy language and framing, Epstein et al. write that policy language is a human-made artifact. The process of creating (and deploying) policy language is a function of historical and temporal factors, such as social norms, group dynamics, rhetoric, and cognitive processing. As such, policy discourse is reflective of both the power structures and the political dynamics in a given policy context; it is through discourse that policy makers enact the social structures of signification and legitimation within which they act.[46]

    Consider the "state of the nation" speech that Russian President Vladimir Putin gave in March 2018. (A transcript is available here: https://www.rferl.org/a/putin-state-of-nation-speech-annotated/29071013.html.)

a. How does Putin frame his plans to expand the internet in Russia, Russia's investment in new hardware including an expansion of the internet backbone, and plans to store user data in Russia? What other elements of state power are these initiatives related to? How does this language connect to what you know about Russia historically?

2. In international relations, we sometimes refer to the agent–structure problem. This phrase refers to two competing notions of causality in international relations.

   The realist paradigm suggests that the anarchic international system, as a structure, can affect how states behave. That is, states may be driven to compete for resources not because they have chosen to do so but because there is no other choice within the current structure of the international system. Other paradigms, like constructivism, give a lot more weight to agency, or free choice.

   Constructivists, who believe that "anarchy is what we make of it," in the words of Alexander Wendt, argue that states shape the architecture of the international system through the decisions that they make along with the language that they use. If we describe a country as an adversary or a situation as adversarial, we can increase the tension. Similarly, we can reduce tensions as a result of how we view the situation.

   a. How does the agent–structure problem relate to the cyber domain?
   b. Are you a realist who believes that states are driven to adopt an adversarial view of this domain, and therefore to focus on protecting their borders, distrusting their neighbors in cyberspace, and creating a cyber command?
   c. Are you a constructivist who believes that the language used by people like Russian cyber experts are instrumental in creating this hostile environment, and could it be changed?

KEY TERMS

Bulletproof hosting 126
Constructivism 122
Critical infrastructure 127
Cybersecurity 124
Domain name system (DNS) 120

Fifth domain 124
Internet Protocol (IP) address 120
Landing station 126
Referent object of security 132
Weapons of mass disruption 128

FOR FURTHER READING

Betz, D., and T. Stevens. "Analogical Reasoning and Cybersecurity." *Security Dialogue* 44, no. 2 (2013): 147–163. https://doi .org/10.1177%2F09670106 13478323.

Epstein, D., M. Roth, and E. Baumer. "It's the Definition, Stupid! The Framing of Online Privacy in the Internet Governance Forum Debates." *Journal of Information Policy* 4 (2014): 146–147.

Hansen, L., and H. Nissenbaum. "Digital Disaster, and the Copenhagen School." *International Studies Quarterly* 53 (2009): 1155–1175.

Quigley, K., C. Burns, and K. Stalard. " 'Cyber Gurus': A Rhetorical Analysis of the Language of Cybersecurity Specialists and the Implications for Security Policy and Critical Infrastructure Protection." *Government Information Quarterly* 32 (2015): 108–117.

Wendt, A. *A Social Theory of International Politics* (Cambridge, UK: Cambridge University Press, 1999).

6

GOVERNING THE INTERNET

Learning Objectives

At the end of this chapter, students will be able to do the following:

1. Define governance, and relate it to ideas of power, sovereignty, and rule making.

2. Describe multistakeholder governance in internet regulation.

3. Name major agreements and events in the evolution of multistakeholder governance.

4. Describe the players who participate in multistakeholder governance in the internet area and how this differs from other types of international governance.

As we have seen previously, the internet can be viewed as an international "territory" that brings together a variety of actors to carry out a variety of functions in the online environment—from participating in commerce to sharing resources like information, data, and entertainment. It has also been described as an international common in which participants from nations and groups come together to share resources as well as to share in the risks that might arise in this environment. In the liberal internationalist lens, the internet is seen as a vehicle that fosters interdependence through creating situations in which states need to work together cooperatively, both relying upon and creating an atmosphere of trust.

At the same time, as we have noted, the realist view suggests that the internet is fundamentally a space of anarchy. Risks arise and are challenging to deal with precisely because there is no one central governing authority whose job it is to regulate this environment. For this reason, the internet was initially described as a frontier, or even as the Wild West.

In this chapter, we consider several questions related to the structure of the internet as an international space. As noted previously, in the "real world," the global system has emerged over a period of hundreds of years, evolving structures of organization, agreement, and cooperation among its members. In some narratives, the creation of consensus among states about what constitutes right or ethical behavior in the international system is described as "evolving"—or emerging naturally from the bottom up as a result of political development. For example, those who write about human rights often tell a story about how, as people have become more educated and scarcity has lessened, people and states have reached a consensus internationally regarding the fact that all humans have individual rights.[1] In this view, states can cooperate in, for example, observing human rights agreements like the United Nations Universal Declaration of Human Rights on the basis of these shared values and norms. Similarly, analysts describe how states naturally, over time, evolved the notion of state sovereignty, or the idea that a state can control what happens in its territory. Finally, customary international law, which forms the legal basis for the resolution of many disputes among states in the global system, is a system of legal understandings that has evolved over hundreds of years. States may accept that a legal obligation—or a constitutional prohibition—exists regarding carrying out a specific action in the international community because doing so has become a "custom," and there thus exists an expectation that an issue will be handled in a particular fashion. Such customs evolve as legal suits are undertaken, legal rulings take place, and problems are resolved. The Universal Declaration of Human Rights is an example of customary international law because it serves as a codification of a consensus about the meaning and place of human rights in the global system that has evolved gradually over time.[2]

However, as noted in Chapter 1, the internet environment differs from real territorial space because this technology has emerged and expanded so rapidly, quickly becoming a vital part of our lives today. Many of the critical building blocks of the international system in the real world appear absent in cyberspace. Currently, there is a lack of consensus in three areas: Not all actors in the international system agree that states should be the primary organizing unit for cyberspace, as they are in the global order. Also, states disagree about whether or not the internet should be construed as territory that can and should be subdivided along state lines. Is it reasonable to speak about Russian cyberspace or American cyberspace, or is cyberspace better understood as a global commons or international territory like the ocean or outer space? Thirdly, states disagree about whether there are norms and values that states should be compelled to observe in cyberspace.

NORMS AND CYBERSPACE NORMS

Here, we can also point to a disagreement about where a norm comes from. Norms are "collective understandings of the proper behavior of actors."[3] Norms can be either informal or formal. Formal norms are codified into law and are enforceable, whereas informal norms do not have the force of law. An informal norm or rule of behavior might be something like "world leaders can expect that other world leaders will not publicly call them names," whereas a formal norm would be something like a prohibition on torturing prisoners of war, which is codified and enforced by the Geneva Convention. Both informal and formal norms together, in the words of Barnett, form a "normative web that constrains (a state's) foreign policy in general and its use of force in particular."[4]

Although some analysts have argued that norms about how states should behave (e.g., in regard to conflict and respect for one another's borders) emerge organically in the international system, other analysts believe that norms can be imposed upon states from the top down and that wealthy and powerful states may act to impose those norms upon less affluent, less powerful states. Because the internet is so new in comparison to the international system (with an age of only forty, as opposed to nearly four hundred years for the Westphalian state system), analysts disagree about whether norms truly exist in cyberspace and whether it is possible to either create formal cyber norms from the top down or bring about their creation from the bottom up. Finally, we can return to the uniqueness debate that we introduced in Chapter 2 to ask about whether international laws should be expanded to also apply to cyberspace or whether new rules and regulations need to be created in this new space.

Thus, a central question in this chapter is: If structures of governance and organization for cyberspace have not yet emerged organically, then can they (and should they) be created and imposed from the top down? That is, can the major players in cyberspace today—from states to international organizations to corporations—come together to agree on what sorts of regulatory frameworks should exist in cyberspace, and can humans thus act to build cyberspace, not merely as a technical entity but as a political entity as well?

This chapter considers three issues: First, is it feasible or desirable to create some form of international institution or international structure (or structures) to regulate the internet? Here, we consider the concept of governance. Next, in the absence of an overarching governance structure for cyberspace, can states still engage in policy coordination in cyberspace on regional and international levels?

Finally, we consider the matter of norms and values. Is it reasonable to expect that a consensus will emerge regarding the norms and values that states and other actors should adhere to in resolving conflicts in cyberspace?

Creating Structures of Governance

We begin by considering how creating a governance structure for cyberspace is and is not a unique problem. Although some arrangements of governance (like customary international law) have emerged or evolved organically, rather than being steered from above, states have also routinely sought to explicitly create structures of governance in a variety of arenas, particularly in the period since the eighteenth century. That is, states do regularly cooperate to regulate activities and actions within the international community. They engage in rule making and standards setting—establishing normative understandings regarding how states should treat other countries within the global system as well as how states should treat their citizens within their territory. International organizations like the United Nations and the World Trade Organization exist to create and enforce both formal and informal standards in the areas of conflict, conflict resolution, human rights, and free trade.

Here, some authors argue that states engage in rule making when a consensus already exists. In this way, regulation can be seen as merely the formal acknowledgment of an agreement that has already been made or that already exists. (Here, analysts may speak of a convergence of standards and concepts regarding what a good or right order would look like.)

However, critics of international organizations ask whether organizations like the United Nations are acknowledging a preexisting consensus or imposing Western standards upon other nations under the guise of behaving as though such norms and values are universal values. Some states, particularly in the developing world, have argued that wealthy nations like the United States, who contribute the majority of funding to the United Nations, actually play an outsized role in the events that occur in this policy body.[5] They argue that the United Nations often seems to impose its agenda and its values upon other nations, who then comply because they need foreign aid rather than because they necessarily agree with the policies.[6] For example, current initiatives within the United Nations to guarantee and uphold the rights of women, as well as the LGBT community, are fiercely opposed by many African and Middle Eastern nations. These leaders argue that the values of the United Nations, in this instance, are not universal values but rather Western values that are not in keeping with their own nations' historical and religious sensibilities.[7] The United Nations has seen contentious policy debates on issues ranging from whether it is appropriate for states to draft child soldiers into conflict, whether children should be allowed to marry, and whether children have the same rights as adults or a more limited set of rights, with the final authority belonging to their families.[8]

Other critics have argued that in the final analysis, bodies like the World Trade Organization and the United Nations are relatively weak bodies with no real authority to enforce the standards and rules that they are attempting to set. The chaotic environment of the international system, such critics feel, mitigates against the ability of global governance to ultimately work.[9]

Issues in Internet Governance

We can see echoes of these same debates in the pages that follow, as we consider what it means to establish international governance in cyberspace. In this chapter, we consider some key ideas from international relations theory—like state sovereignty—which analysts use to understand and describe the role of states within the global system today. Throughout this chapter, you will be asked to think about how well or poorly concepts like sovereignty and territorial integrity can be "borrowed" and applied to thinking about interstate issues in cyberspace. Here, we can refer back to the uniqueness debate in asking whether it makes sense to think of cyberterritory as an extension of physical territory (in which case we can take traditional international relations concepts and graft or map them onto cyberspace) or whether we should think about cyberterritory as something so fundamentally different from physical territory that such theories do not apply.

Some critics suggest that the environment itself is far too chaotic and that the interests that currently exist in cyberspace are too different and too disparate for them to be effectively incorporated into a formal institutional body that would rule and guide the internet. Moreover, some critics, notably Russia, have argued that any organization that might be created to regulate cyberspace will not be apolitical.[10] Here Russia claims that in the past, the United States participated in the United Nations when it suited its interests to do so, often utilizing the United Nations as a vehicle for carrying out US foreign policy interests under the guise of internationalism. In some instances Russia has accused the United States of hypocrisy, in arguing that the United States has sometimes adopted policies formally while informally seeking to violate them—in, for example, officially supporting the notion that states are sovereign in their domestic affairs while simultaneously intervening in others' sovereign affairs on the grounds of preventing human rights violations or humanitarian disasters. In the same way, Russia argues, any international organization that is created to regulate the internet is more likely to embody the values of the United States, which created the internet, than it is to represent an international consensus about the role and meaning of the internet—if, indeed, such an agreement even exists.

As we will see in this chapter, each of these issues—whether an organization is genuinely international or merely a cover for the agenda of a few powerful states that use the organization for their purposes, the degree to which the creation of international organizations represents a threat to national and territorial sovereignty, and whether there are genuinely global values that an international organization should uphold and defend—has been debated within the context of cyberspace as well.

Also, we can ask whether there has indeed been convergence or evolution of shared norms among states regarding issues like the proper use of the internet, the values that the internet should be governed by, and the rules that should govern activities online. If such shared norms have not evolved, we can also ask whether they can be created by the players currently working to shape cyberspace, including states, international organizations, technical groups, and global corporations like Facebook and Twitter.

The Global Governance View

As we saw in Chapter 1, in the heady initial days of the internet's birth or creation, technology specialists like John Perry Barlow claimed that traditional international relations ideas like state sovereignty, citizenship, and even states were irrelevant in cyberspace. In this view, citizens were instead netizens with no particular loyalty to a state. Barlow envisioned cyberspace as a place where the major actors would not be states but where instead the internet would be regulated by loose confederations of volunteers, many with technical expertise, who would administer the internet. That is, they believed that nonstate actors like the Internet Society, and volunteers such as those who manage the root directories of the internet, would be able to perform the work of keeping the internet running on a technical level.

This **open information viewpoint** was based on specific values, including the benefits of transparency, openness, and freedom of information. Advocates of this view believed that cyberspace should not be carved up into territorial domains and that so-called digital sovereignty was neither possible nor desirable. Furthermore, they thought that it was possible for all of those involved in building cyberspace—technology specialists, corporations, nongovernmental organizations, and states—to work together to create a secure cyberspace without imposing ideas like sovereignty or territorial control or ownership on the space.

Today's internet, such analysts argue, is being built from the bottom up by a broad coalition that includes nonstate actors like the International Telecommunications Union and the Internet Society, corporations like Facebook and Twitter, and international organizations like the United Nations Intergovernmental Group of Experts. As a result, these analysts believe that the best vehicle for building a stable and orderly internet for the future is to create institutions of global governance through a multistakeholder process in which states would be one of many actors involved in building institutions, policies, and norms for the internet.

In this view, global governance requires a system in which authority is granted to actors beyond the state, including to regional and international bodies. Also, it requires the ability to make and administer policies on a suprastate level and the distribution of governing resources among a diverse number of actors.[11] Global governance advocates, then, see the evolution of multistakeholder global governance in cyberspace as a logical outgrowth of the internet's unique history and organization. They also present the development of global governance and the waning of state power as the outcome of an inevitable process—or an evolution of the environment—and suggest that there is little that states or particular leaders can do to alter or change the shift toward this new form of organization and policy making.

THE CYBER SOVEREIGNTY POSITION

However, many states—including those that are the most cyber powerful—disagree with this orientation toward global governance and do not feel that the best way to evolve or create a stable, peaceful internet is through a multistakeholder approach. Instead, these actors argue that states should remain the dominant unit of organization within cyberspace and that states should act as the guarantors of a stable internet. This position can be titled the cyber sovereignty position in contrast to the global governance position.

Many analysts credit the United States with "inventing" the cyber sovereignty position, and they trace the idea back to the 1996 decision to form a US Commission on Critical Infrastructure Protection. The United States was also the first nation to draft a National Strategy to Secure Cyberspace under President Bush in 2001 as well as to create a cybersecurity branch within the Department of Homeland Security. The US Department of Defense also played a key role in creating the cyber sovereignty paradigm. Arguing from a realist perspective, the US Department of Defense established the understanding that states could claim sovereignty in cyberspace—that is, that states had a claim to territory in cyberspace as well the claim that states should get to be the final authority regarding actions and activities that occurred in "their" cyberspace. In this view, then, cyberspace was not merely international, ungoverned waters but instead could be broken into Russian cyberspace, American cyberspace, and Chinese cyberspace. Indeed, in 2010, Russia first defined the notion of a military cyber command, which it then began establishing. That same year, the United Kingdom defined a cyberattack against its critical infrastructure as a Tier One Threat.

And as far back as 1999, the United States began asking when a cyber operation might be said to violate another state's sovereignty. That is, when might a state be able to make a claim to an international body, like the United Nations or the International Criminal Court, because a cyberattack had violated state sovereignty? By 2014, the United States in particular had begun enforcing its claims to sovereignty over its internet. That year, the US Department of Justice indicted five Chinese soldiers for hacking and espionage against US companies.

States Enforcing State Sovereignty in Cyberspace

Cyber sovereignty proponents thus believe that the internet is not merely an abstract idea but one based on physical geography or topography. The internet cannot run without crucial components such as undersea cables and cable operators, search engines, and social network sites. Each of these elements has strategic significance for a state because it represents a bottleneck through which information flows and a place where it could be monitored, stolen, attacked, or blocked. Indeed, in recent years, many states have acted to shut down their citizens' access to the internet through what has become known as an **internet kill switch**. Repressive nations have shut down or cut off citizen access to the internet to prevent domestic demonstrations or as a way of prohibiting the free exchange of information in the run-up to an election. In 2015, Congo's government shut down citizen access to the internet as a response to demonstrations calling for the imposition of term limits that would have prevented Congolese President Denis Sasou N'Guesso from running for another term in office.[12] Turkey's government introduced legislation in 2016 allowing authorities to suspend citizen internet access in situations that presented a threat to the public order. India has implemented regional internet cutoffs in response to minority activism and social unrest, and Egypt cut off internet access during the 2011 Egyptian Revolution. Most recently, Zimbabwe has engaged in internet cutoffs as a response to social demonstrations. Moreover, even democratic nations like the United Kingdom and the United States have entertained the possibility that all states should have the ability to shut down the internet to protect critical infrastructure from threats or prevent a virus from spreading online. Here, the ability of a state to control citizen access to the internet seems to bolster states' claims that they do indeed "own" their national cyberspace—although, in some instances, international organizations like telecommunications providers have succeeded in overriding these controls.

Most recently, Russia's parliament has begun considering a law that would require Russian internet providers to ensure the independence of the Russian internet. By 2020, Russia hopes to route 95 percent of its internet traffic locally rather than having it pass through the international network.[13] Russia will conduct its first test of the ability of its internet to function internally through disconnecting from the international network in 2019. Here, Russia's leadership has referred to **digital sovereignty,** arguing that each state has the right to determine what its state interests are in cyberspace along with the ability to structure its cyberspace in a way that best reflects and achieves those interests. Here, Russia's leadership argues that just like a state can control which goods and services can transit through its territory through the use of trade agreements, economic legislation, and export regimes, the Russian state should be able to control what sorts of content and ideas can transit through its information space. They also argue that just like you go through customs and are monitored when you enter a foreign country, the Russian government should be able to look at and control all communications that transit in and out of Russia.

And in 2015, China enacted its own China Cybersecurity Law, which provided the legal basis of China's claim to comprehensive control of its domestic cyberspace. This same law also noted that China would engage in active cyberdefense to defend its cyberspace.

Cyber Sovereignty in Military Doctrine

The notion that a state owns and controls its cyberspace also appears in the military doctrines of many countries. Here, states, beginning with the United States, argued that states had the right to control and administer cyberspace as a "domain." In military doctrine and strategy, the state recognizes five domains of warfare: land, air, space, maritime, and cyber. International legal rulings have created an understanding that a state has the right to control its territory (land domain) as well as the airspace above it (the air domain) and that others cannot transit through it without asking permission. It also controls its territorial waters (maritime domain), although it does not control any part of outer space (space domain). Thus, satellites can travel freely in orbit.

The US Department of Defense thus contends that an unauthorized intrusion into a state's computer systems would constitute a violation of their cyber domain and thus a violation of state sovereignty. Also, if an act led to the effects being felt in a state, that state could also claim its sovereignty had been violated.

The US Department of Defense defines the cyber domain as

> a global domain within the information environment consisting of the interdependent networks of information technology infrastructures and resident data, including the Internet, telecommunications networks, computer systems, and embedded processors and controllers.[14]

From this perspective, an actor could be said to have violated a state's sovereignty in the cyber domain through carrying out a physical (or kinetic) attack on hardware like a cable that carries data to and from a state, or it might include an activity like someone hacking into a computer that belongs to the Pentagon. It might also include an attack on a state's critical infrastructure, defined by the Department of Homeland Security as those sectors whose assets, systems, and networks, whether physical or virtual, are considered so vital to the United States that their incapacitation or destruction would have a debilitating effect on security, national economic security, national public health or safety, or any combination thereof.

Norms and Laws in Cyberspace

That is, adherents of the cyber sovereignty position believe that the norms governing state behavior in the real world of physical territory can also be exported and applied to the world of cyberterritory. If we apply these understandings to addressing conflicts in cyberspace, then an actor could be said to be violating a state's sovereignty were it to attack targets that are physically within a state's borders or owned by a state. In this view, then, a state could claim to have been invaded or attacked if another country or actor attacked targets such as its critical domestic infrastructure—even if these targets are private companies (like your telephone company) rather than state-run or state-owned enterprises.[15] In 2016, NATO recognized cyberspace as a military domain, following the lead of the United States. In subsequent years, it has issued documents such as the *Tallinn Manual*, which puts forth the understanding that international law applies to cyberspace.

However, there is still a debate about whether cyber norms merely codify an existing consensus or whether they more accurately reflect the preferences of strong states. Thomas argues that norms can and do reflect both a state's foreign policy interests and the distribution of power. He writes that "a strong state can thus help to structure the international system in ways that are favorable to it through acting to impose certain norms and lend them legitimacy."[16]

A Consensus regarding Global Cyber Norms?

Today, many leading global powers, including the United States, China, and Russia, would all like to be the state that gets to define global norms regarding cyberspace, its values, and what constitutes sovereignty. And today these states do not agree on what these values are or on the extent to which global norms for structuring cyberspace and interactions within that space are truly international. Here, the United States argues that cyberspace is indeed territory that states can defend, claim, and own. However, at the same time, the US position is that states do not, therefore, have the right or the ability to do anything that they want within the confines of "their" cyberspace. Here, the United States has historically identified "universal" values such as the right to assemble and the right to freedom of speech as existing within cyberspace, regardless of who claims to own that cyberspace. Thus, US policy makers believe that states have limited sovereignty in relation to what takes place in "their cyberspace."

Russia and China, in contrast, describe that the norm of state sovereignty in cyberspace as more absolute. A state that owns its territory, they argue, also has a right to protect its citizens from sometimes immoral and corrupt foreign influences, even if that means imposing what outside observers might label as surveillance or censorship. Here, both China and Russia reject the claim that individuals who use the internet are somehow, therefore "global citizens." Instead, as Cho and Chung note, people have IP addresses that are attached to physical locations as well as e-mail addresses that may contain geographic prefixes. They access the internet through ISPs that are registered in a particular state and access platforms that are also registered to physical addresses.

As a result, states utilizing the full (rather than limited) cyber sovereignty perspective claim full legal jurisdiction over their citizens and their activities as well as the activities of ISPs and related providers that act within their geographical space. In both Russia and China, this claim justifies establishing **digital identification systems** that would allow the state to track all of a citizen's online activity and to aggregate all of the data streams produced by an individual.[17] Such data streams can then be used in making decisions about whether an individual should be permitted to borrow money for a purchase like a house or to have access to state or private-sector jobs that might require them to have a large amount of responsibility or access to classified materials. That is, they can predict whether someone would be a credit risk or a security risk.

Furthermore, the full cyber sovereignty position justifies states' claims to own their citizens' data and communications. These claims may include the right to store data within the geographic confines of their state or to access the data of others stored within their country. In this view, states can also exercise control over how their citizens behave in cyberspace. This may mean removing the option of anonymous browsing or participating in the internet in favor of a system where citizens may be required to register as internet users using only their real names.

The Future of Cyber Sovereignty

Proponents of the cyber sovereignty view, then, believe that states will eventually evolve an understanding that has been described as Cyber Westphalia, based upon the 1648 Treaty of Westphalia, signed in Europe at the end of the Thirty Years War. The Treaty of Westphalia is seen as a hallmark because it represented the first time that states were able to create a new political order from the top down on the basis of mutual recognition by states of each other's sovereign control over their territories. Similarly, Demchak and Dombrowski argue that an interstate system is evolving in cyberspace. In this Cyber Westphalia system, they believe that states will be recognized as the predominant actors in the environment and that states will recognize each other's autonomy or ability to build, administer, and control their cyberspace. Within this environment, then, states will be able to identify when another country or actor has carried out a territorial incursion into their cyberspace, and they will be able to respond accordingly, just as they would if a foreign army invaded their real territory.[18] As these analysts write, "The frontier era of the global cyberspace 'substrate' that increasingly underpins the world's critical socio-economic systems is thus nearly over. A further transition towards what will eventually be the cybered interstate system is now taking place."[19]

Here, analysts point to the decision by the United Nations in 2001 to create the Group of Governmental Experts (GGE) for cybersecurity as the beginning of the cyber Westphalia model. They argue that the equating of cyberspace with cybersecurity made it inevitable that states would take a leading role in securing and building cyberspace. They also point to a 2013 activity report by the GGE working under the United Nations Office for Disarmament Affairs (UNODA), which stated that states should have jurisdiction over the information communications technologies infrastructure within their territories.[20] The publication in 2013 of the *Tallinn Manual on the International Law Applicable to Cyber Warfare* is also seen as a critical development in the growth of cyber Westphalia because Chapter 1, Paragraph 1, of that document specifies that "a state may exercise control over cyberinfrastructure and activities within its sovereign territory."[21]

Realism and Cyber Westphalia

In this view, if international organizations (including international technical organizations like ICANN) play a role at all in global governance of cyberspace, they exist primarily as manifestations and extensions of a particular state's power. Also, in this view, because so many technology-based international organizations either arose in the United States or are funded by the United States, such entities exist primarily as extensions of American state power in the global system rather than as separate actors.

In this realist view, then, cyber sovereignty is a critical component of a state's cyber power and its overall power.[22] In this view, a state needs to control its own "cyberterritory" to be considered a cyber power. A nation that depends on another power—like a stronger state or an international organization—to defend its critical infrastructure from attacks is considered to be a weak cyber power. Moreover, in this view, a state that ceded any amount of sovereign authority to an international organization to create cybersecurity as a collective good would be viewed as displaying weakness. Cyber Westphalia advocates then view cybersecurity as an individual good that states create for themselves rather than a collective good that countries create together in cyberspace.

Cyber Sovereignty: The Isolationist Variant

In the most extreme cyber sovereignty view, then, a state might aim for autarky or a situation in which it is utterly dependent upon its resources and did not depend on any other nation for its existence politically or economically. A fully autarkic state would thus aim to have its internet operate from its own indigenously supplied search engines, news sources, and social media platforms. The state could therefore effectively have complete control over the resources that its citizens could access and how news and other information would be presented to them and used by them. In many instances, this may mean that a state does not aim to eventually have a 100 percent internet penetration rate among its citizens where all have internet access; instead, it may confine internet access to a smaller or self-selected group of individuals.

An autarkic model, thus, rejects the claim that there are universal values that either reside in the internet itself (such as a desire for openness and transparency) or that all citizens should have a claim to by virtue of their global internet citizenship. Instead, the state claims the right to administer its cyberspace and to shape and create that cyberspace in line with its ideas and values derived from its own culture and not from the internet itself. Today, we can point to North Korea as the most restrictive information environment because its "internet" does not actually connect to the international community's systems. Also, we can see how both Russia and China are moving toward situations in which citizens would utilize their own state's search engines, auction sites, and social media rather than relying on those created by international platforms like Twitter or Facebook.[23]

Cyber sovereignty advocates also reject the claims that there are specific human rights that all citizens throughout the world have by virtue of their humanity, which can be grafted onto the regulatory regimes, norms, and values associated with the internet. That is, a state that claims cyber sovereignty may reject the United Nations' claim that internet access is a human right that needs to be extended to all citizens. It may also deny the claim that allowing citizens access to a free and open, unregulated internet is a state's responsibility. Instead, countries claim their right to engage in censorship, filtering, and monitoring of their citizens because they control and administer the territory of their internet.

In evaluating the growth of cyber sovereignty, then, critics have warned about a growing Balkanization of the internet, suggesting that in the future, we may not have merely one international internet but, rather, a system in which there are multiple different internets: a Russian internet that reflects Russian values and interests, an American internet, and a Chinese internet, for example. The problem with Balkanization, however, is that groups of people no longer come into contact with one another in an international space where all ideas are welcome. Instead, people may encounter an echo chamber where they interact only with others who share similar values. Scholar Cass Sunstein has warned that this increasing tendency for users to wall themselves off into their internets where like-minded individuals surround them is likely to lead to people developing more polarized or extreme views than they might in a place where all opinions and ideas were welcomed and considered.[24]

The Downside of Cyber Sovereignty

However, what are the pros and cons of a cyber sovereignty model of internet governance? In her work, Cavelty notes that there is indeed something compelling about breaking up the internet along national lines. It appears to offer states a large measure of control—in that they can establish their internets, protect their citizens from harmful outside influences (including real threats like cyberterrorism or perceived threats like "spiritual pollution" by Western ideas), and better carry out cybersecurity and protection of critical infrastructure. However, she and others warn that establishing the precedent that states alone are responsible for structuring "their cyberspace" may also mean creating a recipe for autocratic control and abuse of human rights.[25]

And technology scholar Berman argues that states have a unique power in the cyber arena to not merely forbid activities that are not socially sanctioned but rather to create an online environment or **architecture** (through the use of code) in which the ability to exercise choice and engage in anti-state activity, for example, does not exist. He argues that, for example, it is preferable to have a law against speeding that citizens must decide to follow than it is to have a state that produces cars that are incapable of speeding. Granting states unlimited ability to shape their national internet architecture, he argues, is giving them unprecedented regulatory power and robbing citizens of the ability to choose how they behave in cyberspace.[26]

Most worrying to those who are advocates of the multistakeholder model is that digital sovereignty appears to give states the right to engage in almost unlimited surveillance of their citizens' online activities. States would be free to declare certain types of online behaviors illegal, often based on national norms and values. States would be able to wall off their citizens from the whole international internet, allowing them instead access only to those parts that are seen to be in keeping with the state's values and policy priorities. In this model, then, citizens who live in a repressive society would not experience a markedly different environment in cyberspace. Instead, all of the same repressive structures, like press censorship and surveillance, that occur in the real world would merely be reproduced in that nation's cyberspace.

In this state-led model of internet regulation, then, other players, like ISPs or content hosting platforms, are subordinated by the state to state interests with only limited autonomy to act on their own. In some cases, ISPs and online service providers may be state owned directly. In other instances, they have been "responsibilized," or been enlisted as guardians of public morality, national security, and individual privacy.[27] We will return to this question in our discussion of online privacy under the digital sovereignty model.

RUSSIA'S CYBER REALIST VIEW OF CYBERSPACE

In considering the cyber sovereignty view of internet governance, it is useful to consider how Russia's leadership has articulated this view because they are a leading proponent of this view. In the Russian view, as in the American military view, cyberspace is seen as anarchic. It is an arena of conflict. Also, in keeping with the realist position, Russian military planners believe that the most crucial goal in creating a national cyber strategy should be the preservation of the state or the assurance of state survival. This lens, then, assumes that other countries are not potential partners for cooperation but are rather potential enemies whose motives are to challenge Russian survival both in cyberspace and in real space.

In the Russian view, then, the Russian segment of the internet (known as RU-Net for the prefix .ru which accompanies all Russian internet addresses) is considered an extension of existing territory in the Russian information space, and RU-Net is viewed as a **platform** for the Russian state. The Russian cyber sovereignty view then believes that each state can and should administer its own information space—in terms of providing security of its hardware, software, and information quality in addition to content and information flows. In this view, then, the ideal situation may be one in which Russia's internet is mostly inwardly oriented, based on the Russian language and dependent on Russian language platforms (like the Russian equivalent of Facebook, V Kontakte).

Here, the Russian view echoes the older Soviet Communist language about the danger of "capitalist encirclement." At the height of the Soviet empire, the leadership had a somewhat paranoid view, believing that the United States, in particular, wanted to support satellite states and engage in proxy wars around the world to encircle the Soviet Union with states hostile to the communist belief system and way of life. Today, Russia feels threatened by the growth of NATO and the European Union (EU), with the offering of membership or provisional membership to Eastern European nations that were previously part of the Soviet Bloc. An article published in 2018 by Sergei Shoigu, Russia's minister of defense, also suggests that Russia reads the establishment of cyber operations centers in Europe as a sign of "intense military preparations" by Europe against their neighbors to the East, including Russia. In this same article, Shoigu evinces concern about the establishment of CERTs throughout European states that are modeled upon the US CERT and voices suspicion regarding US motives in assisting in establishing a European Center for Excellence in Countering Hybrid Threats opened jointly by the EU and NATO in Helsinki in 2018.[28] In this way, Russia's fears about participation in the internet—which it sees as Western in origin, orientation, and values—is related to its fear of territorial encirclement in the real world. In the Russian mind, having its citizens participate in a free and open internet that includes having unrestrained contact with Western citizens and Western ideas thus represents a sort of virtual capitalist encirclement.

As Ristolainen points out, Russia uses different terms to understand and describe cyberspace. Their view of "information security" is broader than the Western view of cybersecurity, which focuses on defending and protecting internet software and hardware. In contrast, in the Russian view, information security refers to defending and protecting internet software and hardware as well as protecting the information that people are exposed to as well—through keeping it free from falsehoods, extremist ideas, and ideas that may constitute a form of "spiritual pollution." Here, Russia worries as well about the fact that the majority of information available on the internet is in English. Instead, the government wants to make sure that the Russian language is preserved by producing or assisting in the production of high-quality Russian language information for its citizens.

Not all analysts see these issues from the same viewpoint, however. James Lewis argues that the "information revolution" is more of a threat to state survival for authoritarian regimes. He writes:

> Information technologies create an existential threat for authoritarian regimes that they are hard-pressed to manage. Authoritarian regimes, with their brittle relationship with their citizens, have reacted by trying to suppress this political effect by restricting access to information, providing counternarratives for both domestic and foreign consumption, and by creating ubiquitous surveillance regimes in a powerful effort to maintain control.[29]

In this view, then, for authoritarian regimes in particular, there are few benefits to cooperation and few reasons to cooperate in cyberspace.

Russian Suspicion of International Organizations

Moreover, as noted, this digital sovereignty model also rests on suspicion of international bodies such as ICANN, which works internationally to administer and assign domain names. As we saw in Chapter 1, ICANN began as a nonprofit organization incorporated in the state of California in 1998. Initially, funding for this international body was provided by the US Department of Commerce through a contractual arrangement. However, ICANN signed an Affirmation of Commitments in 2009 with the United States, which formally ended this relationship.

Currently, ICANN is "formally independent" and administered through multi-stakeholder governance. ICANN has a board of directors that includes individuals from the technology community as well as supporting organizations including the Address Supporting Organization (ASO); the Country-Code Name Supporting Organization (CCNSO), which includes members of country-specific DNS providers; as well as the Generic Name Support Organization (GNSO), which includes individuals involved with the administration of domains like .com, or .biz. Also, there is a Government Advisory Committee (GAC), which provides a forum for states to weigh in on issues related to technical global internet governance.[30]

However, although ICANN thus provides a forum for state actors' involvement in internet governance, the governments of both Russia and China have objected to participating in this forum. In explaining their objections to participating on a state basis in this forum, China's government has stated that they resent the large role granted to private-sector organizations within ICANN. They have also objected to the fact that the United States still plays the most prominent role in the organization. China has even undertaken attempts to establish its Chinese version of ICANN, which would administer Chinese IP addresses.

In this Russian view, then, a state feels most secure in cyberspace when it exercises autonomy and agency over its cyberterritory, when it can control the information flows that enter and leave its territory and when it can defend its cyber infrastructure against threats both domestically and internationally. Cybersecurity is thus an individual good best pursued by a state acting on its own through a self-help system.

Russia has therefore acted consistently to introduce resolutions to the United Nations in the area of cybersecurity. Beginning in 1998, and annually every year after that until 2011, Russia has launched a resolution titled, "Developments in the Field of Information and Telecommunications in the Context of International Security." This resolution, which has been described as controversial, set forth the idea that there should be an international code of conduct regarding cyberspace that all states should agree to. Specifically, states should agree not to interfere in the sovereign affairs of other nations concerning cyberspace. The resolution (which was backed by many states, many of them deeply repressive) stated that signatories would not "use their resources . . . to undermine the right of . . . independent control of information and communications technologies or to threaten the political, economic, and social security of other countries."[31]

Russia's Alliances for Cybersecurity

At the same time, Russia has worked to form its own regional and international alliances with states who share their suspicion of international governmental bodies and who remain equally committed to a vision of national internets administered in line with national values and priorities. In 2003, Russia acted to create a multinational organization called the Shanghai Cooperation Organization (SCO). The SCO is a bloc of nations, including China, Kazakhstan, Kyrgyzstan, Russia, Tajikistan, and Uzbekistan, who have worked to voice concerns and put forth proposals of non-Western internet users. The SCO has advocated for these states' rights to develop their national internets along national lines and has acted to oppose attempts to create an international vision of the internet's mission and goals.

Here, the term *multilateral governance* (as distinguished from multistakeholder governance) is sometimes invoked to describe this situation where states, taking the lead, reach out to other countries to create specific agreements among themselves regarding procedures for addressing conflicts and disagreements in cyberspace. That is, the cyber sovereignty perspective is not inherently conflictual; instead, it is suspicious of the use of multistakeholder approaches as the overarching framework for structuring cyberspace as well as the claim that states need to be participating on an equal footing with other types of organizations, such as civil society organizations. We can point to the conclusion of an agreement between the United States and China in 2018 in the area of cyber conflict to show that cyber sovereignty approaches have merit and that they can play a useful role in helping create global order, even if only on a limited scale.

Also, states like China and Russia have participated in multistakeholder governance organizations like the World Information Society (which we address later in this chapter). However, within these organizations, they have advocated for a stronger, more hierarchical role for states in particular and specific recognition of the state's interests in the conduct and structuring of cyberspace. Cuihong describes Chinese officials as seeing a complementarity between multilateral and multistakeholder approaches, with both being necessary.[32]

As this short analysis shows, then, Russia remains deeply suspicious of the motives of other nations in cyberspace. Cyber sovereignty is thus seen as the best mechanism for limiting the overall societal effects of internet connectivity, allowing states to benefit economically in global commerce, for example, while choosing not to participate in the growth of democratic institutions. This model also will enable countries to view the internet not as a global phenomenon that will inevitably connect them to others but rather as a tool that states can use and shape as they wish in line with their history and values.

Should America Adopt a Cyber Sovereignty Approach?

However, American analysts have also made a strong case for states adopting a cyber sovereignty viewpoint rather than a more cooperative model. In writing about cyber power, analyst Joe Nye describes how power transition theory can be applied to cyberspace. This theory suggests that conflict is most likely to break out in a situation in which power formations in the international system are changing. Power formations might change because a great power begins to lose its leading role, or they might change due to a rising hegemon, or a state that is increasing in power, thus threatening to destabilize the preexisting balance of power. Here, Nye worries about "power diffusion," noting that that although the United States has clearly been the hegemon in cyberspace for the past thirty years, other players are beginning to catch up to it.[33] Brezhnev et al. write that it is easier and cheaper for a middle power to become a great power in cyberspace than it is in conventional military conflicts. They write, "Cyberspace is an offense-dominated domain with low barriers to entry, one that diffuses power away from traditionally powerful states and towards historically marginalized actors."[34]

Here, analysts differ about what the US response to these rising hegemons (like China) should be. Some recommend that the United States should take strong measures to keep its leading edge, but they also worry that other rising powers might band together against the global cyber hegemon that is the United States. In such a situation, it might make more sense for the United States to cooperate than to attempt to go it alone.

What Is Global Governance?

Although many states appear to be committed to the reproduction of traditional forms of organization in cyberspace, a second model has also emerged in recent years. In her work, Halbert describes the emergence of global governance—characterized by the internationalization of policy making, the diffusion of authority beyond the state, the development of procedural norms on a level beyond that of the state, and the distribution of governing resources among an increasing range of actors.[35] She describes this emergence as a "fundamental shift" in the way that international relations function.

We can trace the term *internet governance* back to 1996 in the United States, when scholars at the Harvard Information Infrastructure Project (which later became the Berkman Center) published two volumes on the subject. In this study, scholars asked if the internet was in fact "governable." That is, they interrogated Barlow's claim that the imposition of state control and the development of institutional bodies to administer the internet were impossible. Here, Barlow argued that cyberspace was too different from regular space and that it was inherently ungovernable due to the existence of networks of actors without a clear hierarchy.

Those who advocate for the creation of supranational (beyond the state) governance structures to administer the internet as an international space argue that Barlow was wrong in describing cyberspace as fundamentally unique. Instead, they say that broad coalitions of actors—to include private and public sector partners—have cooperated to make policies internationally in many highly specialized areas (like public health, nuclear weapons regulation, or cyberspace). For example, pharmaceutical manufacturers may have a seat at the table when a body like the World Health Organization is discussing how best to respond to the threat of a global pandemic or a crisis like AIDS. In each of these situations, many functions that we previously thought of as the exclusive province of states—such as the authoring of treaties or international legislation—are today undertaken by networks of actors working interdependently and sometimes autonomously from the state. Here, Liaropoulos notes that internet governance refers to a situation in which the borders or boundaries between countries and business interests in cyberspace are "fuzzy."[36] However, as we will see in Chapter 7, on the role of the private sector in cyberspace policy making, the notion of public-private partnerships is again not unique to cyberspace.

However, what specifically is governance? We can define governance as a form of deliberate steering aimed at rule making. That is, governance refers to a process by which an order is created rather than merely evolving spontaneously or from the bottom up. Governance is also described as "intentional interventions directed towards solving public policy problems and enhancing the common good."[37] Whereas opponents of global internet governance describe it as a mechanism whereby a supranational organization might impose control over subordinate units, including states, Hofmann et al. focus on governance as a mechanism of coordination. In their view, governance occurs when groups of people come together, often through highly interconnected networks of people or things.

GLOBAL GOVERNANCE IN CYBERSPACE

In this perspective, then, the term *governance* can be applied to describe the work done by a body like ICANN but also to define mechanisms by which ISPs might share information about emerging threats among themselves as well as the ways in which users in the technical community might come together to share and regulate the use of a technology like open source code. Governance also occurs when organizations and content platforms share information and techniques for monitoring user behaviors—including norms regarding when users should be banned for, for example, using hate speech. Finally, Singer and Friedman argue that governance in cyberspace often aims at creating systems for interoperability among different types of systems internationally. Here, they point to the work of groups like the Internet Engineering Task Force (IETF), which is an international body that works to set voluntary standards, as well as the US National Institute of Standards and Technology (NIS), which sets standards for internet architecture. They also describe the work of the Internet Architecture Board (IAB). Both the IETF and IAB are subgroups that grew out of the Internet Society, an international group formed in 1992 that oversees most of the technical standards processes.[38]

Here, Hoffman et al. suggest that governance is a process rather than a product or an institution. They argue that governance often involves not merely recognizing a situation in which all parties agree but instead may include de-conflicting a position in which multiple different entities disagree strongly or sources of authority to which participants might refer in resolving a dispute. Governance thus becomes a way of unraveling and sorting out these contradictions through, for example, establishing a hierarchy of existing rules and procedures that might apply to a situation that arises in the international system. In the global environment of the internet, in particular, we can identify many conditions in which there may be multiple actors claiming legal jurisdiction over an issue whose claims would need to be considered, sorted out, and coordinated.[39]

For example, we can point to the Budapest Convention on Cybercrime, signed in 2001 by members of the Council of Europe.[40] This agreement established mechanisms for capacity building, allowing all members to strengthen their ability to track, react to, and punish incidents of cybercrime online—through sharing resources and information or data between EU members through a central clearing house. Before the establishment of the Budapest Convention, a French policing agency would encounter difficulty in, for example, responding to a situation in which French citizens had been the victims of identity theft by a group operating elsewhere in Europe. Before the Budapest Convention, they would have been required to formally request information and assistance from the second nation's police forces, and the procedure might be bureaucratic and lead to a slow response. The agreement put in place in 2001, however, allows states to respond quickly and efficiently to instances of suspected cybercrime through the creation of a mechanism for data sharing and cooperation.

Also, governance processes may focus on harmonizing regulations, including evolving commonly held definitions of key legal, political, or technical vocabulary. Thus, multistakeholder governance becomes a useful process for resolving issues like what constitutes an act of force in cyberspace and whether or not the Law of Armed Conflict (LOAC) applies in cyberspace. More recently, international bodies like the World Summit on the Information Society (WSIS) have examined questions like this: How do we understand election meddling and information warfare as well as psychological operations? What are the responsibilities of nonstate actors, including platforms like Twitter and Facebook, in supporting values like upholding the integrity of electoral systems? Who should regulate these activities, and how might actors be penalized who violate these accords?

As noted, governance is meant to be a cooperative process in which solutions are not imposed (as happens in a regulatory process) but instead are sought out on the basis of mutual interests. Governance is understood here not as something that emerges or evolves but rather as a process that can be "steered." All of the actors involved act in a bottom-up fashion, feeding ideas up to a central authority that can then act to formalize these agreements. Here, Hofmann et al. suggest that this definition resembles Krasner's definition of a regime, a vehicle for coordination in a specific subject area within international relations—that excludes contracts and policies. The description itself, therefore, fits within a liberal internationalist paradigm, suggesting that states and other actors will cooperate to produce global internet governance as a sort of collective good, which would be shared by all actors to enrich them all.

Moreover, in the governance paradigm, the state is understood to be just one among many actors involved in this cooperative process. It does not have a privileged role, nor does it occupy the top tier of some hierarchy. That is, whereas the traditional model of the international system assumed that states and international organizations were "rule makers" and other actors were "rule takers," this distinction does not hold in multistakeholder governance in the cyber environment. Instead, in considering international questions like how best to defend freedom of information and freedom of the press online or how best to secure free electoral discussions in cyberspace, private actors including social media platforms often appear to be leading the way in making policy.

Multistakeholder Governance in Cyberspace

In applying the term *multistakeholder governance*, then, we refer specifically to the fact that administering and de-conflicting international issues in cyberspace today often involves a process that includes the participation of a broad coalition of actors—from states to civil society organizations, to education organizations, to business to technical specialists.[41] As Take suggests, there are three possible international forms of governance that might emerge in cyberspace: those enacted by intergovernmental institutions; transnational forms of governance (which include networks among international, national, and non-state actors); and private forms of governance (networks consisting only of nonstate actors). [42] As he notes, in each case, the organization created is a cross-border arrangement that doesn't have formal authority or central enforcement power. Thus, as he notes, such mechanisms depend on the voluntary cooperation of participants.

But what causes participants to want to comply with the organization and to regard it as legitimate? That is, what are the conditions that the organization must meet for all players to buy into its existence and leading role?

Multistakeholder governance advocates often point to 2003 as the starting point for this way of governing the internet. They look to the first United Nations-backed World Summit on the Information Society (WSIS), which functions as a coordinating organization allowing states and other actors to work together to finance and carry out regional projects such as the creation of internet infrastructure. This group also works to increase access to the internet for citizens internationally, focusing mainly on those in developing countries. At this meeting, the WSIS formulated the Geneva Declaration of Principles. This document states that

> international management of the Internet should be multilateral, transparent and democratic, with the full involvement of governments, the private sector, and civil society and international organizations. It should ensure an equitable distribution of resources, facilitate access for all and ensure a stable and secure functioning of the internet, taking into account multilingualism.[43]

WSIS has been praised for its incorporation of experts from telecommunication and information technology sectors as well as those from civil society and epistemic communities.[44]

Tensions regarding internet governance came to a head in 2012 at the so-called Dubai Summit of the World Summit on the Information Society. At this meeting, many states signed an agreement that would give many internet governance functions over to the supervision of the United Nations. The United States, however, opposed this measure and passed a congressional statement voicing its opposition to either national sovereignty or international organization vision of internet governance.[45]

Objections to Multistakeholder Governance

In his work, Take notes that not all multistakeholder governance arrangements are regarded as legitimate, nor are the rules, norms, and values that these organizations identify as being common to all necessarily accepted by all members. He identifies several threats to the legitimacy of multistakeholder arrangements. In some instances, both participants and outside observers may conclude that the party that is making rules and establishing understandings is not representative of everyone who should be included in these deliberations. They might also raise questions of equity in, for example, asking if all of the stakeholders have been able to participate freely and equally—without undue boundaries to their participation erected (such as high dues or fees for participation). Critics of multistakeholder governance in cyberspace have raised concerns about the exclusion of representatives from developing nations that sometimes cannot afford to send a representative to conferences, such as the summits of the World Information Society. Other critics have criticized US-based groups like Google for playing an outsized role in deliberations at the expense of other smaller civil society groups and members.

However, the two most significant objections to global internet governance—the allegation that international organizations often serve the needs of wealthy actors better than they serve the needs of the disenfranchised and the assertion that at worst such organizations are "colonialist" in that they provide mere window dressing for a process in which wealthy nations impose their values and norms upon less powerful, poor nations—are not actually arguments unique to the cyberspace environment. Rather, both of these arguments can be traced back to earlier discussions within the United Nations about how issues of international development and income equities affect and are affected by global policy making overall.[46] Allegations that developing nations mostly seek new global markets to buy Western information communications technologies, rather than genuinely seeking to empower those in the Global South, have been raised before concerning the extension of telephones and even telegraph service to the developing world. Moreover, the debate about whether those in developing nations need to share the international commitment to paying for information, rather than engaging in information theft or intellectual property theft, is again an older debate that has simply reemerged in the online environment.[47]

Other critics have raised concerns related to transparency. That is, stakeholders may feel that they are merely being informed of all decisions made on behalf of the group but that a small inner group is not acting to make decisions without telling the group as a whole. Other concerns relate to accountability. Does the body possess clear rules and procedures regarding how group requirements will be applied and how those who fail to comply should be treated? Finally, critics have raised concerns about expertise. Here, they have voiced concerns that state representatives, in particular, may not possess the necessary knowledge to understand and administer rule making in this subject area or sector.

Those who support structuring the internet through a process of multilateral stakeholder governance tend to be reasonably optimistic about the prospects that all actors will be able to identify shared interests (including the avoidance of shared risks) and move therefore to cooperate to achieve these interests. That is, this view assumes that there are shared principles, norms, rules, and decision-making procedures that exist and all actors can discover them through some coordinated process. Here we can consider the definition of internet governance put forth in 2005 by the Internet Governance Forum, a working group associated with the World Summit on the Information Society. This group wrote that "internet governance is the development and application by Governments, the private sector, and civil society, in their respective roles, of shared principles, norms, rules, decision-making procedures and programmes that shape the evolution and use of the internet."[48]

In contrast, as we saw, advocates of cyber sovereignty tend to be much more pessimistic about the threats they see as emerging within the cyberspace environment, which they feel states are unlikely to avoid through cooperation. Critics of the multistakeholder governance model, therefore, understand this process as doomed to failure because it appears to be messy and chaotic as there are no clear rules as to who might lead this process or how.

Case Study: Online Privacy, Anonymity, and Global Governance

One way to think about the question of internet governance and universal norms is to consider the related issues of privacy and anonymity online. From the earliest dates of online activity, one of the draws of the medium for many individuals was the ability to participate in events like web browsing in an environment where one was anonymous. Indeed, early internet enthusiasts described anonymity as an unchangeable characteristic of the technology that they saw as built in by its designers. However, in recent years, many states have taken active steps to roll back this characteristic of anonymity, instead undertaking new legislative initiatives in the areas of surveillance and online privacy.

In some instances, states have implemented laws and procedures to limit their citizens' ability to act anonymously. For example, in South Korea, in 2007, the government decided to require that users verify their identities online through submitting a resident registration number. (This would be similar to requiring US users to enter a social security number to access or create content online.) This registration requirement, however, made it difficult for non-Koreans (such as those of Korean descent who lived abroad) to access a great deal of material. In 2011, South Korea reversed this decision and no longer requires that users register with their real names.

In other instances, states have worked with ISPs, co-opting these organizations by asking them to perform activities that support state surveillance. For example, in China, bloggers and microbloggers must register their real names and personal information with their ISPs. Also, in the United States, the US Department of Homeland Security has required technology companies like Apple to provide so-called back doors to their technology, so that, for example, the government could bypass a suspected terrorist's password security to access his devices to gather evidence.

States can also co-opt platforms like Twitter and Facebook, requiring that they furnish information about citizens' online activities as well as offering state security organizations access to materials collected. For example, the US National Security Agency has utilized social network analysis to map terrorist networks. By analyzing terrorist use of tools like social media, counterterrorism analysts have been able to map linkages between key players in terrorist networks and establish who is the leader of a terrorist organization and how parts of the organization work together and with other organizations.[49]

Indeed, in the aftermath of terrorist events throughout the 2000s, including the September 11, 2001, attack in the United States and the July 7, 2005, London bombings in the United Kingdom, states have begun to cooperate internationally, creating both bilateral and multilateral regulations and mechanisms to govern how states should collect and share users' social media and online data for counterterrorism and anti-crime policing purposes. For example, the 2004 EU Data Retention Directive (DRD) attempted to harmonize data retention regulations among EU member states in addition to making data available for sharing among countries.

However, from the beginning, different groups with different interests have clashed in considering how best to protect user privacy and civil rights while simultaneously creating safe cyberspace. Whereas those in the field of international cybersecurity worried about the growth of dangerous threats online, other analysts were concerned about what they saw as the massive and unbridled growth of global surveillance. These analysts began to ask what a global privacy regime that established norms and procedures for preserving citizen rights online might look like. (This approach, then, assumes that citizen privacy is a value or norm that all internet users internationally should value and seek to safeguard. It is viewed as a universal norm rather than a subject about which states can and should have different views.)

Cyber Sovereignty and the Problem of Jurisdiction

Thinking back to the digital sovereignty debate, the question that arises in considering whether citizens have a right to privacy and anonymity online is whether a state should actually have the ability to alter the terrain or working of the internet in this way to lessen citizen privacy or increase government surveillance capacities, even within its own online "territory." In the instances described here—China requiring an ISP to furnish data regarding usernames and activities and the United States requiring Apple to provide a back door into their devices—the state has claimed to have legal jurisdiction over technological actions occurring within its physical space and within its online territory as well as over those corporations and individuals acting within that space. As a result, Western companies doing business in China have felt strong pressures from the Chinese government to comply with Chinese rules regarding user registration—and Google has withdrawn from China due to disputes regarding whether China's government should, for example, be allowed to access the web search results of its citizens. In response to claims that the state has harmed citizen rights through surveillance practices, countries will often claim that the risks posed to national security from online organizing in cyberspace of anti-state activities (from terrorism to democracy activism) are severe enough and that they are justified in taking such steps in seeking to control cyberspace.

However, not all players in the internet governance debate agree with state claims in this regard. Particularly in the aftermath of the 2013 revelations by whistle-blower Edward Snowden regarding the extent of US National Security Agency surveillance of citizen activities in cyberspace, European states as well as international organizations like the United Nations have attempted to speak back to what they see as state or government overreach in cyberspace and the rampant growth of state-sanctioned surveillance.

Here, we can identify two related issues in the field of internet governance. First, we can point to the legal question of jurisdiction. Here, digital sovereignty advocates would state that a nation has the right to do what it likes within its cyberspace. However, as Schmitz points out, in a globalized world, there can be many overlapping claims and many different lenses through which we can view the problem of jurisdiction. Here, she asks us to consider the matter of whether Facebook, an American corporation, has the authority to require that users everywhere use their real names rather than a pseudonym when participating in the online platform. Facebook, the corporation, is a US multinational corporation headquartered in the United States. However, Facebook also has a European branch that was established in 2008 in Dublin, Ireland. In addition, Facebook has a German subsidiary, Facebook Germany GmbH, which sells advertising and other services to German companies trying to reach German Facebook users. However, all users sign a set of agreements when they establish a Facebook account that state that they understand that all disputes are to be resolved in California, United States, under Californian laws.

Schmitz writes that Facebook's "real name policy" might be legal in the United States but that it is also in conflict with EU laws. She notes that the German Telemedia Act "requires tele media providers to allow for anonymous or pseudonymous use of services insofar as this is reasonable and technically feasible."[50] Here, Schmitz argues that because Facebook's activities regarding privacy are covered under the European General Data Protection Directive, there is, therefore, a case to be made that European law should have precedence in resolving the dispute related to anonymity.

Ethical Issues Related to Cyber Sovereignty

In addition to the legal jurisdiction issues raised when considering problems of online privacy, anonymity, and surveillance, we can also point to ethical issues that arise—specifically in the field of human rights. Here, the American organization

Freedom House has suggested that states that take away their citizens' rights to browse and participate anonymously online are depriving them of their universal human rights, including the right to freedom of speech.[51] Freedom House claims that citizens' rights to online privacy are not rights that their government can choose to confer or not confer upon them because they are universal human rights that all citizens everywhere have by virtue of their humanity. Therefore, they argue, states cannot deprive their citizens of such rights, even if they are sovereign states with legal authority over what happens in their territory.

CAN INTERNATIONAL NORMS REGARDING HUMAN RIGHTS BE GRAFTED ONTO CYBERSPACE?

Can existing treaties regarding human rights be extended to apply also to cyberspace rights? Some analysts believe that two international treaties—the 1966 United Nations International Covenant on Civil and Political Rights (ICCPR) and the 1998 European Convention on Human Rights (ECHR)—might be extended to incorporate human rights as they exist in cyberspace. Here, we can consider Article 17 of the ICCPR, which states, "No one shall be subjected to arbitrary or unlawful interference with his privacy, family, home or correspondence nor to unlawful attacks on his honor and reputation," as well as Article 8 of the ECHR, which states, "Everyone has the right to respect for his private and family life, his home and his correspondence," and that "there shall be no interference by a public authority with this exercise of this right except such as is . . . necessary in a democratic society in the interests of national security."[52]

Reflecting these understandings, in October 2013 Brazil and Germany submitted a draft resolution titled "On the Right to Privacy in the Digital Age" to the third committee of the UN General Assembly. The resolution was adopted, including the line that "the same rights that people have offline must also be protected online, including the right to privacy." Many analysts point to this resolution as the beginning of a conversation within the international community about whether international human rights norms apply to state behaviors in the areas of surveillance, interception, and data collection.

Here, privacy advocates suggest that states must come to an understanding globally about how to balance the interests of privacy and security and whether too much surveillance can ultimately pose a threat to democracy internationally.

CONCLUSION

As we conclude this chapter, one might pessimistically find that it will be impossible to resolve international issues related to the conduct of cyberspace. The two positions described here—the global governance perspective and the cyber sovereignty perspective—do indeed rest on different assumptions about the likelihood and desirability of cooperation. They disagree regarding who should have the authority to make decisions in cyberspace (the state or some other entity or coalition of entities). They differ as well as to what cyberspace should look like in the future.

Here, again, however, it is useful to return to our starting point—and to consider that the mechanisms that exist to govern and prevent conflict in the real world did not arise overnight but instead were created in fits and starts over several hundred years. Therefore, as we consider this issue, it may be worthwhile to look forward and to ask what cyber governance might look like ten, fifty, or even a hundred years in the future.

In the next chapter, we consider explicitly the role of the private sector in establishing and controlling the internet environment as well as the challenges and opportunities that arise as the result of the leading role which such actors play.

QUESTIONS FOR DISCUSSION

1. In his work, Klimburg describes cyberspace as a four-layered pyramid with the pyramid standing on its head. He describes the first layer as "the bones of cyberspace"—the bones are the hardware of the physical layer, such as undersea cables. The second layer, which he describes as "the neurons and nervous system of cyberspace," is "the coded behavior of the domain: the various computer protocols and software programs." The second layer, which he compares to human muscle systems, is data—business documents, scientific inquiries, and all of the information that the internet houses. Finally, the largest layer is the social layer, which he describes as "the actual internet of people, the total sum of human actions and aspirations in cyberspace."
   a. As you think about these four layers—hardware, software, data, and social media—which layers do you think should be regulated by a particular state as a matter of sovereignty, and which layers would need to be regulated internationally through either multilateralism or a multistakeholder approach?
   b. Also, how optimistic or pessimistic are you about the ability to define and create norms regarding state behavior in relation to each of these layers of the internet?

2. What constitutes a violation of sovereignty in cyberspace? What are the controversies regarding these principles?

3. Read over the Geneva Declaration, available at this address: http://www.itu.int/net/wsis/docs/geneva/official/dop.html.

a. What values do you see reflected in this document?
b. What assumptions did the writers make about the future evolution of the internet, about its origins, and about the values that the internet represents?
c. Imagine that you are a policy maker from Russia or China. How might you read this document? What parts would you agree or disagree with? How specifically might you respond to the writers of this document in arguing for cyber sovereignty?

KEY TERMS

Architecture   147
Digital identification system   144
Digital sovereignty   142

Internet kill switch   141
Open information viewpoint   140
Platform   148

FOR FURTHER READING

Cuihong, C. "China and Global Cyber Governance: Main Principles and Debates." *Asian Perspective* 42 (2018): 649.

Demchak, C., and Dombrowski, P. "Cyber Westphalia: Asserting State Prerogatives in Cyberspace." *Georgetown Journal of International Affairs* (2013): 29–38.

Zajko, M. "Telecommunications Regulation: Internet Governance, Surveillance and New Roles for Intermediaries." *Canadian Journal of Communications* 41, no. 1 (2016): 75–93.

7

CYBERCRIME

Learning Objectives

At the end of this chapter, students will be able to do the following:

1. Describe major types of cybercrimes, distinguishing between high and low policing and cybercrime versus cyber-facilitated crime.

2. Describe the ways in which globalization and the growth of technology can both make crime more likely as well as facilitate new types of policing.

3. Describe attempts to combat cybercrime, including legislation, on the state and international levels.

4. Formulate a position on the ethical, social, and legal issues related to criminal data sharing among states.

5. Formulate a position on the ethical, social, and legal issues related to preemptive policing and surveillance.

In 2018, criminologists began posing an interesting hypothesis. They noted that since the 1990s, there had been an overall drop worldwide in certain types of crimes, including violent crime. At the same time, however, criminology researchers saw an increase in new types of cybercrimes, including cyberstalking, cyberbullying, cybertheft, and types of online scams. Could the increase in cybercrime, they ask, be responsible for the drop in some types of real-world conventional crimes? Did having the ability to carry out crimes online make people less likely to carry out crimes in the real, terrestrial world? And if so, how were the two types of crimes related?[1]

The analysts, Farrell and Birks, suggested that it might be preferable if criminals turned to cybercrime because online criminal encounters have less potential to be violent than real-world encounters do. Wouldn't most people prefer to be mugged or held up online rather than being beaten and left for dead in real life? In the end, however, the authors found little support for the hypothesis that criminals were engaging in "displacement," that is, choosing to engage in cybercrimes instead of real-world crimes. Instead, they suggested that certain crimes became more likely due to people's increased online presence but that there appeared to be little displacement occurring in which real-world criminals turned to cybercrime instead.

This debate is interesting, however, because it causes us to once again ask questions about the uniqueness debate. What is a computer crime, and how do such crimes differ from more traditional types of crimes? What's new about cybercrime, and is criminal behavior in cyberspace related to traditional criminal activity, or does it represent a brand-new arena of behavior that needs to be governed by its own rules and its own unique institutions? How can states respond to the threat of cybercrime both individually and within the international system?

Today, there is no question that cybercrime is big business. A company targeted in a ransomware attack typically loses about $5 million in revenue, and 25 percent of companies internationally now have their own computer security offices. More than half of all companies have had their systems targeted at some point, and nearly 90 percent of European companies have spent greater than $1 million to bring their companies into compliance with the European General Data Protection Regulation.[2]

Although these statistics may seem alarming, and it can seem that one of the major developments that have emerged from the growth of the internet is growth in crime, the news is not all dire. Indeed, new developments in the fields of crime prevention have also taken place, with the ability to collect data about criminal behavior and to make predictions about where crime is likely being credited for drops in certain types of traditional crimes, like breaking and entering.

Thus, we have a somewhat paradoxical situation—the internet's growth has apparently made the world both more dangerous and safer. New types of crimes have been created, facilitated by the internet's growth. At the same time, new types of crime management strategies have been created.

DOES THE INTERNET ENCOURAGE CRIME?

Earlier in this textbook, we introduced the realist paradigm in international relations. Realists believe that the internet is necessarily an environment that is dangerous and where conflict is likely. Here, they cite the speed at which interactions can occur in cyberspace, the environment's global nature, and the ways that actions carried out in cyberspace can be deceptive, threatening, and misinterpreted. But is the internet an environment that encourages crime?

At first glance, the answer appears to be yes. The internet's global nature means that diverse people and groups now frequently come together to carry out economic, political, and social actions in an environment where they may not know each other personally and where they may have little inherent reason either to trust one another or to behave in a trustworthy manner. Today, however, more than half of all internet users have made a purchase online, and half of all online purchases are made from overseas retailers.[3] As a result, we have seen a sharp increase in criminal activities like fraud, including relationship fraud, bank fraud, and identity theft. That is, the internet environment may create more opportunities for a violation of trust. And trust violations may be more likely because so many transactions or activities are one-off events rather than a series of events in which participants develop a relationship with each other over time (as you might develop a relationship with a local merchant in your community).

And, as we have seen, the internet's anonymous nature, along with its transnational nature, means that law enforcement organizations often struggle to identify the perpetrators of crimes that occur in cyberspace. The attribution problem therefore may make crime more likely in cyberspace. Today, sites exist on the dark web where citizens can purchase illegal drugs, engage in human trafficking, and sell and resell computer weapons like viruses online. Although drug trafficking has always existed, new technological developments have created increases in the scale and scope for these crimes, with more people participating due to the ease with which one can do so.

Furthermore, the transnational nature of these crimes has created problems of jurisdiction and has challenged traditional national crime-fighting organizations because international cooperation is needed to fight crimes that may span multiple countries.[4] Here we can consider the May 2017 WannaCry ransomware attack, which affected more than 300,000 computers in more than 150 countries in less than 24 hours. This attack affected numerous players internationally, including Russia's health ministry and its state-run railways, Chinese students' master's and doctoral theses, the French carmaker Renault, Brazil's social security administration system, and the international corporation FedEx.[5]

As a result of crime's globalization, it may be harder for victims to provide useful evidence to law enforcement to enable a good investigation of events. In addition, the cross-border nature of crimes has created issues related to territorial jurisdiction and the harmonization of multiple sets of conflicting national laws in prosecuting a crime. Indeed, perpetrators today may intentionally target victims where law enforcement mechanisms are not as strong or well developed.

In addition, states are only a set of actors on the internet today. Crimes may also be carried out using private infrastructure (ISPs, etc.), necessitating private cooperation with public law enforcement.[6]

And due to the speed at which technology changes, governments, including law enforcement, have scrambled to keep up with technological developments, and development of legal mechanisms has lagged behind the technology itself. Here, law enforcement personnel may be more concerned with devoting manpower and resources to act on what they perceive as "real crimes" occurring in their actual territorial jurisdictions. They may therefore see cybercrimes as nebulous and somehow less real. In addition, they may encounter jurisdictional and legal constraints on their ability to join the investigation of such crimes due to their lack of technological expertise and the lack of existing binding regulations.

Online Deviance and Antisocial Behavior

In addition, individuals have always engaged in criminal and deviant behavior. Even prior to the internet's advent, individuals committed sex crimes, including engaging in prostitution or viewing pornography. People stalked one another or engaged in voyeurism. Today, however, all of these crimes can be carried out over a wider geographic range and against a greater variety of individuals through reliance upon the internet. In addition, individuals have always engaged in reputational crimes, including engaging in slander and libel, and individuals have also engaged in threatening behaviors, including threatening to assassinate public figures or bullying classmates and neighbors. Individuals have engaged in types of harassment and hate speech against one another and against protected groups in society as well.

Thus, some analysts believe that the internet presents a venue (or toxic environment) that encourages deviant and antisocial behaviors. Because anyone can post to the internet, the usual gatekeepers (like newspaper editors) do not exist, and harmful ideas (like racism, sexism, and homophobia) can find their way into public discourse online in ways that they may not in traditional venues like a conference or a journal. But do people actually engage in crimes on the internet that they might never engage in in real life? Wolff suggests that the internet has emboldened individuals—the relative speed at which one can carry out activities and the anonymity that allows people to hide their activities may make some people more likely to engage in practices like trolling or hate speech. And there appear to be few costs associated with engaging in so-called extreme speech, including hate speech (defined as "speech that expresses hatred toward any individual or group based on a certain biological or cultural attribute or expression").[7] Johnson and others further believe that the sharp increase in online extreme speech, including public support for ideas like genocide, anti-Semitism, and Holocaust denial, is having real-world repercussions, leading to a society that is increasingly characterized by intolerance and polarization.

At the same time, specific technological facets of the internet itself—such as the ability to clone or make multiple copies of materials like ledgers, novels, or songs as well as the ability to quickly share these materials—are said to facilitate the carrying out of crimes such as intellectual property theft. Today, the internet's existence makes it easier for criminals to engage in forgery, counterfeiting, and intellectual property theft including piracy and copyright breaches. The existence of peer-to-peer networking technologies means that users can more easily share stolen content, including video and audio files, through linking directly to one another without going through a node or central point. The internet can thus serve as a venue for carrying out "traditional" crimes in faster, more efficient ways as well as a venue for the creation of new and novel types of criminal behavior. Here, we can consider a new type of bank robbery that occurred in 2003, when a criminal cloned the pages of a bank in Hong Kong (The Hong Kong and Shanghai Banking Corporation). As a result, users logged into the fake site and provided details that were later used for identity theft. We can also consider the creation of altogether new types of crimes. Here, Broadhurst describes how in 2003, a teenager in Hong Kong was able to create a credible-looking web page that purported to convey information about an outbreak of severe acute respiratory syndrome (SARS). (This virus, which has the potential to cause severe respiratory distress and even death, is airborne and therefore highly contagious.)[8] When he posted information stating that the port of Hong Kong was to be closed, he provoked a run on food stuff in Hong Kong as residents rushed to stock up. The potential for creating panic was quickly apparent.[9]

Using realist language, then, we might describe the internet as a force multiplier in the field of crime because the internet can lower the costs and perceived risks of committing a crime. The internet also lowers the barriers to entry for someone embarking upon a criminal pursuit because anyone anywhere can set up a false website or online presence to lure victims of financial crimes for a relatively small price.

New Types of Criminals

The internet environment has also created new types of criminals. Among those who engage in crime in the cyberspace environment, we can identify four different groups of individuals. Hackers present a new threat. These technologically savvy individuals can range from young amateur students to more sophisticated professionals. Hackers may engage largely in harmless behaviors aimed at demonstrating their technological savvy (so-called white hat hackers) by penetrating systems like the Pentagon or Wall Street, or they may engage in dangerous breaches of critical infrastructure. **Hacktivists**, in contrast, are individuals who hack for social or political reasons (i.e., hacking into a database maintained by an animal testing firm on behalf of an animal rights group) or releasing data by a group like WikiLeaks to protest government surveillance. In recent years, we have seen the increased growth of so-called cyber vigilantism, a situation in which nonstate actors have sought to respond to issues of what they view as criminal behavior or injustice through acting unilaterally online. One of the most well-known cyber vigilante groups is Anonymous, a collective of anonymous computer hackers who have taken steps to take down Twitter accounts and websites believed to have been created by ISIS and its supporters. The group has also carried out cyberattacks against financial firms when credit card companies like Mastercard and Visa agreed to stop accepting transactions for donations to the WikiLeaks website.[10]

Traditional organized crime families and groups have also moved into cyberspace. Such groups have the advantage that they may already be skilled in operating transnationally and may already be engaged in activities like intellectual property theft with conventional materials. And just as they have cooperated with terrorists in real-world crimes, organized criminal groups may also work on behalf of states or with cyberterrorists. Finally, states have been implicated in the carrying out of cybercrimes—from state-sponsored hacks carried out by Israel and China to the recent charges of interference in electoral politics.[11]

Combating cybercrime is thus both a political and a technological issue. Technological fixes include the development of mechanisms like encryption for ensuring the security of financial transactions and the creation of services like those that eBay and other vendors offer for dispute resolution. Currently, many cybercrime analysts believe that the development of distributed ledger technology will play a vital role in building trustworthy and safe relationships in cyberspace.

THE STATE'S ROLE IN COMBATING CYBERCRIME

States today face unique challenges in combating cybercrime, including problems related to jurisdiction in addressing crimes that take place across state borders; the need to work closely with nonstate actors including corporations in combating crimes that are often of a highly technological nature; and the challenges that states may face in simply defining agreements internationally about what actually constitutes a crime in cyberspace.

The Problem of Jurisdiction

The first challenge that states face relates to the problem of jurisdiction. Jurisdiction refers to "the limits of legal competence of a state . . . to make, apply, and enforce rules of conduct upon persons."[12] In addition, states can encounter legal difficulties in attempting to prosecute cybercriminals because such activities often create situations involving several different state actors. In such situations, it may be difficult to determine which nation's laws should prevail when a legal conflict exists. In the 2014 case of the *United States v. Microsoft*, the US Department of Justice asked Microsoft to provide evidence that they needed to prosecute cybercrime. However, although Microsoft was an American corporation, the evidence that the United States sought was actually being stored on a server in Ireland. The question was thus whether the United States could compel Microsoft to provide the information using a US warrant or whether furnishing this information would in fact constitute a violation of Ireland's state sovereignty. Here, Currie writes:

> States tend to be quite chauvinistic about their domestic criminal laws and thus guard their sovereignty closely. . . . The investigation of any transnational criminal matter is meant to be shaped by sensitivity to the prohibition on extraterritorial enforcement jurisdiction. After all, enforcement activity on a state's territory that is not sanctioned or even known undermines the entire rule of law in that state and in particular any human rights protections.[13]

In other words, although it might seem rational for the United States to compel Microsoft to furnish information that is stored in Ireland, dangers might arise if an authoritarian nation was compelling Microsoft or another company to furnish information being stored in the United States or about US citizens. Currently, most states strongly oppose cross-border electronic data gathering when actors are being compelled by force to furnish this data and when there is not cooperation between the two states regarding the sharing of information.

However, here we can ask again whether the internet is not somehow permanently changing the international system, including how we understand sovereignty and territorial jurisdiction. Indeed, we are seeing a sharp growth in the ways in which states are creating mechanisms for international information sharing as part of cooperative measures to combat cybercrime. Here, we can point to the establishment of new treaties supporting these practices—including Article 32 of the Budapest Convention on Cybercrime, the Arab Convention on Combatting Information Technology Offenses, and the Common Market for Eastern and Southern Africa Cybersecurity Draft Model Bill. Altogether, these new legal arrangements add up to a significant amount of cross-border data gathering taking place, with that amount only likely to increase.

In the United States, the Federal Rule of Criminal Procedure 41 has also been amended to allow the US Department of Justice and the Federal Bureau of Investigation to issue search warrants permitting the remote accessing of data across state and national borders. Companies like Microsoft have, however, objected to these amendments. Here, the legal question is whether by accessing data across borders the state (here, the United States) is actually engaging in "extraterritorial actions" that could be construed as a violation of international laws regarding state sovereignty. Colangelo argues that "by circumventing the United States-Ireland MLAT, the procedure amounts to a breach of the treaty."[14]

However, in the case of the *United States v. Microsoft*, the court of appeals found that the United States had indeed exceeded its jurisdiction in compelling Microsoft to turn over data being stored in Ireland. However, Currie notes that since 2014, more states have attempted to behave in such a unilateral fashion, compelling corporations to turn over data stored elsewhere. In most instances, they have justified such actions on the basis of national security, and there has been significant domestic support for states doing all that they can to keep their citizens safe.

Public-Private Partnerships for Crime Fighting

In addition, the problem of sovereignty and the limits that states encounter in prosecuting international cybercrimes is that states are sometimes unprepared to respond quickly and effectively to situations in which fast-moving cybercrimes can occur because these crimes are of a highly technical nature. As a result, states today may find themselves compelled to work closely with nonstate actors, including corporations, in both preempting and responding to cybercrimes. In some instances, it may even seem as though corporations are playing the leading role in crime prevention, with states coming in a distant second. Here, we can consider the testimony furnished to the US Senate Committee on the Judiciary in 2014 by leading cyber organizations, including Symantec and Microsoft. In that testimony, a Symantec representative described how his company cooperated with the US Federal Bureau of Investigation, the UK's National Crime Agency, and international law enforcement agencies to carry out a major operation against the financial fraud botnet Game over Zeus and the ransomware network Cryptolocker.[15]

Today, public-private partnerships include the Online Trust Alliance (OTA) and the Industry Botnet Group (IBG). In addition, groups like the National Cyber-Forensics and Training Alliance (NCFTA), with more than 80 businesses, provides cyber threat intelligence to national and international CERTs.

In that same congressional hearing, Microsoft described its **cyber threat intelligence program** (C-TIP), which makes information about botnets available to both ISPs and US-government-sponsored CERTs. Microsoft is also working with states internationally, including making an agreement with Spain's Computer Emergency Response Team INTECO. Today, Microsoft maintains a digital crimes unit (DCU) with more than 100 technical and legal experts who work to fight cybercrime and improve cybersecurity.

We can view public-private cooperation in one of two ways—as a positive sign that the public and private sector are working together to combat cybercrime or a negative sign of the waning of state influence. Here, cyber pessimists are concerned about the downgrading of the state role in crime prevention, worrying that states may be at the mercy of international corporations when it comes to fighting cybercrime. Here the danger is that states and corporations may not always share the same interests when it comes to deciding how, when, and under what circumstances to react to instances of cybercrime, both nationally and internationally.

CRIME AS A SOCIAL CONSTRUCT

Finally, international crime prevention is complicated because states may not all agree about which acts in cyberspace are criminal and illegal or even morally wrong. For example, should maligning a public official on the internet be considered a criminal act that should result in the imposition of substantial penalties, or should it instead be considered merely an important part of freedom of speech?

Here, critical theorists argue that some types of crimes are a cultural construct. (For example, in Afghanistan a woman might encounter criminal penalties for going without a head covering or wearing makeup, but such activities would not be considered a crime elsewhere.) Similarly, attempting to evade or go around a national internet filtering system (like China's Great Firewall) would be considered a criminal activity within China, but in point of fact, representatives of other nations—including the US Department of State—are actively encouraging and even aiding citizens to evade the nation's internet filtering system. (Here, China would consider US activities to be criminal acts—indeed international crimes. The United States, however, would see such activities as merely part of their quest for free speech and internet openness.)

And today, states differ regarding intellectual property theft crimes in cyberspace. As we noted in Chapter 2, early internet designers did not believe that anything that existed in cyberspace should be viewed as private property. These designers advocated for the removal of barriers like paywalls in cyberspace and encouraged all internet users to instead share resources freely among themselves without charge. Even today, some hackers believe that by sharing materials and information (including classified information) in cyberspace, they are fulfilling the values that they associated with the internet, even if doing so violates specific laws in specific nations.

In contrast, the leading international body for the preservation of intellectual property, the World Intellectual Property Organization (WIPO), defines intellectual property as "creations of the mind, such as inventions, literary and artistic works, designs and symbols, names and images used in commerce."[16] WIPO has helped nations write laws to protect the creator's copyrights regarding the compensation they receive for their work as well as how their works are used. However, today, some states, particularly those in the developing world, do not support extending laws to criminalize and prosecute intellectual property theft. They argue that current legal thinking about intellectual property rests on Western legal traditions and history that do not apply to their national situations. They regard WIPO's actions as colonialist in orientation and an abuse of power. In addition, the ways in which individuals today can create mash-ups and memes, mixing together existing creative works with their own unique takes on these works, means that the concept of what constitutes intellectual property itself is changing.[17]

Nations today also disagree about freedom of speech in cyberspace. In the years since the internet was created, we have seen a rise in legal cases both within the United States and internationally that have attempted to establish rules and practices related to the ways in which individuals and groups can express their opinions online. As we noted in Chapter 2, authoritarian societies like China and Belarus may have strict laws governing the sorts of speech that is permissible in "their" cyberspace, and in those societies committing an act like criticizing an elected official or passing along a rumor or meme that paints the government in an unflattering light might be regarded as a criminal act; in contrast, such behaviors might be relatively commonplace in a more open society like the United States.

Indeed, in recent years, the United States has accused China of violating international regimes regarding freedom of speech through its conduct of internet filtering—taking complaints to bodies such as the UN Human Rights Commission. Most recently, the United States has spoken out about the ways in which Chinese internet censorship is a barrier to trade between the two countries. Here, US attorneys argue that censorship creates friction in international communication that makes it more expensive to do business between the two countries. They argue that Chinese internet censorship thus violates WTO rules on what constitutes a trade barrier. Indeed, the US Trade Representative has threatened to file a WTO case against China challenging the restrictions. In response, China argues that it has the right to engage in internet censorship until such time as both the United States and China have an equal amount of soft power in international affairs so that Chinese people will not be unduly influenced by American ideas.[18]

As this short example shows, there is little international consensus regarding what is seen as acceptable and unacceptable speech online. Although in the United States individuals may make viral online memes that include jokes about individuals, like senators, mayors, and even the president, in other countries like Russia, such behavior may be strictly prohibited. And because what constitutes deviant behavior is also socially constructed and varies greatly from one culture to another, states may have different laws governing, for example, whether it is permissible for citizens to utilize the internet to learn about queer life, to find a partner for an extramarital affair, or to view pornography. Such acts might be criminal in one society but not in another.

The Problem of Hate Speech

Here, we can also consider the rise of hate speech and how it might be regulated. Regulating online speech across social media platforms presents numerous legal challenges.[19] First, there is no universally accepted definition of cyber racism, nor do all cultures even agree on what racial categories exist and can be applied.

In addition, although states might like to regulate and respond to instances of online racism, sexism, or gender-based harassment, the only actors who are truly empowered to respond are commercial ISPs and hosting platforms (like Facebook and Twitter) because states do not actually own or control the platforms upon which these crimes are occurring. Here, both ISPs and platforms might have terms of service or community norms that they use to police such behaviors, but thus far states have not been able to come together internationally to draw up legal regulations that would regulate what is available on content platforms or apply consistent punishments for offenders in these areas. The most wide-ranging vehicle for combating cybercrime, the Budapest Convention on Cybercrime, currently includes the Additional Protocol that deals with questions of racist and xenophobic (anti-foreigner) speech. The Additional Protocol to the Convention on Cybercrime, Concerning the Criminalization of Acts of a Racist and Xenophobic Nature Committed through Computer Systems requires states to criminalize making available or distributing racist or xenophobic material. However, not all states that have signed the Budapest Convention have also signed onto this additional protocol. Most recently, Twitter CEO Jack Dorsey has been criticized for having an inconsistent stance in policing materials that some see as advocating for the practice of genocide. In particular, he has been criticized for what some see as his support of the Burmese government despite indications that Burma has practiced genocide against the Rohingya people.[20]

And, as noted earlier in this text, although states may act to limit citizen access to sites or platforms that are found to be hosting material that contradicts their own domestic laws, it may be difficult to draw the line between legitimate state actions in this arena and acts of censorship and violations of free speech. For example, in Australia, ISPs have been asked to restrict access to content hosted overseas that constitutes hate speech according to Australian laws. However, some critics are concerned that by giving an ISP the power to restrict information from coming into Australia, ISPs are in fact carrying out censorship, similar to that provided by China's Great Firewall.

SHOULD PEOPLE AND ORGANIZATIONS BE "BANNED" FROM THE INTERNET?

As we have seen throughout this chapter, states throughout the international system have committed to work together to create binding international laws against certain types of cybercrimes, including violations of intellectual property. However, although states may agree about the seriousness and unlawfulness of the acts being committed, as well as the dangers they pose, states do not always agree about the penalties that should be levied against those who commit such acts.

In recent years, controversy has arisen both within the United States and within the international community regarding one possible solution to eliminating certain types of criminal acts in cyberspace—namely the "internet ban." (Here, we can distinguish between internet banning and internet blocking. Blocking occurs when a platform censures an individual through implementing his or her access to a particular platform, like Twitter or Facebook, temporarily. Here, moderators use specific code to block this person or organization's access to the platform for a specified period of time, usually because the individual has violated the platform's specific code of conduct. Moderators may block users on Twitter, for example, who post violent, offensive, or incendiary content.) Internet banning refers to a situation in which a court might order an individual not to access the internet as part of the terms of his or her probation or release from prison.

(Continued)

CRITICAL ISSUES

(Continued)

The first person to be banned from accessing the internet was Chris Lamprecht, an internet hacker, also known as Minor Threat. Lamprecht, an American, was sentenced to prison for developing the ToneLoc software, which searched for modems using a phone line to carry out early internet hacking. He was also banned from the internet until 2004.[21]

Since then, courts in Australia, Britain, Canada, and the United States have also handed down sentences that included banning an individual from utilizing the internet. Individuals have been banned from utilizing the internet if they have been found to be accessing child pornography or engaging in so-called revenge pornography (releasing private photographs or videos of an individual with whom they may have had a romantic relationship). In Malta, the Court of Magistrates banned an individual from using the internet after he was found to assassinate the country's prime minister using an online platform to make threats.[22]

In 2009, in *United States v. Thielemann*, the US Third Circuit court argued that banning an individual from accessing the internet for a period of ten years involved a "deprivation of liberty" but that this deprivation of liberty was not greater than that which someone might experience during imprisonment. Thielemann's lawyers argued that banning someone from utilizing the internet was "impossibly restrictive." Other lawyers have subsequently argued that banning someone form the internet would be nearly impossible to enforce due to the ubiquity of the internet.[23]

In 2017, the US Supreme Court heard *Packingham v. North Carolina*, which sought to establish a uniform ban on access to social media for individuals tried within that state who were convicted of sex offenses. In this instance, the US Supreme Court argued that this law was too broad and might have the effect of denying too many people their constitutional right to free speech. Here, the Supreme Court was worried about establishing a precedent that allowed entire groups of people to be banned from the internet. Although today it might seem logical to ban sex offenders from utilizing social media, could such restrictions later be used to silence legitimate political or social dissent? The Supreme Court felt that this was too great a risk to take.[24] Indeed, as we have seen throughout this chapter, "crime" can be understood as a social construction with rules changing over time regarding what is and is not considered to be criminal behavior.

In addition, some critics suggest that states should not have the right to ban users from accessing the internet because doing so violates international law. Here, Howell and West note that Article 19 of the UN Universal Declaration of

Human Rights declares that "everyone has the right to freedom of opinion and expression." In some instances, this has been interpreted to mean that everyone has (and should be permitted) the right to access the internet. They note that "Article 19 is . . . considered a 'soft law' in that it only recommends actions for nation-states and lacks any enforcement mechanisms as a 'hard law' would."[25]

Providing a global and open internet is also seen as a crucial step toward the achievement of the Agenda 2030 Sustainable Development Goals (SDGs). These goals are again nonbinding.

Finally, for states that are within the European Union, it is also presently unclear as to whether states have the ability to implement separate laws banning their citizens from accessing the internet or whether such laws need to be decided uniformly on a European level.

Sources

GVZH Advocates. "Malta: Can Internet Use Be Banned?" *Mondaq* (October 26, 2015). http://www.mondaq.com/x/437770/Social+Media/Can+Internet+Use+Be+Banned.

The Harvard Law Review Association. "Criminal Law—Supervised Released—Third Circuit Approves Decade-Long Internet Ban for Sex Offender." *Harvard Law Review* 123, no. 3 (2010): 776–783.

Howland, C., and D. M. West. "The Internet as a Human Right." Brookings Institute. Last modified November 7, 2016. https://www.brookings.edu/blog/techtank/2016/11/07/the-internet-as-a-human-right/.

Masnick, M. "Supreme Court Says You Can't Ban People from the Internet, No Matter What They've Done." *Techdirt* (June 20, 2017). https://www.techdirt.com/articles/20170620/10455137631/supreme-court-says-you-cant-ban-people-internet-no-matter-what-theyve-done.shtml.

Wikipedia. "Christopher Lamprecht." Last modified February 10, 2019, https://en.wikipedia.org/wiki/Chris_Lamprecht.

AN INTERNATIONAL CONVENTION ON CYBERCRIME?

Due to the problems noted here—the limited role that states may ultimately play in policing online interactions, the social construct of crime and lack of common global norms regarding what is lawful in cyberspace, and the jurisdictional problems created in a global environment—many analysts are skeptical about whether there can ever truly be an effective international convention on cybercrime. Initially, analysts believed that the UN would play a leading role in addressing transnational crimes, and indeed the United Nations has had some success in that arena. In 2000, the UN Convention against Transnational Organized Crime (TOC) was signed by 147 states, largely to cope with jurisdictional issues raised by the advent of e-commerce and cybercrime. This convention defined an offense as transnational if it was committed in more than one state; committed in a single state but planned, prepared, directed, or controlled by another state; committed in one state but involved an organized group whose activities cross national boundaries; or committed in a single state but with substantial effects in another state.

However, the rapid creation and expansion of the Council of European Budapest Convention mean that this is now the dominant framework. The Council of European Cybercrime Convention (or Budapest Convention) was first ratified in December 2001 with 42 signatories. The convention had three aims: to lay out common definitions of certain criminal offenses—enabling relevant legislation to be harmonized at the national level; to define common types of investigative powers better suited to the information technology environment; and to determine both traditional and new types of international cooperation. The convention criminalized illegal access, including hacking, cracking, and computer trespass. It also criminalized acts of computer sabotage or acts hindering the lawful use of computer systems. Title 3 of the convention defined content-related offenses, including using computers as a vehicle for sexual exploitation and acts of a racist or xenophobic nature. Title 4 defined offenses related to intellectual property and copyright. The Budapest Convention's provision concerning jurisdiction requires states exercising jurisdiction to coordinate when victims are located in different countries. Through the agreement, signatories agree to cooperate to the widest extent possible to minimize impediments to cooperation. The convention also creates a legal basis for the establishment of an international computer crime assistance network, located in Europe, which is available 24/7.

As of December 2016, fifty-two states had ratified the convention and four states had signed but not ratified. Although the Budapest Convention was initially developed within the Council of Europe, it has subsequently been opened up to nations beyond the Council of Europe. Nonmember states of the Council of Europe include Australia, Canada, the Dominican Republic, Israel, Japan, Mauritius, Panama, Sri Lanka, and the United States.

However, the Budapest Convention is not the only international body concerned with preventing international cybercrimes. Multiple agencies are active in addressing cybercrime including the UN Office of Drug Control and Crime Prevention (UNDCP) and its center for international crime prevention (CICP); Interpol; and the Organization of Economic and Cultural Development (OECD). In addition, the Group of Twelve nations (which actually includes thirteen countries—Australia, Belgium, Canada, France, Germany, Italy, Japan, the Netherlands, Spain, Sweden, Switzerland, the United Kingdom, and the United States) has been active in coordinating international banking and financial mechanisms that have been used to fight cybercrime. Finally, the International Criminal Police Organization (Interpol), an international organization that has existed since 1923, has increased its profile in fighting cybercrimes. With 181 member states, Interpol has created the Interpol Payment Card website, which informs law enforcement and payment card investigators about criminal conspiracies, sharing information about frauds and schemes that may begin in one nation but later spread to other nations as part of organized crime or copycat crimes.

At the same time, regional bodies such as the European Union, the Organization of American States, the Association of South East Asian Nations (ASEAN), the African Union, and the Asia Pacific Economic Council (APEC) have drawn up cooperative agreements in the areas of cybercrime prevention. Most recently, the BRICS nations (Brazil, Russia, India, China, and South Africa) have begun to share information and cooperate in the prosecution of cybercrimes.

Today, critics differ as to whether or not the international community is succeeding in creating strong mechanisms to combat international cybercrime. Broadhurst, a cyber optimist, argues for a developing international consensus on norms in the area of cybercrime.[26] He argues that the transnational nature of crime today means that states alone are insufficient to act to either prevent violations or address them when they occur. He argues that actors now need to form networks between police and other agencies within government, between police and private institutions, and among police across national borders. He writes, "There is now a positive 'moral climate' for enforcement action, whether by civil, criminal or administrative measures and this cross-border cooperation recognizes what sociologists call 'communities of shared fate.'"[27]

In his analysis, he argues that what is needed is a national strategy, coordinated with an international strategy, which includes the establishment of transnational policing networks and the cooperation of both public and private sector players. Here, he argues that "digital footprints are fragile and ephemeral." They vanish quickly, and thus speed becomes of the essence in collecting evidence, disseminating this evidence internationally and acting to address violations that occur. In his analysis, he provides the example of an ATM crime that occurred in the United States that was quickly replicated across the globe. By providing information about the cyber tools used and the ways in which the crime could be detected, police in South America were able to quickly arrest cybercriminals using similar methodologies and tools. In his work, Broadhurst argues that the digital divide means that wealthy nations will always have to play a dominant role in combating cybercrime through leading international organizations. Consumers in developing nations may not be able to afford the latest, and safest, new technologies, and police forces in developing countries may struggle to keep up with technological developments and responses to them. As a result, he argues, "the fight against cybercrime is either a global fight, or it is nothing at all."

In contrast, cyber pessimists point to the weaknesses of existing vehicles like the Budapest Convention. They argue that the Budapest Convention is largely symbolic with few "teeth" to enforce the treaty's provisions. The convention seeks to harmonize existing international legislation, but many signatory states do not actually have strong and binding domestic laws regarding the investigation and prosecution of cybercrime. In addition, many of the most effective players in combating cybercrime have been not states but private corporations. Thus, it is unclear whether an international convention can solve the problems presented by cybercrime's growth today.[28] And as the long list of regional bodies created to combat cybercrime illustrates, there exist multiple overlapping sets of actors, not all of whom share the same orientation and values toward the internet, the role of the state in cyberspace, and the definition of cybercrime. One can argue that combating cybercrime currently is characterized more by competition among states than it is by cooperation.

Finally, we should note, as we have throughout this textbook, that cyber issues are rarely stand-alone issues. Rather, cybercrime issues are frequently entangled with issues of national security, economic competitiveness, and national power in the international system. States may thus accuse other states of engaging in cybercriminal behavior, including cyber espionage or cyber human rights violations—not because of a true commitment to combating these issues but rather as part of a longer-range strategy of state competition. For example, some analysts today note that it is impossible to speak about steps the United States is taking to combat and counter Chinese cyber espionage, including the theft of US trade secrets, without taking into account the larger US-China relationship, including the ways in which the United States and China are competing for economic power and political influence in the global economy. Here, Bacchus argues that the Trump administration's policy of responding to perceived Chinese cyber espionage has been somewhat inconsistent. He argues that the Trump administration might be using these charges as a pretext to carry out a policy that it was committed to anyway. He argues that the Trump administration wants to increase tariffs on Chinese-made products, which would make Chinese goods more expensive and US-made products more desirable for US consumers. Therefore, he says, the Trump administration will likely increase these tariffs as "retaliation" for Chinese espionage. However, he suggests that such a policy would be illegal. He writes that "where an international dispute falls within the scope of coverage of the World Trade Organization treaty, taking unilateral action without first going to WTO dispute settlement for a ruling on whether there is a WTO violation is . . . a violation of the treaty."[29]

DEFINING CYBERCRIME

As we have noted, then, there is not a broad international consensus among states regarding what constitutes cybercrime. However, those in the information assurance industry have nonetheless put together several typologies that are useful as we think about causes of cybercrime and responses to these crimes. Here, analysts distinguish among the types of acts that are carried out in cyberspace, their potential victims, and the repercussions of these activities.

First, analysts are concerned about so-called computer-enhanced crimes, or computer-facilitated crimes. As we saw in the introduction to this chapter, some crimes—like fraud, deception, deviant behavior, and relationships crimes—are not fundamentally new types of criminal behavior. Rather, they are existing crimes (like identity theft) that are now being carried out in the online environment. Computer-enhanced crimes can be targeted toward individuals, corporations, or groups of actors—and they can be carried out by professional criminals including criminal syndicates as well as more amateur criminals. A crime's ramifications can range from personal embarrassment (as when, e.g., a public figure's privacy is violated and embarrassing personal information about him or her is revealed) to large-scale financial ruin.

The second type of crime concerning criminologists is computer crimes. These acts are fundamentally new because they were invented only when the internet itself came into being. Such crimes include the sending of malware or viruses in which the specific target of the act is a victim's computer system. In contrast to computer-facilitated crimes, computer crimes include any acts that interfere with the lawful use of a computer through cybervandalism, cyberterrorism, DDOS attacks, and the use of viruses, worms, and malicious code. Computer crimes also include cyber hostage taking, surveillance, and the illegal interception of communications. These types of crime emerged in tandem with the development of internet technology and could not exist without it.[30] The targets can include individuals and groups and their computers, computer-related equipment, and other devices or their information technology networks.

The ramifications of such acts can vary widely. In some instances, a computer virus might cause an office to shut down for an afternoon. However, attacks on SCADA systems, which govern public utilities like dams, water treatment facilities, electrical grids, and air traffic control mechanisms, can create much larger effects. For this reason, in the United States, the SCADA systems of many public utilities are considered as part of US critical infrastructure—even though such systems are neither owned nor administered by the US government. The 2001 USA PATRIOT Act defined critical infrastructure as

> systems and assets, whether physical or virtual, so vital to the United States that the incapacity or destruction of such systems and assets would have a debilitating impact on security, national economic security, national public health or safety, or any combination of those matters.

Sectors that are described by most nations as belonging to critical infrastructure include services such as heating, agriculture, water supply, transportation, public health, electricity, telecommunications, and the financial sector. For that reason, attacks on these sectors may be treated not as mere cybercrimes but as acts of war because an attack that shuts down water treatment or heat or hospital services could have the effect of creating thousands of civilian casualties.[31]

The first legislation to impose criminal penalties for computer use and misuse was drawn up in 1978 in Florida. Today, in the United States, the Computer Fraud and Abuse Act (CFAA) provides the most comprehensive set of statutes regarding the criminal use of computers, covering everything from hobby or nuisance hacking up to and including espionage and state-sponsored hacking. The CFAA also covers criminal enterprises such as trafficking in passwords or the theft of trade secrets. In addition, the CFAA has also been used creatively to charge individuals who have engaged in cyberbullying and cyberstalking through the creation of fake websites and identities online.

Congress passed the first version of the CFAA in 1984. Since then, it has been modified and expanded upon in several areas. In addition, the CFAA will require amendment again in response to technological developments tied to the expansion of cloud computing. The CFAA can be used both to seek criminal charges against those regarded as having misused computers as well as for the application of civil penalties to those harmed by computer misuse. The CFAA also provides key definitions used in the prosecution of cybercrime.[32]

High Crimes and Low Crimes

As we saw in our discussion of SCADA systems, we can identify crimes that are specifically related or threatening to state security. Here, we can consider acts such as cyberterrorism or cyber espionage. The United Kingdom has identified cybercrime as a "tier 1" threat, alongside terrorism, as one of the most serious national security threats.[33] Cybercrime is seen as a national security threat because of its crippling economic repercussions for individual businesses and for the economy as a whole. Analysts have estimated the annual cost to the US economy from intellectual property theft at approximately $600 billion.

Here, we can also distinguish between computer crimes committed by individuals or criminal syndicates from those that are state-sponsored. In considering the threat to the US economy from cyberattacks, analysts use the term *advanced persistent threat* (API) to refer to targeted weapons, likely created by highly technologically sophisticated and advanced adversaries (including China and Russia). Such weapons are seen as too complex for ordinary thieves to have created and are instead regarded as the product of a robust **cyberweapons** or cybermunitions complex, likely led by the defense industries in adversary nations. For this reason, among the players in combating cybercrime, we can identify government agencies like the British GCHQ, Britain's MI5, and the US Department of Justice.

Crimes like APTs are sometimes referred to as "high crimes" because in these instances the victim is the state, not an individual. Here, the criminal actor aims not merely to steal material or to harm a victim but rather to carry out activities aimed at threatening state security or state survival in the international system. The adversary may do so through creating societal chaos to prepare the battlefield for a follow-up conventional military assault or may seek to damage a military's command, control, and communications capabilities during wartime through first targeting domestic telecommnications infrastructure.

Finally, an adversary may engage in **psychological operations (PSYOPS)**, utilizing social media platforms to plant rumors and false information that can serve to degrade citizens' trust in their elected leaders and political processes. In the July 2018 Intelligence Community Assessment Report of Russian Activities and Intentions in Recent US Elections, the intelligence community stated that Russian actors had attempted to "undermine the US-led liberal democratic order" through conducting cyber operations against targets associated with both major US political parties. They were found to have targeted global audiences in carrying out an influence campaign against US voters.[34]

This third group of crimes, then—crimes that present an explicit threat to national security and that are most often carried out by state-sponsored cybercriminal groups—differ greatly from mere nuisance crimes or those that are carried out merely for monetary gain. In his work, the prominent criminologist Sheptycki refers to "high policing," which the state itself may carry out (through organizations like the National Security Agency, the Federal Bureau of Investigation, or the Central Intelligence Agency). Here, he acknowledges that the state and its representatives may behave differently to secure the state than they do when their task is merely to protect an individual homeowner or business targeted by a criminal. High policing (as opposed to regular or low policing) frequently includes preemptive policing, including the use of surveillance to gather evidence about potential crimes or anti-state acts.[35]

Today, we can classify such acts as cyber espionage carried out by states aimed at stealing commercial or military technologies of other states, psychological operations aimed at undermining a state's reputation and relationships with voters and citizens, and cyberattacks on critical infrastructure as not merely criminal activities but as high crimes against a state. The US Criminal Code provisions that deal with cybercrimes currently make such a distinction. Provision 18 of USC Section 1030(a)(2) has the most stringent criminal penalties for those accused of seeking or achieving unauthorized access to government computers. Accessing government computers can carry a sentence of up to ten years in prison, with longer sentences for repeat offenders.

Acts against the State: Crimes or Acts of War?

However, many analysts today think that such cyber high crimes against the state are better responded to utilizing the instruments and institutions associated with warfare rather than those associated with crime. The United States defines espionage as "the act of obtaining, delivering, transmitting, communicating or receiving information about the national defense with intent or reason to believe that the information may be used to the injury of the United States or the advantage of a foreign nation."[36] However, the international law system has no official policy on espionage—it is regarded as "neither lawful nor unlawful under international law." It is, instead, an open secret that nations can and do engage in espionage, with those accused of engaging in espionage often going unpunished instead of being dealt with through informal mechanisms such as the revoking of diplomatic credentials and expulsion from a state.[37]

In contrast, there are strict international laws and protocols governing cyberwarfare. However, it can be difficult for those who are targeted to distinguish between whether they have been the subject of cyber espionage or cyberwarfare. In both cases, the perpetrator seeks unauthorized access to a system, may steal information, and may cause harm to a computer system as the result of actions performed within the system. In both situations, actions may take place across international territorial lines, resulting in violations of national sovereignty. Currently, legal definitions distinguish between the two activities, with cyber espionage referred to as computer network exploitation in contrast to the cyber activity, which constitutes an act of force or act or war. (We explore this distinction more in the following chapter.)

The United States has been quite vociferous in prosecuting those engaged in economic espionage through cyber means. Here we can consider the 2014 US decision to undertake legal proceedings against five Chinese military officers accused of cyber espionage as well as the 2015 joint US-China agreement prohibiting cyber espionage for commercial gain.

REGULATION AND RESPONSIBILITY: WHO IS LIABLE?

Today, some critics argue that the US government (and other governments) overemphasize securing the state from cyberattacks by adversary nations and underemphasize securing and protecting individual citizens who suffer from personally devasting acts like identity theft.[38] These critics suggest that the government places too much responsibility on individual users and corporations to practice good cyber hygiene through installing software patches and choosing good passwords rather than acting broadly to keep users safe in cyberspace. Cyber hygiene campaigns, they argue, seem to blame users and corporations when they are unable to respond to cybercrimes that occur.

But whose responsibility is it to secure cyberspace from cyber harm? It is the responsibility of the user, the corporation, the state, or the international community? In an analysis published in 2018, David Weitzner argued that part of the reason why it has been so difficult for states to respond to and prevent cybercrime is because of the internet's history as a largely unregulated space. He argues that a feature of this technology, from its inception, has been a sort of buyer-beware ethos, in which firms were free to experiment and grow quickly in cyberspace due to the fact that they had only limited liability for harm generated by their users.[39] That is, firms—and platforms—did not have to behave cautiously in this new space, bound by fears that they could be sued or punished for unexpected actions that might take place in this new, somewhat unpredictable space. In this way, the internet represented the ultimate free market, characterized by states' laissez-faire approaches.

At the same time, liberal internationalists argue, the state—in its hands-off regulatory approach—created opportunities for firms themselves to take the lead in policing this new space. Indeed, firms have played the leading role in establishing international agreements on e-commerce, with governments getting involved later only at the firms' request. Furthermore, often sectors (like banking) may formulate their own rules regarding what it is permissible and what actions should be punished or sanctioned. These rules are then approved by the government. Here, analysts point to the establishment in 1989 of the Computer Systems Policy Project (CSPP) in the United States. This group acted like a lobby or consultative group. Because its members were technology experts and most legislators were not, the group in essence wrote legislation on issues like international trade, internet taxation, and e-commerce, which was then adopted by the US government.[40] These analysts argue that self-regulation by platforms and ISPs is actually a much more effective mechanism for addressing cybercrimes than either the adoption of international norms or the creation of laws and legislation.

The notion that firms and governments can cooperate with police activity in a certain social or economic sector is not, however, unique to the internet. Indeed, the same regulatory space is often occupied by both governmental and nongovernmental organizations that may have overlapping regimes in many areas. For example, a trucking industry organization may have its own rules and regulations governing who may be licensed to drive a commercial vehicle and how many hours a driver can drive per day. At the same time, there are national laws regarding these same issues. And doctors and lawyers can be governed both by their own professional regulations as well as by national laws.[41] Jamal et al. note that "law, auditors, reputation, business norms and practices, warranties, disclosure and industry associations are competing trust-creation mechanisms associated with markets. The value of each mechanism depends on which other mechanisms are available in a particular market."

STATES AND FIRMS COOPERATE: THE EXAMPLE OF A BOTNET TAKEDOWN

As we have seen throughout this chapter, law enforcement personnel encounter many obstacles in attempting to combat cybercrime. Jurisdictional questions arise when crimes take place across borders, and it may be difficult to secure the cooperation of all states in confronting these crimes. In addition, states may have different legal understandings of what constitutes a crime (e.g., in the case of intellectual property) and different levels of skills necessary to combat cybercrime. In addition, crimes can be aimed at individuals, at corporations, or at states, and therefore acting to punish offenders may require the cooperation of multiple different types of actors—including private companies, organizations, individuals, and states.

Here we pause to consider one example of how states and private firms have begun cooperating to prevent and respond to cybercrimes. A **botnet** is a specific mode of organization in which multiple computers may be linked together through a system of command and control. That is, malware or instruction software can be installed on a number of different computers through an infected software download. Once the malicious code is installed on computers worldwide, these client computers are then instructed to connect with a host or server that will then direct them to engage in targeted, coordinated actions and activities. The host or server can be a computer located in a third country where regulations regarding computer crime are much less developed and where the rules regarding liability are less developed. (Some nations perform what is known as bulletproof hosting, essentially serving as foreign hosts for types of activities that a client may be unable to perform in his or her own home country. For example, countries like Estonia have become havens for the hosting of sites like neo-Nazi and Nazi propaganda sites because such activities are illegal in many Western nations.) In some instances, bots will connect to a "zombie computer" that runs programs somewhere within the system; in these instances, even the owner of the computer may be unaware of the fact that the computer is being used in this way.

The creation of a botnet thus allows the creator to command seemingly hundreds or thousands of computers rather than merely one or two. In this way, he or she can carry out malicious activity utilizing a virtual army of computers. Because a botnet can span hundreds of computers in multiple geographic areas, the challenges to law enforcement in shutting down and capturing the lawbreaker can be formidable.

Botnet "armies" can be deployed to carry out many different kinds of actions, including DDOS or denial of service attacks, in which many computers simultaneously attempt to access a program or server to overload the system and shut it down. Botnets can also carry out activities like mining for Bitcoins (a type of cryptocurrency), which can then be used for activities like terrorist finance. A botnet attack perpetrator can thus be a private individual, a group like a terrorist cell, or even a state, which can utilize its own computer networks to establish a botnet to engage in cyberwarfare activities like DDOS attacks. (Both China and Russia have been accused of engaging in such behaviors.) Some botnet attacks may be relatively harmless, such as the activities of a group of computer hackers who merely wanted to increase their chances of winning at Minecraft.[42] However, other attacks, including those that include the downloading and installation of ransomware onto infected computers, can have serious physical repercussions if, for example, hospitals are unable to access medical records until a ransom is paid.

One of the major challenges that law enforcement personnel encounter in attempting to shut down botnet attacks is that it may be difficult to even be aware that a botnet system has been created or that it is engaged in malicious activity. In many instances, a botnet system may be set up, and then the participant computers may go dormant, lying in wait for the command that will wake them up and set them into action, carrying out activities like destroying data. That is, the groundwork for the attack may be laid significantly in advance of the actual activities, but law enforcement may become aware of the existence of a botnet only when it begins to act in a malicious manner.

In addition, today a great many different types of internet-connected devices can be utilized in carrying out a botnet attack. Any device that comprises part of the internet of things—from a video doorbell to an internet-enabled thermostat to a wired refrigerator to a cell phone—can be included in a botnet attack. Thus, computer security personnel warn of the greatly expanded threat surface that law enforcement personnel must contend with today in a system where there are more internet-enabled devices on our planet than there are humans. (Our population is nearly 7 billion, and the number of internet-enabled devices on earth is approaching 50 billion.)

Because of the complex technological challenges that law enforcement faces in identifying and responding to botnet attacks, private corporations have begun to take on a leading role in identifying, responding to, and taking down botnet systems. Private corporations can use computer forensics to identify suspicious patterns taking place within computer systems that may indicate that a botnet system is being established. Symantec Corporation has played a leading role in establishing the Global Threat Intelligence Network and has worked with the US Federal Bureau of Investigation to combat a number of serious botnets in recent years.[43]

In addition, nations have begun sharing information about suspicious patterns of activity that they may have observed, particularly in key sectors like the banking industry.[44] However, computer security experts stress that consumers play a key role in securing their own systems and remaining aware of the activities that are taking place on those systems. In addition, some analysts have suggested that liability laws need to change because currently device manufacturers have little incentive to worry about the security of their devices or to work to secure them from these attacks as they are not held liable for security breaches in their devices.[45] They argue that there needs to be better international security standards that devices should meet as well as more liability attached to ISPs whose systems are used to facilitate botnet attacks. However, manufacturers are opposed to these measures because increasing security will undoubtedly make these devices significantly more expensive.

Today, bots may receive their commands through a variety of methods, including through commands carried by social media channels like Twitter and Instagram. It is relatively cheap to set up a botnet attack, and the technological requirements are not great. (The botnet attack thus represents a type of asymmetric warfare, as we will see in Chapter 7, because it is significantly cheaper to establish this type of attack than it is to defend against it.) Thus, some computer security specialists worry that even if one group of botnet manufacturers is captured and prevented from engaging in this behavior, hundreds of others could immediately pop up and continue to engage in this behavior.[46]

THE RISE OF ANTICIPATORY POLICING

Another issue facing those engaged in crime prevention today is the matter of intelligence-led policing. Today, law enforcement personnel have access to more data about their communities and their citizens than ever before. As a result, it is possible for police and other community services providers to make predictions about incidents, including crimes, before they actually occur. By looking at past patterns of criminal behavior, law enforcement leaders can deploy police resources to the areas where crimes are most likely to occur—based on previous patterns—at the times when crimes are most likely to occur there. As a result, they hope that police personnel can move beyond merely responding to crimes by instead preventing or deterring crimes from occurring. Ideally, the use of intelligence-led policing could make law enforcement cheaper, with fewer resources wasted monitoring the wrong areas, and could also make our communities safer.

However, critics of this preemptive policing approach have raised several objections to this practice: First, some legal analysts argue that when police respond to crimes that have not yet occurred, they are in fact judging some citizens and some types of citizens as guilty until proven innocent, which violates both the Sixth and Fourteenth Amendments of the US Constitution, which mandates that all citizens should receive the right to due process, including the right to a speedy, fair trial in which they are presumed to be innocent until evidence is given attesting to their guilt. Citizens also have the right to know what the charges being levied against them are so that trials are transparent. In contrast, critics allege, intelligence-led policing sets up an opaque system in which citizens may not know that they are being preemptively accused of crimes or what those crimes are.

In addition, some critics worry that predictive criminal analytics are based on racial, ethnic, or socioeconomic profiling. They argue that in deciding that certain types of people are more likely to be guilty, police are in effect prejudging members of these ethnic or racial groups and thereby treating them differently than other citizens through engaging in increased surveillance of those groups.[47] For example, in Los Angeles, some blocks of the city are listed as "red blocks" where crime is more likely. Police may overfocus on those blocks and allow those who live outside those blocks to get away with more criminal behavior.

Other critics note that intelligence-led policing efforts often rely on algorithms and the use of artificial intelligence. For example, Vaak, a Japanese company, introduced a program that analyzes individuals' body language in a store to predict who is likely to shoplift. Patrons who appear to be ready to shoplift are approached by store personnel with offers of assistance in finding goods. Such efforts may preempt shoplifting. To carry out such efforts, however, every patron who visits a store must be placed under video surveillance, often without their knowledge.[48] (Although the European Union requires that citizens be informed via signage when they are in a public place where they may be under surveillance, many other countries do not.) Human rights activists oppose the creeping extent of ubiquitous surveillance as well as the fact that machines, rather than humans, are often being used to make decisions about people's lives.

In addition, Braman is concerned about the accuracy of data used in making such judgment calls. She warns against "statistics as policy" and what she sees as the "dissolution of the individual into a probability."[49]

In addition, government policing departments often do not own, manufacture, or administer the software on which intelligence-led policing depends themselves; instead, they are likely to outsource such functions to contractors and subcontractors. For-profit purveyors of this software may be more concerned with their economic bottom line than they are with the rights of citizens because they are not formally members of the government.

The Growth of the Surveillance State

A final concern relates to the growth of the surveillance state and the ways in which individuals may lose their right to privacy as the state seeks to track and predict who is likely to commit a crime. Here, critics first began speaking out in 2002, when it was reported that the US Defense Advanced Research Projects Agency (DARPA) was seeking to create so-called Total Information Awareness (TIA). The United States was concerned about perceived weakness in its intelligence-monitoring mechanisms in the aftermath of the terrorist attacks of September 11, 2001. Officials were concerned that there were multiple sources of intelligence information that had been available—from airplane booking logs to immigration records. However, intelligence personnel had failed to connect the dots or to draw these disparate sources together. TIA was seen as a way to connect multiple databases that collect information in the United States to be better able to predict and monitor citizen activity that could potentially present a threat to state security.[50] Although the United States never fully implemented TIA, other nations, like Singapore, utilize data mining (also known as data discovery or knowledge discovery) to search for patterns in citizen data to better understand and respond to criminal activity and possible criminal activity.[51]

Information Sharing among States

Today, states are creating agreements to share citizen data among states for the purposes of predicting and responding to criminal threats. The Stockholm Program, part of the 2010–2014 European Union Framework, seeks to create interoperable criminal databases for all European Union members so that members can more easily share data such as airline passenger name records (PNRs) and the issuing of visas to non-European Union visitors and residents.[52] Such data is also compared to other sources like the Interpol database. Critics of these information-sharing practices have suggested that they may violate two European Union values: nondiscrimination and data protection. They argue that the flagging of specific ethnic or religious groups would violate European Union regulations regarding nondiscrimination and fair treatment of all European Union citizens, specifically the "principle of equality" or "nondiscrimination clause," which appears in Article 21 of the Charter of Fundamental Rights of the European Union and in Article 14 of Protocol of the European Convention on Human Rights.

In addition, the use of PNR data in particular by policing authorities goes beyond the goal of merely preempting crimes from occurring. Leese argues that PNR data analysis is utilized through the application of a "precautionary principle framework," which asks users to make decisions based on the assumption that something is dangerous unless it is proven not to be. (That is, we assume everyone and everything could potentially be a risk and then look for reasons not to treat it as risky rather than assuming that it is not a risk initially.)[53] Proponents of this data mining approach argue that machines do not have the same sorts of prejudices and biases that humans do and that therefore it is preferable to rely on machines to make these decisions regarding who poses a risk. We will look at these issues in more depth in Chapter 10, which considers ethical issues, including the ethics of privacy.

BUT IS IT A CRIME? THE CASE OF WIKILEAKS

You may have heard the expression, "One man's terrorist is another man's freedom fighter." That phrase is often used to convey the sentiment that one's position in reference to an event or phenomenon can affect how one views the phenomenon. In other words, the actions of someone who plants a bomb or even holds a protest in a public place might look like anti-state activity and a security threat to a government official. However, for someone who is disenfranchised and disempowered in their political system, carrying out such an act may seem like a logical and even moral way of forcing change in a stagnant authoritarian political system. That is, definitions of legality and even morality may be quite different depending on one's own status.

In thinking about new types of political activism that have arisen as a result of the advent of the internet, we can consider the situation of WikiLeaks, an organization that has been both praised as a beacon of freedom of speech and the press and condemned as an unlawful, anarchist organization. WikiLeaks, a website founded in 2010 by Australian citizen Julian Assange, has been described as "a high security anonymous drop box fortified by cutting-edge cryptographic information technologies."[54] WikiLeaks describes itself as an international nonprofit that carries out the original principles of the internet's founders through using information dissemination technologies to promote radical transparency.[55] Sometimes quoting the famous slogan "Information wants to be free," WikiLeaks has posted classified government materials from the United Sates and other nations, seeking to open up conversations in society through reducing government secrecy. Readers logged onto WikiLeaks to read US government diplomatic cables, e-mails from the US Democratic National Committee, the Hillary Clinton for President campaign, and classified US Department of Defense documents detailing US military activities in Iraq and Afghanistan.

To WikiLeaks, individuals who have leaked these documents, often at great personal risk, are heroes and whistle-blowers who acted according to their consciences by seeking to make government secrets (and errors) public. On November 16, 2018, former Central Intelligence Agency contractor Edward Snowden—who is best known for having leaked hundreds of thousands of documents from the Central Intelligence Agency and the National Security Agency through the WikiLeaks platform—tweeted the following: "You can despise WikiLeaks and everything it stands for. You can think Assange is an evil spirit reanimated by Putin himself. But you cannot support the prosecution of a publisher for publishing without narrowing the basic rights every newspaper relies on."[56]

However, states reacted quickly and decisively to these releases of classified materials. Although the exact charges filed against WikiLeaks founder Julian Assange are not being revealed, he will likely be charged under the US Espionage Act. In addition, Chelsea Manning, a former US Army private who was responsible for passing hundreds of thousands of classified Defense Department communications to WikiLeaks, was convicted in 2013 of violating the US Espionage Act. She served jail time for this offense. In the United States, Special Counsel Robert Mueller, who investigated election hacking in reference to the 2016 presidential election, has also investigated WikiLeaks and its part in election hacking because it published e-mails that were illegally procured from the US Democratic Party headquarters during the run-up to the election. Edward Snowden, the former Central Intelligence Agency contractor who leaked information to make Americans and Europeans aware of the extent of US government surveillance of their communications, has sought political asylum in Russia as he would likely be charged under the Espionage Act if he returned to the United States.

CONCLUSION

As we have seen in this chapter, the brave new world of cyberspace presents both new challenges and opportunities as well as new variants of old challenges and opportunities. For criminologists, the advent of cybercrime represents a new challenge—as existing crimes can now be carried out more quickly, across greater distances, utilizing mechanisms that leave little to no trace. At the same time, the internet's advent has also given birth to new types of crimes, including financial crimes and identity theft. The risk associated with the rise of both types of crimes has, however, led to genuine global commitments to work together cooperatively to combat these crimes and their effects upon nations and their citizens. In the conclusion to this text, we explore the ways in which new technologies—from quantum computing to the advent of artificial intelligence—will present even more challenges in the field of criminology.

QUESTIONS FOR DISCUSSION

1. How can states deal with attribution and enforcement of internet crimes when different states have different and/or conflicting laws on the matter?

   a. Can or should states appeal to "universal rights"?

2. Manufacturers and consumers frequently think about trade-offs when deciding how to manufacture or purchase internet-enabled devices. For example, securing all internet-enabled devices to the highest degree possible might make them prohibitively expensive and inaccessible to individuals in the developing world. It might also result in a significant loss of consumer privacy.

   a. In thinking about securing devices and combating crime, should safety be the only concern, or do concerns for safety have to be balanced against other competing interests, such as equity, value, fairness, and accountability?

3. Do you believe that individuals behave differently in cyberspace than they do in real life? In what ways? What, if anything, can be done to cause people to behave in a socially responsible way in cyberspace?

KEY TERMS

Botnet 183
Cyber threat intelligence program
  (C-TIP) 170
Cyberweapons 180

Hacktivist 167
Psychological operations
  (PSYOPS) 180

FOR FURTHER READING

Bannon, S. "The Tao of 'the DAO' or: How the Autonomous Corporation Is Already Here." Tech Crunch. https://techcrunch.com/2016/05/16/the-tao-of-the-dao-or-how-the-autonomous-corporation-is-already-here/.

Braman, S. *Change of State: Information, Policy and Power* (Cambridge, MA: MIT Press, 2009), 142.

Finnemore, M., and B. D. Hollis. "Constructing Norms for Global Cybersecurity." *The American Journal of International Law* 110, no. 3 (2016): 425–479.

Manjikian, M. *Cybersecurity Ethics: An Introduction* (New York, NY: Routledge, 2018).
See Chapter 6 on intellectual property.

Mason, G., and N. Czapski. "Regulating Cyber-Racism." *Melbourne University Law Review* 41, no. 1 (2017): 324.

8

PRIVATE ACTORS IN CYBERSPACE

Learning Objectives

At the end of this chapter, students will be able to do the following:

1. Define the following terms: *corporate social responsibility*, *net neutrality*, *gatekeeping*, *active/passive global ethics*, *data monopoly*, *capabilities approach*, and *natural monopoly*.

2. Apply the uniqueness debate to argue that technology actors either do or do not have unique ethical responsibilities within the international system in comparison to other types of corporations.

3. List economic and political objections to the development of monopolies, and argue for or against breaking up Facebook.

4. Compare and contrast the evolution of US-based Facebook and China-based Alibaba in terms of their relationship to government and their understanding of national responsibilities.

In this chapter, we consider how nonstate actors have helped build and administer cyberspace. International relations theorists have long noted that international relations are no longer solely the province of states as actors. In recent years, analysts have identified transnational advocacy networks in which nonstate actors reach across national borders to engage in activism. A transnational advocacy network is "those actors working internationally on an issue, who are bound together by shared values, a common discourse and dense exchanges of information and services."[1] Transnational advocacy networks include among their members nongovernmental organizations, research and advocacy organizations, foundations, the media, and religious organizations. Transnational advocacy networks often play a crucial role in articulating concerns previously identified within the international system (from the importance of ending the use of landmines during wartime to the need to combat gender-related abuses like female genital mutilation or child marriage). In some instances, a transnational advocacy network may be seen as pursuing policies at odds with the policy preferences of state actors, or they may even embarrass states internationally by calling attention to state actions not previously well-known.

At the same time, transnational corporations also play a role in international politics. Here analysts often focus on issues of corporate social responsibility in considering how a corporation carrying out trade or mining activities in a developing country, for example, might consider the political consequences of these economic decisions on local, regional, and international levels of analysis.

Policy makers have also begun grappling with the increasingly large role that private corporations and private actors play in the provision of cybersecurity and internet governance. As the revelations by Edward Snowden made clear, the US government in particular had contracted out many of the surveillance functions that it sanctioned to defense contractors, often because the government itself lacked the necessary technological expertise and manpower to carry out these functions itself.[2] In addition, the maintenance of the hardware that runs the internet, including undersea data pipelines, is administered almost exclusively by private-sector actors like international telecommunications providers. The contracting out of state functions is not unique to cyberspace. Indeed, in the period since 9/11, private defense contractors have played a variety of roles in combat and combat support actions in both the Iraq and Afghanistan conflicts. But some policy makers have been critical of what they see as a blurring of lines between state and private-sector activities. They ask if private-sector actors involved in cybersecurity or military security actually have the same values and priorities as the state does. They also suggest that private actors are less accountable than states might be in the event that a threat to national security emerges and is not satisfactorily addressed.

Consider, for example, a terrorist incident that occurred in San Bernardino, California, in 2016, when an employee and his wife carried out a fatal workplace shooting. In the incident's aftermath, a US court ordered the Apple corporation to "break into" one of the dead terrorist's cell phones so that the US Federal Bureau of Investigation could access its information. (A private company was eventually able to get into the system, so the suit was withdrawn.) In the San Bernardino case, some politicians suggested that companies making devices like cell phones should be required to build in a "back door" that would allow governments to access communications in situations like terrorism. But it was (and still is) unclear what the legal responsibility of a private corporation was in providing cybersecurity, particularly because Apple regarded itself as an international rather than an American corporation. When Apple objected to working with federal authorities to unlock the terrorist's cell phone, some policy makers accused Apple of being unpatriotic and of valuing the profit motive over safeguarding US national security.[3]

The question of whether companies like Apple and even Facebook are American or international companies—and whether they owe allegiance to their customers or to their host nation—came to a head in 2016. In 2016, Facebook was accused of having utilized its power—either wittingly or unwittingly—to aid Russia in interfering in the US presidential elections. In February 2018, Robert Mueller, the White House special counsel investigating Russia's role in the election, arrested thirteen Russians for having engaged in electoral interference in US social media including Facebook, Twitter, and Instagram. In his report to the US Congress, Mueller showed that a Moscow-based "troll farm" named the Internet Research Agency had created fake Facebook pages with names like Blacktivist, Defend the 2nd, and Secured Borders where they posted information aimed at changing voters' opinions. Some estimates are that 150 million people were exposed to this content. A related scandal broke in March 2018. The Cambridge Analytica scandal showed that Republican presidential candidate and now President Trump and his Republican advisers had hired the Cambridge Analytica consulting firm, which was able to utilize user data from Facebook to create targeted advertisements sent to 87 million people. Facebook users were unaware that their data was being used in this way.

WHAT IS A PLATFORM?

In 2018 congressional hearings about these events, Mark Zuckerberg, Facebook's founder, argued that Facebook is not actually a news provider but is rather a platform hosting content created by others, such as quizzes and online shopping opportunities. Zuckerberg compared Facebook to the computer operating system Microsoft Windows, arguing that Windows was not responsible for content that anyone created using the program. The same software, he argued, could be used to write a terrorist manifesto or a poem. The impetus to use it wisely thus rested with the user, not the platform's creator. Windows itself did not produce content, nor did it have rules governing what people could do with the software or the sorts of activities that they could engage in with it.[4] Zuckerberg thus argued that Facebook did not have a responsibility to police the content that was on the platform. Although Facebook knew that large amounts of targeted presidential advertising in 2016 was being purchased by individuals with .ru, or Russian internet addresses, his corporation did not feel a responsibility to investigate this further or to alert US authorities.

Here some analysts questioned whether Zuckerberg should have conceptualized of himself as an American whose primary loyalty would be to US national security or as an international businessman. Facebook is currently being investigated by the Federal Bureau of Investigation, the US Securities and Exchange Commission (SEC), the US Department of Justice, and the US Federal Trade Commission. It is also being investigated by a number of foreign governments, including Australia, Belgium, and the United Kingdom.

In addition, some groups, like the Freedom from Facebook coalition, have asked the US government to undertake anti-trust legislation to break up what they see as a monopoly on information. In an analysis of the situation, Osnos quotes Leslie Berlin, a historian of technology who asks, "Should (Facebook) be the arbiter of truth and decency for two billion people? Nobody in the history of technology has dealt with that."[5]

In this chapter, we consider the many legal, political, and ethical challenges that arise when states are no longer the only actors involved in administering cyberspace.

WHAT ARE TECHNOLOGY ACTORS?

In this chapter and the following one, we examine the role that technology actors play in international relations through considering three types of activities they engage in: the provision of cybersecurity, the provision of information, and the provision of communications.

But what separates these actors from other types of private corporations that have participated in international relations in the past? What is unique about technology actors?

First, the scope of this company's reach is unprecedented. A recent analysis of the Facebook notes that it "has as many adherents as Christianity," with its more than 2.2 billion members.[6] Facebook, along with Google, Amazon, and Apple, has been described as dominating the internet, with a combined stock value larger than the gross domestic product of France.[7] These corporations owe some of that influence to their positions as monopolies. There is no real competitor to an international platform like Facebook, Twitter, or Instagram, although some nations have attempted to create national equivalents. Today, analysts debate whether a company that has a monopoly position as the sole provider of some commodity or service (such as serving as a communications platform) also has unique responsibilities as a monopoly player in that space. Taddeo, for example, argues that online service providers today play a unique role in shaping the information environment as well as in influencing people's experiences within it. For this reason, she argues, as technology actors, they have a unique set of responsibilities because they need to consider not only the ethics of their own actions but the effects that such actions might have on the information environment.[8]

Here, we can invoke international relations theory to ask whether Facebook now plays a role in the international system similar to that which the United States played in the aftermath of World War Two. At that time, the United States recognized that it had a unique set of responsibilities not only to its own citizens but also globally. The United States was sometimes referred to as "the world's policeman" because it frequently became involved in peacekeeping and humanitarian missions that were arguably only of peripheral importance to US policy interests. In certain cases, US leaders understood that if America did not step in to respond to a global pandemic, the spread of AIDS or the devastation caused by a tsunami in Southeast Asia, no other nation would because only the United States had the economic and military manpower and logistics resources available to respond.

ARE TECHNOLOGY ACTORS COMPETITORS TO STATES WITHIN THE INTERNATIONAL SYSTEM?

Today analysts and policy makers worry about the inordinate amount of power that actors like Google and Facebook have. That is, if Google has a larger gross national product than Portugal, some analysts worry that its voice will eventually be louder than that of Portugal or other small states in venues like the United Nations. And on a local level or domestic politics level, citizens might feel powerless to use their abilities to petition their government to oppose zoning changes or housing laws, for example, when international corporations like Airbnb have more money and trained personnel whose job it is to lobby Congress to change rules regarding the provision of housing in a state or local area.

For this reason, some analysts describe technology actors as competitors to states in the competition for power within the global system. If we think back to the debate about multistakeholder forms of global governance versus the state sovereignty model, we will remember that some states, like Russia and China, have opposed adopting a multistakeholder model because they see it as a threat to state power. That is, they feel that the multistakeholder model of governance is a first step toward the evolution of an interstate system in which states are no longer the most important actors in the international system. They view the privileged position that states have held within the hierarchy of actors who participate in the international system since the Treaty of Westphalia in 1648 as under threat. As we look into the future, it is possible that states will simply be one player among many rather than serving as the standard-bearers and rule makers within the international system.

In addition, some analysts have expressed concerns about the ways in which monopoly corporations or "bigness" present a threat to democracy. We can compare the heads of corporations like Facebook to the "robber barons" who built America's railroads and America's electrical system in the 1800s. Here analysts point out that figures like the steel baron Andrew Carnegie and the railroads and shipping magnate Commodore Perry played an outsized role in the creation of America's industrial policies and priorities, advising presidents and working internationally—even though no voters ever elected either of these men.[9]

Other critics point to problems of transparency and accountability. In a democratic system, individuals elected to Congress or the presidency have an obligation to their constituents, the citizens who elected them. They are bound by the Constitution to share information with citizens and to obey the nation's laws. However, the heads of corporations are under no similar obligation to share information about the inner workings of their corporations, nor are they obligated to be responsive or attentive to the needs of their users or those who are affected by decisions made by the corporation. Today, internet activists in groups like the Electronic Frontier Foundation have expressed concerns that technology actors like Facebook can make decisions about how your personal data will be collected, used, and shared with little to no public discussion or input. The policies that a corporation may create regarding user privacy, what constitutes hate speech, or which groups are considered to be political extremists are not debated in Congress, and users do not have the option of voting a technology actor out of office if they disagree with the policies implemented. Indeed, technology actors like Twitter often do not have human operators who are directly tasked with making these decisions, relying instead on computer-generated algorithms and bots that decide which posts to delete or flag. Individual users may not be aware that such activities are occurring, and they may not understand the process by which such decisions are made.[10]

TECHNOLOGY ACTORS AS GATEKEEPERS

The CEOs of corporations like Google and Facebook have long been aware of the ethical responsibilities that they are seen to bear in the current environment. However, the corporate conceptualization of ethical responsibility may be different from the conception that policy makers have. The two groups use different language. Congressmen and congresswomen may speak of patriotism and one's duty to one's country in, for example, arguing that corporations should cooperate with the US government bodies in investigating the use of their platforms or equipment in terrorist incidents. CEOs, however, are more likely to speak about their duties to their customers and to their shareholders. They may also speak of the ways in which the obligations of patriotism do and do not fit into their corporate responsibilities.

In Chapter 2 of this textbook, we asked how a technology acquires its meaning and function in society. We described the ways in which a technology's meaning can evolve and change, as users reshape a technology, according to the social construction of technology model. The technology that eventually emerges may bear little resemblance to the designers' original vision for the technology and may surprise even the creators themselves with what it has become. This view helps explain why CEOs of platforms like Google and Twitter have responded as they have to calls for them to exercise greater social responsibility and even patriotism in shaping their corporate policies. Today, corporate CEOs are aware that their technologies are often necessary for the functioning of society and that, in many cases, their companies may be the sole providers of a particular type of technology (such as a ride-sharing platform). They are also aware of the roles that such technologies may play in shaping the information environment and thus the actions of people within that environment.

However, in many cases, technology actors have been reluctant to embrace this role, often stating that they felt unprepared to carry out the numbers and types of functions they were being asked to undertake. For example, today, social media organizations are often asked to serve as gatekeepers—deciding who may access a platform to participate in discussions and share information in an environment and deciding what sorts of information and discussions will be permitted within an information environment. Social media platforms are thus expected to regulate their information environments through making decisions (often automated through algorithms) that affect what information is available to users, the order in which information is displayed, as well as the types of information that may not be available. In addition, social media platforms can revoke a user's ability to participate in discussions on a particular social media channel. (This activity is referred to as deplatforming.) Today, users and groups may be deplatformed for a set period of time such as a twenty-four-hour period or may be permanently deplatformed.

Although regulating an online media environment is sometimes straightforward (e.g., in removing links to photos containing nudity or posts by terrorist organizations), it may also become a highly political undertaking. Here we can consider, for example, a decision by Facebook in 2018 to no longer allow posts by supporters of the US right-wing extremist group Proud Boys. This decision was seen by some group members as an unreasonable act of overreach by the organization because being banned from Facebook can make it harder for a group to share information, coordinate activities, or raise funds.[11]

In thinking about technology actors' political role today, we can ask: Should Facebook have the right to decide who is an extremist and which groups should be banned from expressing themselves on platforms both domestically or internationally, or is that a job for governments or perhaps the international community through an organization like the United Nations?

In addition, as gatekeepers, search engines like Google have been blamed for contributing to the rancor and polarization now present in American politics. Because Google's search engine algorithms learn what sorts of stories you like and then engage in custom tailoring, showing you more of them, over time, you will see more and more tailored results that reflect your own biases back to you. Thus, Republicans are more likely to see news from right-wing sources, whereas Democrats are more likely to see news from Democratic sources. Taddeo and Floridi note:

> Customer-tailoring of search results challenges the basic underpinning of a deliberative democracy insofar as it undermines the possibilities of sharing cultural background and experiences and reduces the chances of being exposed to sources, opinions and information that may support or convey different world views.[12]

TECHNOLOGY ACTORS AS PLATFORMS

In comparing the role of technology actors—in comparison to traditional economic actors like oil companies or agricultural concerns—it is important to define the term *platform* and to understand how a platform differs from a traditional corporation. A platform is like a virtual marketplace where customers and producers can come together to exchange services, with the platform administration then taking a percentage of the resulting economic transactions. That is, Uber and Lyft provide a platform through which drivers and riders can contract for transportation arrangements, but neither company actually owns any automobiles. Uber and Lyft do not service automobiles, nor do they inspect them—although they do run background checks on the individuals who serve as drivers for the service. Similarly, Airbnb is a platform through which individuals can list their apartments for rent or contract to rent other people's apartments. But Airbnb does not actually own any real estate.

Platforms thus differ from traditional corporations because arguably the platforms' owners do not have the same sort of stake in creating a stable system that a traditional corporation might. Here, Herder suggests that the platform model itself is fundamentally unethical. Utilizing Marxist terminology, he suggests that platforms profit off of the labor of others. By taking a percentage of the workers' profits, he argues, the platform robs the workers of the fruits of their labor, whereas the platform itself doesn't create anything. (Here we can think of Etsy, a platform that allows skilled artisans to market their crafts internationally. Although the crafters create, Etsy merely extracts a percentage of their labor without making anything itself.) Platforms have thus been accused of engaging in "rent seeking" through taking a percentage of the profits that others have earned without putting these profits back into the system in some way. Furthermore, they can be seen as limiting the worker's bargaining power because they tend to have a monopoly on the services for which they serve as platforms. Because Lyft and Uber can be seen as setting the rates for transportation, it thus becomes more difficult for any single worker to ask for a higher rate for his or her services.[13] At the same time, however, a platform like Airbnb can be described as "democratizing" because it allows people to profit off of selling a good or service (like a spare room in a house) for which they otherwise might not find a buyer. In addition, it allows individuals to trade directly with one another, thereby bypassing the larger, more established vendors of lodging such as a hotel, which might charge a higher price and also not be amenable to bargaining for that price.

Policy makers have praised platforms for fulfilling a need through providing a quick and efficient means of creating additional housing options, for example, in areas that might have a housing shortage. However, they have also been accused of violating local zoning ordinances as well as leading to shortages of more traditional housing (like monthly and yearly leases) in areas where homeowners can command high prices for temporary housing.

Critics argue that whereas a local landlord might also be a member of the community, and therefore cares about issues like keeping up the appearance of one's property, making sure that safety rules are followed, or making decisions that would lead to a community maintaining its home price values over time, a platform is not local and has no local stake in the community. A corporation that is led purely by profit motives, they argue, is at base utilitarian. But it is unable to consider larger issues like the ways in which a corporation might contribute to a community or the provision of collective goods over the long term.

This utilitarian ethos is evidenced in an internal Facebook memo. The document states:

> Maybe it costs a life by exposing someone to bullies. Maybe someone dies in a terrorist attack coordinated on our tools. And still we connect people. The ugly truth is that we believe in connecting people so deeply that anything that allows us to connect more people more often is "de facto" good.[14]

The question for political scientists, however, is whether this utilitarian ethic is sufficient to drive the policies of powerful technology actors in a highly complex international environment today. Do corporations need more than a utilitarian ethic? Do they need a foreign policy?

TECHNOLOGY ACTORS, RESPONSIBILITY, AND LIABILITY

In considering technology actors' roles and responsibilities in the international political system, both American domestic and international legislation are vague regarding the legal, political, and ethical liability that private corporations have in situations where people's rights are violated or negative consequences accrue from their actions. It is also not clear whether and under what circumstances these actors are liable—legally and ethically—for the consequences of their actions in cyberspace.

That is, states' legal responsibilities within the international system are clearly specified in treaties with other states as well as in the founding documents of organizations like the United Nations. The responsibilities that states have to their citizens domestically are spelled out in the United States in documents like the Constitution and the Bill of Rights. And in both instances, there is a set of normative understandings that have evolved over hundreds of years that can be referred to if a dispute comes about regarding a state's rights and responsibilities.

In contrast, the responsibilities that corporations have to the international system, to the states where they are located, and to their customers are somewhat more ambiguous. There are no sets of binding international laws that regulate how corporations should behave within the international system, and many of the issues that technology actors in particular are facing within the current international system have no historic precedent. Some of these questions—like the degree to which a corporation should consider itself to be a "corporate citizen" with an obligation to the state and its citizens in a location where it does business—have been asked previously in other settings. However, other issues are new and with few historic precedents. In addition, some analysts argue that technology actors themselves are fundamentally new and different from other types of corporate actors that might have preceded them.

As we consider the responsibilities of corporate actors in cyberspace, we can consider the words of Facebook's CEO, Mark Zuckerberg, who famously stated that Facebook never expected that its organization would come to play an important role in the provision of political information or that it would have the power to influence elections. (Remember, it was originally designed when he was in college as a way to increase his dating options by putting him into contact with more students on campus.) Facebook's political role is a role that neither he nor his corporation sought and that they did not want to play. He portrays himself as an unwilling leader, as his organization has strived to take on new types of political and social obligations that it often feels underequipped to handle and unaware of. However, as he notes, Facebook has nonetheless found it necessary to evolve policies regarding many different issues, both domestically within nations and internationally. Today, Facebook has divisions coordinating responses to messages that might be interpreted as suicide notes, divisions that take down explicitly violent and brutal content, and divisions analyzing and responding to messages that appear to advocate terrorism and genocide. Due to the sheer volume of content generated every day on platforms like Facebook, however (approximately 1 billion posts per day), a great deal of content monitoring is carried out through the application of algorithms that apply specific rules to classify content. Because the technology is still in its infancy, it is not always accurate.[15] Today, some academics feel that a technology company should not be the one to draw the line between which groups are mainstream and which are extremists.

The Example of Facebook's Targeted Advertising

As we consider these issues of responsibility and liability, we can consider an example. In August 2018, the Facebook corporation responded to a study undertaken by the state of Washington, following charges that Facebook allowed its advertising clients to engage in "targeted advertising." That is, individuals purchasing ad space on Facebook were allowed to specify which demographic groups could and could not see the advertising that would run. Therefore, it was possible to show advertisements for a new housing development to clients who were identified on Facebook as white while excluding users who were identified as African American or Hispanic.

If we think of Facebook as merely an economic entity, then we might argue that it can sell its products (e.g., advertising space) to anyone who wishes to buy them, and it should not be held ethically or legally accountable for the fact that some individuals chose to buy advertising space segmented by race or economic class. (Here, we could think of Facebook as similar to a weapons manufacturer who is not ultimately responsible for how someone uses a gun that they purchased from the manufacturer.)

However, we might hold Facebook to a higher ethical standard by claiming that they should have realized that this economic decision had political implications and that by selling racially targeted ads, they were contributing to the problem of housing inequity in the United States. Here, some critics would argue back, noting that it would be extremely expensive for most corporations to employ analysts to consider the political implications of every economic choice they offered consumers and to then make policies that ensure that there were not unexpected or unwanted political consequences that resulted from their economic decisions. That is, it would unfeasible to ask corporations to meet this standard.

But another analyst might say that Facebook is not just "any corporation" but a uniquely powerful corporation with a unique ability to affect politics domestically and internationally. Thus, Facebook has a unique responsibility to consider how its product might be used to influence an election, start a riot, or affect people's housing choices. Thus far, participants in US congressional hearings on subjects like election meddling have put forth this "unique responsibility" argument, and Facebook has responded by committing resources to set policies on issues ranging from what sorts of speech on the platform constitute hate speech to what sorts of political issue advertising should be allowed. However, this issue is far from resolved.

Distinguishing Ethical and Legal Responsibilities

Here, we can distinguish between a company's ethical responsibilities and its legal responsibilities. The term *normative* refers to what an individual or corporation "should do" as a matter of principle. When speaking about a company's ethical responsibilities, we can refer to their normative agenda, or statement of principles that specifies what they should do in an ideal situation. Normative agendas can be more subjective, with what a company should do subject to a variety of competing explanations and values. In contrast, the legal responsibilities to which a company is subject are more straightforward.

Nonetheless, determining when a technology actor is actually legally liable for an action that occurs in cyberspace can be challenging. For example, we can ask if a service like Facebook should be held legally liable if individuals post hate speech on the site or if advertising sold on its site is found to have exercised undue influence on a country's national elections. Should a medium like Twitter be held legally liable if it is found that users have utilized its functionality to engage in transactions related to drug dealing or human trafficking? Should an ISP that provides web hosting services be held legally liable if a user is found to have set up a site featuring child pornography? What are Twitter's legal responsibilities if someone tweets that they intend to harm a public figure, like a senator or president? Today, these issues are particularly complicated because much of the data that users access and store are hosted not within a specific country but rather in a data cloud that can span multiple geographic distributions.

When Are Technology Actors Legally Responsible?

States can and often do establish laws granting technology actors immunity from prosecution for certain types of activities that take place on their systems. This is an acknowledgment that a technology actor cannot always know everything that takes place on a system, nor can it always predict what is likely to take place.

Most commonly today we see voluntary types of arrangements between states and technology actors in which states agree to participate in some form of cooperation with private actors and also acknowledge that these actors cannot be held liable for all of the consequences that might occur on their systems.

There are, however, two areas where the law is clear regarding the legal responsibilities of technology actors. Both in the United States and abroad, there are clearly defined legal understandings regarding a corporation's responsibility not to host material that violates copyright law as well as in situations where illegal activities like human trafficking or the sale of child pornography are taking place on its platforms, servers, or devices. Within American law, technology actors are subject to the provisions of two major laws, Section 230 of the US Communications Decency Act (1996) and Section 512 of the Digital Millennium Copyright Act (1998). Within Europe, technology actors are regulated by the Responsibility regime set up by EU Directive 2003/31/EC on e-commerce. This regulation states that "there is no general obligation to monitor the information which ISPs transmit or store, nor a general obligation actively to seek facts or circumstances indicating illegal activity." But once an ISP is informed about an activity, they can be held liable. That is, in specific circumstances, including possible trafficking in child pornography, as well as copyright infringement or intellectual property theft, ISPs are regarded as legally bound to act to combat these situations once they are informed of them. These laws recognize that ISPs and online service providers are merely intermediaries and not producers of this content. Therefore, their responsibility includes complying with notice and takedown procedures and acting promptly to remove and disable access to copyrighted material. However, in neither instance is the ISP required to, for example, set up its own police force to investigate whether such things are occurring or to act preemptively to keep them from occurring.[16]

The issue regarding the responsibilities of private actors, including platforms, for policing the content on their sites is far from resolved, however. As of 2019, the European Union was still working out the details of the European Copyright Directive.[17] Here, much of the debate centers on Article 13, which details how platforms in particular should act to prevent copyright infringements on materials that are hosted on their platforms. This issue is particularly complicated today because it is not always clear if, for example, a meme that utilizes content found elsewhere is an entirely new creation or an unauthorized misuse of the original material. At present, Google has voiced opposition to some of the provisions of Article 13, whereas European politicians have stated their opposition to the role that platforms have had in providing input into this legislation, feeling that it overrides states' rights to resolve these issues as they see fit.

The Analogy of the Post Office

As we think about issues of legality and liability, we can consider an analogy. Taddeo suggests thinking about online service providers as similar to the post office. The post office merely moves packages of content from one place to another. It does not open the packages, nor is it considered to be liable if someone misuses the post office by, for example, mailing drugs or sending threatening letters by mail. Here, the post office is merely the conduit, whereas the immoral behavior belongs to the user. Indeed, the principle of net neutrality, as originally designed by the internet's developers, states that the internet itself is merely a conduit along which information travels. The ISP is not meant to interfere with the information that travels but rather to treat all information in a similar manner. That is, the ISP is not supposed to prioritize certain types of information, allowing it to travel faster or more directly, nor is it supposed to censor other types of information.

However, in recent years, national governments have begun to query whether net neutrality is a necessary principle for ISPs to adhere to or whether it has gradually become less relevant as the internet has changed. Most recently, the Body of European Regulators for Electronic Communications (BEREC) has suggested that internet access providers are not merely neutral vehicles or conduits for internet communications. Instead, they have suggested that certain types of traffic are already blocked or controlled and that in some instances ISPs should have the ability to treat different types of communications differently. (A similar debate is also taking place within the United States.) For example, a hospital's medical information might in the future travel at a different speed than, for example, someone's download of a video, because it has priority. That is, it is possible that net neutrality will someday be replaced by principles of content discrimination, including agreements among states to allow content among them to travel more efficiently. However, for ISPs to discriminate among content on their services, to treat it differently, they would be required to open the information and be aware of its content. This, according to some analysts, makes it likely that ISPs' liability will increase in the future.[18]

In addition to complying with state and regional level legislation, many social media actors today have also come together in voluntary groups to engage in the process of self-regulation. Just as banks may come together to regulate the banking and securities industry, or insurers may band together to regulate the insurance industry, companies like AOL, Apple, Dropbox, Facebook, Google, LinkedIn, Microsoft, Twitter, and Yahoo have come together to create the Reform Government Surveillance (RGS) group. This group seeks to create an industry-wide set of understandings regarding appropriate surveillance as well as to work together with the state to enforce and legislate these understandings.[19] That is, whereas private corporations do not act as lawmakers, they can nonetheless act as regulators—establishing rules and norms that affect how people behave. In the cyberspace arena, private actors can use code to create certain types of online environments and to administer these spaces, allowing certain types of actions and disallowing others.

WHAT IS CORPORATE SOCIAL RESPONSIBILITY?

Thus far, we have focused on the legal liabilities of technology actors. But what moral and ethical responsibilities do these actors have within the international system? What responsibilities do global technology actors have toward the international system, including those members of the international system in the developing world? The notion that corporations should use a wider lens to examine their role in the world, and that they should think about who—beyond their shareholders—might be affected by their business decisions is not of course new. It has long been acknowledged that corporations' economic decisions have political ramifications and that citizens can be affected by those decisions.

Corporate social responsibility is defined as "voluntary activities by private business that claim to promote societal welfare ... beyond any benefits of economic activity per se."[20] The literature on corporate social responsibility describes corporations as having three types of obligations: They have an ethical obligation to "do the right thing," they have an economic obligation to maximize corporate profits for their shareholders, and they also have an obligation to behave as "corporate citizens."[21]

Corporate social responsibility is often conceptualized primarily as a negative responsibility. That is, corporations are asked to think about actions they can take to prevent harms to the environments where they operate, for example. It may also mean creating an ethical workplace where, for example, employees are able to conduct their business activities free from sexual harassment or other forms of bullying.[22]

CRITICAL ISSUES

CRITICAL ISSUES: INTRODUCING THE BAT: MONOPOLY TECHNOLOGY ACTORS IN CHINA

Thus far, we have examined only technology actors who began operations in the United States. But not all powerful technology actors were born in the United States. We now examine three of China's most powerful technology actors, the BAT. BAT is an abbreviation for three of the leading technology actors currently operating in China. Baidu is China's leading search engine. Alibaba is an online commerce platform that acts like "the Chinese Amazon," and Tencent is a leading messaging and online gaming platform.

The term *monopoly* has been applied to each of these companies, with the term *duopoly* sometimes used to describe Tencent and Alibaba together. Each actor also has additional holdings beyond its technology platform. Alibaba has a significant footprint within the financial services industry today, whereas Tencent has a number of related businesses within its portfolio, including a movie studio.

A Symbiotic Relationship between China's Government and Chinese Technology Actors

BAT's evolution shows that there is more than one way to become a powerful technology actor within the international system. The successful rise of the

BAT is particularly striking because all three arrived somewhat late to the game in contrast to their American and international counterparts. Whereas eBay, the American auction firm, was well established during the e-commerce revolution of the late 1990s, all three Chinese actors began building in earnest only in the mid-2000s. So how were they able to compete, driving their rivals out of the marketplace and capturing the huge Chinese market share for themselves?

One important factor here is the close relationship that all three actors have with the Chinese government. Whereas Google and Facebook began their rise largely free from governmental intervention and support, actors like Baidu worked closely with the Chinese government as they grew their customer base and functionality.

As noted, China came late to the game of e-commerce and social media. Despite the e-commerce revolution internationally in the 1990s, China did not begin opening its markets to significant foreign investment until 2001, when it joined the World Trade Organization. Prior to the signing of that agreement, Chinese firms had a significant advantage in capturing Chinese market share. China is thus said to have had a protectionist economic policy that favored domestic firms over their international competitors prior to 2001. In addition, critics argue that whereas World Trade Organization rules state that foreign and domestic actors should be treated equally with regard to doing business in a nation, China actually favored Chinese rivals over foreign actors attempting to do business in China.[23]

Because foreign firms did not have a long history of doing business with China, their start-up costs were significant, and they had much to learn about the new environment.[24] In the initial stages, then, Chinese firms moved quickly to utilize this advantage. By establishing themselves in their internet environment from the beginning, they thus had a first-mover advantage.

As a result, by 2003, Alibaba began to take a commanding lead in the Chinese internet. From the beginning, Alibaba (and its founder, Jack Ma) specifically saw itself as in competition with Western and other foreign internet actors in China, including eBay. Alibaba therefore created its own online payment system to compete with PayPal, eBay's online payment system. The Alibaba payment system, called Taobao, was offered to businesses wishing to conduct transactions via Alibaba free for three years. This payment system was seen as a key strategic tool for Alibaba's growth because China's official banking system had no structure for making online payments. Alibaba, with the cooperation of the Chinese government, formed alliances with leading banks and financial institutions throughout

(Continued)

(Continued)

China.[25] In 2013, again with the support of the Chinese government, Alibaba began a money market fund for Chinese investors. By 2014, the US company eBay had closed its Chinese operations.[26]

China's alliance with Baidu, the internet search engine, allowed the government to monitor information being disseminated on the internet as well as to control it. As Baidu was building a market share, China's government worked to interrupt Google's operations in China. First, it banned the Google.cn domain. When China moved its operations to Hong Kong, where Chinese citizens could still access it, the Chinese government intervened, sending searchers not to the Google site but to Baidu.[27] Later, both Google and Amazon withdrew from operations in China.

As the examples of Alibaba and Baidu show, the relationship between China's firms and its government can be described as symbiotic. The state implemented protectionist policies that created a space favoring Chinese firms, and then the BAT actors acted preemptively to create a Chinese solution to the need for internet commerce and social media sites.

Chinese Tech Actors as Regulators

As these two examples show, for these BAT actors, the question of corporate ethics and legal and social responsibilities is answered differently than it is for a company like Google. All three BAT actors conceptualize of themselves as international actors but with an explicit loyalty to Chinese values and to the government of China. And although Google and Facebook only reluctantly embraced their political roles and their responsibility to act as regulators to administer the online environment, this is a role that Chinese actors like Baidu and Alibaba have explicitly sought out.

Chen and Ku argue that China has lagged in its development of state regulations in regard to internet functionality, instead relying upon the BAT actors themselves to act as rule makers or hegemons in Chinese cyberspace. In a sense, these actors set the regulation, and then the Chinese government formally ratifies the arrangements and alliances that these firms have already created (such as legalizing the arrangement between Alibaba and Chinese banks only after the relationships had been established). This arrangement again favors Chinese firms and makes it more difficult for international actors wishing to work in China as well as for any firms wishing to set up businesses once the initial regulations have already been established.

They thus describe the Chinese internet economy as "half open and half closed" because it is legally open to all economic actors, but in reality, it favors some actors over others, including those that are already established.

In describing how the BAT firms in particular have worked with the Chinese government, Chen and Ku write:

> They create public goods to fuel the industry growth and establish rules to maintain orderly trade on the internet. They follow the policy winds closely and always act before the government to foreclose possible intervention. When disputes arise with the government, they compromise to preserve their core business interests.[28]

Monopoly Practices by Alibaba

The practices utilized by China's BAT actors resemble techniques that monopolists have used in other settings to gain market share by driving out competitors. First, Alibaba engaged in "price fixing." That is, it held the prices of its banking and cash transfer services artificially low for a period of several years, enabling it to gain market share in the financial services sector while also driving out competitors from this space.

In addition, Alibaba moved quickly to absorb competitors and, with the Chinese government's blessing and support, moved into the financial sector. Today, Alibaba's payment service (Alipay wallet) serves as a payment service not just on the Alibaba platform but for many other services as well. And the national shipping infrastructure created by Alibaba is now also utilized by many other services. Finally, Alibaba is taking on state-run banks, attempting to compete and perhaps even drive them out of business through offering lower interest rates and new types of financial products.

Alibaba in particular is also seeking to become a regional economic power, expanding its financial services to other nations in Asia and concluding agreements with other East Asian companies for carrying out data storage and processing.[29]

Pros and Cons of the Chinese Approach

As this history illustrates, with the support of the Chinese government, the BAT moved quickly to capture market share for their products, took on social and political responsibilities, and in many cases provided vital services for consumers in China and throughout Asia. Yet they are not without their critics. What is wrong with the Chinese approach?

Critics have accused the Chinese government of providing preferential treatment to Chinese technology actors and even of colluding with these actors

(Continued)

(Continued)

to create conditions such that international competitors would be driven out of China. The preference for Chinese technology actors is seen as part of a longer-range Chinese strategy aimed at creating a "Chinese internet," which would be governed by Chinese values and laws, rather than allowing China—and China's citizens—to participate more broadly in the internet as an international phenomenon. Some ethicists have thus criticized these firms for cooperating with China's government in terms of implementing censorship and supporting surveillance of China's citizens.

We can also consider the problems monopoly actors present to the internet and to international economies as a whole. Is it possible that a company like Alibaba (currently valued at $2.5 billion) has become "too big to fail"? As noted, Alibaba and Tencent, like Facebook, are also not merely Chinese companies but rather large regional companies doing business in Thailand, Vietnam, and elsewhere in the region. Thus, their policies will have implications far beyond just China. That is, if Alibaba's interests in China collapsed, could it affect the whole economy, not just in China but throughout the region?

Finally, although at present these companies appear to have the same interests and agenda as the Chinese government, it is possible that in the future, the alliance of these firms and the government could split or waver. In particular, if Alibaba's founder, Jack Ma, decided at some point to challenge the Chinese government's stance on the cyber one-party state, he would be in a strong position to do so. Sender, an analyst for London's *Financial Times,* argues that currently most Chinese internet companies are administered by their original founders, who likely grew up under communism. However, she wonders what these companies may look like if their founders are succeeded by a new type of leader from China's new generation.[30]

In closing, the evolution of these actors within China suggests that it may indeed be possible for states to have an internet that is efficient and functional without it being international or open to the world. China's BAT actors thus provide an alternate view to the descriptions provided earlier in this chapter of Facebook's corporate ideology, ethos, and practices—suggesting that Facebook's evaluation to its present state was not actually inevitable but rather the product of a series of choices.

Sources

Beilinski, T. "Competition between Chinese and US companies in the Internet Market." *International Studies, Interdisciplinary Political and Cultural Journal* 22, no. 1 (2018): 137–152.

Chen, T., and Y. Ku. "Rent-Seeking and Entrepreneurship: Internet Startups in China." *Cato Journal* 36, no. 3 (2016): 659–678.

Gough, N., "Tops in E-Commerce, Alibaba Is Now Taking on China's Banks." *New York Times* (September 18, 2014). https://dealbook.nytimes.com/2014/09/18/tops-in-e-commerce-alibaba-is-now-taking-on-chinas-banks/.

Sender, H. "China Fears Threaten the Bullish Case for Tencent and Alibaba." *Financial Times*, June 16, 2017. https://www.ft.com/content/ac7d1120-51ba-11e7-a1f2-db19572361bb.

Shim, Y., and D. Shin. "Analyzing China's Fintech Industry from the Perspective of Actor-Network Theory." *Telecommunications Policy* 40 (2015): 168–181.

Zacks Equity Research. "Zacks Investment Research: Alibaba (BABA) to Expand in Asia with 2 New Data Facilities." *Newstex Finance and Accounting* (blogs). Last modified June 12, 2017. https://www.zacks.com/stock/news/263881/alibaba-baba-to-expand-in-asia-with-2-new-data-facilities.

Corporate Social Responsibility or Global Business Ethics?

By many objective measures, a multinational corporation like Google scores well in terms of corporate social responsibility. Google in particular has been awarded high marks for its commitment to environmental sustainability goals. Buildings are frequently built to demanding environmental specifications and may use recycled materials. Google also strives to implement sustainability practices to reduce its carbon footprint.[31] Google is also highly rated in its commitment to encouraging a diverse workforce. It awards scholarships to women students to combat gender disparities in technology leadership and has been particularly supportive of its lesbian, gay, bisexual, and transgender (LGBT) workforce.

Yet at the same time, Google has struggled, like many multinational corporations, with articulating a strategy and set of values with regard to its larger international commitments, including commitments in the areas of human rights, equity, and social justice. For this reason, it is useful to distinguish between corporate social responsibility and global business ethics. The lens of global business ethics is a relatively recent development, and those who ask questions about global business ethics are particularly interested in how corporations can act ethically in a globalized world, where their customers and employees may come from diverse nations with diverse cultures and cultural and social values. Global business ethicists also strive to help corporations answer questions regarding their commitments to their home nation and the larger global community.

Here, the struggles that global technology companies face are not unique. Other types of businesses, from global energy corporations to global manufacturing concerns, have articulated similar concerns. Here, we can distinguish between passive global ethics goals (i.e., seeking not to harm the environment in which one operates) and active global ethics goals (i.e., seeking to improve the arena in which one operates through acting proactively). Economist Jeffrey Sachs refers to active global ethics as "being part of the solution," noting that it may involve taking on new roles and responsibilities that are not directly related to one's marketplace activities. He writes, "This does not mean to turn the company upside down or into a charitable institution, but rather to identify the unique contribution the company may make as part of a broader effort to solve a major social challenge."[32] For this reason, multinational corporations in particular are sometimes referred to as "politicized actors."

Echoing the global ethics approach, Taddeo argues that technology actors have inherent moral responsibilities due to the power that they have to affect the information environment. She argues that they should strive to perform their tasks according to the principles of justice, fairness, and efficiency as well as to link their values to those of the information society. Here, Taddeo and Floridi argue that actors like search engines and ISPs have the same obligations to all users regardless of the environment in which the actor is operating.[33] They argue that ethics are universal and that the obligation that a technology actor has as a gatekeeper–to provide users with free, high-quality, unbiased information—should be the same everywhere in the world. In contrast, Brenkert argues that there are situations in which people in business must confront the possibility that they must compromise some of their important principles or values to preserve other ones.

Today, many ethicists utilize a "capabilities approach" to describe how both states and corporations involved in international affairs should support activities that allow individuals throughout the world, including the developing world, to maximize their human potential. The capabilities approach, initially expressed by philosopher Martha Nussbaum in 2000, describes ten capabilities or opportunities that every political order should strive to provide for citizens. She argues that every individual in a society should be provided with basic capabilities such as the ability to live a healthy life, to express one's opinions and thoughts, to have one's own beliefs, and to live a life that is meaningful. Many of these capabilities can be found in international policy documents like the UN Universal Declaration of Human Rights. States and corporations concerned about ethics are thus asked to consider how their actions can lead to an expansion or decrease an individual's capabilities as a result of their policies.

Technology actors might thus be asked to contribute (often financially) to programs that endeavor to make internet access available to everyone globally, including those who are poor and in the developing world. Technology actors may also be asked to contribute voluntarily to efforts such as those aimed at making technology accessible to citizens, including those who are elderly or disabled. Technology actors may also be enlisted in international efforts to accomplish goals such as combating hate speech including racism, anti-Semitism, and misogyny on the internet. Here we can consider the activities that the Gates Foundation (created by Microsoft founder Bill Gates) is involved in, actively seeking to combat child mortality in the developing world, for example, through making vaccines and medical care more widely available.

Some of the capabilities that Nussbaum describes appear to align almost exactly with missions of social media platforms like Facebook or Twitter. For example, Nussbaum argues that states and corporations should work to nurture people's capabilities for affiliation, or the ability to create and live in communities. The capability for affiliation has been described as being able to live with and toward others, to recognize and show concern to other human beings, to engage in various forms of social interaction; to be able to imagine the situation of another and to have compassion for that situation, to have the capability for both justice and friendship.[34]

However, the capabilities approach is a set of ideals, and achieving and supporting these ideals may not always be possible. Indeed, corporate policies aimed at increasing citizen capabilities are sometimes at odd with other corporate goals, such as the maximizing of profits. Thus, an actor might not be able to achieve a goal due to feasibility concerns.

Can a Corporation Be Profitable and Socially Responsible?

Today, some political scientists are critical of the corporate social responsibility approach in particular, feeling that it falsely claims that a corporation can fulfill different and opposing missions. They see a conflict of interest between a corporation's responsibilities to its shareholders and its responsibilities to other actors, like those affected by its policies. They ask, for example, whether it makes sense to ask a gambling corporation to simultaneously conduct corporate social responsibility activities aimed at helping people identify their gambling addictions and to seek treatment. If the casino wants to maximize profits through encouraging people to return and spend money there, then it makes little sense for them to identify some subset of people who should never return. These analysts argue that much of the discussion about corporate social responsibility doesn't address these fundamental conflicts that exist, nor does it acknowledge that there may be times where corporations will have to choose who to serve—their shareholders, their clients, or those who are harmed by their activities.[35]

Similarly, we might ask if technology actors like Google can simultaneously provide products to their users, provide value to their shareholders, and also uphold international human rights and US security interests. Is it possible that these values may in fact be in conflict with one another?

The Problem of Complicity

In considering corporate social responsibility issues for technology actors, we can also consider the issue of complicity. What happens, for example, when a company like Google is asked to share its data with a government for the purposes of ensuring national security, but there also exists the possibility that that same government might rob citizens of their capabilities for freedom of thought and expression through engaging in surveillance? In this situation, Google has not directly violated citizens' rights, but it could be seen to be guilty by association because it aided the government that took the citizens' rights. To what degree should corporations be able to anticipate possible violation of citizen rights, and what is their obligation to identify and prevent such violations?

Here we pause to consider two dilemmas that private corporations may face in deciding how to act in a socially responsible way. The first case takes place in Saudi Arabia, whereas the second takes place in China.

Case Study: Absher in Saudi Arabia

In the spring of 2019, Western readers became aware for the first time of the existence of an app for smartphones and tablets called Absher. The app, which has been available since 2015, can be purchased through Apple's and Google's online app stores. Absher allows Saudi citizens to interface with the Ministry of the Interior of Saudi Arabia for the purposes of conducting online transactions.

Among the transactions that Saudi citizens could engage in using Absher were those related to the cultural and political practice of male guardianship. In Saudi Arabia, until quite recently, Saudi women were not allowed to obtain a passport without the permission of a male relative, and a male relative had to grant her permission before she could travel abroad. Thus, the app allowed male guardians (husbands for those women who are married and fathers or brothers for those who are unmarried) to carry out activities such as allowing or restricting their female relatives to renew their passports or to travel abroad. (The legislation allowing women to have access to their own passports and to travel abroad without a male's permission was amended in August 2019, granting women these rights.)[36]

In addition, the app tracked all of a user's trips outside of Saudi Arabia and, until recently, sent text messages to male guardians when women traveled abroad. To Western feminists, the app might seem like a way of facilitating or supporting human rights abuses because a male guardian can use such an app to track and restrict his wife's movements.

In thinking about the ethics of such an app, there are several questions to consider: Should developers of apps be willing to create apps that they believe might be utilized to engage in surveillance or the ability to deny citizens their right to mobility? Should Google and Apple refuse to sell such apps on their platforms due to the likelihood that they could be used to deny some citizens their rights?

Here, Human Rights Watch, an international nongovernmental organization suggested that Google was complicit in unethical behavior in agreeing to sell the app on its platform. They felt that Google should refuse to carry the app and that, furthermore, it should put pressure on Saudi Arabia to change these discriminatory practices.[37]

The UN Guiding Principles on Business and Human Rights suggest that companies should engage in due diligence before engaging in business practices abroad. Due diligence includes assessing the human rights violations that might occur as a result of these business practices.

Human Rights Watch also advises that companies need to be particularly careful every time they carry an app that is developed by or designed to interface with a government. They write:

> Companies should always assess apps to determine whether they may undermine or violate rights. . . . They should also revise their terms of service to prohibit apps expressly designed to violate rights and make

every effort to mitigate any human rights harms before making such apps available.[38]

However, other technology analysts argue that the app is merely a tool and that if there is an ethical issue, the ethical issue is that governments (and cultures) allow the creation of unequal sets of practices in which women, for example, have fewer rights than men. Indeed, they argue that men may be more likely to allow their wives the freedom to travel abroad if the paperwork to grant this freedom is simplified through the provision of an app.[39]

The Ethical Responsibility of Gatekeeping: Google's Policies in China

Next, we can consider the history of Google's activities in China. By 2000, Google had developed a Chinese-language version of its search engine widely used by China's citizens, although it was located on servers outside of China. By 2002, some of these users began reporting that some of their search results were being blocked and that the search engine was operating slowly (as the result of overlays that the Chinese government was attaching to the engine). Google became aware that China's government was blocking user access to information about certain politically sensitive topics. Because few people wanted to use the search engine, which now ran so slowly, Google had to decide whether to reconfigure the search engine so that it was located within China, and in conformance with Chinese government regulations, so that it would run quickly and be competitive with other search engines.

Initially, Google decided to conform with Chinese requirements, but it was quickly criticized by human rights groups like Reporters without Borders and Human Rights Watch. They accused Google of complicity in agreeing to conform to China's requirements.[40]

As Brenkert points out, what Google did might be morally suspect, but it was not illegal. As he notes, documents like the UN Declaration of Human Rights are not binding upon corporations because only states are parties to these agreements. He asks, thus, whether private organizations should be viewed as having a duty not to violate people's rights to freedom of information. Here, he also distinguishes between not standing up for someone's rights versus actively taking them away. He argues that Google merely did not prevent the Chinese government from engaging in censorship, which is not the same as engaging in censorship itself. However, it might still be seen as being complicit because it complied with the Chinese government's directives. Further, he argues that whereas the United Nations does not create binding obligations upon private corporations, it has nonetheless furnished them with guidance regarding how they might support human rights as part of ethical business practices.

However, other analysts argue that there is such a thing as a "permissible moral compromise." Thus, for example, some platforms might continue to do business with a repressive government like China's, arguing that even if users in China can only access an abridged or limited version of a search engine or online source, the users still receive more value from accessing that platform than they would if nothing were available.

Nonetheless, in 2010, Google announced that it was withdrawing from business operations in China. At that point, Google had been subjected to cyberattacks that were believed to have been carried out by China's government, aimed at securing information about Chinese citizens who China believed were engaging in anti-state activities.[41] Tan and Tan argue that much of Google's incentive to continue conducting operations in China, despite the need to comply with censorship, rested on what they saw as their duty to shareholders. China offered a large market with hundreds of millions of users, and shareholders may have seen it as fiscally irresponsible for Google to simply refuse to pursue such a lucrative business opportunity. Thus, they argue, Google was willing to accept mandatory state regulation and even to accommodate a repressive system. In doing so, Google placed its business ambitions over its moral principles and stated company philosophy. However, in the final analysis, Google made a decision that prioritized ethical and corporate responsibilities above purely monetary returns.

Thus far, technology actors have defined their moral positions regarding user rights themselves. Some corporations have continued to do business in China or Russia, whereas others have not. Thus far, there is no binding set of legal agreements regarding how corporations should weigh user rights, economic considerations, and broader international principles. Indeed, given that states themselves do not agree on these issues, it is difficult to see how an international consensus, which would then be binding upon corporations, would emerge.

Thus far in our analysis, we have considered the legal and normative responsibilities of technology actors in cyberspace. Now we turn to the legal and normative responsibilities that technology actors might be said to have toward the nations where they are headquartered. Is Google, in the final analysis, an international corporation or an American corporation, and should the United States expect to be able to influence its foreign policy or to expect that it would cohere with the foreign policy of the United States?

IS FACEBOOK A MONOPOLY, AND DOES IT NEED TO BE BROKEN UP?

A monopoly is a company that plays a leading role in controlling access to a product or service within a market. Monopolies can exist for a number of reasons: Sometimes, an early entrant into a market for a good or service will accrue an advantage that allows this company to play a leading role in steering how the market develops, driving out competitors as a result. A natural monopoly is said to exist when a company has a particular advantage—such as owning the land upon which a natural resource is located—that cannot easily be replicated by competing firms.

Finally, a monopoly may arise over time as companies engage in mergers. Some less-profitable companies may be bought or absorbed by a stronger competitor, and a strong company may also engage in business transactions that result in its establishing control over the original industry plus a number of peripheral or related industries. (For example, many analysts of the financial crisis that occurred in the United States in 2008 suggest that one of the root causes of this crisis was a situation in which many smaller banks failed and were absorbed by larger banks. The result, they argue, was a situation in which the remaining banks were "too big to fail." That is, the failure of a bank that affected a large percentage of America's economy would have been a disaster for the American economy. As a result, the US government was forced to bail out the large banks after they made poor financial decisions, including extending too many mortgages to individuals and corporations with bad credit.[42] In this scenario, the creation of a monopoly is seen as increasing risk to all participants in a market economy.)

Ethical Risks of Monopolies

But what's wrong with a company playing a leading position or "cornering the market" on a good or service? The larger a company is, the better positioned it is to deliver a good cheaply through economies of scale. And the more likely it is to create new innovations in the field because its budget for research and development might be larger.

However, one can identify both ethical and legal arguments against monopolies. Ethically, a monopoly can be seen as likely to create an inequitable situation. If one company owns all or most of a good or service, then this company can then engage in practices like price gouging, that is, raising prices for the desired good to a price that is as high as the market will bear. Monopolies are thus said to create inequities because some customers will be shut out and unable to access the good or service.

For example, we can think of a situation in which only one company is able to make a necessary drug or vaccine, and in which monopoly practices might mean that many people go untreated as they cannot afford the medicine. Or monopolies may be created, for example, after a natural disaster if other businesses have been destroyed or driven out of business. In situations like this, governments will frequently intervene rather than letting a free market set prices. The need to respond to social needs is seen as greater than the need for companies to be able to do business completely freely.

In addition, if there is only one company in which trained workers in the industry can work (e.g., auto workers or coal miners), then it is more difficult for those workers to bargain for a fair wage because there may only be one employer in a region. Monopolies are thus sometimes described as less accountable both to the governments of the states in which they work as well as less accountable to customers and employees. If a company has a preponderance of power in one sector, then it is less likely to need to form cooperative relationships with the government and indeed may seem like a competitor to the government. It may also be less likely to consider its corporate social responsibilities.

Monopolies, Duopolies, and Oligopolies

An **oligopoly** refers to a market situation in which there are only a few participants. In oligopolies, companies may band together to create a cartel, working together to fix artificially high prices for the good or service rather than engaging in healthy competition that would actually lower the price of the good.

For example, the gas shortage—and resulting high prices—that occurred in the United States in the 1970s under President Jimmy Carter was the result of the thirteen major oil-producing nations (Organization of Petroleum Exporting Countries [OPEC]) forming an export cartel. OPEC nations worked together to limit the amount of natural gas that was sold to Western nations.

Similar to an oligopoly, the term **duopoly** refers to a situation in which two companies own all or nearly all of the market for a product or service.[43] The existence of a duopoly is also seen as often leading to collusion between companies and the absence of a free market and healthy market competition.

Many nations, including the United States, have strict laws that limit the formation of monopoly situations. However, there is no binding international legislation that forbids the creation of cartels.

Monopolies and Duopolies in the Tech Industry

US government analysts have warned about the emergence of monopolies and duopolies in the tech sector since 2011. In that year, the US Federal Trade Commission raised concerns about Google's plans to acquire software and mobile phone companies.[44]

We can identify both ethical and legal arguments against allowing technology actors like Facebook or Google to acquire a monopoly position within the information economy.

Google and Facebook have been described as a duopoly in the provision of information to American citizens in particular. Some analysts worry that Google and Facebook have the ability to engage in collusion because they control a significant share of the information that Americans view daily through newsfeeds. The two leading companies often make specific agreements with content providers to feature their content in daily newsfeeds as well as selling advertising. Epstein believes that both providers favor liberal news outlets over conservative news outlets and worries that this can skew the news coverage available to American readers.[45]

Monopolies Pose a Security Risk

As Wu illustrates in his history of critical industries in the United States, the creation of a monopoly also poses a security risk. He argues that the Sherman Antitrust Legislation of 1890 was created as a result of the first Industrial Revolution, when technological advances in fields like electrification, hydroelectric power, railroads and other forms of public transportation often meant that there was a single powerful provider for these services.[46]

What's wrong with a single provider? Thinking back to the original military decisions that created the internet, we remember that initially military planners were trying to create redundancies. That is, they supported the creation of the internet as an alternate mode of communication if, for example, an enemy nation targeted the US telephone or telegraph system during wartime. The internet would then provide a backup system of communications, providing flexibility in the American response to an attack. However, if over time, the companies that provided internet telecommunications became centralized, then this military advantage would no longer exist. That is, if there are only one or two providers of a service that is essential (composing part of critical infrastructure), then an attack on that service can be particularly devastating as there are no other companies that provide redundancies to the system.

For this reason, the US government has, in the past, acted strongly and quickly to oppose the creation of mergers that would lead to centralization of services and the elimination of redundancies. One of the most well-known examples of such government action was the decision in 1984 by the US federal government to mandate the breakup of the Bell telephone company, which controlled much of the telephone market in the United Sates. The company was broken up into seven regional companies (known as the "baby bells"). This decision has been credited with leading to innovation in the telephone sector.[47]

The Uniqueness Question

As the examples of the banking crisis of 2008 and the breakup of "Ma Bell" in 1984 show, the situation that the United States faces at present—with the existence of a duopoly of technology actors—is not unique. And a government response that sought to limit the effects of a monopoly in the tech sector would also not be unique. Indeed, the duopoly in the tech sector is not the only monopoly currently existing. Currently, two credit card companies (Visa and Mastercard) control 80 percent of the payments market in both the United States and Europe. The European Central Bank has sought to take steps to break up this duopoly. Military planners also worry about the strength of Boeing and the dependence of the air industry on Boeing's Airbus airplane.

Finally, critics have identified **antitrust** issues with relation to other platforms in the sharing economy, including lodging provider Airbnb and transportation providers Uber and Lyft.[48] Both Germany's competition authority and the US Federal Trade Commission have raised questions related to competition between new and more established competitors as well as issues related to taxation and employment policy.[49]

We can also consider Amazon.com's position in the American and international marketplaces. Today regulators often consider whether a monopoly should be broken up by asking, "What is best for the consumer?" Khan argues that Amazon has for many years been able to present itself as a benevolent actor because its overall strategy is to sell a large quantity of merchandise cheaply. The low prices that consumers profit from are therefore seen as a reason to allow the monopoly to exist and for regulators to look the other way, even as Amazon has branched out into more and more service sectors, including supplying goods and services to clients like the US military.[50]

Historical Precedents: The Case of Microsoft

In thinking about how monopoly regulations apply in the technology sector, it is useful to look back to an early antitrust case that involved Bill Gates, the founder of Microsoft. In 2001, Washington, DC's, Circuit Court heard the case of *United*

States v. Microsoft Corporation. The case concerned arrangements that the Microsoft Corporation had made with stores and companies selling personal computers. In many instances, personal computers were sold with Microsoft Windows preinstalled as an operating system, and in some instances, it was extremely difficult for vendors or customers to uninstall Microsoft Windows. The US government worried that by steering consumers to adopt Microsoft Windows as their computer's operating system, consumers were being deprived of choice in a free market.

However, Microsoft won the case. In deciding the Microsoft case, judges described a **natural monopoly**—a situation in which one company naturally has the majority of shares in an industry due to built-in factors that are difficult to correct without unduly influencing a free market economy. In Microsoft's case, it did not make sense for computer companies to have multiple operating systems because a goal of each company was to provide resources that were interoperable or transferable among machines (e.g., being able to move files between one's home and office computer). Thus, Gates's legal team argued, it made sense to preinstall Microsoft Windows on most computers. Doing so wasn't forcing anyone to use Microsoft products but rather acknowledging that this was in fact what most people desired to do with their computers.

Lessons for Facebook and Other Technology Actors Today

What lessons does this case hold for states trying to regulate actors like Facebook today? Is Facebook a natural monopoly? Why or why not?

Some analysts argue that Facebook is actually a utility—a conduit for providing necessary services within a society. Just as societies depend on electricity or water to function, states now depend on Facebook to provide information in crisis situations, like a natural disaster. State and local governments use Facebook as a conduit to provide information to their citizens, and citizens depend on Facebook to access news and information.

However, states have previously stepped in to regulate utilities—particularly those that are considered part of critical infrastructure. States can inspect public and private utilities. Utility companies can be fined when safety violations occur, and states can implement strict procedures and protocols that must be followed for a utility to have a license to operate.

In recent years, states have begun using similar language to talk about regulating Facebook. Sifry suggests that states should have the right to "audit" Facebook in, for example, asking to see its financial records regarding to advertisements sold during the 2016 US presidential election cycle. He suggests that regulations could be put in place requiring Facebook to exercise due diligence in investigating who is purchasing election ads on its platforms and ensuring that only US actors should be allowed to purchase ads aimed at influencing US voters during an election cycle.[51]

The US Federal Trade Commission has also stepped in to examine complaints against Facebook related to privacy. In 2011, the FTC alleged that Facebook had violated Section 5a of the Federal Trade Commission Act. Facebook settled with the US government and promised to implement stricter regulations in which individuals would have to explicitly consent before their information was shared. Facebook could be fined if these terms are violated. [52]

Individual US states have also sought to regulate Facebook. The state of Missouri has laws against allowing teachers to contact their students on Facebook, which Facebook has been required to help enforce.[53]

Internationally, Facebook is subject to the regulations of the European Data Privacy Regulation (EDPR) legislation, and since September 2011, Facebook has implemented a voluntary code of conduct in Germany to protect user data. Canada and Ireland have also investigated Facebook for privacy complaints.

Should Facebook Be Broken Up?

In his history of social media, Chander describes "Facebookistan," which he portrays as an international actor. He argues that Facebook encompasses a community of 1 billion people, utilizing forty-nine national currencies, and that Facebook has its own de facto diplomats whose job it is to reach out to governments around the world.[54] He argues that it would be difficult for any one nation to attempt to regulate—or even break up—Facebook because of this international character.

Given these issues, it is difficult to see how the suggestions of those, like US presidential candidate Elizabeth Warren, who wish to break up Facebook could be implemented. And some analysts today ask: If we cannot trust Facebook to safeguard our data and privacy, why would we trust another, newer company that might have fewer highly trained employees and procedures in place to carry out these tasks?

In addition, it is possible that in the future, Facebook will not enjoy the same international monopoly. Already, Russia has its own platform, V Kontakte, which fulfills many of the same functions as Facebook. And Chinese-made social networking apps may play a similar function in Asia.

Although US regulators in particular are concerned about the ways in which foreign electoral interference could be conducted through platforms like Facebook, the best solution may be to have tighter regulations regarding these activities rather than seeking to break up the utility itself.

CONCLUSION

However, questions related to tech monopolies are likely to persist as technology continues to develop. In some cases, a technology company may come to occupy a monopoly position due to its unique ability to collect, store, command, or exploit data. Data has famously been referred to as "the new oil"; that is, data is a resource that is necessary to fuel almost every type of activity that occurs in the economic marketplace today. For this reason, perhaps in the future, we should worry not about monopoly actors but about so-called data monopolies.

In addition, we might worry about the fungibility of Facebook's monopoly power. There have been articles suggesting that Mark Zuckerberg is considering running for president, translating the authority that he has as a monopoly supplier of services into political power.[55] Both of these are interesting issues to consider in the future.

QUESTIONS FOR DISCUSSION

1. Imagine that you are the CEO of an international technology company, and you just found out that the government of a country in which you are operating has been spying on people using your platform as well as engaging in blocking so that users only have limited access to the material you carry online.

   a. Do you continue to do business in this country?

   Your first adviser, Mrs. Jones, states that continuing to do business there represents a permissible moral compromise and that allowing users' access to limited content still gives them some access and still allows them to utilize functions like messaging, which would allow them to communicate with family members abroad. She also advises you to consider your duties to your shareholders, noting that your business there is profitable.

   She advises continuing to do business in Country X.

   Your second adviser, Mr. Smith, states that a human rights violation is a human rights violation and that by continuing to do business with a government that violates people's human rights would be signaling that human rights don't matter. He advises withdrawing operations from Country X.

   b. Whose advice do you take and why?

2. Compare and contrast the stance of Facebook and Alibaba regarding patriotism or government regulation.

   a. Why do you think the two firms act so differently in relation to their host nation and their policies? Give specific examples.

   b. Why are there so many identified conflicts of interests between Google and the US government but *not* between Alibaba and Chinese government?

   c. What benefits do BAT actors accrue from a close relationship with the government? What benefits does the Chinese government get from allowing BAT to act relatively freely in the e-commerce space?

3. Do you think Facebook needs to be broken up, and is doing so possible? Give at least three reasons for your answer.

4. Do you believe that technology actors, including platforms, have unique corporate social responsibilities in contrast to other types of corporations? What is the basis for their unique responsibilities, and what specific unique responsibilities do they have?

5. There are several videos on YouTube that include interviews with Microsoft CEO Bill Gates in particular talking about corporate social responsibility. For example, see the following:

    Bill Gates Describes the Gates Foundations Efforts in India (20 minutes, filmed in 2017): https://binged.it/30shIjC

    a. What evidence do you have that Gates is using a capabilities approach?

    Bill Gates Addresses Harvard's Graduating Class (10 minutes, filmed in 2018): https://binged.it/30pvNyd

    b. How does Gates conceptualize corporate social responsibility? To whom does he think researchers and scientists, as well as corporations, are accountable?

KEY TERMS

Antitrust 217
Duopoly 216

Natural monopoly 218
Oligopoly 215

FOR FURTHER READING

Chander, A. *The Electronic Silk Road: How the Web Binds the World Together in Commerce* (New Haven, CT: Yale University Press, 2013).

Global Justice Information Sharing Initiative. *Public Safety Primer on Cloud Technology* (Washington, DC: Bureau of Justice Assistance United States Department of Justice, October 2016). file:///C:/Users/Mary/Desktop/FINAL%20Public%20Safety%20Primer%20On%20Cloud%20Technology.pdf.

Maak, T. "The Cosmopolitical Corporation." *Journal of Business Ethics* 84 (2009): 361–372.

Taddeo, M., and L. Floridi. "The Debate on the Moral Responsibilities of Online Service Providers." *Science and Engineering Ethics* 22 (2016): 1575–1603.

United Nations. *United Nations Guiding Principles on Business and Human Rights* (Geneva, Switzerland: United Nations Press, 2011). https://www.ohchr.org/Documents/Publications/GuidingPrinciplesBusinessHR_EN.pdf.

STATES AND PRIVATE ACTORS COOPERATING IN CYBERSPACE

Learning Objectives

At the end of this chapter, students will be able to do the following:

1. Define *public-private partnership* (PPP).

2. List at least three ethical, political, economic, and social issues associated with the provision of services by PPPs.

3. Define *military industrial complex* and *cyber industrial complex*, and describe the political, legal, and ethical issues raised by the existence of both.

4. Compare and contrast the ways in which technological innovation is carried out in an authoritarian versus a democratic regime.

In January 1953, President Eisenhower nominated Charles Erwin Wilson, who was then president of the General Motors automobile manufacturing company, to hold the position of Secretary of Defense in his cabinet. During his Senate confirmation hearings, Wilson explained that there was no conflict of interest created by the fact that he was a majority stockholder in General Motors and did not plan on selling his stock if he became Secretary of Defense. In explaining his decision, he famously said, "What's good for General Motors is good for America."

This remark summarized an understanding that US corporate interests can be quite tightly tied to US foreign policy interests. In the case of General Motors, the company's strong economic position and skilled work force meant that it was part of the US industrial base. The resources of General Motors could be diverted to support US military operations during wartime if needed, and GM's policy priorities were seen as aligned with US policy priorities.

However, as we look at the world today, can we say that what is good for Google is good for America? During the nearly ten-year period in which Google's search engine was located in China and operated in cooperation with the Chinese government, Google appeared to be following a policy that explicitly clashed with US foreign policy statements about human rights and refusing to cooperate with repressive governments. So, are the policy priorities of technology actors like Facebook and Google (both corporations that began in the United States whose leaders are American and who are headquartered in the United States) best understood as supporting US policy interests, leading US policy interests, or diverging from them?

To understand this relationship, it is necessary to begin to unpack our technology actors. Here, we will distinguish between technology actors whose resources comprise part of America's critical infrastructure—including ISPs and communications and power corporations within the United States that depend on internet technology—and platforms, which were defined earlier.

In considering which actors have policy priorities aligned with US foreign policy priorities, the situation is more straightforward with reference to those companies that provide cybersecurity and that are associated with critical infrastructure.

WHAT ARE PUBLIC-PRIVATE PARTNERSHIPS?

The term *public-private partnership* (PPP) describes a relationship between national governments and the many types of technology actors that may be involved in the provision of goods and services within a nation. A PPP is an arrangement whereby certain aspects of governmental activities have been privatized. These functions are carried out by a private, for-profit corporation through an agreement made with the state.[1] The PPP is thus a hybrid arrangement, existing halfway between a totally free market and a state-run economy. That is, in a state-run economy, the state might simply force corporations to provide a public good like cybersecurity through coercion, whereas in a totally free market, the state might merely hope that corporations would volunteer to participate in arrangements with the state. The first model does not provide enough freedom and rights for the organization, whereas the second might not provide enough security for the state. Ideally, the PPP arrangement would be mutually beneficial and attractive for both parties. The private corporation might provide a highly technological service that state workers do not have the expertise to provide, or it might be in a position to react more quickly and efficiently to changing market conditions. In some instances, a corporation might be prevailed upon to produce a good (like vaccines) for which there is a grave need but not a strong market incentive to produce it.

PPPs are a key building block in the provision of cybersecurity today in the United States and internationally. Most critical networks are privately owned, and even the majority of US government and military communications travel over private networks.[2] Presidential Policy Directive 20, signed in 2012, describes the PPP as the cornerstone of America's cybersecurity strategy.

In this arrangement, the private organization is not merely a subordinate organization or contractor hired by the state for the provision of these services. Rather, the private organization and the state are co-equals. They work together to shape goals, to create plans to carry them out, and to provide goods and services, including security as a collective good. In doing so, private organizations see a broadening of their roles. They are not merely economic actors but are also political actors whose activities may be mobilized in the pursuit of state or international goals—such as the combating of disease, the preservation of the environment, or the preservation of cyberspace. These private actors have thus been given a new role as responsible actors through serving as intermediaries, mediating between the clients they may serve and the state on whose behalf they work alongside.

However, critics of the PPP approach have raised several concerns. Some analysts worry that private industries do not have the same values and goals as government agencies. In particular, they worry that private corporations may be less committed to safeguarding the privacy rights of citizens.

Others worry that government actions that result in sharing classified information about vulnerabilities with private actors create new threats.[3] In addition, historically there have been problems with trust between commercial and government actors in the cybersecurity sector.

THE EMERGENCE OF PPPs IN THE CYBERSECURITY ARENA

By the late 1990s, American policy makers had acknowledged that the private sector was better equipped to handle responding to many types of cyberthreats much more quickly than the public sector could. The private sector was better resourced, had more highly skilled specialists, and could respond quickly in ways that a large bureaucracy could not. Despite the recognition that states needed the private sector to prevail in cyberspace, many analysts nonetheless saw the decision by democratic states to utilize PPP-type arrangements to guarantee cybersecurity as a signal that states had failed because they were unable to produce cybersecurity by themselves. That is, in an ideal world, each state might like to be fully self-sufficient and able to provide its own cybersecurity through government agencies, including its own cyber command. Indeed, in the realist view of international relations, this is clearly the preferred scenario. However, given the internet's own history—as a structure largely developed by academic and private industry personnel—this was simply not possible.[4] The term **sovereignty gap** refers to the gap between a state's capacity to carry out the activities of a sovereign state within the international system (such as policing its borders and providing a strong infrastructure) and its actual ability to do so.[5] In recent years, analysts have begun to point to a "technology sovereignty gap," noting that even highly developed states sometimes fail in their ability to satisfactorily monitor and control what goes on within their "digital borders."[6] That is, many (perhaps all) states simply do not have the ability to singlehandedly guarantee and provide cybersecurity within their regions, even if they wished to do so. Rather, they are dependent on technology actors to work with them to provide this public good.

As a result, within the democratic capitalist world, governments have created PPPs, or economic arrangements in which players cooperate in the market for cybersecurity. Private corporations—including those that constitute or provide critical infrastructure—make investments in providing cybersecurity to ensure their own economic prosperity and, in doing so, help guarantee America's economic prosperity as well. In addition to providing capital, private companies have provided highly specialized expertise, providing services that help shore up US cybersecurity. In recent years, the US government has worked with the private sector to carry out four types of activities. Private corporations like Microsoft have engaged in "botnet takedowns"—disrupting networks of infected computers used by transnational crime groups. They have also worked to identify and disrupt zero day exploits (ZDEs) through sharing patches for software vulnerabilities. Corporations have also carried out attribution activities, working with national governments to identify the perpetrators of online attacks. Finally, corporations have worked to defend private-owned systems and networks from sophisticated nation-state sponsored attackers.[7]

PPPs AND THE CONDUCT OF CYBERWAR

Military analysts have also embraced the notion of PPPs for the conduct of cyberwar, noting that cyberspace is a unique terrain for warfare that requires different sorts of relationships among states in the international system as well as between states and other actors. Klimburg describes the need for a whole of nation or **whole of government approach** to building a state's cyber power position within the international system. Drawing upon the experiences of the United States in recent conflicts, including in Iraq and Afghanistan, Klimburg argues that a country's power often rests on its ability to coordinate functions that might be shared across many different actors or agencies of different types. Today, he argues, a state that wishes to be powerful—whether in the real world or cyberspace—needs to know how to work with civil society actors, skilled technologists, and nonstate actors including corporations, from Google to defense contractors. Thus, Klimberg's "integrated capability model of cyber power" has multiple dimensions. He argues that the cyber-powerful nation should be able to carry out actions on a host of different activities—from responding to natural disasters, to protecting critical infrastructure, to responding to cyberattacks. The nation also needs to be able to work with a variety of international alliances and partnerships—like NATO and the United Nations as well as with groups like ICANN. Finally, it needs to be able to work with "nonstate cyber elements" to include private actors such as those associated with critical infrastructure.[8]

Within this approach, he argues, a state's government may play a coordinating role but not necessarily a leading role. Some traditional state activities, including those in the cyber sphere, might be outsourced to private organizations or even international organizations like the United Nations. At the same time, some technology actors, such as digital media platforms, will find themselves playing a role that goes beyond the mere provision of communication to become an inherently more political role.[9] In this model, the best way to calculate a state's power is not to look at the size of its military or the weapons that it owns but rather to look at its integrated capabilities, which might be shared with and among a variety of different actors. Thus, the strongest states will be those that are effective in working with private groups like ISPs, in some instances compelling these organizations to share the communications of ISP customers if doing so is in the state's interest.[10]

But other analysts see the evolution of these new hybrid relationships not as an opportunity but as a threat. They suggest that states are not moving toward working with other actors because they favor such an approach. Rather, states are recognizing an inevitable reality that is beyond their control. States are no longer the dominant players in the cyberspace arena. Today, global technology actors are playing a role not only on the state level but also on the international level, cooperating with foreign governments to build cyber infrastructure as well as domestically to secure America's electrical grid.[11] Carr suggests that the term *PPP* may be too narrow to describe all of the roles that technology actors play today— from serving as government contractors, to participating in international building projects, to working with states to combat cybercrime.

Here Macak argues that states have already begun ceding their leading role in the shaping of cyberspace to global technology actors, whereas Carr suggests that states might wish to "hide behind" the PPP rather than taking full responsibility for their actions in cyberspace. Macak argues that states have ceded many of their traditional roles to other types of emerging actors. In doing so, they have created a vacuum or lack of authority that other actors have been forced to step in to fill. Here, he points to the creation of the *Tallinn Manual*, which describes how international laws regarding armed conflict can be applied to cyberspace. This highly influential manual was developed not by a single state but rather by a cooperating group of experts sponsored by NATO. Here, he also points to the efforts undertaken by actors like Microsoft, which has put forth its own initiatives regarding what norms should apply to cyberspace in areas like security and freedom of speech.[12]

CRITIQUING PPPs: IS WHAT'S GOOD FOR GENERAL MOTORS ALSO GOOD FOR AMERICA?

Critiques of the PPP approach can be both functional and ideological. Functional critiques focus on whether a PPP is indeed the best, most efficient way of achieving a public policy objective. Ideological critiques (such as those put forth by critical theorists in international relations) instead focus on whether "collusion" by public and private actors is ultimately harmful to consumers and citizens.

Functional Critiques

Some analysts find that a PPP may provide less protection and reliability to a state than a more formalized arrangement would and thus support the creation of formalized arrangements over PPPs. That is, PPPs tend to have more of an ad hoc, dynamic character in contrast to more traditional types of official agreements made among states. In PPP arrangements it is not always clear exactly what the responsibilities of nonstate actors are, nor is it clear how such arrangements will be enforced if technology actors fail to uphold their obligations within the arrangement. In some instances, it may seem like private actors are volunteering their services and that they can withdraw from arrangements at any time if they are not to their liking.

Indeed, over time, we have seen some states simply compelling private actors to comply with the state for the provision of cybersecurity rather than establishing PPPs. For example, Russia has passed legislation that grants the Russian security service (the FSB, the successor organization to the Soviet KGB) the authority to store and analyze all of the data that passes over Russian networks. The System for Operative Investigative Activities (SORM) requires virtually all ISPs to install equipment that in effect allows the intelligence services to directly monitor all internet traffic within the country.[13] France has made it mandatory for identified critical infrastructure operators to participate in their programs, and even the United States has abandoned a completely voluntary approach to the private sector within critical infrastructure protection and has introduced legislation to compel cooperation where required. Here, Carr has argued that whereas at present private corporations and states seem to be working well together utilizing the PPP approach, this is perhaps simply a fortunate set of events, but it doesn't necessarily mean that this sharing of interests and complementary nature of activities is destined to go on forever.[14]

In addition, PPP arrangements seem to create situations where a nonstate actor, particularly an economic actor, may find itself subject to multiple, competing sets of expectations. Here, Zajko uses the term *intermediary* to refer to technology platforms in particular, which may be situated halfway between the state and individual citizens. He asks whether a technology actor can be expected to serve both the interests of the state (by, e.g., sharing information about people's Google searches with the Federal Bureau of Investigation or another government agency) and the interests of individual users (through safeguarding their personal information and integrity). He and others worry that PPPs seem to muddy or erode the boundary between what the state does and what corporations do. Corporations seem to be taking on political roles that they may not wish to have and that their customers may not be aware that they have. PPP arrangements also do not always clearly specify how risks will be shared between both parties, and it may be difficult to determine under what circumstances a nonstate actor is liable for any negative consequences that result from the arrangement.[15]

Finally, organizations that exist as for-profit corporations in particular may inherently have functions and values that are at odds with the values and procedures that states may have in the same situation. Although it makes sense, for example, for a state to engage in significant financial outlays to provide for state cybersecurity, it might not make sense for a profit corporation to do the same.[16] Here, we can consider the example of the petrochemical industry at the Port of Rotterdam in the Netherlands. Despite the knowledge that cyberattacks on petrochemical storage facilities could have major repercussions on society, private actors have been slow to meet and articulate standards for securing these facilities. Here, van Erp argues that whereas governments seem to expect businesses to invest in cybersecurity despite a lack of market incentives to do so, in point of fact this does not happen.[17]

Ideological Critiques: What Is the Cyber Industrial Complex?

Although some analysts are thus concerned that PPPs may create inefficiencies, other analysts are more concerned with questions of equity and justice. Here, scholars ask us to consider the following: Can a commercial company in particular, whose emphasis is on continuing to sell a product and make a product, ever fully behave in the best interests of citizens and consumers, as we might expect a state to behave?

Some analysts and policy makers are fearful of the alignment of corporate and governmental interests, fearing that citizens and consumers may be at the losing end of this bargain. Corporations may be more interested in keeping their military client than in serving the needs of customers, and government might utilize its relationship with corporations to engage in activities that are actually harmful to citizens, such as spying.

The phrase **cyber industrial complex** was first used in the aftermath of the 2012 revelations by former Central Intelligence Agency contractor Edward Snowden, who revealed classified information to American and international citizens regarding the level of surveillance being carried out domestically and internationally through the US National Security Agency. As policy makers and citizens became aware of the violations of their privacy, which had been put in place by government agencies in the aftermath of the 9/11 terrorist attacks, many people began to ask questions regarding the ways in which private corporations had been aware of National Security Agency surveillance. In some instances, corporations had even seemingly been supportive of these activities and had shared citizen information with the National Security Agency.

Making Corporations Responsible for Cybersecurity

The policy dilemma here is the following: Given that private corporations are increasingly responsible for the conduct of activities that are vital to a nation's national security, what is the best way for a government to make sure that corporations are taking this responsibility seriously, including implementing best practices for ensuring the security of their systems? The first option would leave corporations largely free to implement their own cybersecurity protocols. In this option, corporations might merely be subject to strict regulation, including the implementation of fines when breaches occur.

A second option was, however, proposed in 2012. The Cyber Intelligence Sharing and Protection Act (CISPA), a measure introduced to the US Congress, called for the creation of a "hub" for cybersecurity information. Corporations would all be tied into the US National Security Agency, which would act as a clearing house, making sure that information was shared about breaches and attacks among corporations and working to implement action plans when a breach occurred. Congressman Ron Wyden of Oregon, who spoke out against the passage of the CISPA, used the phrase *cyber industrial complex* to describe a possible future in which the US National Security Agency was privy to all consumer information and data and in which corporations and government worked together to implement security at the expense of individual privacy rights.[18]

Other analysts have used the phrase to draw a historic parallel with the Vietnam-era military industrial complex. This phrase, first used by outgoing US President Dwight D. Eisenhower in a farewell address in the 1960s, was used to describe a situation in which military equipment manufacturers and suppliers were seen as allied closely with the US government. The phrase gained resonance during the Vietnam War (although never formally declared as a war, the United States was involved in Vietnam and Laos from 1955 until 1975). At this time, critics suggested that because war was so profitable, military corporations had a vested interest in prolonging the conflict rather than seeking to resolve the conflict and make peace.

In thinking about for-profit companies that provide cybersecurity products, some analysts have suggested that these corporations have a similar vested interest in never solving the cybersecurity problem through eliminating viruses and malware. Rather, they argue it is in a corporation's interests to continue to sell subscriptions to security patches and updates. In this way, they argue, cybersecurity strategies will always be ongoing rather than leading to a long-term solution of the problem.[19] In addition, cybersecurity experts have been also faulted for using scare tactics and exaggerating the seriousness of the threat posed by cybersecurity breaches to create a profitable industry, particularly around Washington, DC's, Capital Beltway—aimed at servicing the needs of government clients. Some critics of the cyber industrial complex believe that terms like *cyber Armageddon* or *cyber Pearl Harbor* have been popularized by cybersecurity vendors to convince the government to spend resources on the provision of cybersecurity over other types of societal needs that government should provide for its citizens.[20]

PLATFORMS AS FOREIGN POLICY ACTORS TODAY

Today, whereas private cybersecurity actors and the US government share several goals in relation to the preservation and defense of America's cybersecurity environment, it would be wrong to assume that all technology actors have the same goals in cyberspace and that US foreign policy is aligned with the foreign policies of technology actors like Facebook and Google.

In his work, Segal identifies two phases in the history of US–private sector technology relations. He describes a honeymoon phase through the 1990s and up until 2013, during which Washington and Silicon Valley shared a vision of the internet as a borderless "territory" characterized by ideas like freedom and open access. However, he argues that this happy connection was severed in 2013 with the revelation that the US National Security Agency had spied on private citizens and public officials—utilizing privately owned platforms.

Today, he argues, Silicon Valley has interests that have diverged from the stated policy positions of the United States. And as a result, the heads of software firms like Microsoft and Google have sought to establish themselves as separate foreign policy actors, independent from the United States and its interests. Private corporations also have business dealings in many parts of the world, and thus they must juggle the opposing views and interests of actors as diverse as China and the United States. Thus, they have responded to international customer concerns regarding the security of their data by building hardware in some instances that bypasses the United States so that the United States cannot tap into communications data from other nations. (For example, the Brazilian government is working to create a fiber optic cable between Brazil and Lisbon, Portugal, so that their traffic no longer goes through Miami). They have also worked with nations that wish to have their data stored locally or within their own countries (rather than in a server farm in the United States). These international companies, headquartered in the United States, feel that they have been hurt by the perception that they are "American" companies. For example, Beijing recently announced that it is working hard to reduce dependence on foreign technology companies and that it will give preference to local Chinese firms.

In addition, Segal argues that even in the field of cybersecurity, private corporations often define cybersecurity differently than the United States does. Whereas the US definition focuses on state interests like counterterrorism and safeguarding

US economic interests, he argues that private corporations are more interested in safeguarding their users' assets, and keeping their information private. As a result, some corporations may be moving away from PPPs toward instead formulating coalitions of private actors that engage in self-regulation, setting their own standards for cybersecurity, and working together to address issues that arise. For example, some international companies have attempted to create what they call a **Digital Geneva Convention**, which would be focused on the needs of civilian or private internet users rather than the needs of states. Here, Segal describes how companies act as "first responders" when citizens have their data stolen, noting that in conflicts among states, many of the victims are private citizens in cyberwar, unlike conventional war.[21]

A final issue to consider as we examine technology actors as agents within international relations relates to issues in which potentially incendiary content carried by platforms and ISPs can result in detrimental political consequences both domestically and internationally. Previously we asked if technology actors had an ethical obligation to consider how their services might affect human capabilities and human rights. But we can also ask if technology actors should be regarded as complicit in situations where a platform might be used in ways that cause political polarization and strife within a society or when practices like the dissemination of "fake news" lead to the destabilizing of political institutions, such as the carrying out of free and fair elections.

Previously in this chapter we referred to platforms and search engines as gatekeepers, or doorways that allow users to access information. But whose interests should the gatekeeper serve? Is the gatekeeper's primary obligation to the user because technology actors are primarily economic entities? Or does the technology actor also have a broader obligation to society in terms of working to maintain stability and order within a political system?

And are these interests always the same? Should an ISP do what the user wants (i.e., provide him or her with the ability to read a left-wing or right-wing view of last night's presidential debate, depending on his or her inclinations, through offering tailored or customized search results)? Or should Google do what is best for society (i.e., to provide him or her with a more diverse set of views regarding the debate, with analysis from both sides of the political spectrum)? If the second option is preferred, then the gatekeeper role can be seen to override the economic role of the organization. That is, if Google's job is merely to provide content to the customer, then we might expect Google to behave more like a clothing store, where "the customer is always right." Stores don't usually force customers to try on clothes that they haven't selected from the racks out of some sense that the customer needs to be exposed to a variety of fashion looks. If Google is merely a type of store for information, then, it would seem strange for it to seek to shape customer preferences and affect customer behavior in this way, through forcing information upon them that they hadn't requested and didn't want.

Furthermore, in this scenario, by overriding the customer's wishes in the pursuit of a greater social good, the platform has moved away from its purely utilitarian, economic role into one with much greater social responsibilities. But can the platform serve both the government (and social good) and the customer? Here, one might worry that whereas today Google is acting as a gatekeeper through exposing you to a wider spectrum of political views, tomorrow Google might decide that you don't need to be viewing pornography, or foreign media, or religious material. Is it possible to ask Google to act selectively to serve the collective good, and should the determination of what that good is being made by Google, by the government, or by some other authority?

In response to these concerns, analysts have proposed a variety of solutions. Richard Allan, a member of Britain's House of Lords, has proposed the establishment of PPPs between the UK government and content platforms, where the players would work together to establish and maintain standards for content moderation. US Senator Elizabeth Warren has proposed taking government action to break up Amazon, Facebook, and Google. Under her plan, platforms with more than $25 billion in revenue would be designated as "platform utilities" and required to "spin off" subsidiary businesses rather than existing as large aggregations of bundled services.[22] And Anne Marie Slaughter, adviser to former US State Department head Hillary Clinton, has proposed the adoption of a multistakeholder model for internet governance in which coalitions of actors—to include states, private corporations, and nonprofit organizations—would work together to formulate policies in areas like content regulation and the combating of hate speech.

Case Study: States, Corporations, Shared Risk, and the Cloud

Thus far, our discussion of interdependence and shared risk has been rather abstract. We turn now to an analysis of one specific technological development that illustrates interdependence and shared risk in more specific terms through looking at cloud computing.

Cloud computing is a general term that refers to models of computing in which calculations and services are not carried out on an individual user's computer or where data and information are not stored on an individual's computer. The cloud is thus defined as "a networking solution in which everything from computing power to computing infrastructure, applications, business processes to personal collaboration can be delivered to you as a service wherever and whenever you need it."[23] Individual users interact with types of clouds in carrying out everyday functions on their computers, often without being aware that they are doing so. An individual might utilize cloud-based infrastructure, like storage functions, in uploading photos to a photography printing site like Snapfish or in engaging in e-commerce activities like bidding on an item on eBay or making a purchase on Amazon. A user might utilize a cloud-based content platform when applying to college through the Common Application, uploading a video to YouTube, or putting together a tax return through a service like TurboTax. Finally, a user might utilize cloud-based software in, for example, making a meme using a meme-generating program like Meme Creator.

In each case, the information uploaded to the cloud is no longer resident merely on the user's computer, but instead resides elsewhere (the user may not and often does not know where), and may in point of fact reside in several locations or be shared seamlessly among a variety of actors. And although data may seem like an amorphous or immaterial entity, in point of fact, the data produced by each user also has a physical component, because it is stored on a physical server farm that can be located anywhere in the world. Here, businesses that conduct activities in the cloud may decide where to site server farms based on economic calculations tied to these physical entities—choosing a country with low real estate costs or a highly educated workforce to serve as the site of its server farms. Thus, for example, an American company might decide to store the data produced on its websites in another country, including one in the developing world.

"The cloud" thus encompasses one location or several (and may easily traverse geographical boundaries, including national boundaries). Entities participating in a cloud may include government actors as well as private actors. Clouds can be entirely private (perhaps requiring a password or some other form of authentication to access them), shared within a community, entirely public, or they can exist in a hybrid format, containing elements of public and private ownership.

The existence of data clouds thus presents unique challenges for the interstate system, which has thus far made assumptions about territories and borders that no longer hold true in relation to cloud computing, big data, and the role of actors like those involved in e-commerce. Beginning in the 1980s with the advent of e-commerce, states found themselves in situations where both individuals and corporations were increasingly participating in economic transactions (both legal and illegal) that took place in cyberspace and across national borders. And in more recent years, as we have noted, data itself has achieved the status of a resource—again one that is being produced internationally, across national borders, as well as stored internationally.

Thus, states have found themselves in positions where it has become necessary for them to cooperate—drawing up international regulations in the areas of e-commerce, cybercrimes, and international data governance. However, thus far, both domestic and international laws regarding how data and transactions are to be administered and treated in a cloud-based environment are not clear. Experts have raised questions of jurisdiction. In the event that data housed in a cloud is stolen or corrupted, where is the crime to be tried, and where exactly do we consider that the crime occurred—at the place where the individual accessing the data was located, at the physical location where the data was stored, or at the location where the cloud's proprietor has its legal headquarters? It has thus far been difficult for those seeking to protect data, as well as those who may have suffered harm through insufficient data protection, to determine which set of laws (national, regional, or international) are applicable in considering the act as well as which entity exercises jurisdiction over the platform and its activities. In addition, as a recent European Union study indicates, it can also be difficult for cloud providers to carry out activities aimed at deterring those who might seek to breach or attack them—because it is not always clear to adversaries when and under which conditions the cloud provider would be likely to respond offensively or defensively to a possible breach. Responding to breaches can be particularly challenging when doing so requires the coordination of multiple entities, both public and private, who might be associated with the cloud.[24] (We look more at the phenomenon of deterrence in Chapter 11, on military cyber issues.)

In cases where data may be managed or stored on a commercial platform, it is also thus far unclear who owns and may access the data in a situation where the commercial entity goes bankrupt or is absorbed or subordinated to another entity at a later date. For example, should users be made aware that their stored data is being transferred, and should they have a right to opt out of such an arrangement? It is also unclear which entities are responsible for dispute resolution in the event that a user might have a complaint against a service provider in the cloud.

Cloud computing also presents unique challenges to law enforcement when it comes to carrying out activities like surveillance and collecting evidence. Does a law enforcement office require a search warrant to access data held in the cloud, and if so, which entity should set the conditions regarding when such warrants might be authorized? In addition, prosecuting a criminal is difficult if all of the specific legal conditions regarding the collection and preservation of evidence are not adhered to, and these conditions can vary by jurisdictions—not only internationally but even within the United States. Greiman notes that a criminal investigation may require interception, search orders, protection orders, mutual legal assistance (carried out among states on the basis of a mutual legal assistance treaty) and the preservation of evidence in other countries.[25]

Cloud Computing and the CLOUD Act

In March 2018, the US government passed the Clarifying Lawful Use of Overseas Data (CLOUD) Act, and the European Commission is in the process of proposing legislation regarding so-called e-evidence to the European Parliament. Supporters of these initiatives argue that they are necessary to modernize existing legal understandings regarding how data can be used and shared, whereas detractors argue that both the CLOUD Act and the proposed European Union legislation represent a threat to user privacy rights.

However, currently, not all actors within the international system regard the creation of this far-reaching legislation as a positive development. A spokesperson for the US-based digital privacy advocacy group, the Electronic Frontier Foundation (EFF), invokes the constructivist language of securitization in arguing that the CLOUD Act was passed in the United States quickly with little public discussion or debate about its provisions. EFF notes: "It was never reviewed or marked up by any committee in either the House or the Senate. It never received a hearing."

EFF argues that the CLOUD Act provides the US government and the foreign governments with which it makes bilateral executive agreements with unprecedented access to user data across a variety of platforms.[26] Here, some legal analysts argue that this provision of the CLOUD Act actually violates the US Constitution, including the Fourth Amendment, which forbids unreasonable search and seizure.[27] After the passage of the legislation, nine human rights organizations—including EFF, Human Rights Watch, Access Now, Demand Progress, Fight for the Future, Freedom of the Press Foundation, Government Accountability Project, Restore the Fourth, and World Privacy Forum—wrote a letter to the US Department of Justice detailing their objections to the CLOUD Act.

At the same time, the existing legislation will end up governing the actions not only of states but, as we noted earlier, of many other entities that conduct business in the cloud, including ISPs, providers of internet security, and international corporations like Google and Microsoft.

And although one might expect that commercial services providers in particular would welcome legislation aimed at creating a more stable and predictable ecosystem for the conduct of computing activities, in point of fact it becomes clear that not all actors that will be governed by the regulations have the same interests. A corporation like Microsoft, for example, may place a higher value on safeguarding the rights (and data) of its users rather than prioritizing the increased law enforcement capabilities that the CLOUD Act provides.

Here, we can see the ways in which legal remedies and norms or values governing cloud-based interactions can thus be at odds. In introducing the legislation on a blog written for consumers, a spokesperson for Microsoft has emphasized the fact that the corporation is still firmly committed to consumer privacy. In a statement, Microsoft's spokesperson has argued that despite the provisions of the CLOUD Act, Microsoft believes that all of its users have a universal right to be notified when the government accesses their data as well as a right to transparency, which means that users should be made aware of how and when governments are seeking access to their data. They have called for the establishment of specific legal bodies within states that would consider government requests for access to user data following specified legal processes as well as the creation of an international legal framework to de-conflict issues that might arise among nations regarding the provision and authorization of access to user data internationally. In its statement, Microsoft clearly articulates an understanding that "enterprises have a right to control their data," which implies that users themselves do not own their data but that rather, in creating data on an entity's platform or agreeing to share their data with that platform, they have in fact given that entity ownership of that data.[28]

Norms regarding Cloud Computing

In the approximately twenty-five years that civilians have had access to the internet, scholars and policy makers have frequently clashed when considering the matter of norms in cyberspace. Here, major areas of disagreement include the matter of how norms regarding cloud computing emerge and whether they are the product of the space itself or the product of actual decisions and actions taken by states and other entities acting within that space. That is, analysts disagree about the source of norms governing online behavior, including in the area of cloud computing. Next, analysts disagree about whether there are in fact universal norms regarding how states, corporations, and individuals should behave in regard to data sharing, privacy, and other issues within a cloud computing environment. Here, some analysts suggest that one can identify clear rules that all players within an environment should support, whereas others argue that those entities (both states and corporations) that enjoy a preponderance of power are actually imposing norms on other, weaker actors (including states) while claiming that such norms are universal. Finally, analysts disagree about whether norms should remain an informal mechanism governing behavior within an environment, like an information cloud, or whether norms should be codified into legal frameworks.

INTERNATIONAL LEGAL CHALLENGES IN CLOUD COMPUTING

None of the issues raised here are fundamentally unique. Rather, as we have noted earlier in this text, states have in the past created international intergovernmental organizations—or global partnerships—to harmonize regulations and work jointly to address sector-specific problems. For example, the International Atomic Energy Agency (IAEA) exists for the purposes of regulating and overseeing the peaceful and safe development of atomic energy, with input from a wide variety of states committed to this effort. Here, states may have different forms of economic and political organization, but all share a commitment to work together for the peaceful and safe creation of atomic energy. Similarly, the International Civil Aviation Organization (ICAO) brings together experts and practitioners to standardize and harmonize protocols and procedures regulating international civilian air travel so that states can cooperate in this arena. The term *interoperability* refers to the ability of different entities to work together in a cooperative manner through the standardization and harmonization of procedures.

Thus, the formation of a new organization such as the proposed International Cloud Policy Center for Law Enforcement (ICPCLE) would not therefore represent a new approach to regulating activity within the international system. Rather, such an international private or intergovernmental organization might be structured in a similar fashion to Interpol or the World Trade Organization.[29] However, the phenomenon of cloud computing does present a unique challenge to policy makers today largely because of how quickly the technology has developed and because, at the moment, the development of mechanisms to govern, regulate, and harmonize state approaches to these issues have lagged behind the technological developments themselves.

Case Study: Hua Wei Corporation and US-China Relations

Earlier in this chapter, we suggested that corporations that are headquartered in the United States have a particular responsibility to work with their national government to share information and initiatives that would benefit both corporate and private cybersecurity strength. Perhaps not surprisingly, foreign corporations also have similar arrangements with their national governments.

Here, we pause to consider the issues posed by Chinese public-private cooperation—from an American perspective. We do so through a case study of the issues posed to American consumers due to the availability and use of Chinese cell phones.

Today, many consumers, including those in the United States and Europe, might choose to use a Hua Wei cell phone. Hua Wei Technologies Company Limited, founded in 1987 by Ren Zhenfei, a formerly high-ranking Chinese government official, is headquartered in Shenzen, China. The company provides telecommunications equipment and is best known for its consumer electronics, including smartphones, which are available throughout the world. These phones, which are made in China, may seem like a good value to an American consumer because they have a reputation for being cheap and reliable. But should Americans be using Chinese phones—and if not, why not?

The story of the Hua Wei Corporation illustrates the ways in which the creation and maintenance of today's technology infrastructure depends on a wide-ranging constellation of actors working together. These actors are public and private and international in scope. For example, although Hua Wei makes phones (or hardware), these are not self-standing products. Rather, in Europe, Hua Wei users frequently depend on Google, an American corporation, to provide mobile phone services and software, including the platform upon which these Chinese-made phones run. In particular, the phones depend on other platforms like Google's Android to provide the apps and interfaces that users need to make their phones do all the things they would like to do. And in utilizing facial identification services to allow users to sign in to their phones, Hua Wei users depend on technology produced and sold by Apple, another American corporation. Hua Wei phones may also include data chips made by companies (including American companies) like Qualcomm, Xilinx and Broadcomm, and Intel and Microsoft. Hua Wei users throughout the world can also regularly receive security updates from Hua Wei, thus choosing either automatically or with permission to upload information from China to their phones.

The result is a cell phone product or experience that is thus not wholly Chinese, wholly European, or wholly American. Instead, the "system" created allows each company to specialize in what it does best, thereby driving down costs for the whole product. Until recently, consumers took the existence of such a system for granted, and most people were unaware of just how many nations might have been involved in creating and supporting your personal actions, from tweeting to Instagramming.

For a liberal internationalist, the example of Hua Wei represents the phenomenon of complex interdependence.[30] Complex interdependence refers to the existence of multiple forms of interaction among societies and an interplay between issues and linkages in which issues may have a changing priority in the list of issues that exist between states and other actors. The example of Hua Wei also shows how multiple types of actors from different nations must come together to produce our global telecommunications environment, how fragile that interplay among actors can actually be, and the ways in which this type of cooperation can come about only if all players in the system are willing to trust others within the system.

Who Owns Hua Wei?

However, in recent years, the US government in particular has voiced public objections to the creation of a system in which US and Chinese products are interlinked and has taken steps to make it more difficult for US users in particular to use these Chinese products. Instead of viewing the advent of cheap Chinese cell phones as a positive development for the international economy and for American consumers, the US government has begun to voice security and surveillance concerns, suggesting that the Chinese government may have motives in making these devices available that are not purely commercial in nature.

Huawei maintains that it is a private company whose employees own stock in it through an employee union, and that is not owned by the Chinese government.[31] However, American policy makers in particular view it not as a private company but rather as a company that works closely with the Chinese government.[32] They are therefore suspicious that China, which has a reputation for conducting corporate espionage, might be utilizing Hua Wei telephones to conduct some of these spying activities.

Here, we can ask: Does the existence of an option for buying a Chinese cell phone in America represent a success story for the spread of free trade and international global commerce, or does it represent a creeping threat as China uses private corporations as a vehicle for espionage and even cyber warfare against the United States?

America Reacts to the Hua Wei "Threat"

In recent years, the US government in particular has become increasingly worried by what they see as a security threat emerging from US use of Chinese cell phones. In August 2018, the US Congress passed the John McCain National Defense Authorization Act, which dictated that US government employees, including those working for private defense contractors, should surrender their cell phones if they were made by two Chinese companies, Huawei and ZTE.[33] In this act, policy makers expressed concerns about two issues: the fact that Chinese cell phone manufacturers appeared to have fewer controls in place to ensure that user information and user privacy were protected and the fear that the Chinese government was acting to install spyware on Hua Wei cell phones made in China. This spyware would then be used to collect data on users for purposes of cyber espionage, including industrial espionage.

In May 2019, the US Department of Commerce placed Hua Wei on the so-called Entity List after Hua Wei was accused of doing business with the government of Iran. The international community has passed economic sanctions legislation that forbids companies that are UN members from doing business with Iran.[34]

The Entity List refers to a group of countries in which US businesses are forbidden to engage in international commerce with unless they have a government-issued Export Administration license. This regulation thus prevents American companies to do business independently with these firms and increases US government oversight of such transactions. Thus, a decision by the US Commerce Department to restrict the licenses that these American companies who do business abroad with foreign corporations will have international repercussions.

Applying the Paradigms

The Realist Paradigm. If we examine the statement that the US Department of Commerce has issued regarding the ban on US companies doing business with Hua Wei, we can identify the use of a realist framework. The Department of Commerce believes that the Chinese government is utilizing the Hua Wei corporation to conduct espionage against non-Chinese individuals who use these products. This view, then, does not distinguish between private companies located in adversary nations and adversary nations themselves. Rather, it rests on the assumption that companies do not have a separate foreign policy or set of interests but that instead their policies reflect the policies of their governments. This same view, then, expects Google to act "Americanly" in going along with US policy statements and expects Google to make decisions that reflect US foreign policy interests.

The Trump administration also attempted to pressure European allies to go along with this ban. European allies were warned against allowing Hua Wei to play any part in constructing their hardware as they move toward the adoption of 5G technology. (5G refers to the fifth generation of cellular wireless technology, which telecommunications companies believe will be in place worldwide by 2021 or 2022. 5G technology will provide more flexible internet connections carried by radio waves streamed from cell phone towers. This system will allow companies to install internet connections on a house by house basis rather than laying internet cable for streets or neighborhoods. It will also allow users to have a faster internet connection and more capacity. This will enable the adoption of more streaming services as well as providing the necessary support for a future in which almost every device in someone's house is internet-enabled through the internet of things.)[35]

Some analysts have described the tensions between US and foreign telecommunications providers as part of a "new Cold War in cyberspace." China has been active in building the telecommunications hardware system (or backbone) used by many nations in Africa as well as in the Mideast. Thus, it is possible to picture a future in which some countries are American oriented whereas others are China oriented, depending on which company built their infrastructure. Countries might be seen as allied with one cyber power over another, and each cyber power might be seen as having its own bloc or group of nations who support them. Instead of a world in which nations and technology actors act freely in an international framework, these actors might be seen as having more limited freedom, with the expectation that they will act along national or ideological lines.

In addition, each bloc might potentially have its own self-standing infrastructure. Thus, for example, Hua Wei executives have noted that they are working on a Plan B for how to proceed if they are no longer allowed to use or have interoperability with American and European products and interfaces. Hua Wei Corporation spokespeople have already noted that should Hua Wei products no longer be able to depend on the use of US or European software and telephony services, Hua Wei is ready to expand its business to provide these products and services to its users by itself. In the future, Chinese hardware users might thus utilize a Chinese variant of Android to host apps rather than interfacing with the international internet system as a whole. However, they also note that the end of transnational business partnerships, like the partnership between Hua Wei and Google, is not in anyone's best interest.[36]

It is easier here to see a future in which instead of working together cooperatively, international corporations instead depend only upon themselves and their national partners. In this way, the internet itself will have less of an international character and more of a national character—with some companies choosing to give their citizens access to American services, American hardware, and American platforms, whereas others choose to give their citizens access to Chinese or Russian services. Internet technology will thus be parallel, rather than global, with different countries utilizing parallel operating systems.

The Liberal Internationalist Paradigm. Although US policy makers have used a realist framework to describe their disagreement with Hua Wei, the company's own leadership utilizes a liberal internationalist framework to discuss these events. In an interview in May 2019, a Hua Wei official described the dispute as being about "free trade, not security." He stated, "We are in the middle of a trade war between two big countries. . . . We're a football in between this trade war."[37]

Hua Wei thus believes that the US government has used talk about security and surveillance concerns as a cover for its real concerns, which are the limiting of economic competition. Hua Wei, as the world's largest telecommunications provider and a leading producer of cell phones, believes that the United States is mostly interested in erecting trade barriers and tariff systems so that Chinese products will not compete with American products on the American or even the world market. And as retaliation for the US ban on Hua Wei products, some Chinese policy makers have called for Chinese citizens to boycott American products, whereas Chinese corporations might refuse to do business with American companies that supply components for their production, instead choosing to work with other producers.

Although realists thus fear that America might lose its competitive advantage if China is able to use its products to engage in commercial espionage, liberal internationalists worry about losing the collective benefits created through free trade and an international market for goods and services. If nations begin closing their borders to economic competition, the economic advantages that corporations can accrue from sharing risks and outsourcing services to others will cease to exist. Specialization will be less likely as single corporations are forced to carry out more functions themselves.

As a result, the costs of internet services may be higher for both commercial companies and individual consumers.

The Constructivist Paradigm. Finally, we can use the constructivist paradigm to see how both sides are talking about this dispute and to consider the ways in which language is being used to create a situation within the international system. The constructivist paradigm allows us to suggest that it is not inevitable that states engage in either a trade war or a cold war in cyberspace. Rather, constructivists would suggest that tensions can be both built and resolved throughout the international system.

Just as Mikhail Gorbachev was able to end the Cold War between the United States and Russia largely through using the phrase "our common home" to emphasize the shared interests of all nations in ending the Cold War, it might be possible for the United States and China to both use language emphasizing the shared nature of the internet space that hosts international commerce. Nations might begin to think about how best to address security and surveillance concerns through creating trust and cooperation.

Recently, Roff has suggested that there is perhaps not an actual arms race in cyberspace (including an artificial intelligence arms race). Rather, she suggests, there is a perception that such an arms race exists due largely to the language that has been deployed to describe competition between the Great Powers in relation to cyber issues.

She writes that "talking about technological competition—in research, adoption and deployment—in all sectors of multiple economies and in warfare is not really an arms race."[38] She suggests, however, that by using the term, policy makers risk escalating competition and rivalry as well as the likelihood of actual conflict between rivals. Furthermore, she notes, by adopting the arms race framework, we risk giving some actors (like military actors) a privileged voice within the debate, meanwhile closing out other actors and ways of addressing the situation.

Perhaps the deployment of different terms, then, might enable states to come together to address issues raised by the use of foreign technology by consumers and government officials. Ideally, states might be able to create new regimes of trust in which each side agreed not to install spyware or to engage in cyber espionage—without invoking the specter of war or an arms race if issues arise.

CONCLUSION

In this chapter we have considered the phrase "what's good for General Motors is good for the United States" and asked whether what's good for technology companies is also "good for the United States." In short, we have considered the relationship between a nation's business interests and its other foreign policy interests and the connection between the two sets of interests. Thinking back to Chapter 1, we can remember that the internet arose as a commercial undertaking albeit with governmental and military support. And in Chapter 2, we considered the phenomenon of path dependence—or the ways in which design decisions made early in a product cycle can have repercussions throughout the life cycle of a technology, including the establishment of constraints regarding how and under what circumstances a technology can be used. As we saw in this chapter, the establishment of PPPs between ISPs and technology platforms offers the promise of creating more efficient solutions to many problems that states face today. At the same time, the relationship between public entities and private service providers is a delicate one, and many critics have voiced warnings about the ways in which democracy itself may look different in a situation where businesses are (or threaten to be) coequals with government in the provision of goods and services to citizens and to the state. We pick up this discussion again in Chapter 10, as we delve more deeply into the question of ethics and ways in which technology can support or erode state efforts to create a more ethical international system.

QUESTIONS FOR DISCUSSION

1. In her essay on public-private cybersecurity, analyst Kristen Eichensehr argues that when it comes to working with private-sector corporations as actors in the international system, "the state may sometimes act more like a market PARTICIPANT than like a regulator—as government functions are contracted out to private parties."

   a. What do you see as the dangers associated with state reliance upon private sector actors, either as participants working together with the state, or even in a leading role vis-a-vis the state?

   b. How would a realist respond to this question? A liberal internationalist? A constructivist?

2. Alec Ross, a White House official, recently made the following statement:

   "I think the Internet is the single most disruptive force for the sovereign nation-state since the concept was founded with the 1648 Treaty of

Westphalia. I don't think the Internet is going to take an eraser to state wars, but it is inherently anti-state."[39]

a. Do you agree with Alec Ross's statement that the internet is inherently anti-state? If so, what specific features of the internet have combined to render it anti-state?

b. If you disagree, explain how the internet can strengthen the power of the state.

3. What are some risks associated with the rise of private actors in the spheres of the economy, social media, and the international system?

KEY TERMS

Cloud computing 232
Cyber industrial complex 228
Digital Geneva Convention 231

Sovereignty gap 225
Whole of government approach 225

FOR FURTHER READING

Carr, M. "Public-Private Partnerships in National Cyber-Security Strategies." *International Affairs* 92, no 1 (2016): 43–62.

Eichensehr, K. "Public-Private Cybersecurity." *Texas Law Review* 95, no. 3 (2017): 467–538.

McCarthy, D. "Privatizing Political Authority: Cybersecurity, Public-Private Partnerships, and the Reproduction of Liberal Political Order." *Politics and Governance* 8, no. 2 (2018): 5–12.

Segal, A. "Bridging the Cyberspace Gap: Washington and Silicon Valley." *Prism* 7, no. 2 (2017): 67–73.

van Erp, J. "New Governance of Corporate Cybersecurity: A Case Study of the Petrochemical Industry in the Port of Rotterdam." *Crime Law and Social Change* 68 (2017): 75–93.

10

ETHICS, NORMS, AND RULES

Learning Objectives

At the end of this chapter, students will be able to do the following:

1. Define key terms, including *ethics*, *emerging technology*, *stewardship*, and *infosphere*.

2. Describe salient ethical issues related to cyber policy today, including online privacy and surveillance and state accountability.

3. Argue for the likelihood or unlikelihood that states will establish strong and shared norms regarding ethical behavior in cyberspace.

4. Describe unique ethical issues arising among nations in cyberspace, including problems of trust and deception.

If we look back over the nearly twenty-five years since states first began conducting business in cyberspace, we can identify several different types of international incidents that have arisen. Since states started taking ownership of cyberspace, defending cyberspace, and conducting political, economic, and social relations in cyberspace, policy makers have sought to establish understandings regarding what is and is not considered acceptable behavior by states in that arena.

In 2013, as a result of the revelations made public by former US Central Intelligence Agency contractor Edward Snowden, several European states expressed outrage at what they saw as unethical and possibly illegal behavior by the United States. The US National Security Agency was found to have hacked into e-mail accounts and government databases belonging to West

European leaders as well as UN officials. The United States was accused of having violated these individuals' rights to privacy as well as to have violated the sovereignty of these nations.

In 2014, North Korea's leadership was found to have hacked into the servers belonging to the US-based Sony Pictures Corporation. Upset about what they saw as an unfair and unflattering portrayal of North Korean leader Kim Jong Un in the film *The Interview*, North Korea retaliated by releasing hundreds of private e-mails between famous Hollywood stars, their agents, and the organization. The public release of private information of a possibly compromising nature is referred to as doxing, and it is seen as a type of cyberattack. Those who were publicly embarrassed by the e-mail release felt that they had been slandered and libeled and that their privacy rights had been violated. Sony Pictures regarded the events as a criminal act—because it was a type of electronic breaking and entering—as the theft of materials.

In 2017, a report compiled by the US Central Intelligence Agency was released to the US Congress regarding the role that Russia had allegedly played in attempting to sway the 2016 presidential election. Russia was accused of having hacked into the Democratic National Committee's private e-mail servers, resulting in the release of e-mails that were politically damaging to the organization and to Democratic presidential candidate Hillary Clinton.

And at a recent conference held in South Africa, a high-ranking US official working in the information security arena discussed the Russian strategy of conducting psychological operations against the United States.[1] This official argued that Russia is following a strategy first articulated by Russian General Gennady Gerasimov, which aimed at taking advantage of existing social cleavages within a society or group through using false information, propaganda, and "fake news" to increase polarization among group members to create social unrest. This strategy includes, according to this official, utilizing Russian trolls to post stories and comments in social media that play upon Americans' fears that vaccinating their children could have adverse effects on their health. Some American officials now feel that the large-scale outbreaks of measles, chicken pox, and other childhood diseases may have been caused by adversary states using a targeted social media strategy to dissuade Americans from vaccinating their children.

Each of these events—the National Security Agency's unauthorized surveillance, North Korea's hacking, and Russia's electoral interference—resides in a complicated legal and ethical space. In all of these instances, one can positively state that these actions feel wrong and are likely something that states should not do, but what exactly makes them wrong, and what is the basis for this understanding?

WHAT ARE ETHICS?

In many cases, the law is not entirely clear regarding whether these actions are legal acts of state self-defense or unauthorized violations of state sovereignty. Because many of the acts described here are so new and indeed novel or unique, existing laws and regulations have not caught up with actual practices. As noted in Chapter 1, international law is a complex body of decisions that has grown up over the course of hundreds of years as the result of judicial decisions that have established precedents. Thus, it has been difficult for states to reach resolutions or to implement legal findings that would cover all of these cases. Also, as noted previously, it is not always clear whether existing legal understandings regarding territory, sovereignty, and possession or ownership can merely be grafted onto cyberspace and whether these concepts are unique and different in cyberspace and new legislation is needed.

In the absence of a clear set of binding laws for such cases, policy makers and analysts will often, therefore, speak not of laws and legal or illegal behavior but instead about norms and ethics. That is, an act does not need to be unlawful to be viewed as unethical. Ethics is not a set of predetermined moral stances tied to a particular religion, nor is it only a set of legal limits regarding what behavior is acceptable within a society or the international community. Instead, ethics is a branch of philosophy that attempts to answer eternal questions such as "What is the nature of truth?" and "What should a just society look like?" Today's ethical understandings often have their roots in Western ethical sources, including the writings of philosophers like Plato and Aristotle. However, all cultures have ethical traditions, and all of these ethical traditions can and do have a place in thinking about state behavior in cyberspace today. That is, even if there is no specific binding law internationally that articulates the limits to which a state can go to influence another state's elections, for example, there are often nonetheless normative understandings among members of the international community regarding what constitutes acceptable and unacceptable ethical and moral behavior by states.

The practice of ethics is particularly important in rapidly developing fields like cybersecurity because we can identify **gray areas**, or vacuums where the law may not be clear on whether or not a behavior is lawful and under what conditions. Many internet technologies today—including video and document sharing, the use of social media, and the use of search engines—are emerging technologies. Emerging technologies are radically novel and relatively fast-growing technologies that have the potential to exert a considerable impact on a state's socioeconomic domains. This impact may include the creation of new actors and institutions and new patterns of interactions among them.[2] Emerging technologies tend to quickly exert their influence on society, often in unpredictable or even ambiguous ways. Here, we can point to events like the Arab Spring in 2010, which was fueled by social media platforms like Twitter. Here, few analysts expected that Twitter would one day fuel social revolutions around the world, nor did they expect that states would need to establish regulations and procedures for limiting or multiplying the impacts of this technology.

That is, particularly in gray areas or when a novel problem occurs, practitioners and policy makers may have to rely on ethics to determine whether or not to embrace a particular practice—at least until the law catches up. Throughout this text, we have seen examples of novel problems or gray areas where the law has not yet caught up to the regulation of practices. For example, there is not yet an international consensus regarding who owns materials being held in cloud storage, what ethical practices should govern data generated by the internet of things, and how governments should regulate monetary issues arising from the use of digital currencies like Bitcoin. Scholars differ regarding what they see as the rights and responsibilities of users regarding safeguarding their electronic data and the situations in which they can be compelled to relinquish it.

As noted earlier in this volume, there is not yet a clear international consensus regarding how and under what conditions cyberspace and real terrestrial space are connected, on whether or not the same rules apply to both areas, and whether a violation that occurs in cyberspace is the same or different as a violation that happens in real terrestrial space.

Philosophers known as objectivists believe that it is possible to identify universally applicable rules regarding what is and is not ethically acceptable behavior. They feel that even if the environment has changed over time, there are still universal values that would be applicable (e.g., there would never be a situation in which it would be okay to engage in torture, regardless of the type of war one was engaged in or one's position in the war—i.e., whether one was winning or losing). Objectivist philosophers, therefore, strive to elucidate a set of ethics regarding how an individual or state should conduct themselves in regard to violence, for example. An objectivist would articulate a standard of behavior that would not be substantively different because one was engaged in cyberwar rather than conventional war, for example, nor would they perceive that standards for how a newspaper should treat information would be different in an online environment than they are in a traditional environment.

Moral relativists, however, believe that different ethics may apply in different situations. In this view, ethics may differ according to the culture in which one resides. (For example, a Confucian culture might emphasize granting additional rights to the elderly in a society based on filial piety as a value of that society. In other societies, however, the elderly might not be granted those same rights.) And in this view, an ethic might evolve or change over time. (For example, individuality is a value that is more prized today than it might have been in previous generations, whereas chastity is a value that is less prized today.) Thus, moral relativists might argue that online and physical environments are not always comparable and that different norms regarding reputation management, how one treats information, and how one treats others might prevail in the two distinct spaces.

ETHICAL LENSES FOR CONSIDERING CYBER VALUES

Thus far we have spoken about cyber norms and ethics in general terms. However, it is important to consider what specific ethics currently exist and the bases on which they rest.

Here, we can ask ethical questions regarding state behavior in cyberspace from a variety of different perspectives. We might ask about acceptable and unacceptable uses of technology—focusing on the ethics embedded in the technology itself. Alternately, we can ask about what constitutes ethical human or state behavior regarding the use of a particular technology. This stance assumes that technology does not have specific right or wrong uses, but rather the agency to decide what constitutes a right or wrong use resides within the human social and political environment. Finally, we might ask whether humans—and states—have a particular ethical obligation to the information environment itself. We can consider each of these stances in turn.

Embedded Values within Technology

First, some technology ethicists focus on defining acceptable and unacceptable uses of the technology itself. We see the approach reflected in the creation of norms such as a prohibition on using biological or chemical weapons. The International Convention on the Prohibition of the Development, Production and Stockpiling of Bacteriological (Biological) and Toxin Weapons and on Their Destruction, ratified by the United States in 1975, is a codification of the normative principle that certain types of weapons, including biological weapons, chemical weapons, and blinding agents, are unethical and inhumane and should not be allowed in warfare. Similarly, in recent years, activists have called for an international ban on the use of so-called killer robots, or unmanned autonomous vehicles used in combat.[3] In addition, both professional organizations and states have attempted to create international principles that would govern the use of artificial intelligence in computing through specifying acceptable and unacceptable applications of artificial intelligence.

The ethical argument in these cases is that some facet of the technology itself is incompatible with the goal of human flourishing or the development of human capabilities and capacities. Here, philosophers of technology argue that when a new technology is introduced, there may be a period during which there is not a consensus regarding how this technology should function and how it should be used. However, they note that over time, communities arrive at a site of technological closure, where appropriate uses of the technology are defined and accepted as a matter of consensus. Here, we might argue that the international community has not yet arrived at technological closure concerning what it regards as ethical and unethical uses of social media because the technology is still too recent. Thus, we do not currently have a consensus regarding how the international community should respond to events like the use of trolls and false accounts in social media to sway outcomes in the United Kingdom's vote on withdrawing from the European Union or in elections on the local, state, and national levels. In this view, over time an ethical consensus is likely to emerge, which can then be codified and enforced.

Ethical Limits on Human Use of Technology

In this case, the ethics regarding technology use derive from facets of the technology itself. However, we can also obtain ethical principles by thinking not about what technology is for but about how humans should use a technology that is available to humanity. Here, analysts describe an ethic of restraint—or a situation in which a specific use of technology might be practical or feasible but where it is nonetheless still regarded as ethically unacceptable. For that reason, individuals and societies might make a reasoned decision to forgo the benefits of using such a technology if its implementation is regarded as violating greater moral, ethical, or humanitarian principles.

Here, we can consider debates about the ethics of genetic enhancement. Enhancement refers to a situation in which individuals might undergo "medical or biological interventions . . . designed to improve performance, appearance or capability besides what is necessary to achieve, sustain or restore health."[4] That is, enhancement refers to a situation in which an individual might receive a medication, medical procedure, or implant not to cure an existing defect but instead to become "more than human" through receiving an increase in a human capacity like intelligence, memory, processing speed, or physical strength. Ethicists who suggest that humanity should forego the potential benefits of this type of enhancement (such as advances that might arise as the result of creating human-machine hybrids) often voice two objections: First, some ethicists worry that by merging the boundaries between man and machine, we risk giving up some essential qualities of our humanity as well as the opportunity to learn and grow as humans through experiencing all facets of the human experience, including experiencing fear or even physical pain. (Such ethical concerns have also been voiced concerning practices related to transhumanism—or the creation of technologies that would allow a human individual's consciousness to be uploaded to the internet after the person's physical body has expired. These practices are also seen as blurring the lines between human and not human.) In addition, ethicists are concerned about the issue of equity, believing that if the ability to adopt human enhancements is made available, it is unlikely that everyone everywhere will benefit equally from these technological advances, in which case some humans may end up with more material and physical advantages than others.

Human Ethics for Technology Use: The Example of Surveillance

However, debates about restraint can also revolve around states and state activity. Here, for example, we can consider disputes that have arisen in many societies in the aftermath of the Edward Snowden revelations of US government surveillance activities. Whereas it might be possible today to create a situation where almost all of our daily activities could be tracked, and where that information might be shared with government law enforcement, ethicists still ask whether the conduct of such actions would be ethical. Should states automatically embrace all of the new surveillance capabilities that are available to law enforcement today, or are there situations in which states should refrain from utilizing these technologies, acting instead to preserve people's rights to privacy and autonomy?

In reacting to revelations in 2013 that Australia had conducted electronic surveillance in Indonesia, Indonesia's foreign minister described such activities as "just not cricket" and "outside the norm." He expressed the ethical position regarding the duties of states to engage in restraint in stating:

> Countries may have capacities, technical capacities to intercept and carry out activities that have been reported and information may have been gathered.
>
> But whether you would want to put that into effect and therefore potentially damage the kind of trust and confidence that has been nurtured and developed over many decades and years, is something that we may want to ponder.[5]

The ethical principle of restraint is not new and indeed can be traced back to Aristotle. Moreover, there is a precedent for applying it when speaking about the ethics of information. For example, journalists engage in restraint when they do not publish the names of minors who have been accused of crimes or of rape victims.[6] Here, journalists have decided that the individual's right to privacy is more important than the public's right to know specific facts about these people.

CRITICAL ISSUES

INFORMATION PRIVACY

What is privacy? We might define privacy as the right to engage in activities without being observed or monitored. But it is more complicated than that. Different individuals, like celebrities, might be expected to have less privacy than others due to their status as public figures. Their lives might be said to belong to the public domain. In addition, we might have different expectations of privacy depending on whether we are in our homes, which are regarded legally and ethically as private spaces, or whether we are out in public. And this right of privacy can also be extended to cover not just our rights to have our physical persons and activities go unobserved by those we have not authorized but also to cover privacy rights that extend to our personal information, including educational or medical information. We might even claim to have a right to privacy regarding the data that we generate while we are online, claiming that others do not have the right to view the information that may be compiled regarding our web searches or online communications.

Privacy is thus a multifaceted set of rights. The understanding of what is private, who has the right to privacy, and the penalties associated with violating privacy rights can thus differ depending on the historical period, the specific culture in which one resides, or the status of the individual. (That is, children and those who require special care due to physical or mental disabilities might in some situations have less of an expectation of privacy.)

Indeed, Mark Zuckerberg, the founder of Facebook, has claimed that since the advent of social media, each subsequent generation has had less of an expectation of privacy. Young people today may feel comfortable, for example, filming a video inside their family home and posting it online, whereas some older people might think that the family home is private and should only be viewed by those whom the family has explicitly invited in. In addition, anthropologists have noted that those individuals who grow up in cultures where family spaces are often small and shared by a large number of individuals may have significantly different expectations of privacy than those who grow up in a traditional nuclear family occupying a detached house. And in many Middle Eastern cultures, women may follow cultural practices that require them to conceal their physical bodies through wearing traditional garments like an abaya or a chador. These practices may be less common in other cultures because societies differ in their expectations about whether one's physical body should be displayed in public or kept private.

Some private rights are a matter of legal policy. For example, within the United States, the Health Insurance Portability and Accountability Act (HIPAA) regulates who may see an individual's medical information, whereas the Family Education Rights and Privacy Act (FERPA) determines who may know an individual's educational records. Within the European Union, the European Data Protection Regulation addresses issues of online privacy. This legislation mandates that users be told when they visit a website that installs cookies on their computers to track their online activities. Users must explicitly consent to be tracked in this way before cookies can be installed. And in Britain, where law enforcement experts frequently utilized closed circuit television cameras (CCTV) to monitor public spaces for reasons of counterterrorism or counter-vandalism,

(Continued)

(Continued)

laws require that citizens be informed via signs whenever they are in areas where their images may be collected and viewed via CCTV. We use the term *normative expectations of privacy* to refer to ideas about what is socially appropriate in terms of privacy, although normative expectations of privacy often line up with legal understandings as well. Because norms, or unwritten social expectations or rules, are usually specific to a culture, norms regarding privacy may also differ from one society to another.[7]

However, in other areas, normative and legal understandings regarding data and online privacy are still evolving. In thinking about privacy, cyber ethics expert Luciano Floridi distinguishes among types of privacy, including physical privacy (the right not to be observed or to be left alone), decision privacy (the right to make decisions about your own life without interference by others), mental privacy (the ability to have your own thoughts), and information privacy (the right to control what others know about you and what information is collected and shared about you).[8]

Today, it is particularly challenging for policy makers to define norms regarding privacy for three reasons. First, today the demarcations between what is public and what is private space seem to be shifting. Practices like coworking, working from home, and utilizing video-sharing technologies like Facebook in public spaces have helped blur the public-private distinction in new and intriguing ways.

At the same time, privacy issues are arising in the area of data privacy. Here, many ethicists suggest that individuals have the right to know who is collecting their data, where it will be stored, what it might potentially be used for, and who might possibly have access to it. In addition, ethicists suggest that citizens should be informed if they are in places where their data is being collected (e.g., if your grocery store is tracking your phone to see what products you are most interested in while in the store) and stored.

However, some ethicists argue that privacy is not a right but a responsibility. They feel that users of technology need to pay more attention themselves to the types of data they are producing and sharing as well as whether or not they are in situations where they are being tracked.

Sources

Grodzinsky, F., and H. Tavani. "Cyberstalking, Personal Privacy, and Moral Responsibility." *Ethics and Information Technology* 4, no. 2 (2002): 123–132.

Manjikian, M. *Cybersecurity Ethics: An Introduction* (New York, NY: Routledge, 2017).

Within international relations, the notion that states should engage in restraint in the arena of spying is often traced back to a statement made in 1929 by then Secretary of State Henry Stimson, when he said, "Gentlemen do not read each other's mail." Here, he established the principle that a state's identity within the international system was determined by its ability to behave ethically, including not violating the rights of other states through, for example, engaging in unauthorized surveillance.

More recently, David Orman, head of Britain's GCHQ (the UK equivalent of the American National Security Agency) has argued for the application of the principle of proportionality in relation to engaging in surveillance. Proportionality, or the ability to apply only enough force to achieve a specific objective, provides the basis upon which states are mandated to participate in restraint in conflict according to the international Law on Armed Conflict (LOAC). In the arena of warfare, proportionality means that a state should use only enough force to expel an invader from its territory to engage in territorial self-defense. However, the state should use restraint in that it should not attempt to either destroy an invader and its territory, nor should it pursue the invader outside the bounds of the state's territory, once it has been expelled. Here, again, the virtue of proportionality is seen as a value or ethic that serves to create an international community that both respects the existence of other states and seeks to avoid the escalation of conflict. Orman, therefore, argues that in considering whether to engage in surveillance of an adversary, states should consider possible harms and should also exercise restraint in deciding whom to surveil and under what conditions.[9]

Enforcing the Human Commitment to Ethical Behavior in Cyberspace

Within the branch of philosophy known as ethics, there are many subdisciplines whose work is relevant to our discussion of what sorts of acts—by individuals, groups, and states within the international system and within society—could be considered ethical or unethical. When considering what constitutes ethical behavior in cyberspace, we can look to the field of professional ethics to see how professional computer programmers and technology designers have articulated what they regard as acceptable and unacceptable uses of these new technologies. Here, we can refer to the epistemic community—or the international professional community of those who work in computer science—which has gradually over time articulated a set of normative understandings regarding the rights and responsibilities of those who work in this field. Such understandings are codified in documents such as the Ethical Code of the Association for Computing Machinery. In addition, the epistemic community offers training to new professionals in the area of computer ethics, including providing Certified Ethical Hacker (CEH) certification. Epistemic communities play a role in codifying and articulating ethical understandings in building a consensus in favor of these principles and often also serve to export these principles, particularly to developing countries that may have less established ethical and professional traditions.

Some of the principles articulated in the Association for Computing Machinery (the largest and oldest professional organization for computer scientists in the world) code of ethics include a requirement that members adhere to overall national norms regarding the securing and registration of materials with national security implications. They are also required to adhere to regimes for publicizing information about scientific advances. They must conform to export regimes and undertake ethical and legal training at conferences and professional workshops.[10] In addition, the technology community has provided input on the European Union's General Data Protection Regulation, and the European Regulation on Electronic Identities and Trust Services (eIDAS), as well as serving as permanent stakeholders within the European Network and Information Security Agency (ENISA) of the European Union.[11]

Of course, as with other professional norms—such as those governing the ability of a biologist to work with and on biological agents that might lead to the development of biological weapons—not everyone working in a profession will adhere to these norms. In 2013, it was revealed that Edward Snowden had previously obtained a certificate in ethical hacking, which had, in reality, furnished him with the skills he needed to carry out his hacks against the National Security Agency. Thus, although professional organizations can serve an important role in socializing individuals into professional norms as well as building international support for the export of norms and values, they cannot fully protect against the actions of rogue actors who may not be successfully socialized into professional norms or internalize those norms. Occupational norms are thus not legally binding, although they do sometimes overlap with laws. (For example, medical professionals who sold prescription drugs to consumers could be sanctioned legally within their state as well as losing their license through sanctions by their professional organization.)

Just as professionals within a particular profession have the ability to shape norms of ethical behavior, so do states within the international community. Within international relations theory, the English School or international society lens highlights the fact that states that share similar values or a commitment to similar virtues can create international structures of cooperation.[12] In describing international society, Hedley Bull described the international system as coming into existence when states come into contact with one another and come to realize that their decisions have an impact on one another, thereby causing them to take into account the effect of their actions on others when choosing a course of action. Here, Bull assumes that all states have a common interest in the preservation of the international system itself in a peaceful form—thus sharing a Kantian sensibility.[13]

Some analysts view the internet as a type of international society. That is, although the internet is anarchic, there is nonetheless a pre-existing set of values, norms, and expectations that govern online interactions. Internet users understand and are aware of their shared interest in preserving the internet as a usable technology, which involves recognizing and agreeing to conform with rules that help govern and establish peaceful and nondisruptive online interactions. In this way, states that use the internet can be seen as having a common sort of citizenship due to their shared commitment to preserving the internet's functionality. And states that violate those shared commitments can be regarded as rogue states or pariahs, subject to the censure of the international community or even to exclusion from international society.[14]

Using this lens thus helps us understand Germany's reaction when they found out that they and their leaders had been the subject of unauthorized US surveillance through the auspices of the National Security Agency. In using the internet to conduct surveillance on its allies, the United States violated an unspoken and unarticulated set of ethics or normative commitments that other states had subscribed to. This ethic includes the idea that even if a state has the technological capabilities to learn all of its allies' secrets, it should engage in restraint and not take advantage of those capabilities. Instead, states should take their allies' commitments at face value without utilizing unauthorized means to seek proof of those commitments.

The Ethic of Stewardship: Ethics Derived from the Internet Environment

In addition to asking about ethical uses of technology itself, we can also pose ethical questions about the obligations that users have as stewards of the information environment. Here, we draw a parallel with the school of environmental ethics known as Deep Ecology. In applying the ethics of Deep Ecology to thinking about animal and environmental rights, ethicists assume that the rights that the Earth has to remain undisturbed and to flourish are as important as the rights that humans have to exploit the resources of the Earth. Thus, using this lens, they might conclude that the right of a corporation to develop a pristine natural environment so that humans may enjoy it is not as important as the right of that environment itself to continue undisturbed.

Floridi, in his work *The Fourth Revolution*, puts forth an ethic in which the infosphere itself has rights. He suggests that all humans reside in an information environment that is governed by laws, just as laws like gravity govern the physical environment. He proposes that humans should regard themselves as the stewards of the information environment, working to create laws and regulations that would safeguard that environment and conform to the laws of that environment. Within the infosphere, information is said to move in information flows. The information has a right to move unimpeded throughout the infosphere, and humans must allow the infosphere to flourish without either interfering with or "polluting" the information environment. In this view, then, erecting a paywall or filtering system that censors information or excludes some users from the full experience of the infosphere would be unethical. It would be seen as an act of human overreach that robs the infosphere of its rights. In this view, utilizing false accounts on Twitter or Facebook, or posting information that one knows is false, would violate the infosphere. In this view, the infosphere is an environment where information should remain in its purest, truest form—and actively inserting false information into the infosphere would be an act similar to polluting a pristine stream.[15] Creating false information also "poisons" the infosphere, creating long-run harms because it makes it harder for people to trust information found there in the future.

In Floridi's view, the infosphere is moving toward a mature information society, where accurate information will be available for user needs in much the same way that drinkable clean water flows out the tap today in most developed countries. The assumption is that everyone everywhere has a right to receive such accurate information, just as they have a right to unadulterated food or clean water. Those who impede that right are said to have engaged in ethical violations,[16] not against other states or even against the technology but against the environment itself. In Floridi's view, then, conducting unauthorized surveillance against allies is wrong because it creates friction within the infosphere, which could impede the flow of information.

Thus far, we have considered only the ethics of the internet itself. However, we can also ask whether ethical violations that occur in cyberspace are the same or different from ethical abuses that arise in real space. Also, we can ask about the relationship between ethical violations in the two areas and whether there is something unique about cyberspace that encourages unethical behavior.

Does Cyberspace Allow Unethical Behavior by States?

As we have noted throughout this text, the internet in its earliest incarnation was perceived and described as a unique space. The internet founders expected it would be a world apart where people and states would somehow behave better than they did in real life. These early internet pioneers believed that there were values and norms that somehow resided within the technology of the internet itself, which individuals would put on and acquire as they went online. Now, however, we are more likely to believe that people bring their preexisting values (including preexisting attitudes toward gender and racial politics, commitments to one's national or religious convictism, and so forth) to the internet space and that people, therefore, use the internet as an extension of real space, behaving in ways within cyberspace that enact their preexisting values and behaviors. In this way, the internet is no longer conceptualized of as space apart but rather as an extension of real, physical space.

At the same time, some analysts suggest that the nature of cyberspace itself and its features make it a more inviting space for states to behave unethically. Here we can identify characteristics like the ability to act anonymously in cyberspace, the speed at which transactions occur, and the ability to transcend geographical boundaries between states through the wonders of technology. The most pessimistic of analysts suggest that the unusual terrain of cyberspace means that some types of unethical behaviors will always occur in cyberspace because they are an unavoidable outgrowth of its geography. They are also pessimistic about the achievement of such sustained long-term objectives as the articulation and enforcement of strong cyber ethics or cyber norms for the global community.

Here, cyber pessimists note two reasons why this is unlikely. First, they believe that it is easier for states and individuals to evade accountability or to escape taking full responsibility for their actions online in the same way that they would in the real world. Because of facets of the internet's architecture, including the attribution problem and the possibility of participating online in an anonymous fashion, they argue, people and states may be willing to do things in an online environment that they would not do in the real world. For example, people are more likely to harass others online when they believe they are anonymous.

On an interstate level, we can argue that the availability of certain types of technologically mediated activities—including electronic warfare, the use of psychological operations in social media, and technologies of surveillance—allow states to avoid public accountability for their actions. That is, states can behave in more covert rather than overt fashions and can engage in more activities and more types of events that can be publicly disavowed.

The internet's environment is also seen as one that allows for or even facilitates practices of deception. Remember, the internet is a place where there are multiple sources of online information of varying quality because there are few barriers to entry in establishing oneself as a purveyor of information in that environment. Because information can be created and disseminated so quickly, and because there is no central authority, there are few resources for policing the quality of online information or for taking down inaccurate information. Instead, users need to adopt a "buyer beware" attitude as they choose their practices for ensuring that the information they access is accurate and unbiased.

Recently, critics have identified a variety of online threats—from **deep fakes** (video footage that has been artificially created but that purports to show a public figure making a speech or engaging in an activity) to phishing attacks to pervasive online harassment of protected groups. Here we will examine the problems of accountability and deception in turn.

The Problem of Accountability

States have always kept secrets. Information classification practices existed in the Roman Empire, with details about warfare plans or one's military capabilities being tightly held. However, within the democratic tradition of government, leaders generally believe that they should govern in transparent ways (i.e., moral leaders should have nothing to hide) and that citizens have a right to know about the decisions that leaders make on their behalf.[17] American citizens can thus utilize a Freedom of Information Act (FOIA) request to inquire about government activities through requesting declassified research reports, telegrams, and cables.

However, the public right to transparency is not absolute, and states sometimes need to be able to keep certain facets of their activities private, or concealed from the media and citizens. The phrase *arcana imperii* refers to "secrets of state," or the things that citizens do not need to know. Even in the real world, then, newspapers like the *New York Times* or the *Washington Post* may agree not to publish details, such as the locations of troops or future troop movements, if doing so would endanger an ongoing military operation or lead to a loss of life. They also enact the virtue of restraint in, for example, not sharing information such as the names of rape victims or underage victims of crime.

However, the majority of a state's activities are not carried out covertly but rather are carried out overtly in ways that can be observed both by their citizens and outside observers. In the United States, the War Powers Act requires that the US Congress formally adopt a resolution before going to war against an adversary. In this way, citizens can weigh in through the force of public opinion, urging their legislators to back or reject the resolution and demonstrating publicly in favor of or against the resolution. In contrast, covert activity is a broad term that can refer both to long-term strategic plans by states (as, e.g., a plan to destabilize an adversary's government through creating sources of opposition to the ruling political party) or immediate short-term activities (such as mining an enemy's harbor to prevent its use during a specific activity). Although any activity that violates a state's sovereign right to conduct its domestic affairs free from outside interference is considered illegal within international law, states have always acknowledged that intelligence services engage in covert activities. The term *secret war* has been coined to describe a situation in which a state carries out activities against an adversary outside the scope of congressional oversight or domestic public opinion.

Covert activity is problematic for two reasons: First, a president might use covert activity to achieve his or her foreign policy priorities in situations where they differ from those of Congress or the citizens. In this way, he or she is seen as behaving outside the bounds of the democratic system through engaging in presidential overreach. In addition, states may use covert activity in situations where some of the options for state behavior might be regarded as ethically or morally unpalatable (e.g., choosing to torture prisoners to obtain information in violation of the Geneva Convention). By keeping their activities secret, states can avoid having to deal with negative public opinion domestically and can also prevent any censure or discipline that might be meted out by the international community. (In this way, the state can maintain its public face as a democracy while secretly acting in an anti-democratic fashion.)

Today, however, covert activity is more likely to be embraced by states within the online environment, and over time states may prefer to fight covert wars in cyberspace rather than fighting overt land, air, or naval battles. Indeed, Valeriano and Maness argue that in the period since 2001, the vast majority of conflicts fought in cyberspace by states are better understood as covert activities than they are as wars. They foresee a future in which there will be ongoing low-level cyber conflicts between states. States will utilize cyber warfare to conduct espionage against each other, to carry out low levels of sabotage, and to spy and attempt to undermine rival states, particularly those within the same region. However, most will not rise to the level of an international diplomatic incident.[18]

Although in many ways, the conduct of perpetual low-grade cyberwar among rivals sounds ethically more palatable than the conduct of traditional conventional wars, which might result in mass casualties, as we have shown, these actions are ethically problematic because state leaders can carry out these activities outside of the public's awareness and knowledge. In this way, arguably, societies become less democratic because citizens are no longer as invested in or aware of the actions of their leaders.

The Problem of Deception

If the internet's architecture makes it more likely that states will seek to avoid ethical responsibility through conducting covert actions, it also makes it more likely that states will engage in other types of deceptive behavior. But what is deception, and why it is unethical?

Deception refers to practices of deliberately presenting false information or allowing people to believe false information when you know it to be false, although not identifying it as such. Deception is neither absolutely wrong, nor is it always justified. For example, it is commonly accepted that military personnel may engage in deception during wartime for purposes of self-defense.[19] Deception is considered an acceptable stratagem or ruse of war. That is, a state may utilize a decoy ship during wartime to draw away enemy fire from one's navy personnel by encouraging the adversary to fire on the false ship instead.

However, using deception online may be particularly ethically problematic for two reasons. First, it is easier to lie online than it is in real life—both for individuals and for states—because the online environment is only loosely linked to the real world in many ways. For example, the ability to have multiple online accounts on different platforms, or even to have multiple accounts within one platform, means that individuals can present themselves in a variety of ways. At the same time, the existence of the attribution problem makes it difficult to always trace actions back to their sources.

Thus, it is possible to create a freestanding identity online that is not explicitly linked to one's real-life person—at least in some nations currently. As psychologists note, individuals often present only their best face online and may engage in practices from digitally altering their photos to enhance their appearance to reporting just good news on Facebook. Psychologists often describe such practices as mentally unhealthy, reporting that individuals who spend a great deal of time on social media may be more depressed as a result because they compare their real lives to the idealized lives of others as presented on Facebook or Instagram.

But are acts like creating a false website or allowing a Russian military intelligence operative to impersonate an American citizen in an online interaction thus a stratagem or ruse of war—which is allowable—or is it instead some form of illegal or unethical activity? As Bagge points out, Russia's intelligence services have utilized **maskirovka**—defined as "activities such as the use of dummies, decoys, execution of demonstration maneuvers, camouflage, concealment, denial, deception and disinformation"—since before the Soviet Union was created in 1917. Indeed, he notes that they were taught at a military school founded by Tsar Nicholas II.[20]

Here one might argue that today's maskirovka activities are different because, in seeking to change the outcome of a US presidential election in 2016, Russia violated America's ability to conduct its sovereign affairs. One might also argue that maskirovka activities that target civilians, rather than military personnel, are also a violation of the military agreements that allow for deception as a stratagem and ruse of wartime.

Here, different ethical traditions might see such activities differently. The tradition of virtue ethics suggests that one's actions are best understood within the context of one's identity and that all of one's actions together serve to constitute one's identity. That is, an individual should seek to be someone who doesn't lie, and to be that person, one should always be truthful. Similarly, a nation that sometimes engages in deception might find that it is perceived as overall less trustworthy within the international arena than a nation that is always truthful. Here, detractors argue that there are situations in which lying might be ethically appropriate. For example, if you were hiding a Jewish family in your home during World War Two in Europe and Nazi soldiers knocked on your door and asked who was living in your home, utilitarian ethicists argue that the honorable or moral thing to do would be to lie to the Nazi soldiers about the presence of the family in your home.

Utilitarians apply a cost-benefit calculus in which the most moral thing to do would be the action that produces the greatest good for all. In this case, they would argue that the good created by lying to the Nazi soldiers is offset by the bad of telling a lie. Within the Russian context, maskirovka activities online have been justified using a utilitarian calculus. Russian analyst Pasentshev describes what he views as a Russian defensive strategy in which Russia seeks to find the point at which an organization might be split open and destabilized through the application of targeted psychological operations aimed at sowing distrust among organization members so that they will lash out at one another.[21] He describes Russia's creation of such strategies but argues that they are not being used against targets like the US electoral system but rather against terrorist organizations operating both within and outside the borders of Russia itself. He argues that the social good realized by ending a terrorist threat overrides any ethical questions that might arise regarding this methodology. Indeed, the US intelligence community also has programs to recruit and train American civilian and military personnel to become members of online chat rooms frequented by Islamic fundamentalists to gather information about them as well as to dissuade chat room members from becoming radicalized as terrorists. In both of these situations, the utilitarian calculus suggests that the good or value that should be prioritized is in ensuring the best possible outcome through using this technology rather than seeking to use the technology itself most ethically.

A third ethical lens is deontological ethics. This approach asks the decision maker to consider whether he or she would be willing to live under any ethical rule or model that might be created. A related ethic, that of Rawlsian justice ethics, says that the most just ethical rule is one that does the least amount of harm to the most vulnerable subject of any rule. That is, this approach would not say that deception in and of itself was always wrong, nor would it seek to articulate the sets of outcomes that might justify its use. Rather, it would ask who, if anyone, is likely to be hurt by the use of deception, including online psychological warfare. Thus, it would focus on how those who lack education or experience might be particularly "duped" by deceptive online practices.

Deception and the Degradation of Trust in the Infosphere

Returning to the infosphere ethic approach, we find that the ability of individuals, corporations, and nations to behave in deceptive ways online (along with the ability to evade accountability or responsibility for their actions) can affect the online environment, degrading the quality of all online interactions as a result. That is, deception and lying have an impact on trust as an absolute quality as well as trust within relationships.

But what does it mean to trust an individual or an organization? Philosopher Russell Hardin describes trust as a willingness to delegate the authority to another to carry out some task, from providing information to watching one's children or protecting one's country, on our behalf. He argues that the decision to trust results from a rational calculation of the costs and benefits of doing so.[22] That is, because we cannot always carry out all actions by ourselves (i.e., one cannot simultaneously be a full-time artist and a full-time soldier), we allow other people or groups, in certain situations, to act on our behalf. In thinking about whether or not to allow someone to act on our behalf, we weigh the risks (such as the possibility that a website might take our money but never send us the product) against the savings that results from trusting (i.e., I would prefer that the store manufacture a sweater for me rather than spending my time to make one myself). In a sense, whenever we visit an online journalism site, we are engaged in a trust relationship. Because I myself cannot go to Jerusalem to check on the progress of the Middle Eastern peace negotiations, I instead delegate that task to CNN, trusting that they will carry it out on my behalf, reporting back accurate and unbiased information about what has transpired.

Although trust is ultimately a decision, there are some conditions that make the development of trust more likely. We are more likely to trust those, for example, with whom we have long-standing personal relationships and with whom we have ties outside of the specific transaction we are considering undertaking. (For example, I might trust my neighbor to watch my house while I am away because I see him or her frequently and we are friends.) In international relations theory terms, the decision to betray or trust an interlocutor is a strategic interaction between two players. Each player needs to consider the other person's motives and what that player can gain from either behaving as expected or "defecting" from the trust relationship.

On the internet, however, the ties created among people tend to be shallow rather than deep. They tend to be of short duration and revolve around only specific interactions. Due to the attribution problem, and the existence of anonymity on the internet, you may not know the person providing you with news updates via Twitter or posting videos on Instagram. In addition, the person may have a motive that does not align with yours: A troll may purposely be attempting to elicit a reaction from you by providing news that is false or incendiary. The other person has more to gain from engaging in deception than he or she does from being truthful.

Fixing the Problem of Deception Online

Currently, policy makers propose two types of fixes for this trust problem. First, technology experts are working to create better systems for identifying the computers with whom you are interacting, and for checking that information is traveling safely from point A to point B without being corrupted by a third party that might insert itself between the players in the relationship. (For example, one might be less apt to trust the news from major news outlets if there are multiple news outlets that have names that are almost the same as the trusted news source. News seekers might mistakenly go to an incorrect site that has less of an interest in providing unbiased news.) Online marketplaces have developed rating systems so that you can see whether a seller is credible, and software systems use certificates to check that individuals are interacting with trusted sources. Firewalls can also help make sure that only trusted sources can communicate with you online.

Some states, however, believe that the best way to address this trust problem is to fundamentally remake the internet in such a way that it is no longer open or anonymous. That is, in the absence of trust or when trust is insufficient, we may turn instead to regulation. Regulation may be used in situations where the stakes are too high to rely on trust alone or when an industry is too complex to self-regulate. Thus, we have a Food and Drug Administration to regulate the quality of our food supply and pharmaceuticals rather than merely relying on farmers and pharmacy companies to police themselves or to engage in only trustworthy interactions. In addition, the American medical professions engage in self-regulation but are also the subject of specific laws regulating their behavior. In China, the state regulates online identities. They have adopted a "real name" policy in which users must use their names rather than pseudonyms. In addition, China's rating system for users ties together people's identities online with other facts about them, such as their financial stability and education.[23]

However, there is a trade-off in substituting state-led regulation for the development of norms and ethics. By requiring internet users to use their real names, China has made online activism and genuine intellectual inquiry less likely and also strengthened state power vis-à-vis the power of democratic activists. Although requiring all users to act only under their real names creates stability, predictability, and ultimately trust in online interactions, the creation of this trust is not free. Indeed, it can be quite expensive.

In this chapter's final section, we consider the relationship between ethics and norms and the likelihood that states will over time evolve a shared consensus about acceptable and unacceptable online behaviors by states.

THE EMERGENCE OF CYBER NORMS

What is a norm? The term refers to "an expected or established rule of behavior." It is what we might typically expect individuals, or states, to do.[24] An individual who violates a norm is said to be engaged in deviant behavior or that which does not conform with societal norms. Non-normative, or deviant behavior, could be something that is regarded as strange or improper (such as wearing a bathing suit when one is not at the beach), but this does not mean that it is explicitly illegal either nationally or internationally. Instead, norms often reflect social conventions, and social norms can change or evolve. (For example, one hundred years ago, many nations had laws against interracial marriage and the practice of homosexuality because such activities were viewed as morally wrong within that social and temporal context. Today, norms and laws are quite different.)

Norms can be prescriptive (or aspirational), defining expected or ideal behaviors, or they can be descriptive, illustrating shared understandings that already exist. Norms are related to state identity in the sense that a state might think of itself as a law-abiding and norm-respecting member of international society or as a pariah or rogue state that does not conform with international norms.

Where Do Norms Come From?

Where do norms come from? Some analysts believe norms evolve organically over time and that the only reason there are not currently strong international binding norms in cyberspace is because of the newness of the venue. However, others[25] argue that norms are built deliberately (rather than evolving organically). In their model, certain states, acting as norm entrepreneurs, work to consciously export and build consensus around norms within the international community through a three-stage process. First, norms emerge through the actions of a norm entrepreneur, who might be a transnational actor (such as a human rights organization) or a powerful state that acts to frame the norm and that reaches out to norm acceptors within a nation. Norm entrepreneurs (both transnational actors and states) can build support for the norm until a tipping point is reached, with the vast majority of actors accepting the validity of the norm. Once a tipping point is reached, a norm cascade occurs with more actors signing on to the norm—which might be codified in legislation or a treaty or through a more informal mechanism. The final stage is norm acceptance, when the norm becomes part of the international system.

In thinking about creating cyberspace norms within the international community, we can point to the actions of professional groups like the Association for Computing Machinery (which established professional norms for cyber practitioners) or the members of the group that authored the *Tallinn Manual* (thus establishing norms in relation to cyber conflict) as norm entrepreneurs. And the United States itself serves as a norm entrepreneur in seeking to establish the right of all people to have access to the internet as a universally accepted principle. American foreign policy initiatives—both on a unilateral and multilateral basis through cooperation with organizations like NATO and the United Nations— focus on taking steps to establish certain values as universal norms, acting as front-runner states through modeling secure cyberspace policies that can then be emulated by other states.[26] Documents like the 2015 Department of Defense Cyber Strategy and the 2011 US International Strategy for Cyberspace describe the United States as working with allies and adversaries to create agreements aimed at creating "secure cyberspace." Secure cyberspace is presented here as a global good from which all would benefit.

In the case of norms regarding cyberwarfare and cyber aggression, the United States, in conjunction with NATO, the Organization for Security and Cooperation in Europe (OSCE) and the European Union, has sought to make the claim that existing international laws about conflict, including the LOAC, are universally valid and that they also extend to the conduct of cyberwar.[27] The United States has worked to extend existing normative frameworks—including those related to human rights or related to use of force—to talking about cyberwarfare.[28] Furthermore, the United Nations and the United States have sought to codify these understandings in international and bilateral treaties, including an attempt to include cyberweapons within the confines of the Wassenaar Agreement, which establishes the requirement that states consider how adversarial regimes might use software and code before agreeing to their export.

Early norm entrepreneurs' success may depend on their ability to frame issues in ways that resonate with the public and specific constituencies. Here, professional organizations may be uniquely suited to carry out this role. For example, discourse related to the CEH credential notes how a programmer's job prospects may be enhanced by pursuing such a certification. The international appeal of the credential suggests that these professional norms can cross borders and take hold in other cultures, even when they do not match preexisting professional norms.

In each case, we see the second stage, norm cascade, emerging when a critical mass of actors adopts the norm. At this stage, states may wish to demonstrate that they have adopted the norm, and they may push others to do so as well.[29] And over time, many international laws that are seen as having emerged and become the subject of an international consensus have later become codified into both national and international laws, thus assuming the force of law. That is, understandings that states should not use assassination as a tool of foreign policy, that diplomats have a sacrosanct status that means they should not be targeted, or understandings that torture should not be used have all subsequently been codified in documents such as the Geneva Convention and the LOAC.

However, not every attempt at establishing a new norm is successful. In addition, within the international system in the absence of a central authority who serves to enforce norms, it is not always clear if or how norm violators, including states, might be sanctioned or brought into conformance if they have violated a norm. For example, although many states opposed the US National Security Agency's data collection practices, no formal measures were ever taken against the United States or its actions, such as imposing sanctions or censuring them in an international body like the United Nations.[30]

Obstacles to the Creation of Universal Cyber Ethics and Cyber Norms

What obstacles do states and other actors face in attempting to create meaningful cyber ethics and cyber norms? First, not all states agree about the process by which norms emerge. Less powerful states sometimes feel that more powerful states are imposing norms upon them while presenting these norms as universal rather than as a product of the preferences of more powerful states. These states reject the assumption that there are genuine global norms that all nations would necessarily hold to or support—because nations are different, having different histories and cultures as well as different orientations toward their citizens and the international system. They argue that what might look to those in the West like a definition and consensus building around an international norm may look to many others like the imposition of a specific set of norms that they have then been forced to accept. This viewpoint explains why an attempt to establish an international norm may fail to take hold on a local level.[31]

Legal theorist John Austin furthermore argues that legal norms result from diplomatic compromises among states that draft agreements.[32] He argues that a decision to comply with an international norm is the result of a strategic choice by a nation's policy makers—who are considering both domestic and international implications of the norm—rather than the result of some magical convergence in normative understandings among nations. At the same time, we can see that nations might put forth proposals for the adoption of certain norms not out of a deep-seated set of ethical convictions but rather for pragmatic reasons associated with state security. (For example, a nation that cannot compete in a nuclear arms race might want to deprive its adversaries of the ability to create these weapons. Thus, it might sponsor resolutions to slow its development rather than because such weapons are unethical and harmful.)

In considering norms governing internet censorship and surveillance, China has accused the United States of misusing its advantage as a first mover to present its norms as necessary for the proper development and functioning of international cyberspace. Here we can consider "Document 9," issued in April 2013 by China's Communist Party. In this document, Chinese leaders warned against seven perils that could potentially accompany the internet's reach into Chinese society. This included a warning about the dangers posed by Western constitutional democracy and Western culture, both of which had been presented as universal rather than Western values.[33] Similarly, Russian analysts believe that it is unfair of the United States to say that the internet must reflect America norms of governance and values. Instead, they argue, each state should have the ability to steer technology so that it is congruent with its own nation's norms and values.

In this instance, both China and Russia would, therefore, oppose the compilation of a list of "internet enemies" put together annually by the group Reporters without Borders. The list, which aims to call attention to nations that engage in practices of censorship and surveillance online, rests on the understanding that the right to free and unfettered internet access is absolute and that states should not impede that access. However, as noted, not all states currently agree with the contention that there exists such an internationally valid and accepted ethic regarding internet access.[34]

One can also identify situations of norm mismatch between international and domestic norms concerning cyber activities, and this perspective can be useful in understanding why some attempts to establish an international cyber norm have failed. In particular, one can identify multiple competing norms in the area of intellectual property, including in the online environment. One viewpoint emphasizes the responsibility to share scarce academic or cultural resources through making material available to all who might need it, whereas another view prizes the rights of the author over the need to share information. In particular, ethical thinking in contemporary Africa rests on tribal values such as Ubuntu, or concern for harmony within society and groups. We can contrast the Western philosophical and ethical interest in the preservation of individual rights with the African tradition, which often emphasizes group or societal good rather than asking, "What is best for the individual?"[35] Similarly, in discussing the problem of intellectual property in China, Feldman argues that "all developing countries tend to be IPR violators," going on to explain that states and citizens in the developing world have made a conscious decision to violate international intellectual property regimes because they cannot afford to forgo the wealth they would lose if they upheld intellectual property. In addition, he states that there is no domestic tradition of intellectual property in many Asian nations, where again the emphasis on sharing and the collective may be stronger than the focus on individual rights. Here, Feldman suggests that developing nations, in particular, might be allowed a period of transition in which they gradually align their policies with international norms in this regard rather than expecting them to immediately disregard domestic norms developed over thousands of years in favor of imported foreign norms that may not match.[36]

Resolving Competing Norms

We can also identify situations of norm conflict in which an individual, group, or state finds itself bound by two contradictory sets of obligations. For example, a law enforcement officer might find him- or herself in a position where he or she is bound by human rights norms regarding offering asylum or sanctuary to refugees, including children, while simultaneously being bound to enforce immigration laws. In such a situation, he or she may struggle to disentangle the hierarchy of the competing norms in deciding which obligation should be addressed first.

The Example of Edward Snowden

Concerning cyber norms, here two brief examples can illustrate this point. First, we can consider the actions of Edward Snowden, who acted in 2013 to release close to ten thousand classified documents belonging to the US National Security Agency. Some defenses of Edward Snowden have argued that he was not acting unethically but rather was acting according to the so-called hacker code of ethics,[37] which assumes different values as a starting point for specifying which actions are and are not ethical in cyberspace. In deciding to release information, Snowden was acting in accordance with the norms of the hacker community. The problem thus stems from his dual identities as a member of the hacker community and a member of the US national security community, which created a norm conflict. Although the United States has thus taken the lead in international forums in arguing for a norm against hacking into identified critical infrastructure of another nation, the actions of Snowden suggest that this norm may not be fully internalized among all domestic actors in the United States, including those working within the national security establishment.

The Ethics of Cryptography

The second example of this conflict between state-level norms, corporate norms, and professional norms exists in the fields of encryption and cryptography. Those who make encryption programs for consumer computer products may feel that their first ethical duty is to protect the privacy of the consumer's information, whereas states may argue that no such right exists if a citizen is accused of lawbreaking.[38] In each case, the United States may behave in international interactions as though the United States has already achieved consensus internally on issues like what constitutes an act of cybertrespass, cyber espionage, or unauthorized hacking. However, these issues may still be far from resolved among the actors in the US cyber community. Here we can state that corporate employees have failed to internalize a norm, saying that the state should always have the ability to override encryption mechanisms. The problem here is that corporate actors may ultimately be the individuals who are asked to propagate, enforce, and adhere to norms that the United States has proposed as norms for the international system as a whole.

This is not to say that prospects for the development of healthy cyber norms and ethics are hopeless. Indeed, one area in which we can identify a normative or ethical consensus is in the need to protect vulnerable populations from encountering harm on the internet. Thus, as noted in Chapter 7 on crime, most nations have regulations in place that forbid the posting or using of online child pornography, and states have achieved a consensus allowing them to cooperate in this area.

Levels of Normative Compliance

Furthermore, it is unhelpful when thinking about legal and political descriptions of cyber norm violations to believe in purely dichotomous (or yes/no) terms. Today, many rankings of "internet enemies" or "cyber violators" describe states as either compliant or noncompliant with cyber norms and either accepting or not accepting of cyber norms.

However, compliance with norms is seldom dichotomous. Here we can think about nuclear nonproliferation regimes—in which some cases of noncompliance are clearer than others and where there is a range of actions that would constitute noncompliance—not all of equal severity. That is, a state can be mildly noncompliant through failing to report certain activities (perhaps through oversight rather than a desire to deceive) or in major noncompliance or violation, such as through carrying out an unauthorized nuclear test. In thinking about cyber norm violations, it may be possible to establish levels of compliance as well as to acknowledge that there may be multiple reasons why a state can be out of compliance, not all of which are malicious. Noncompliance may be a function of either an inability to police and enforce or a lack of desire to police and enforce. That is, theoretically a nation could accept a cyber norm but fail to comply (to a greater or lesser degree) with that norm. (Here, however, the problem is that the regime as a whole is endangered if a sufficient number of states are noncompliant or display degrees of noncompliance.)[39]

In addition, it is important to understand why states do not comply with cyber norms when this occurs.[40] Particularly in developing nations, states may have a strong desire to comply with a mission of, for example, combating fake news or trolling online but may lack the resources needed to comply. This presents a different situation than one in which states are noncompliant due to a perceived sense of coercion or failure to accept the norm.

State and Private Cooperation Issues in Norm Adherence

Finally, nations differ in the relationships that they have with the technology communities themselves, the ways in which their input is solicited and taken into account, the nature of the relationship that tech experts enjoy with government (adversarial vs. cooperative), and the existence of functional mechanisms for securing expert input into national and international cyber policies. In America, the relationship between the federal government and the technology community is relatively ad hoc, with few formalized relationships. Technology initiatives are viewed as the province of entrepreneurs within a free market economy, and for the most part, efforts to bring connectivity to regions of the United States (including rural areas) to address security concerns and breaches and to develop new modes of security have been seen as the province of corporations rather than the government.[41]

In contrast, in the developing world, most nations have created a new Ministry of Information Technology within the past twenty years. At present, the nations of India, Bangladesh, Pakistan, Egypt, Ethiopia, Kenya, Saudi Arabia, Nepal, Mauritius, and Thailand all have a Ministry of Information Technology, led by a minister who steers the development of the technology community and its initiatives in the areas of connectivity, education, commerce, and security.

Normative issues that have been the subject of great debate within the United States and many nations of Europe—such as whether states have the right to request that internet users register their IP addresses and/or provide biometric identification of themselves as information technology users and whether the government should have access to a so-called internet kill switch, allowing it to shut off internet communications within the nation during times of national disturbances—have already been decided centrally by these ministries in many developing countries. If such nations accept the norms, then achieving compliance by private companies may be easier.

CONCLUSION

We began this chapter by considering three recent international technology events that reside in a legal gray zone but that nonetheless present ethical issues to the international community. We considered the Sony hack, the Russian hack on the Democratic National Committee headquarters, and the unauthorized surveillance conducted by the US National Security Agency in 2008. In each case, there is not a clear-cut international consensus by states regarding the harms inflicted or the responsibility of those who carried out the actions, nor is there a clear consensus regarding how such actions should be addressed by and within the international community. In this chapter, we considered the ways in which expectations regarding behavioral norms can be universal as well as culturally or situationally specific. We also examined specific virtues or ethics, including restraint, or the notion that just because an actor has the ability to do something, an actor might still choose not to exercise the power to do so. We also considered the roles that epistemic and professional communities have played historically in establishing international norms regarding behavior in cyberspace. We concluded by focusing on the challenges that states will face as they attempt to frame binding, internationally accepted norms governing behavior in cyberspace. In considering the likelihood that they will be able to do so, we can consider again the debates that have arisen among states regarding the establishment of international governance of cyberspace as well as the connections between debates about internet governance and internet norms of state behavior.

QUESTIONS FOR DISCUSSION

1. As we think about Russia's Gerasimov Doctrine—or the idea that states should seek to identify sources of social cleavages within a society and then use psychological operations to stir up discontent and divide the societies of their enemies—we note that many portray this doctrine as an illegitimate use of social media.

    a. Why do you think this use of social media is regarded as unethical or illegitimate, and what makes it a less legitimate use than others?

    b. Is it because on some level, the Western nations, led by the United States, believe that they "own" the right to define normative and nonnormative uses of social media?

    c. How does the idea that the 2016 election hack represented a violation of international law rest upon assumptions that we have made about acceptable and unacceptable uses of social media technology, and where do those notions come from?

2. How should the international community negotiate the role that a technology hosting platform like Google or Twitter should play in enforcing use norms within the global system, and how does the timing of technological closure affect that role? Can we expect any actor, including a tech platform, to enforce use norms if indeed technological closure has not occurred?

   a. Is it possible for the international community to somehow accelerate the process of technological closure (which is most often presented as an organic process, which occurs gradually over sometimes centuries, in a process that is simultaneously bottom up and top down) to arrive at a specific set of meanings regarding acceptable and unacceptable uses of technology?

3. Do you think it is possible to make changes to the internet's architecture that would eliminate the problem of trust? The problem of equity? What might such changes look like?

KEY TERMS

Deep fake 257
Gray areas 246

Maskirovka 259

FOR FURTHER READING

Bagge, D. *Unmasking Maskirovka: Russia's Cyber Influence Operations* (Washington, DC: Defense Press, 2018).

Bok, S. *Lying: Moral Choice in Public and Private Life* (New York, NY: Pantheon Books, 1978).

Cohen-Almagor, R. "Responsibility of and Trust in ISPs." *Knowledge, Technology and Policy* 23, no. 3–4 (2010): 381–397.

Floridi, L. "Mature Information Societies: A Matter of Expectations." *Philosophy of Technology* 29, no. 1 (2016): 1–4.

Manjikian, M. *Cybersecurity Ethics: An Introduction* (New York, NY: Routledge, 2017).

11

CYBER CONFLICT

Learning Objectives

At the end of this chapter, students will be able to do the following:

1. Describe key terms related to cyber warfare including *information warfare, advanced persistent threat*, and *crisis stability*.

2. Describe unique features of the cyberwarfare environment.

3. Discuss proposed solutions to regulating or decreasing conflict in the cyber environment including weapons bans and the use of deterrence.

As long as people have been alive, people have gone to war with one another. There have always been objects that were scarce, desirable, and necessary—from food, to tools, to sexual partners—and as a result, humans have always engaged in defending their own resources while simultaneously organizing to take others' resources. Indeed, conflict has been cited as the driving force behind humankind's desire to explore the world and to invent new technologies, creating useful objects and institutions as a result.[1]

But how does cyberwarfare fit into our understanding of war as a human activity? Does the invention of cyberweapons and actions like offensive and defensive cyberattacks mean that war is now a fundamentally new type of activity from what it has been in the past? Do governments need new definitions of warfare? And do they need to develop fundamentally new modes of organization, both domestically and internationally, to cope with the threat of cyberwarfare? Should new institutions, laws, and norms be created to form an ethical framework for the governance of cyberwarfare, or can existing laws and ethics of war be adapted to speak about cyberwarfare as well? These are the questions that we ask in this chapter.

WHAT IS CYBERSECURITY?

We begin this chapter by laying out some simple definitions of what is meant by cybersecurity, including the controversies that we encounter when trying to define the term. First, we should note that the term *cybersecurity* itself actually has two meanings—a technical meaning and a political meaning. For scientists and engineers, the term *computer security* or *cybersecurity* refers to "a field of computer science concerned with the application of security features to computer systems to provide protection against the unauthorized disclosure, manipulation or deletion of information and against denial of service."[2] In political science, however, cybersecurity refers to political security.[3] Cybersecurity references the use of technology in warfare and conflict among nations—and specifically the practices of protecting a computer system or its information against a hostile adversary such as a nation-state or a nonstate actor like a terrorist group. National security concerns are at the heart of this type of cybersecurity, which focuses on the state's vulnerability to terrorist attacks.

Computer security is thus part of national security more broadly—in that failing to protect a state's data and critical infrastructure can affect a state's economy, political system, and society. Thus, we cannot speak of a state's cybersecurity strength in isolation because a state's cybersecurity posture—its strengths and weaknesses, the size of its force, and the tools and assets that its commands—can affect other elements of its overall military.

The Whole of Nation Approach

Today, in thinking about how to defend a nation's cybersecurity assets, policy makers often reference a "whole of nation" approach, which includes actions carried out by military assets as well as commercial and business interests, aimed at securing data and information from adversaries.[4] The whole of nation approach was developed by Russian military planners, and it contains both defensive and offensive strands. Although state and nonstate actors, both civilian and military, can work together to defend a nation's cyberspace and cyber assets, they can also work together to carry out campaigns against other states, aimed at destabilizing them militarily and socially. Today nowhere is this entwining of conventional military strength and cyber strength more apparent than in the arena of information warfare. Information warfare is "an extension of ordinary warfare in which combatants use information and attacks on information and information systems as tools of warfare."[5]

Like warfare itself, information warfare is not new. Indeed, the notion that an army could use the element of surprise to render an enemy off-balance and that deception (including the use of decoys) could be used to make one's army seem more powerful and larger than it really is are ideas that appear as early as 5000 BC in the writing of Chinese military strategist Sun Tzu. In particular, states have long used PSYOPS in warfare. PSYOPS are planned operations to convey selected information and indicators to audiences to influence their emotions, motives, objective reasoning, and ultimately the behavior of organizations, groups, and individuals.[6] That is, states have long sought to achieve military and political objectives through influencing an enemy's civilian population through the use of propaganda, using information channels to convey information meant to sow dissent, fear, and confusion among a state's civilian and military population and releasing damaging information about one's opponents to degrade their basis of popular support. During World War Two and the Vietnam War, a state's military might have used airplanes to drop leaflets with information (either true or false) meant to influence a population. Today, these psychological operations can be carried out more quickly and more efficiently and over a greater distance using channels like Twitter and social media.

Here, the aim is often to "prepare the battlefield" by confusing enemy participants in war through supplying false information. Information warfare relies on the use of deception, which is legal according to the internationally recognized LOAC, which permits deceiving one's enemy through stratagems and ruses.

Furthermore, states have long utilized strategies like targeting and destroying an enemy's communications infrastructure to install disorder within the adversary's military or general population, thus facilitating the carrying out of traditional conventional (or kinetic) military attacks. The United States famously used such techniques during the 1991 Gulf War against Iraq, carrying out airplane strikes against Iraqi targets during the early hours of that short conflict, almost immediately rendering the Iraqi leadership unable to communicate with its army, leading to a swift and overwhelming defeat by the US military. Today, such strikes can be carried out quickly over the internet.

However, some cyberwarfare techniques are fundamentally new. For example, states today may engage in cyber hostage taking to coerce other states into giving up key objectives. In a 2016 report, analysts described how a piece of code known as "black energy" (believed to be Russian in origin) had been found in many computer systems across Europe. The analysts claim this code may have been responsible for a number of events that later ensued, including a hacking attack on TV Monde in Paris that kept television personnel from accessing their network as well as a shutdown of circuit breakers and substations across Ukraine that left more than 200,000 people without power. Analysts describe how a state can enter an adversary's computer network, plant malicious code, and then "hold targets at risk."

If the state later finds itself in a hostile situation with that adversary, it then has several possible ways of responding due to the control that it already has over targets in that adversary's cyber territory. In a cyber hostage-taking scenario, an adversarial state could seize hold of your computer system and threaten to destroy all of your data if certain demands are not met. Here we can foresee a scenario where a state might demand real-world concessions (e.g., the release of criminals, the lowering of economic sanctions, or a state's withdrawal from physical territory) as a condition of releasing the data.[7]

Do Cyberweapons Make the World More Dangerous?

Analysts disagree today about a fundamental question: Has the advent of cyberwarfare made our world less safe and secure, or has it in fact rendered the world more secure? Here, some analysts argue that cyberwarfare is an improvement over conventional warfare. They suggest that cyberweapons are more precise—better able to discriminate against targets—and thus less likely to lead to indiscriminate killing.[8]

However, others believe cyberweapons have a number of destabilizing effects. Aside from starting a cyberwar, states could use such weapons to start a conventional or even a nuclear war. That is, states could utilize cyberwarfare tactics to hack into the command and control systems of conventional weapons—for example, by shutting down key safety systems within a civilian or military aircraft or by interfering in the communications at an air traffic control tower. Analysts also worry about the ability of states to utilize viruses and other cyberweapons to either disable an enemy's nuclear weapons or even to send false information to a sensing array, resulting in the launching of a nuclear missile in response. Such activities might occur as part of a "false flag" operation in which, for example, Russia could make it look as though the United States had attacked China with a nuclear missile, causing China to respond by attacking the United States. Such an attack might be considered an act of war, but it might also be considered as an act of cyberterrorism, which is defined as "the execution of politically motivated hacking operations intended to cause grave harm that results in either loss of life or severe economic loss or both."[9]

Thus, cyberwarfare tactics can serve as part of a larger strategy in which a nation uses both cyber and conventional weapons and tactics to achieve a target. Here cyberwarfare is seen as a force multiplier. A nation uses cyber tactics—such as taking down an enemy's communications infrastructure through the use of a virus, for example—to install disorder within the adversary's military or general population, thus facilitating the carrying out of traditional conventional (or kinetic) attacks. A cyberweapon can thus be used as part of a plan to achieve a particular objective in cyberspace (i.e., taking down a nation's communications system) or to achieve a larger objective within conventional or real space.

Hybrid War: Where Is the Battlefield in Cyberspace?

In his work, Alexander Klimburg speaks of the "tragedy of cyberspace." He describes how the internet itself has been weaponized.[10] What was once understood as a "global village" where citizens from throughout the world could come together peacefully to debate and share opinions is now understood as (in the words of military planners) "the digital battlespace."[11] At the same time, even civilian assets, like social media platforms, have become spaces where states may carry out military strategies of information warfare. Social media strategies target not military personnel but rather civilians who may find that they think differently about their state, their national authorities, and their responsibilities as citizens due to the ideas and images they encounter via social media. That is, over the long term, citizens' trust in their elected officials and the legitimacy of their political systems may be degraded as the result of enemy activities.

In addition, military cyber strategies may focus on targeting critical infrastructure—public utilities like water and sewage as well as national resources like our food supply. Such critical infrastructure is not a military target but rather a civilian target because it is often privately owned and used predominantly by civilians. And due to the fact that the internet spans the borders of real territories, such attacks (including those carried out via social media or targeted at critical infrastructure) can occur from anywhere. A soldier who carries out internet warfare does not need to be seated inside a military facility, nor does he or she need to travel to the site where he or she will carry out the attack. He or she may be embedded within a civilian community, or he or she may hack into the code that launches a nuclear missile from a site that is thousands of miles away.

Thus, our traditional military conception of the battlefield is not relevant when we talk about cyberwarfare. Instead, military planners speak about hybrid war, which is defined as "a combination of conventional and unconventional or irregular warfare—extending beyond the battlefield to encompass economic, diplomatic, and information attacks (including psychological, cyber and misinformation) as well as political warfare."[12]

Most analysts credit Russian General Gennady Gerasimov with inventing hybrid war. In 2013, he argued that in the future, wars will be fought with a four-to-one ratio of nonmilitary to military measures—where nonmilitary measures could include actions such as propaganda, subversion, and espionage. Whereas military measures focus on attacking specific targets and inflicting physical damage, nonmilitary measures are aimed at shaping the adversary's social and political landscape. Such attacks could be carried out by remote engagement, with no need to mobilize and deploy conventional troops. Instead, personnel could use the internet to engage in maskirovka, carrying out attacks and maneuvers that could be disavowed and that could often not be traced back to the original actor. And rather than actively engaging in wars, which are expensive, states could engage in activities just short of war, including defacing websites belonging to adversary states and invading their sovereignty through attacking their servers, stealing their information, and engaging in activities to confuse and destabilize an adversary's population.[13]

Gerasimov proposed deploying information warfare to destabilize an adversary. Warriors would use **active measures** (including influence operations, **disinformation,** and propaganda) in a strategy of **subversion** undertaken to weaken the West through splitting the Western community (including organizations such as the European Union and NATO).[14] New products like fake news, conspiracy theories, and fake Twitter accounts could be deployed to confuse the signals that American and European voters received during their elections. Extremist positions would be strengthened, and information warfare could create political polarization and exacerbate animosity among citizens. As a result, some analysts have begun to speak of a new cold war in cyberspace.

Gerasimov famously wrote that when faced with the combination of pressure and interference, a "perfectly thriving state can, in a matter of months, and even days, be transformed into an arena of fierce armed conflict, become a victim of foreign intervention, and sink into a web of chaos, humanitarian catastrophe, and civil war." Russian planners describe how it is possible to find the "tipping point" where a state could become destabilized and "tip over" into anarchy. Here, they consider long-term scenarios such as whether in the future, unemployment might become significant in Western Europe or the United States as the result of widespread adoption of robotic technologies. In such a situation, they ask, what sort of social media and disinformation campaigns might be sufficient to achieve this tipping point? What cracks exist in our societies that an adversary could capitalize on to splinter a state apart?[15]

Hybrid warfare thus represents a type of asymmetric warfare, in which a small actor can take on a much larger and more powerful adversary. Asymmetric warfare, which includes terrorism, has traditionally used surprise and nontraditional attacks aiming to throw a more powerful adversary off of its guard by acting in unexpected ways.[16] Today, a state that lacks a large conventional military can still cause damage and chaos by using cyberweapons, including psychological operations. Developed nations, in particular, depend on the availability of advanced technologies. Their militaries are rendered more effective, more able to respond quickly and accurately, through dependence on robotization, stealth concepts, and warfighting from a distance. However, the fact that so much of its strength depends on technology means that it can be attacked from afar, at relatively little cost by an adversary—even if it is less technologically advanced and smaller in size—without the use of conventional forces.

Russia used hybrid warfare for the first time in Ukraine during the 2014 Russian annexation of Crimea, an enclave within Ukraine with a significant Russian population (as well as a vitally important warm-water port on the Black Sea). Russia's military campaign included an initial attempt to undermine Ukrainian confidence in domestic Ukrainian institutions. Social media was used to discredit the government and the Ukrainian armed forces and to encourage people to engage in separatist activities. Psychological operations thus prepared the battlefield for the actual use of military forces.

SPACE SECURITY

When the public heard about the US decision in the spring of 2019 to form a Space Command under the auspices of the Department of Defense, many people joked about people in space suits going to war with alien civilizations—like something from a science fiction movie.

However, the reality is quite different. Today, many commercial and government activities in the United States and internationally depend on having constant access to large amounts of data. From 1990 until 2019, the amount of commercial bandwidth used by the US military has increased by 150 times. And new technologies like autonomous vehicles enabled by artificial intelligence will require even larger amounts of data to function. In addition, these emerging technologies, like self-driving cars, also require access to Global Navigation Satellite System (GNSS) data, which also depends on satellites to perform functions like locating an object in space.

As the challenges associated with accessing and storing this data increase, both government and commercial providers are considering new solutions for providing this data access. In many instances, data is stored not on a company's home servers, nor is it necessarily stored in the company's home nation. Instead, it may be stored in the cloud. And in the future, this data may be stored in satellites that orbit the Earth.[17]

Space Is Becoming Crowded

Technically, space is considered unowned or belonging to everyone. Nations own the airspace that exists above their nations, but the cutoff for airspace is 18,000 feet.[18] The air above that is considered to be outer space, which is not owned by any nation. However, an international body, the International Telecommunications Union (ITU), must grant permission to any commercial or national body wishing to launch a satellite into outer space.[19]

In 2017, a Department of Defense spokesperson referred to space as "congested, competitive and contested."[20] Although in the twentieth century, most satellite activities were carried out by national governments, including those of the United States and Russia, today, more and more nations have their own satellites in space, as do commercial entities. And although previously launching a satellite required millions of dollars and up to fifteen years of research and development activities, today smaller satellites can be launched quickly

(Continued)

(Continued)

and cheaply. As a result, the ITU has warned about possible collisions that could occur in space if too many satellites are launched or if an event like a hacking attack alters a satellite's path.

Today, military planners and legal scholars are working to develop better international legal regulations regarding who may launch satellites into space, what constitutes an attack on a satellite in space, and who is responsible for guaranteeing the safety of satellites and the data streams they carry.

Are Satellites Critical Infrastructure?

In recent years, officials in many nations, including the United States, Germany, and Canada, have realized that their economic and social systems depend on functions performed by satellites residing in space. Military technologies rely on data applications using global positioning system (GPS) functions, as do commercial shipping and transportation operations. In addition, services like cable television depend on commercial satellites. Satellite communications are necessary for disaster response as well as the conduct of activities like e-governance and e-education. Satellites help monitor game preserves to prevent poaching and national borders to prevent incursions. The space satellite infrastructure has an estimated worth of $340 billion a year.[21]

Thus, analysts suggest viewing satellites as part of a nation's critical infrastructure, as satellite-based services often provide the backbone for other activities (like health care) considered to be part of critical infrastructure.

Vulnerabilities in Space

How safe and reliable are these satellites, and what risks does relying on satellites pose? On one hand, satellites are not vulnerable to events that occur on Earth like earthquakes, storms, or fires. On the other hand, there are several identified vulnerabilities associated with a nation's satellite dependence. First, because satellites navigate above the Earth, there are international legal issues associated with establishing jurisdiction for activities involving these entities.

In addition, satellites are vulnerable to hacking attacks. Defense Department analysts worry about jamming of satellite communications by adversaries including other states as well as terrorist organizations. They are concerned about spoofing[22]—in which an adversary fraudulently obtains access to a computer system through taking on someone else's identity or where an adversary sends communications or data purportedly from one source when, in fact, they are from someone else. For example, an adversary could cause a nation-state to believe that they were under attack by a foreign power and cause them to respond through altering the data that the nation-state saw by entering a system and providing false data. They could also interfere with military activities like targeting through changing a state's awareness of coordinates. A criminal organization might also disguise its own financial dealings or even enrich itself financially through altering data streams passing through satellites that are linked to national or international financial transactions.[23]

Satellite communications may also be impeded due not to adversary attacks but to mechanical failures. As satellites age, they may malfunction and require repairs. If they cannot maintain their orbits, they risk moving into the path of another satellite, potentially damaging it, as well as falling to Earth. And as space becomes more crowded, it becomes necessary for satellites to communicate with one another to ensure that they do not lose position or interfere with others' data streams. Aging satellites may have trouble with these tasks.

As these examples show, cybersecurity and space security issues overlap, and vulnerabilities in one domain can lead to vulnerabilities in other domains as well as responses by conventional or economic means.

Space as a Military Domain

The United States first evinced awareness of the security vulnerabilities created by reliance upon GNSS systems as early as 1997. The US Presidents' Commission on Critical Infrastructure Protection noted that "exclusive reliance on GPS and its augmentations, combined with other complex interdependencies, raises the potential for 'single point failure' and 'cascading effects.'"[24]

Beginning around 2011, governments in the United Kingdom, the United States, and Russia began using military language to describe space. The United States now notes that space needs to be defended and that adversaries need to be deterred and defeated. In a US House Permanent Intelligence Committee hearing, a US representative first broached the idea that an attack on a US satellite could be considered an act of war. At the same time, Russian military officials have called upon the international community to create rules of engagement for fighting in space.[25]

Policy Coordination Problems

Within the United States, implementing regulations to provide for data safety is complicated by the fact that satellites are often mounted and administered

(Continued)

(Continued)

not by states but by commercial entities. And as noted in Chapter 6, commercial technology actors do not always have the same interests and priorities as states do—particularly in areas related to the provision of cyber and space security.

In addition, it is difficult to create policies to administer space security because of the large number of agencies involved in this policy area. However, prior to the creation of the US Space Command, within the military, the only branch that specifically had a space policy division was the US Air Force.

The Space Command, created in 2019, would thus enable the military branches of the US Department of Defense to work together to ensure the safety of satellites. The Space Command will also work closely with the US Cyber Command to counter cyberthreats like hacking. In addition, the Space Command will seek to coordinate the actions of a number of actors with interests in accessing and utilizing satellite data from the US National Reconnaissance Organization, the US Central Intelligence Agency, and the US Geospatial-Intelligence Agency.

Responding to Secure the Space Domain

However, not all actors within the international system support a military solution to secure space. Critics suggest that what is needed is a space regime in which states agree to participate in bilateral and multilateral efforts to secure the space domain. These analysts stress the need for multistakeholder governance, noting that successfully securing satellites and data streams that operate through satellites in cyberspace will require an effort that includes international organizations, states, and commercial entities, including those involved in the supply chain and insurance industries.[26]

Currently, GNSS systems have been created by five different nations or regional groups: The US GPS, Russia's Global Navigation Satellite System (GLONAS), Europe's two systems—EGNOS and Galileo—China's Baidu Navigation Satellite System, and India's regional NAVIC system. Japan is also developing its own system. These systems have the potential to interfere with one another, and international coordination could also preempt problems arising from problems of interoperability.

At present, the UN Committee on the Peaceful Uses of Outer Space (COPUOS) is working on drafting guidelines for the long-term sustainability of outer space activities, and the Group of Governmental Experts on Transparency and Confidence-Building Measures in Outer Space Activities (GGE-Space) is also working to increase cooperation.

Sources

Cilluffo, Frank. *Trends in Technology and Digital Security: Space Satellites and Critical Infrastructure* (Washington, DC: George Washington University Center for Cyber and Homeland Security, 2017), 2. https://cchs.gwu.edu/sites/g/files/zaxdzs2371/f/downloads/DT%20panel%203%20issue%20brief%20final.pdf.

de Selding, Peter B. "ITU Grapples with Small-Satellite Regulatory Challenge." *SpaceNews*, last modified March 13, 2015. https://spacenews.com/itu-grapples-with-small-satellite-regulatory-challenge/.

Federal Aviation Administration. "Airspace Classification." https://aspmhelp.faa.gov/index.php/Airspace_Classification.

Livingstone, David, and Patricia Lewis. *Space, the Final Frontier for Cybersecurity?* (London, UK: Chatham House Publications, 2016). https://www.chathamhouse.org/publication/space-final-frontier-cybersecurity.

President's Commission on Critical Infrastructure Protection. "Critical Foundations: Protecting America's Infrastructures" (1997). Cited in Livingstone and Lewis, 34.

Sabbagh, Karim Michel. "Satellite—a Critical Infrastructure for Defense and Security." SES News. Last modified November 19, 2015. https://www.ses.com/blog/satellite-critical-infrastructure-defence-and-security.

DEFINING ACTS OF WAR

As noted earlier in our study of criminal activity, it is often difficult to classify some types of cyberspace activities. We can consider the actions undertaken by Russia's government in 2016 aimed at altering the outcome of the US presidential election, which fit the definition of information warfare. Hackers who are believed to have been state sponsored carried out activities like electronic breaking and entering through hacking into the databases of e-mails belonging to the Democratic National Committee, then releasing these private e-mails to the online WikiLeaks site.

Can such an attack legitimately be considered an act of war? The US legal code defines an act of war as "an action by one country against another with an intention to provoke a war or an action that occurs during a declared war or armed conflict between military forces of any origin."[27]

One might argue that an act is an act of war if cyberweapons are used. Here, we could consider that the Russian attack utilized cyberweapons, therefore rendering it an act of war. However, many of these same tools—viruses, worms, and Trojans—can be utilized in other situations by other actors for nonmilitary purposes. For example, a program that logs people's keystrokes could be used to steal military information if it were installed in a military facility, but it could also be used by detectives who were seeking to disrupt criminal activities through collecting information on those individuals' activities. Cyberweapons are thus dual-use technologies because they may have different uses and different utilities in different situations. It is particularly challenging for states to create laws and regulations regarding such dual-use technologies because doing so requires establishing and regulating who will have access to this technology as well as how people will use this technology and under what circumstances. In considering conventional weapons and their regulation, states have been successful in establishing export regimens that require weapons producers to carefully track where such weapons will go and who will use them. However, because a cyberweapon is not a physical entity but a bit of code, it has proven much more difficult to track their proliferation and their use as well as to regulate sales and exports of these weapons. Thus, it may be insufficient to argue that just because a particular class of cyberweapon was utilized, what occurred was an act of war.[28]

WHO IS WINNING THE CYBER ARMS RACE?

CRITICAL ISSUES

For many years, the United States was considered to be the clear front-runner in the development of all things cyber, including military cyber. The United States was the first state to set up a military cyber command and a military space command, and the internet itself was born as part of a US Department of Defense project and developed largely in Silicon Valley in the United States. Today, the United States is perceived as having a leading role in artificial intelligence cyberdefense technology innovation. In addition, the United States is seen as being a leader in the development of military strategies for the deployment of these new technologies.[29]

However, several nations have begun to challenge US superiority in the arena of militarized cyber strategy and weapons. China and Russia have devoted money, manpower, and energy to the development of a military cybersecurity strategy, including in artificial intelligence. China has set a goal for itself of achieving global leadership in the deployment of artificial intelligence by 2030.[30] And Russia is regarded as a global leader in the deployment of offensive disinformation weapons and strategies, although it is considered to be less far ahead of its competitor states in terms of developing and deploying artificial intelligence for military purposes.

Today, analysts have begun to speak of an arms race in cyberspace. But what is an arms race, and what is the significance of this developing arms race? And who is actually winning?

What Is an Arms Race?

In simplest terms, an arms race refers to "the competitive and rapid mutual build-up of capabilities between pairs of states."[31]

An arms race is thus a competitive dynamic in which states compete for the leading position in terms of technological innovation and the deployment of new technologies. The earliest example of an arms race was in the late 19th century, when other states, including Russia, attempted to overtake Britain as the leading international naval power. More recently, we can look to the US-Soviet arms race for nuclear superiority.

At first glance, one can identify many positive innovations that have come about as the result of arms races. Arms races can spur technological innovation, prompting states to generously fund research and development and training. States may emphasize the recruitment of high-profile scientists and engineers, and the race to solve a military technological problem often has significant benefits for society as a whole. Today, the space race is credited with the development of cable television, laptop computers, telemedicine, and smoke detectors.[32] And an arms race may even benefit a state's economy, leading to new jobs and investments in key industries.

Why We Should Avoid Arms Races

Yet arms races also have downsides: When technological innovations come about quickly, there may be a tendency to cut corners and to compromise safety in the race to be the first to bring a new technology to market. Scharre argues that "competition raises the pressure to cut corners," warning of the risks that an arms race might cause states to deploy systems before they have been fully tested. He concludes, "A race to the bottom on AI safety is a race no one would win."[33]

A more broad-ranging argument against arms races focuses on the opportunity costs of these political and military developments. If we consider the arms races occurring today in cyberspace, it is obvious that they are expensive! The United Kingdom, for example, has invested nearly $2 billion in combating cyber-threats for the period 2016–2021.[34] Today, some critics have faulted the "cyber industrial complex" for behaving in a parasitical manner, drawing resources from other sectors of the economy to grow at their expense.

In addition, political scientists point to the problem of arms proliferation. If states come to view the ability to produce and deploy a new technology—like nuclear weapons—as prestigious within the international community, more and

(Continued)

(Continued)

more states may clamor to enter the arms race. As a result, a technology that is dangerous and potentially harmful may end up being owned by more and more states. If these states are located within the developing world in particular, then it is possible that they may not have the financial means to secure key components of the technology (like nuclear materials) or to sufficiently train their personnel in the deployment of these technologies. As a result, accidents might be more likely, as might the migration of the materials and expertise from legitimate state actors to other actors within the international system, like terrorists or organized criminal elements.

Indicators of an Arms Race in Cyberspace

So, is there truly an arms race occurring in cyberspace? The US Department of Defense Cyber Strategy from 2018 describes the United States as engaged in a "long-term strategic competition with China and Russia." US planners describe China as poised to catch up and overtake US strategic superiority in the cyberspace field—partially as a result of a strategy of cyber espionage and intellectual property theft. The document contains the line: "The Department must take action in cyberspace during day to day competition to preserve US military advantages and to defend US interests."[35]

In the United States, the push to participate in a cyber arms race has meant the deployment of resources toward this goal from a variety of fields across the US government. The US Department of Homeland Security has participated in evaluating cybersecurity programs at universities and colleges across the United States, designating those institutions that meet the standards as Cybersecurity Centers of Excellence. The Department of Education has made funding available for universities, university faculty, and students who are receiving training or conducting research in the areas of cybersecurity or cybersecurity policy. This social mobilization toward the creation of a pool of talent in cybersecurity has led to the development of both military and civilian training programs. US federal government funding has been made available for the establishment of US computer coding camps for children, cybersecurity internships within federal government agencies, and accelerated paths to hiring for government positions in critical areas. Corporations have been encouraged to increase their cybersecurity through participation in programs sponsored by agencies like the Federal Emergency Management Agency. And the federal government has conducted outreach to the technology industry in particular, including undertaking joint projects with the private sector.

Who Is Winning the Cyber Arms Race?

Despite the significant commitment of US resources toward the achievement of cyberspace superiority, some analysts believe that over time the US competitive advantage has eroded.[36]

In an influential article written in 2018, analyst Adam Segal argued that the United States has ceded leadership in cyberspace to China. He writes:

> President XI Jinping has set his country on the path to cyber dominance by integrating domestic regulations, technological innovation and foreign policy. His aim is to build an "impregnable" cyber defense system . . . [to] lead the world in advanced technologies and give China a bigger voice in internet governance."[37]

In his analysis, Segal quotes Eric Schmidt, a former Google chair, who writes, "By 2020, they will have caught up. By 2025, they will be better than us. And by 2030, they will dominate the industries of AI."

In point of fact, the argument that Segal makes is not new. Rather, he reiterates an older argument in suggesting that centralized, authoritarian regimes have advantages over decentralized, democratic regimes when it comes to producing and supporting technological advantages. Currently, the United States does not have one centralized agency that is tasked with administering all US policies regarding the internet. Rather, different policies are made by different agencies, with the US Department of Justice, the Federal Trade Commission, the Department of Defense, and the Department of State, for example, all contributing to the making of internet policy in the United States. In contrast, China's Cyberspace Administration of China (CAC) plays a leading and coordinating role in creating one centralized cyberspace policy for China. The CAC has the ability to tightly regulate content on online platforms, to shut down websites and hosts, and to control the actions of private actors within China.[38] In addition, the existence of the CAC has also made it easier for China to integrate its goals in the areas of technological innovation into its overall foreign policy—for example, in creating the Digital Silk Road project.

In addition, in authoritarian states, the military innovation infrastructure does not compete with private innovation infrastructures. In addition, because the barriers between state-run and private enterprises may be more permeable, innovations can more easily be transferred between any limited private sector

(Continued)

(Continued)

and the state sector. China, for example, has a model of "military-civil fusion" in which innovations in the civilian sector can more easily be transferred into the military sector.[39]

And in a repressive regime, employees have fewer opportunities (and rights) to mobilize against technology policies that they oppose. In contrast, the United States is facing a sharp divide between Washington and Silicon Valley over the military use of artificial intelligence. In the United States, employees at Google and Microsoft have mobilized to voice their opposition to these company's contracts with the Pentagon, and Google has discontinued work on a project using artificial intelligence to analyze video footage as a result. And, in the United States, legislators like New York State Representative Alexandra Ocasio-Cortez have spoken out against the widespread adoption of facial recognition technology, fearing that it could create a "surveillance state" in the United States.[40]

In contrast, China's innovators have been able to marry together technologies like biometric identification, facial recognition, GPS tracking, and artificial intelligence to achieve goals like tracking citizens and utilizing predictive analytics to identify future sites of political conflict or unrest—without facing similar opposition.

However, as Segal cautions, top-down efforts may not necessarily succeed without the dynamism that may come from internal economic competition among competing firms. In addition, some studies suggest that a country that operates predominantly through imitation—capturing and modifying the technology of others rather than creating its own technology—will eventually encounter built-in limitations in its ability to grow and develop technologically.[41] In other words, for China to truly become a world leader in cyber innovation, including in the world of artificial intelligence, espionage will eventually have to be supplanted with genuine technological innovations that begin in China.

Applying the Paradigms

Each of the three paradigms for understanding international relations—realism, liberal internationalism, and constructivism—can be applied to better understand the issues and threats posed by a cyber arms race.

Realism

The arms race is an idea developed by realist analysts like Jervis. These analysts believe that the security dilemma that exists within the international system is real, not a construct. They believe that the anarchic nature of the international system and the self-help system that states therefore create make arms races likely and that this same system also makes attempts to end arms races by creating norms or rules to control conflict likely to fail.[42]

A realist analyst would likely conclude that other nations' development of cyber expertise constitutes an existential threat to their states' continued existence and way of life. Thus, over the long term, a realist would expect that cyberweapons are likely to proliferate, that states are likely to continue building arsenals of cyberweapons, and that as a result, the international system is likely to be rendered more unstable. A realist policy adviser might thus suggest that states develop a strategy of cyberdeterrence, which would enable states to telegraph their intentions to defend "their cyberspace," in the hopes of creating a stable international environment in which, nonetheless, conflict is always a possibility.

Liberal Internationalism

A liberal internationalist analyst, in contrast, might view an arms race as threatening to the international system because of the ways in which it could threaten global practices like the creation of healthy global trade flows and the sharing of innovation. A liberal international theorist might therefore express concern about events like the US decision to ban the use of Hua Wei technology by US government employees for security reasons or the arrests by nations caught in the cyber arms race of technology actors who are accused of spying. He or she might also be concerned by developments such as one nation banning its citizens' access to an international technology platform (like Instagram) due to concerns about the collection of citizen data or the installation of spyware.

In this paradigm, the development of a conflict about the use of artificial intelligence could represent a closing off of vital enhancing trade. Liberal internationalists might also express concern about the end of innovations like open source code, the extension of encryption practices, and even the eventual creation of separate "national internets" that do not interact. An arms race is thus seen as creating a lack of a trust and a tendency on the part of nations to hoard innovative new technologies. But as nations face problems that can only be solved together, like climate change, it would be unfortunate if they were establishing precedents in which data is not shared due to one state's fear of conflict with its neighbors.

(Continued)

(Continued)
Constructivism

Finally, we can adopt a constructivist viewpoint to suggest that arms races are not real, but they are instead constructs produced within the international system through the strategic deployment of language. Through utilizing the language of conflict, states can exacerbate tensions within the international system, or they can use more cooperative language to decrease tensions within the intentional system. Here, we can point to attempts by US, Russian, and Chinese policy makers to create an arms race in cyberspace by using terms like *catch up* and *overtake*.

In addition, as Dupont notes, the deployment of language about competition in cyberspace has many facets. He suggests that discussions about the arms race in cyberspace are part of a "more fundamental contest of ideas and beliefs about the rules and architecture of the information highway." He identifies many tensions or rifts among those who are viewing cyberspace today and suggests that the language of competition can be used to pit "democrats against autocrats, big tech against government, big tech against consumers, and sometimes governments against their own people."

Here, in addition, he suggests that in choosing to use the language of competition and conflict, including the language of an arms race, policy makers preclude the deployment of other types of language that might instead emphasize cooperation and the achievement of joint goals. Instead, it becomes "all about conflict."[43]

Sources

Craig, Anthony, and Brandon Valeriano. "Conceptualizing Cyber Arms Races." *Proceedings from the 8th International Conference on Cyber Conflict*, Tallinn, Estonia, 2016.

Darnell, Casey. "Concern over Facial Recognition Technology Unites Progressive and Conservatives in Congress." Yahoo News. Last modified May 22, 2019. https://news.yahoo.com/concern-over-facial-recognition-technology-unites-progressives-and-conservatives-in-congress-234327186.html.

Department of Defense. "Summary: Department of Defense Cyber Strategy." Last modified 2018, https://media.defense.gov/2018/Sep/18/2002041658/-1/-1/1/CYBER_STRATEGY_SUMMARY_FINAL.PDF.

Dupont, Benoit. "Bots, Cops, and Corporations: On the Limits of Enforcement and the Promise of Polycentric Regulation as a Way to Control Large-Scale Cybercrime." *Crime Law Social Change* 67 (2017): 97–116. https://doi.org/10.1007/s10611-016-9649-z.

Gan, Nectar. "Cyberspace Controls Set to Strengthen under China's New Internet Boss." *South China Morning Post* (September 20, 2018), https://www.scmp.com/news/china/politics/article/2164923/cyberspace-controls-set-strengthen-under-chinas-new-internet.

Gilli, Andrea, and Mauro Gilli. "Why China Has Not Caught up Yet: Military-Technological Superiority and the Limits of Imitation, Reverse Engineering and Cyber Espionage." *International Security* 43, no. 3 (2019): 141–189.

Jervis, Robert. *Perception and Misperception in International Politics* (Princeton, NJ: Princeton University Press, 1976).

Mead, Rob. "10 Tech Breakthroughs to Thank the Space Race For." World of Tech. Last modified July 20, 2009.

Scharre, Paul. "The Real Dangers of an AI Arms Race." *Foreign Affairs* (May/June 2019). https://www.foreignaffairs.com/articles/2019-04-16/killer-apps.

Segal, Adam. "When China Rules the Web: Technology in Service of the State." *Foreign Affairs* 97, no 5 (2018): 10–18.

Taddeo, Mariarosaria, and Luciano Floridi. "Regulate Artificial Intelligence to Avert Cyber Arms Race." *Nature* 556, no. 7701 (2018).

IS CYBERWAR ILLEGAL OR UNETHICAL?

But are hybrid warfare techniques considered illegal according to international law or immoral and unethical? Is there an existing body of law or knowledge that we can "borrow" or "graft onto" the digital battlefield to decide what actions are and are not allowed in cyber conflict?

As noted, the digital battlefield is a different place from a traditional battlefield. And traditional norms and international laws governing warfare rest on clear distinctions between the spaces where civilians live and the battlefields where uniformed soldiers fight. For example, international organizations like the International Criminal Court distinguish sharply between legal and ethical acts of declared war between professional military personnel acting on behalf of a state versus illegal and unethical acts of terrorism that rely on surprise attacks outside the battlefield, carried out by irregular or nonstate soldiers, usually targeted at civilians. The laws of war are clear on this matter—legal and ethical warfare is that which occurs among uniformed, official soldiers who fight a declared, open conflict between states on the space of a battlefield.

The laws of war also state that the only ethical justification for a state to carry out an act of war is in response to a threat. That is, states can legally engage in aggressive actions for defensive reasons, such as to defend their nation from an invading force. In contrast, states cannot legally or ethically engage in offensive actions or attacks on others, nor may they engage in preemptive or preventive attacks against an opponent. (That is, they cannot legally or ethically strike their opponent as part of a surprise attack in which their opponent has not been warned, nor had time to prepare for an attack—by, for example, getting civilians out of harm's way.)

But what do such conditions mean for the conduct of cyberactivities? Here it is useful to distinguish between active and passive cyberdefense. In the cyber arena, **passive cyber defense** refers to "software or hardware added to the architecture that increased security without consistent and direct interaction from personnel, even if updates and tuning are required over time (i.e. firewalls, anti-malware software, intrusion detection and prevention systems, and application whitelisting)."[44] Passive defense is legal and ethical when speaking of cyberwarfare. Indeed, both state institutions and corporations (including ISPs) routinely engage in passive defense through practicing good cyber hygiene, making sure any system vulnerabilities are patched regularly, monitoring one's system for suspicious addresses, and engaging in practices like quarantining suspicious packets and running antivirus software.

Active cyber defense refers to situations in which security personnel take an active, often preemptive, role in countering threats to their systems, seeking to neutralize threats before they can affect an organization's operations. Active cyberdefense also includes carrying out intelligence activities to understand who might be targeting your system, and what their objectives are.[45] Personnel engaged in active cyberdefense will often act to turn an attack around, sending elements of the attack back to the site from which it originated. Such actions are referred to as "hack backs." For example, at a World Trade Organization meeting in San Juan, Puerto Rico, in 2002, a World Trade Organization server suffered a DDOS attack carried out by an activities group based in the United Kingdom called the Electro-Hippies. The ISP company hosting the World Trade Organization server was able to trace the attack back using the IP address to the e-hippies. That company then redirected attacks back to the e-hippies' server, disabling that server.[46]

Finally, we can distinguish between offensive and defensive cyber operations. Here offensive operations are those aimed at defacing or altering the equipment or terrain belonging to one's adversaries in cyberspace. Offensive cyber operations can include acts like web defacement, DDOS attacks (including botnet attacks), or the uploading of malware including ZDEs to an adversary's system.

But how do we reconcile these rules of engagement with the new rules of cyberwarfare? Today, the cyber battlefield has no clear geographic borders because a cyberattack can be launched from anywhere. This has made it problematic to apply international law to prosecute those who are seen to have acted illegally in carrying out cyberattacks. We can consider the case of the Russia-Estonian cyberwar in 2007. That year, Estonia experienced a massive cyberattack (including DDOS and web defacement attacks) that affected its governmental structures. These attacks were particularly damaging because Estonia is characterized by a high level of e-governance, with most citizen services being provided through the use of a cyber platform. These attacks were believed to have originated in Russia as a response to protests within Estonia calling for the removal of a Soviet-era World War Two memorial. Analysts carrying out cyber forensics found that the attacks had a Russian signature—they had similar command and control features, occurred in highly coordinated waves, and in some cases could be traced back to an IP address in Russia. However, the evidence was incomplete, particularly because Russia did not cooperate with the investigation. In addition, some of the servers involved in the attacks were located in a third country, and it was not clear whether or not investigators could legally seize these computers as part of their investigation. The digital battlefield does not have clear borders, nor are they aligned with traditional territorial borders.

The battlefield also does not have clear temporal borders, with a clear understanding of when conflict begins and when it ends. (In a conventional war, in contrast, conflict begins with a formal declaration of war and ends with a formal surrender.) That is, today, there is not a clear temporal distinction between declared war and undeclared war or when hostilities begin and when they cease. Indeed, US military planners have begun to speak of "fighting through the war," describing a situation in which cyber soldiers would never require a cease-fire or a pause to regroup. Instead, when one target (such as a network) is hit, they envision immediately moving operations to a cloned network that is being continuously updated, in this way continuing to fight on even after being subject to a large-scale attack.

CREATING INTERNATIONAL RULES GOVERNING CYBERWARFARE

This temporal distinction is important because the laws of war clearly distinguish between legal and ethical conventional military attacks on the basis of when they occurred. However, a recent analysis of Russian cyberwarfare cautions us that Russia may have already adopted a cold war mentality, in which it sees the territory of Russia surrounded (or encircled) by hostile ideological forces as the result of activities like NATO expansion and the expansion of the European Union to include states formerly included as part of the Soviet bloc. As a result, analysts suggest, Russia may be less likely to show restraint—either in terms of when it deploys conventional forces or when it deploys cyber forces. That is, they write that today, "the Kremlin will have a relatively low bar for employing cyber in ways that US decision makers are likely to view as offensive and escalatory in nature."[47]

However, because cyberattacks can be carried out so quickly—and indeed, a target may not even know that such an attack has occurred—it is difficult to see how a state could formally issue a declaration of war prior to engaging in a cyberattack.[48] Furthermore, the possibility of acting anonymously and deceptively in cyberspace (known as the attribution problem) means that even when a target is attacked, the authorities may not immediately know who carried out the attack. Instead, they may undertake a **cyber forensic investigation** to identify the perpetrator, sometimes finding the answer only days or weeks after the attack. In addition, it is often difficult to separate out offensive and defensive cyberattacks, given the murkiness that may sometimes accompany a cyberattack.[49]

In addition, in considering the legality and ethics of a particular cyber intrusion, it can be difficult for a state to understand exactly why an adversary has entered your system and what its purposes are for being there.[50] Here, as a technology matures over time, new methods of defending that technology (or making it resilient) may emerge. "Defending" the telegraph from intruders back in the 1800s eventually led to the development of new technologies like encryption.

And the use of deception as a mechanism of defense is an old and widely accepted technique within warfare; computer programmers who today use a "honey pot" or decoy—by planting a file in hopes of drawing system intruders out so they will reveal themselves and their identity—are merely carrying out widely accepted legal acts in cyberspace that have long been carried out in real space. Similarly, spying, or intelligence preparation of the battlefield, is not considered a violation of the laws of war. For example, it would not be illegal for an adversary to use a drone or high-tech imaging system to learn more about the real physical territory of his or her enemy in preparation for a future attack. Similarly, hackers may access an enemy's computer system to engage in "intelligence preparation of the battlefield," mapping the coordinates of an adversary's computer system and learning about its strengths and weaknesses. Here, some analysts see this as a legal act within a cyber conflict (quoting Martin Libicki's famous statement that "there is no forced entry in cyberspace" but only weaknesses created when a company fails to properly secure its system, leaving it vulnerable to outside intrusions), whereas others may see it as an act of cybertrespass.

Furthermore, analysts don't agree regarding the legality and ethical acceptability of active cyberdefense—or indeed whether it is properly understood as defense. Here, they have raised concerns about whether "hacking back" creates a merely proportional response to an attack by an adversary or whether a hack back might inflict a disproportionate response on one's opponent. If a conventional military can only drive an opposing army out of their borders but not pursue the army farther nor seek to destroy it, what is a comparable set of conditions to impose on today's cyber warriors? Would destroying the intruder's computer system be merely a proportional response or something that was disproportionate? Active cyberdefense is also often carried out today autonomously. A program might be established within a state or commercial computer system that instructed its computers to automatically hack back in response to a perceived attack. Here, some analysts are concerned about setting up a system that acts autonomously without a human in the loop to carry out such actions. The norms of warfare also require that acts of war can be traced up a chain of command to a responsible individual (such as a commanding officer) who would then be held legally and ethically responsible for any breaches of the military code of conduct that might occur. But in the field of cyberwarfare, where acts may take place often with only minimal human oversight and supervision, legal issues have been raised regarding who exactly is legally responsible in instances when mistakes might be made.

A Debate: Is Cyberwarfare Really War?

For these reasons, then, analysts disagree about what specific actions constitute a cyberwar and indeed whether cyberwar exists at all. Thomas Rid is the most well-known proponent of the view that cyber conflict does not equal cyberwar. In his book, *Cyberwar Will Not Take Place*, Rid argued that cyberweapons are fundamentally different than kinetic weapons because they cannot by themselves actually kill other human beings. He notes that code can be deployed to, for example, destroy hospital records that might then result in deaths of patients who receive the wrong medication or no medication. However, he argues that such deaths would be secondary effects rather than direct results of a cyberattack. Similarly, even if malicious code could be used to shut down an electrical grid, causing people to freeze to death in a cold climate in the winter, such deaths would not be a direct result of the code itself but rather of the effects that the code had on the electrical grid. Thus, Rid argues that code alone cannot kill anyone, and for this reason, we should abandon any attempt to formulate rules for cyberwar or doctrines of cyberwar. Instead, cyber operations should be understood merely as a force multiplier for conventional conflicts. However, information ethicists claim that destroying an information object is the goal of cyberwarfare and that such actions can indeed be considered as acts of war.

Valeriano and Maness, the creators of the first data set of cyber conflicts, came to a slightly different conclusion. They argue that half of all interstate cyber incidents that have occurred in the last twenty years are best described as cyber espionage or cybertheft rather than cyber conflict.[51] And the Department of Defense designates much of their cyberactivity not as acts of war but rather as CNE, which is defined as enabling operations and intelligence collective capabilities conducted through the use of computer networks to gather data from target or adversary automated information systems or networks. They argue that the vast majority of the time, Department of Defense cyber warriors are not "fighting in cyberspace" but are instead exploring and mapping cyberspace in preparation for future battles. In legal terms, they are engaged in "covert activity," much as spies working on behalf of intelligence agencies are. Covert activities—including surveillance and trespassing—are not part of any nation's official foreign policy and are not publicly claimed by states because such actions violate international law principles of sovereignty.

However, these views—that cyberwar is not warfare or that it is more usefully understood as covert activity—represent a minority viewpoint among scholars, most of whom argue that the LOAC, as well as international law understandings regarding the conditions under which war is legal, can be "exported" to regulate the conflict of cyberwar as well. Here, we can consider the 2011 US International Strategy for Operating in Cyberspace, which states:

> The development of norms for state conduct in cyberspace does not require a reinvention of customary international law, nor does it render existing international norms obsolete. Long-standing international norms guiding state behavior—in times of peace and conflict—also apply in cyberspace.[52]

International Law according to the *Tallinn Manual*

Today, most legal analysts reference the *Tallinn Manual on the International Law Applicable to Cyber Warfare* when discussing the legality of actions in cyberspace. This document was authored between 2009 and 2013 in a series of meetings involving members of NATO. The committee members (including civilian and military analysts) attempted to codify key issues, such as the role of civilians in the prosecution of cyberwar, the conditions under which it is lawful to respond to a cyberattack, and the ways in which one can practice discrimination in cyberwarfare through not targeting civilians.

The *Tallinn Manual* states that nations can respond to cyberattacks with conventional force if the intensity of a cyberattack is such that it meets the definition of an armed attack (according to Article 51 of the United Nations Charter). In 2012, US State Department Legal Advisor Harold Koh reiterated this understanding, noting that a cyberattack whose consequences amounted to an armed attack could trigger the right of self-defense under UN Charter Article 51 and that international law governing armed conflict (such as the requirement that armed forces distinguish between military and civilian targets) also applied to cyberspace.

The *Tallinn Manual* does however recognize some ways in which cyberwarfare differs from conventional or nuclear warfare—in particular through its heavy reliance on civilians as cyber warriors. The manual notes that civilians can participate in cyber activity during wartime alongside military personnel. However, when they do so, they lose the protection normally provided to civilians and may instead be treated as combatants. The *Tallinn Manual* also acknowledges that although one cannot specifically target civilians during a cyberattack, it is permissible to carry out attacks that might nonetheless inconvenience citizens through, for example, taking a banking system offline.[53]

Militarizing Cyberspace

Earlier in this textbook, you were asked to think about the phenomenon of governance, defined as "intentional interventions directed towards solving public policy problems and enhancing the common good."[54] What does the creation of an international consensus that the structures of international law, including international humanitarian law, as well as the LOAC, when applied in cyberspace mean in terms of internet governance?

In 2018, scholars Hollis and Ohlin argued that the decision by *Tallinn Manual* authors that both LOAC and international humanitarian law rules and norms apply in cyberspace meant that policy makers had decided that "cyberspace is for fighting."[55] They believe that creating a strong international consensus about the application of LOAC means that cyberspace is now understood primarily as an arena of conflict, rather than cooperation, and one in which the most privileged international actors are states and by extension their militaries. If anyone has a key role to play in governing or regulating cyberspace, then it is likely to be military actors acting on behalf of legitimate states. That is, they believe that the publication of the *Tallinn Manual* supports the creation of a cyber Westphalia model of internet governance over and above the creation of other models, such as multistakeholder governance.

However, in their final analysis, they conclude that although warfighting might indeed end up becoming one of the primary purposes for the existence of cyberspace, this does not preclude the carrying out of additional activities—including e-commerce—nor does it preclude the possibility that states (and other actors) could come together to form structures of cooperation in other areas, such as e-banking or the regulation of digital currencies. In addition, they note that just as nonstate actors still have a role to play in conflict scenarios (e.g., the role played by the international campaign to ban landmines in advocating for a ban on these weapons in wartime), nonstate actors could still have a role to play in the creation of norms and laws regulating cyber conflict as well as in the conduct of cyberspace hostilities.

In the following section, we examine a different viewpoint—one that suggests that states can indeed learn to cooperate and manage conflict in cyberspace through the creation of structures of cyberdeterrence as well the possible creation of a wide-ranging and widely accepted cyber arms control agreement.

Solutions to End and Regulate Cyber Conflict

We have concluded that cyberwarfare is itself neither safer nor more dangerous than conventional warfare because it is in fact intimately entwined with political and military objectives (rather than mere cyber objectives) and because it is not a stand-alone activity that has effects in many other areas, both military and political. Nonetheless, some analysts believe that it is time for states to consider ways of limiting the impact and utility of these weapons.

In considering how and when to regulate cyberweapons or, indeed, whether such an eventuality is even possible, many analysts look back to other historic conflicts and begin to reason by analogy. For example, although nuclear weapons were first used to end World War Two in 1945, the predicted nuclear Armageddon that many thought would result did not, in point of fact, occur. Instead, states evolved systems for controlling, monitoring, and limiting the creation of such weapons. Could states evolve similar mechanisms for preventing the outbreak of a large-scale cyberwar? In this section, we consider whether concepts like deterrence and arms control can be "exported" and applied to thinking about cyberwar as well.

Cyber Optimists versus Cyber Pessimists

In Chapter 2, we introduced the notion of technological determinism, the idea that a technology has its own destiny and seeks its own end. Today, cyber pessimists share common ground with technological determinists because they believe that once invented, a weapon (including a cyberweapon) will inevitably be used. A rational actor would naturally want to exploit all possible capabilities of such weapons. Thus, cyber pessimists believe that the best course of action is for states to ban the creation, stockpiling, and use of such weapons in conflict. Cyber pessimists point to events like Russia exercising influence over the 2016 US presidential elections, China engaging in cyber espionage to steal blueprints for the US F-35 fighter, and the US intelligence community's engaging in covert activities aimed at disrupting

Iran's nuclear program. They suggest that such events are potentially extremely destabilizing to the international balance of power.[56]

In contrast, cyber optimists believe that states (and policy makers) have a significant amount of agency in deciding how, when, and under what conditions to deploy cyberweapons. These individuals point out that in fact, after World War Two nuclear weapons have never been used in conflict. Instead, states have been able to utilize restraint in not deploying these weapons. The agency belonged not to the weapons but to those who made decisions about how to deploy them.[57]

The Logic of Cyberdeterrence

Cyber optimists and cyber pessimists disagree both about the risks posed by cyberweapons as well as about their specific utility. We know that cyberweapons are useful for achieving specific cyber objectives (i.e., to defend a target, such as critical infrastructure). But can these weapons also be used to achieve larger foreign policy objectives? That is, could a state use a credible cyberthreat to coerce or compel an adversary to carry out some other type of objective—to withdraw conventional troops from a region, for example?

Here, we can look to the past to ask whether cyberweapons can play a similar role to the role that was played during the 1970s and the 1980s (during the Cold War) by nuclear weapons. At that time period, the UN "nuclear umbrella" was extended over much of Western Europe. In other words, the Soviet Union was prevented from invading NATO countries due to the threat that the United States presented, the threat that it would utilize its nuclear weapons against the Soviet Union if such actions occurred. In this way, US nuclear weapons were used to carry out extended deterrence, serving to protect both American and European interests, based on a credible US threat to utilize them against anyone who invaded either American or NATO territory.

The notion that weapons can be utilized to deter another country from taking specific actions is important because it suggests that a state can derive great utility merely from owning such weapons, even if these weapons are never used. Instead, the threat that a country might use such weapons is enough to prevent other states from engaging in specific actions (i.e., interfering in a nation's sovereignty). Here the weapons serve a signaling function; US possession of nuclear weapons served as a signal of US credibility and resolve. The United States could guarantee Western Europe's security because its adversaries knew that it was willing and able to back up its threats with force.

Here, Frank Harvey argues that nuclear weapons were necessary to achieve **strategic stability**.[58] He felt that the mere existence of potentially world-ending nuclear weapons (sometimes known as existential deterrence) would be sufficient to deter nations from actually using them against one another. Here, nuclear analysts described a condition of mutual assured destruction (MAD), which existed as a result of the United States and Soviet Union both possessing nuclear weapons. These analysts argued that both sides knew that allowing any situation to escalate to the point that one side launched a nuclear weapon and the other side felt compelled to respond was foolish because any conflict would likely destroy both the United States and the Soviet Union. Thus, just having such weapons allowed both sides to maintain an uneasy peace (or strategic stability) because the destructive power of these weapons all but guaranteed that they would never be used.[59] And because the weapons were never used, some argue that deterrence is perhaps a cheaper and more ethical form of warfare than other types of warfare (like conventional warfare) in which weapons are more likely to actually be used.

Today, some analysts speak of Mutual Assured Disruption (MAD); Here, these analysts argue that no state actually wants to engage in a large-scale cyberwar against an enemy that could potentially destroy all of its critical infrastructure, resulting in massive civilian casualties and possibly a period of several years without electricity or other basic services until the state could rebuild.

But does this logic hold in cyberspace? Would a state, aware of the danger of cyberwar, engage in the same type of restraint that states engaged in regarding nuclear weapons? Axelrod and Iliev argue that cyberweapons are not the same as nuclear weapons because once a state or nonstate actor possesses a cyberweapon, this entity may feel compelled to utilize it quickly because its utility begins to degrade or decay quickly after its creation—unlike a nuclear weapon, which could be used to deter aggressors for years. In this way, one could argue that although nuclear weapons create crisis stability, cyberweapons do not. Furthermore, cyberweapons might not function effectively as a deterrent because everyone, including one's adversaries, know that these weapons degrade over time.[60]

Andres raises another objection to the application of the nuclear-cyber analogy. He points out that the credibility of a state's nuclear deterrent actually rested on two qualities: the actual technological capabilities that the state possessed as well as the credibility of the state's threat that it would in point of fact deploy these capabilities. (The willingness to use these weapons was referred to as resolve.) Andres argues that the United States may possess a significant cyberweapons arsenal, developed by highly skilled personnel; however, he is not convinced of the US resolve to respond to a cyberattack with "massive retaliation" that could be either cyber enabled or carried out by some other mechanism.[61] Here, he argues that the best deterrent in a cyberattack is to threaten retaliation but that such retaliation does not need to be in kind. That is, the United States could answer a cyberattack with some form of economic sanctions, or with a conventional attack, or by asking the United Nations for a public condemnation or censuring of the state. However, Andres argues that the United States effectively did nothing in response to the 2016 Russian election hacking and argues that when a state fails to respond to a provocation, it makes it likely to be the subject of additional provocations. At the same time, he argues, the United States has not responded in a sufficiently strong way to Chinese cyberattacks aimed at carrying out industrial espionage. And although civilians were keenly and visibly aware of the damages caused by conventional attacks, such as the 1941 attack on Pearl Harbor, or the September 11, 2001, attack on the World Trade Center, cyberattacks may be much less publicly visible, leading the general public to be less supportive of strong state responses to these attacks.[62]

However, some more optimistic analysts do see a future for the creation of cyberdeterrence.[63] These analysts argue that as long as states are able to engage in restraint through not using cyberweapons to attack their opponents, the more likely it is that such restraint will become a norm within the international system.

Does the Cyber-Nuclear Analogy Fit?

Other critics disagree, however, about whether the logic of nuclear deterrence can be extended to speak about cyber deterrence as well. Libicki, for example, argues that there is no cyber equivalent of a "first strike capability," which could paralyze your opponent and make it impossible for them to respond.[64]

Furthermore, it was relatively easy for a state to signal what its intentions were in utilizing nuclear weapons. Given the size of nuclear weapons, their cost, and the numerous support personnel who were involved in their production and deployment, it was difficult for states to keep secrets regarding the size and capabilities of their nuclear arsenals. Nuclear weapons are physical weapons that can be photographed utilizing satellite technology, and deploying them in a particular scenario might involve moving them from one location to another.

In contrast, cyberweapons are mere pieces of code. We cannot see how many cyberweapons another country has, it is difficult to know how much other nations are spending on the creation of cyberweapons, and unlike nuclear weapons, the "life" of a cyberweapon may be relatively short-lived due to changes in technology. And states do not always announce the deployment of a cyberweapon. Instead, such weapons might lie dormant on another state's system until they are deployed through either a human action or an autonomous program. That is, states cannot use cyberweapons to signal resolve and commitment in the same ways that they have used nukes in the past.[65] And Libicki argues that because so few people actually have the training and ability to create sophisticated cyberweapons, states would encounter a finite limit on the number of weapons they could create or the numbers of people they could deploy to create them. Valeriano argues that a cyberweapon is more like a piece of knowledge than it is a piece of hardware. For that reason, he feels that it would be impossible to ever ban cyberweapons because coders would still know how to make new ones.

In addition, many analysts including former Director of Intelligence James Clapper do not believe that a "cyber Armageddon" or "digital apocalypse" is likely. They believe that if cyberwar among adversaries does occur, it will be an ongoing series of low- to moderate-level cyberattacks from a variety of sources over time, which will impose cumulative costs on US economic competitiveness and national security.[66] But they do not accept the existence of MAD.

At the same time, military analysts today acknowledge that cyber is not only a stand-alone platform for engaging in conflict. Rather, they point out that many conventional weapons, such as airplanes or aircraft carriers, depend upon a cyber infrastructure, which provides communications and navigation capabilities. Planners thus worry that a hacker (either private or state sponsored) could hack into the cyber infrastructure supporting both conventional and nuclear weapons.[67] A hacker could provide a naval ship with false information regarding its location or even trigger a launch of a nuclear weapon.[68]

Futter points to a number of risks: Hackers might somehow directly or indirectly cause a nuclear explosion or precipitate the launch of US or Russian strategic forces (including several hundred nuclear missiles). Or hackers might be a hostile state or outsiders, like third parties or terrorist groups, who might seek to create a crisis between states (e.g., through creating a false flag attack that the United States would attribute to Russia or China). The hacker could be a lone wolf. Futter refers to these scenarios as enabling cyberattacks.[69]

Here he suggests that the United States or Russia might carry out a disabling cyberattack. That is, the United States or Russia might intentionally use their cyber capabilities to disable an adversary's nuclear missile—and then either on purpose or accidentally launch missiles. One's adversary would be unable to respond due to cyberattacks having disabled or incapacitated the system. Here the author argues that the only way to secure nuclear weapons in a cyber environment is to seek to significantly reduce US (and Russian) dependence on nuclear weapons as part of our strategic force postures as well as to aim for a build down of existing weapons and perhaps even a ban.

A Cyber Arms Control Treaty?

Should we expect states to come together to regulate or even ban the creation and deployment of cyberweapons? Today, we can point to three different types of state efforts aimed at reducing the costs and risks associated with cyber conflict: the creation of confidence-building measures (CBMs); the creation of cyberweapons bans; and the creation of long-term and comprehensive cyber arms control treaties and agreements.

Confidence-Building Measures in Cyberspace

First, we can consider CBMs, which are defined as "practical actions aimed at creating attitudes of cooperation." CBMs are short-term rather than long-term instruments aimed at creating transparency and trust among actors to prevent the outbreak of war and conflict as well as to resolve existing conflicts among regional neighbors or other actors who may be involved in a long-standing confrontation.[70] In the physical world, we can point to international attempts to create CBMs for two long-standing enemies, India and Pakistan. These two countries have sometimes engaged in territorial incursions or skirmishes along their shared borders. In this scenario, the borders between states are sometimes unclear, while ethnic tensions are great. There is a high risk of either side engaging in a preemptive action (i.e., acting prior to declaring an official war) as well as a high likelihood that an adversary would misread the situation. The scenario is thus a classic example of a security dilemma.

In such a scenario, CBMs have aimed to bring the two sides together to create trust and to encourage those involved to engage in dialogues and information sharing with each other so that when misunderstandings do occur, the conflict does not escalate into war. The operative assumption here is that conflicts often escalate as a result of misunderstandings or misperceptions, in which, for example, a defensive action might be perceived by an adversary as offensive in intent. States are encouraged to behave with transparency, utilizing procedures for warning an adversary, for example, before engaging in an equipment test of military exercise. CBMs often include the establishment of a hotline so that leaders can communicate with each other quickly in crisis scenarios and exchange information to de-escalate a situation. Actors can also engage in simulations or exercises, rehearsing how to behave in a high-tension crisis situation.

In the cyber arena, we can identify rudimentary efforts among states aimed at increasing transparency among actors and reducing the amount of "noise" that exists in our present-day system. That is, states have begun making agreements to share information among allies, as well as to consult (even with adversaries) before assuming that they have been attacked by a cyberweapon and responding with massive retaliation. Cyber CBMs can be freestanding, or cyber concerns can be added to existing CBMs among states. For example, the United States and Russia have engaged in large strategy stability dialogues that now include a cyber component.[71]

States also carry out joint military exercises aimed at increasing their ability to communicate and convey information in an often chaotic wartime environment. States have now begun carrying out joint cyber exercises, whose purpose is to see how quickly breaches can be identified and to practice rules for verifying the sources of breaches.

Critics point out that CBMs don't actually solve the security dilemma but merely create a way of responding when breaches occur. They note as well that not all states are willing to engage in CBMs because even sharing information about one's forces, one's doctrines and strategies, and one's procedures for behaving in conflict may be seen as threatening national sovereignty. In addition, because most CBM agreements tend to be multinational and carried out under the auspices of international organizations like the United Nations, some states may resent the leading role offered to these organizations in addressing a regional conflict that they might prefer to address on a state-level basis.

Finally, some analysts suggest that although CBMs might work in addressing rising tensions in real space, they are unlikely to work in cyberspace. Here, Denning and Strawser argue that cyber warriors often find themselves in situations requiring an immediate response in an environment of incomplete information. And because of the rapid speed at which cyber warfare occurs, active defense may also include provisions to predelegate authority to carry out defensive actions to cyber warfighters or even to create conditions in which machines might respond autonomously to perceived attacks without waiting for or even seeking permission. In such a situation, it is difficult to see how CBMs such as the creation of a crisis hotline would be effective in preventing escalation or preventing misunderstandings.[72]

Should We Ban Cyberweapons?

Next, we can consider efforts to create a comprehensive ban on the development and proliferation of cyberweapons. As early as 2011, China and Russia put forth a proposal to ban cyberweapons. Here analysts differ as to whether what is needed is an extremely broad-ranging agreement that in effect bans cyberweapons or a more targeted agreement such as a pledge by both sides not to use cyberweapons to target their adversaries' nuclear weapons. Analysts also disagree about whether it would be possible to distinguish among types of cyberweapons, as well as between offensive and defensive cyberweapons, to determine who is and is not complying with a ban.[73]

Cyber Arms Control Treaties

Finally, we can consider the likelihood of creating a cyber arms control treaty. Here we can return to the three paradigms for thinking about cyberspace—realism, liberal internationalism, and constructivism. Each paradigm leads us to a different conclusion regarding the possibility of creating an arms control agreement for cyberweapons in the future.

Realists, who conceptualize the international system as a self-help system in which each state's ultimate goal is to ensure its own state survival, do not believe that arms control agreements work in most situations. Instead, they believe that states will use such agreements to achieve aims that are most favorable to their own interests. (For example, a state that was lagging behind its peers in the race to create a nuclear weapon might support a nuclear weapon ban or build down largely because it wanted to slow down its neighbors' or its adversaries' progress in creating such weapons rather than because the state wanted to build a more peaceful world.) They also believe that most states are likely to engage in deception and rule breaking, even if they have publicly agreed to a cyber arms control treaty. Thus, realists believe that most sophisticated states will likely continue to carry out aggressive cyber actions and will simply work harder to avoid detection—exploiting vulnerabilities in cyberspace such as the difficulty of attribution.[74] Here, a realist would suggest that the individual payoff of enhanced state security trumps any shared international interest in preserving a stable, peaceful commons because cooperation under anarchy is unlikely to be long-lasting. The system simply mitigates against it.

However, liberal internationalists are more optimistic about the possibility of implementing a cyber arms control treaty. Under the Obama administration, the US leadership sought to implement a broad international framework of norms, treaties, and institutions to govern cyberspace with a cyber arms control treaty as a first step. Progress was made toward the goal with the creation in 2015 of a limited agreement between the United States and China that stated that "neither country's government will conduct or knowingly support cyber-enabled theft of IP, including trade secrets." The two sides also committed to a joint statement to "identify and promote norms of state behavior in cyberspace within the international community."[75] The efforts under the Obama administration represented an attempt to graft the cold war concepts of deterrence and arms control onto the cyber domain. Here, analysts like Lindsay argue that because cyberspace is a human-made domain (rather than a physical territory that exists independently of human interaction), states must cooperate to preserve it as a domain for all sorts of activities, from warfare to commerce. That is, they feel that the interdependence that is created between states in cyberspace will force states to interact and to learn to cooperate with one another over time, leading to the creation of structures like international arms control agreements.

Finally, we can consider the constructivist view. Constructivists believe that the world is what you make of it or that states can make decisions about how to talk about and how to structure cyberspace rather than assuming that it must be one way (conflictual) or the other (cooperative). Here, Hollis and Ohlin describe the ways in which key actors behave in cyberspace as precedent setting. That is, they argue that if military cyber command members demonstrate that they accept the validity of structuring agreements like the Tallinn Manual through adhering to them and behaving as if they are real, then these actions may have the effect of socializing everyone within the system into accepting these agreements as valid. That is, rather than arguing about whether cyberspace limits or creates the structures of cooperation, we as analysts should look to how people and states actually behave in cyberspace because it is ultimately their behaviors that create the conditions under which states (and nonstate actors) interact.

In the final chapter of this textbook, we consider future developments, including the ways in which autonomous weapons might be used in future conflict.

QUESTIONS FOR DISCUSSION

1. Think about the political polarization that is currently occurring in the United States and the reasons for it. How might an outside adversary take advantage of such a situation to destabilize the state? Do you consider this a legitimate worry? Why or why not?

2. How optimistic or pessimistic are you that a cyber arms control agreement would actually work? Do you regard yourself as a realist, a liberal internationalist, or a constructivist? Give reasons for your answers.

3. Which nations do you regard as Great Powers in terms of their cyber capabilities? What measures are you using to arrive at this estimate? Do you think it is useful to attempt to rank states in this way? Why or why not?

4. List the ways in which the creation of cyberweapons has made the international system more stable as well as the ways in which the existence of cyberweapons might make the world more dangerous. Do you consider yourself to be a cyber pessimist or a cyber optimist?

5. Consider the nuclear analogy at length. In what ways are cyberweapons like nuclear weapons, and how is the nuclear arms race different from or the same as the cyber arms race?

6. Consider the threat posed to the United States by psychological aspects of cyberwarfare versus the threat posed by cyberattacks on critical infrastructure like hospitals or government offices. The aim of psychological warfare is to damage citizens' trust in the integrity of their political institutions, whereas cyberattacks on infrastructure aim to damage the integrity of physical infrastructure. Which is harder to repair—physical infrastructure or trust in political institutions? What is harder to defend?

KEY TERMS

Active cyber defense 290
Active measures 276
Cyber forensic investigation 291
Disinformation 276

Passive cyber defense 289
Strategic stability 296
Subversion 276

FOR FURTHER READING

Bagge, D. P. *Unmasking Maskirovka: Russia's Cyber Influence Operations* (New York, NY: Defense Press, 2019).

Geist, E. *Deterrence Stability in the Cyber Age* (Carlisle Barracks, PA: United States Army War College Press, Strategic Studies Quarterly, 2015).

Klimburg, A. *The Darkening Web: The War for Cyberspace* (London, UK: Penguin Press, 2017).

Manjikian, M. *Confidence-Building in Cyberspace: A Comparison of Territorial and Weapons-Based Regimes* (Carlisle Barracks, PA: United States Army War College Press, Strategic Studies Institute, 2015).

Manjikian, M. "From Global Village to Virtual Battlespace: The Colonizing of the Internet and the Extension of Realpolitik." *International Studies Quarterly* 54, no. 2 (2010): 381–401.

12

LOOKING TOWARD THE FUTURE

Learning Objectives

At the end of this chapter, students will be able to do the following:

1. Define critical terms, including *emerging technology*, *big data*, and *fourth industrial revolution*.

2. Describe political and ethical problems related to dependence on data and algorithms, including algorithmic governance and bias.

3. Define key terms associated with artificial intelligence, including *meaningful human control* (MHC) and *levels of autonomy*.

4. Apply three paradigms (realism, liberal internationalism, and constructivism) to describe and analyze the dynamics of an artificial intelligence arms race.

Thus far in this textbook we have examined cyberspace as it is. In this final chapter, however, we look into the future to consider questions that might arise as well as to think about possible solutions. We begin by exploring what is meant by an emerging technology and explain the specific hazards and challenges presented by these types of technological developments.

We then consider two crucially important emerging technologies—big data and artificial intelligence. In 2013, author James Barrett made the following prediction: "In our lifetime—in the future, all the important decisions governing the lives of humans will be made by machines or humans whose intelligence is augmented by machines."[1]

In examining the rise of both of these new technologies—big data and artificial intelligence—we contemplate a world in which agency is shared between humans and machines or where agency may even in some instances be ceded to the machines themselves.

If in the future key decisions affecting our social, economic, and political lives are made not by humans but by algorithms, hardware, and software—this scenario presents many questions for political scientists and international relations experts. In this chapter we consider the stances that different nations have taken toward supporting or opposing the extension of algorithmic and artificial intelligence-enhanced decision-making. If power is indeed given to machines to make decisions, on whose behalf can we expect them to act? Will they do what is best for citizens, or will they do what is best for our governments at the expense of citizens? Will a new reliance on these technologies lead to a more peaceful world or a more violent one? And can nations decide together on restrictions, norms, and rules for how decision-making and power sharing will occur between humans and machines?

Although we began this text by suggesting that many of the issues initially created by the invention of the internet were heading toward a place of technological closure, where a consensus had been achieved regarding the utility and meaning of a technology, we end this text by looking at new technologies with which technological closure has not yet been achieved. The future of human-machine interactions may indeed turn out to be one of great promise as exciting new goals are achieved. Possibly, humans and machines will work together to solve problems like global warming and world hunger. However, it is also possible that the existence of these new technologies will merely exacerbate existing conflicts rather than solve them.

As you read this chapter you are asked to think about whether you yourself trust machines, what circumstances or restrictions would be necessary in a society for you to do so, and whether you are yourself pessimistic or optimistic about the challenges and opportunities presented by emerging technologies like algorithms and artificial intelligence.

WHAT IS AN EMERGING TECHNOLOGY?

This term refers to new technological developments that differ radically from those that preceded them. An emerging technology as one that is "radically novel and relatively fast growing . . . characterized by a certain degree of coherence persisting over time and with the potential to exert a considerable impact on the socioeconomic domain."[2]

It is often difficult to predict the impact that an emerging technology will have. As we saw throughout this text, computer science has been a field of study since the 1940s, and the internet itself has emerged over a period of about fifty years. It has emerged in ways that its developers and designers never could have fully predicted, and it has altered our world in ways that previously seemed unimaginable. Thus, it is difficult to predict the sorts of laws and social institutions that may be required to cope with the outcomes of such novel technologies.

Policy makers may not be immediately aware of the specific regulatory challenges that it presents. The long-term effects of a technology may be unclear or ambiguous, and questions about access may initially be unresolved. In addition, many new technologies are highly specialized, and it may be difficult to convey to citizens exactly what the technology does and how it works. Thus, it may be difficult to solicit citizen input into such technologies.

Here, we might consider, for example, recent medical advances that have led to a lengthening of the human life span. In 1896, the average person's life expectancy was forty-eight, and today the average life span in Japan is eighty years. The numbers of people worldwide who now live past one hundred years has experienced a sharp uptick, and some scientists think that in the future people may live to be 120 years old.[3] As a result, policy makers are coping with new and unexpected challenges both within their own nations and internationally. For example, Japan is currently experiencing social and economic issues because there are more aging people receiving social security than there are young people who are employed and paying into social pension systems. In addition, people are working longer, and this affects the availability of jobs for young people. And in many communities housing is expensive because older people still live in their houses rather than retiring to a nursing home and putting them on the market for younger buyers.[4] All of these are unexpected and unpredicted consequences of technological advances.

The term *fourth revolution* is sometimes invoked to refer to our current era, in which we are beginning to see a blurring of the distinctions between humans and machines as we begin to influence and be influenced by one another. The fourth revolution also refers to the advent of technologies, like 3-D printing of human prosthetics, voice control over technologies (like a home heating or entertainment system), the use of technology in medical diagnostics, and the growing influence of the internet of things and big data. Here, the first industrial revolution refers to the adoption of steam power and mechanical equipment in manufacturing, beginning in 1784. The second industrial revolution (1870) refers to the adopting of practices like the division and specialization of labor, along with technologies of mass production and a reliance on electricity for power. Finally, the third industrial revolution connotes the move in 1969 to an increased dependence on information technology and automated production.[5]

The fact that we cannot predict the effects of a new technology is not a unique idea. In the European Union, throughout the 1990s, citizens and policy makers asked whether people should grow and eat foods that had been genetically modified. Genetically modified organisms (GMOs) are commonly used today in commercial agricultural operations. The best-known example of a GMO that is widely consumed today is a specific breed of corn that was bred in a laboratory by the Monsanto Corporation. This corn was designed to be disease and drought resistant. Over time, the strain of this corn has come to be the dominant type of corn grown throughout the world. Many people see the adoption of this corn breed as a mark of progress, and they point out that its availability has likely saved many lives in regions where drought is common. But some environmental activists argue that it is impossible to predict what the effects might be in the long term of using technology to alter genetic material. They point to situations in which the effects of a chemical or drug did not become known until many years later. (For example, in the 1970s, in the United States, Europe, and the developing world, many pregnant mothers were given an anti-nausea medication known as Thalidomide. Although the mothers did not suffer any ill effects while they were pregnant, it turned out that the medication caused birth defects in their children.)

These activists suggest that governments adopt the precautionary principle when thinking about the introduction of new technologies whose long-term effects are unknown. The precautionary principle means that decision-makers should assume a technology is harmful until it can be proven safe—rather than assuming it is safe until it is proven harmful. It also means that when thinking about possible harms from a technology, decision makers should consider not only those who are currently present but also those who may be present several generations from now. In the case of the genetically modified corn, decision makers worry that if all other strains of corn are wiped out, then a possible blight or disease in the future that targets the Monsanto corn might lead to a famine because there would be no sources of replacement feed.

We can expect to see similar unexpected, and unpredicted, consequences as a result of advances in artificial intelligence technologies. In considering the social and ethical impacts of emerging technologies, the United States in particular appears to lag behind its counterparts. Beginning in 2011, the European Commission Project on Ethical Issues of Emerging Information and Communications Technology Applications was launched. Also, in Europe, the European Commission's Educational Research and Development Project on Future and Emerging Technologies has been formed. This group is attempting to predict what new technologies might emerge, what regulations might be required for these new technologies, and what the implications of new technologies might be. The European approach thus has been largely preemptive—rather than waiting for issues to emerge, they have attempted to get out ahead of the issues presented by new technologies to build the necessary regulatory frameworks to confront these issues as they emerge. Such an approach represents a change from previous approaches, which attempted to react to events once they had already occurred.

SELECTED FUTURE CHALLENGES: BIG DATA

The best way to understand the import of, and the challenges related to, an emerging technology is to consider a specific emerging technology. Here we consider the emergence in the 21st century of big data as a by-product of the extension of the internet and large-scale computing.

But what is big data? Big data does not simply refer to the existence of a large data set. Rather, big data can be described as a methodology in which existing data collections of all types are aggregated together and made to communicate with one another through sharing data.[6] Data scientists seek to search, aggregate, and cross-reference data to find out information that cannot be gleaned from one data set alone. In addition, big data refers to data that is produced by subjects both consciously and unconsciously, both actively and passively.

Kitchin, a noted data architect, writes that big data has certain characteristics. It exists in high volumes, is accumulated at a high velocity, and is created in real time. There is an extensive variety of this data, which is exhaustive in scope. It is "fine grained" in the sense that one can delve down into tiny details. It can be indexed and classified, and it is relational. Analysts can join together multiple data sets across multiple fields, including adding new fields. It can also be expanded rapidly.[7]

In analyzing big data to look for trends or make predictions, analysts are often not particularly interested in the specific data produced by one individual (i.e., the contents of an individual's e-mails). Rather, analysts often seek to mine metadata—or data about data. Metadata refers to information that can be gleaned from data sets to include the ways in which actors within the data sets are tied together through interactions. Metadata thus might include IP addresses that are seen as interacting with each other, the locations of calls or messages, or the duration of contacts between different sites.

Today, data are often described as a resource. It is "the new oil" in the sense that it is a resource that allows many other types of services to run. Just as a car cannot run without oil, today's organizations depend on data to sell products, to target customers, to track the progress of students in a university, and to make planning decisions about how to configure electoral districts, build roads, or choose sites for community residential and commercial services. For this reason, the data collected in the United States alone has been valued at nearly $70 billion a year.[8]

As noted earlier in this text, data can migrate far from the original source where it was created through mechanisms like cloud storage and cloud computing. Today, the importance (and value) of big data, combined with the lack of clarity regarding who owns data produced, who may access it, and whether citizens in fact have control over the data they have produced, has created many urgent political, legal, and ethical questions.

What's Wrong with Big Data?

Today analysts and ethicists have identified three issues to pay attention to as we consider the rise of big data. First, the existence of more and better data than ever before means that governments in particular may be tempted to utilize data to engage in surveillance of citizens. Today, it would be easy for a government to know who was accessing potentially subversive information online; at the same time, citizens would remain unaware that they were being watched in this way.

In the years since the revelations by Edward Snowden of large-scale US government surveillance of citizens by the US National Security Agency, policy makers and watchdog groups have raised issues associated with data storage. Today, many internet servers and programs automatically archive records of all transactions that take place online and all activities that take place in public spaces. Although this data may potentially never be accessed by anyone, there is always a possibility that at some point in the future, an organization like the police force could ask for this information. They could ask for surveillance footage, for example, that showed you engaging in a public demonstration against the government or even driving away from a crime scene.

The phenomenon of data storage means that although you may temporarily enjoy the privacy of acting independently as a private citizen while you initially engage in the action, this ability to act as a private citizen might later be revoked. Privacy can thus be conceptualized as a dynamic and changing rather than a permanent quality that a state gives to its citizens.

Second, the storage of data also means that your information is being stored preemptively in response to the likelihood that you might in the future commit a crime and the government might require evidence to prosecute you. Here, some privacy watchdog groups have stated that the storage of data for future prosecutions in essence renders every citizen guilty until proven innocent rather than allowing them the presumption of innocence until they are proven guilty in a court of law. Kerr writes that previously, law enforcement did not carry out stakeouts of people or follow them for prolonged periods of time because it was too expensive and resource intensive. However, today, he argues, it would be possible for a law enforcement group to create a bot whose sole purpose was to monitor the communications of someone who was merely suspected of having committed a crime or planning to commit one in the future. Here, the availability of this resource might make it more likely for law enforcement organizations to move to a system of near constant and near universal surveillance of those who fall into certain likely risk groups.[9]

QUANTUM COMPUTING

Quantum computing, a new technology, has been referred to as the next stage of computing. Computing emerged in a number of stages: from the existence of mainframe computers that were found only at scientific and research sites, to the development of the personal computer, to the development of our current environment in which computers are everywhere and embedded in a variety of devices.

At each stage of this evolution, computers became cheaper, easier to use, and significantly more powerful. Moore's Law is the principle that states that the amount of computing power available on a microchip doubles every two years, leading to an exponential rate of technological advancement as each new generation of computers is significantly more powerful than the previous one.[10]

Quantum computing is a major new technological development because quantum computers work significantly differently than our existing computers.

(Continued)

CRITICAL ISSUES

(Continued)

In short, our current computers run on bits, chains of zeros and ones that are used to encode data and instructions. Quantum computers, however, use quantum bits, which can have a value of zero, one or zero, and one at the same time.[11] This new functionality will in turn give quantum computers the ability to solve problems that are too complex for existing computers. They will be able to handle more data, to carry out more complex operations, and will be faster than existing computers.

Implications of Quantum Computing

This new technology is best described as an emerging technology. Emerging technologies may emerge in unpredictable ways, and therefore it is challenging both to regulate them and to prepare for all the ways in which an emerging technology can change a society.

As Marr writes, "Quantum computers will disrupt every industry. They will change the way we do business and the security we have in place to safeguard data, how we fight disease and invent new materials, and solve health and climate problems."[12]

Quantum computing is predicted to have a variety of effects, both in the civilian and military sectors. First, it will make existing artificial intelligence more powerful. Quantum computing will allow systems to engage in faster and more accurate attempts at code breaking, which may render many of our existing encryption technologies useless. However, quantum computing can also be used to develop quantum encryption methods. Here, encryption refers to the method by which data is encoded. In sending data and messages in an end-to-end system, encryption can act like an envelope, shielding the message's contents from those who will handle it along the way. The sender encrypts a message and then provides the recipient with a key (a set of instructions), which can then be used to decode the message at the other end.[13] Encryption is commonly used to secure the privacy of our financial data, for example, when we are engaged in online banking transactions.

Quantum computers can also carry out simulations, for example, of possible drug interactions or the interactions of chemicals. Quantum computing could thus lead to advances in medicine, including the development of new drugs and therapies. Quantum computing could also improve weather forecasting and climate change predictions. In addition, it could be used to streamline traffic control and optimize supply chains, leading to faster, more efficient movement of goods around the globe.

Military applications include the ability to spot stealth aircraft, secure battlefield communications, and allow submarines to travel undetected.[14] Quantum technologies could also be used to make existing military navigation technologies more secure. The development of a "quantum compass" could allow US warfighters to move away from current dependence on GPS technology. (In relying on a GPS system, the danger is that someone could intercept communications between soldiers and GPS, inserting false information.)

A US-China Quantum Computing Arms Race?

Although many of these advances exist largely at a hypothetical stage, it is becoming clear that whichever country is first to develop workable quantum computing will have a significant advantage over its peers. Thus, some analysts describe an arms race between China and the United States—with each vying to achieve **quantum superiority.**

China is investing heavily to set up new quantum computing research facilities, in concert with private actors and universities. China is also recruiting computing specialists with interests in this field. China may be concerned with the development of military applications of quantum computing, but it also has the potential to achieve greater economic superiority if it can develop new scientific advances and streamline existing industrial processes.

In the United States, the government is also working with private actors like Google to develop quantum computing. In recent years, US politicians have voiced concerns that China is winning the quantum computing race through putting more resources toward this goal, with the United States falling behind. Indeed, China has reportedly already developed the ability to send quantum-encrypted messages, using a satellite in space.[15]

Sources

Diamandis, P. "Massive Disruption Is Coming with Quantum Computing." Singularity Hub. Last modified October 10, 2016. https://singularityhub.com/2016/10/10/massive-disruption-quantum-computing/.

Giles, M. "The US and China Are in a Quantum Arms Race That Will Transform Warfare." MIT *Technology Review* (January 3, 2019). https://www.technologyreview.com/s/612421/us-china-quantum-arms-race/.

Marr, B. "Six Practical Examples of How Quantum Computing Will Change Our World." *Forbes* (July 10, 2017). https://www.forbes.com/sites/bernardmarr/2017/07/10/6-practical-examples-of-how-quantum-computing-will-change-our-world/#1191e82380c1.

Tardi, C. "Moore's Law." Investopedia. Last modified April 20, 2019. https://www.investopedia.com/terms/m/mooreslaw.asp.

Tech Target. "Encryption." Accessed June 5, 2019. https://searchsecurity.techtarget.com/definition/encryption.

Finally, critics today suggest that big data has an ideology. They argue that it does not serve individual citizen interests but rather serves the interests of major corporations and the national security interests of government. They argue that citizens are often fooled into sharing their data while remaining unaware that this data is being compiled for use by others. For example, many people might enjoy getting a shopper's card at a grocery store that offers a discount on groceries without realizing that in showing a shopper's card, the customer is actually providing the grocery store chain with information about their purchases and purchasing patterns.

SELECTED FUTURE CHALLENGES: ARTIFICIAL INTELLIGENCE

In considering the implications of large-scale dependence in society upon big data, we cannot easily separate it out from a related technology, that of artificial intelligence. **Artificial intelligence** is defined as "the theory and development of computer systems able to perform tasks normally requiring human intelligence, such as visual perception, speech recognition, decision-making, and translation between languages."[16] Artificial intelligence programs are being used to carry out tasks on the internet, including sorting data, making predictions, and carrying out targeted surveillance of internet users.

Artificially intelligent machines and programs, however, differ from those that are merely automated. An automated weapon, or automated machine, is one that once activated by a person, is then capable of carrying out the person's instructions. However, an automated machine is not a robot because that term refers to machines that can sense, think, and also act independently.

An agent—whether it is a machine, a computer program, or a computer itself—that is capable of deciding for itself what actions to take in response to data that it receives about its environment or its goals is said to be autonomous.

An agent that is capable of learning from its environment and as a result accumulating new knowledge, new routines, or changing its goals is said to be artificially intelligent. Artificial intelligence depends on a process known as **machine learning.** Machine learning is defined as "an algorithmic computer approach to making a determination or prediction in which the computer may act without being explicitly programmed, automatically improving itself." That is, machine learning refers to a situation whereby a system can learn and improve its information through the actions of learning algorithms. Like autonomy, machine learning exists along a spectrum—systems can be fully autonomous in their machine learning functions, or they can be semi-supervised in a scenario where they are fed labeled data.[17] **Deep learning** refers to a system whereby artificially intelligent agents utilize multilayer artificial neural networks that mimic human neutral architecture.[18]

THE POLITICS OF NEURAL NETWORKS

Machine learning is a specific branch of artificial intelligence that includes approaches like the use of neural networks and reinforcement learning to train computers to recognize information and carry out specific actions. A **neural network** is a machine learning technique that is modeled after the human brain. The idea of creating a neural network to carry out computing functions is not new. Indeed, the technology first emerged as an abstract idea in 1943, with research by McCullough and Pitts at the University of Chicago. Over the intervening years, computer scientists argued about whether neural networks were actually possible. The first real attempts at creating this technology began in the 1980s, and experiments are beginning to bear fruit in the years since 2010.

What Is Deep Learning?

Neural networks are said to produce deep learning. Deep learning is a subset of machine learning, where machine learning refers to situations in which an algorithm is able to "parse data, learn from that data, and then apply what they've learned to make informed decisions." In traditional machine learning, a machine learns to perform a task and then gets better at it over time as it gathers more information and performs the task more times. (For example, a bot that serves as a customer service agent at a bank might eventually "learn" that when a customer says "theft," he or she should be transferred to the fraud department, even if he or she has not used the word "fraud.") The machine or technology agent does, not, however, substantively modify the nature of the task, nor does it go on to perform new or different tasks.[19]

In deep learning, however, the machine learns information through three modes: supervised learning, in which the computer is fed data sets with correct answers to a problem; **unsupervised learning** and **reinforced learning,** in which the algorithm receives rewards for arriving at correct conclusions and negative reinforcement when it does not. Deep learning is used for detecting frauds and spam, reading handwriting, and recognizing speech and translation.

For example, a computer might learn to recognize handwriting by looking at examples of how a letter is produced in cursive by different people, coming up with rules for determining if a pen mark is indeed a "g." (When you deposit a check in your bank's ATM, it is relying on this technology to determine the amount written on your check and to check that it corresponds with

(Continued)

(Continued)

the amount you have typed in.) The computer is thus said to have "learned" to recognize patterns to read people's handwriting, but it is also engaging in some amount of independent reasoning and decision-making as well.

Neural networks are used today in stock trading and for tasks requiring pattern recognition and prediction. (For example, recognizing and tagging faces on social media relies on this technology.)[20] The technology has identified applications in fields as diverse as government, business, and education.[21]

Google's Deep Mind Project

One of the best examples of a deep learning project is the DeepMind Project. This project began in 2010 and was acquired by Google in 2014 for a cost of £400 million pounds (approximately $800 million).

DeepMind uses deep neural networks to train algorithms on massive data sets aimed at allowing the algorithm to predict outcomes to a variety of problems. DeepMind famously beat Europe's champion at the strategy game Go in a match conducted in 2015. DeepMind's technology has been used to increase the rate at which artificial intelligence can recognize images and has also been used in text-based searches and speech recognition. DeepMind is often used to illustrate the capabilities of advanced artificial intelligence. Much of the code associated with the project is open source so that other programmers can utilize it in their own artificial intelligence work.

Issues with Relying on Neural Networks and Deep Learning

Sceptics point to several problems with deep learning, suggesting that its proponents might wish to temper their enthusiasm and trust in the technology to solve all problems.

First, there are still activities that humans can and always will perform better than neural nets. Chollet believes that a neural net may never be able to generalize at a high level of abstraction, something that humans do often and easily. In addition, a computer would be unable to easily take information about one environment and decide whether it holds in another environment as well. Instead, it would have to relearn the new environment based on new data.

Chollet's critique relies on the fact that computers still do not "understand" what they are doing but merely match things up, finding patterns and like objects. He gives the example of an image of a bell curve that a computer labeled as a panda because the algorithm merely looked for certain shapes rather than "understanding" that one is a photo of a living animal whereas the other is a graph of a mathematical function.[22] Sandberg writes that "[neural networks] inhabit a potentially alien world where their representations could be utterly unrelated to what we humans understand or can express."

The fact that deep learning computers merely carry out programmatic functions without understanding what they are doing or any implications has created problems in the past. In particular, many analysts have described a problem of algorithmic bias. Because the data sets that neural networks train on are representations of the world as it is rather than the world that we might like to see, a deep learning algorithm may therefore reproduce the worst stereotypes and biases of our society as a whole—whereas a human might exercise judgment and question the patterns that he or she was seeing. (For example, a deep learning network might see that most of the pictures labeled as "secretary" in an archive like Google Images are female, whereas most pictures of a "boss" are male, and conclude that men are always bosses and women are always secretaries.)

That is, as Sandberg argues, deep learning computers may "learn wrong." They can also engage in activities that would be ethically problematic if a human engaged in them as they are unaware of the ethical implications of their activities. (For example, an algorithm that selects which content to show to someone browsing on a website would not be aware of or responsive to concerns like whether images were offensive or whether these were election ads that might constitute undue interference in a nation's sovereign elections.)[23]

For this reason, some ethicists and policy makers have suggested that nations may wish to articulate a formalized framework for **AI governance.**

Sources

Chollet, F. "The Limitations of Deep Learning." *The Keras* (blog). Last modified July 17, 2017. https://blog.keras.io/the-limitations-of-deep-learning.html.

DeMuro, J. "What Is a Neural Network?" Tech Radar. Last modified August 11, 2018. https://www.techradar.com/news/what-is-a-neural-network.

Reese, H. "Google DeepMind: A Cheat Sheet." Tech Republic. Last modified August 3, 2016. https://www.techrepublic.com/article/google-deepmind-the-smart-persons-guide/.

Sandberg, A. "Ethics for Neural Networks." Aleph.se. Last modified 2019. http://aleph.se/andart2/ethics/ethics-for-neural-networks/.

Similarly, US Department of Defense Directive Number 3000.09, "Autonomy in Weapons Systems," defines a fully autonomous weapons system as "a weapon system that, once activated, can select and engage targets without further intervention by a human operator."[24] That is, fully autonomous tools do not merely carry out orders set by humans but also have deciding and planning functions that they can carry out. They can also learn from tier environments and thus alter their plans.

In his analysis of the future of US autonomous warfare, Scharre describes autonomy as possessing three dimensions. An entity is said to be behaving autonomously if it can collect information about its world, sense things autonomously, is capable of making autonomous decisions, and is capable of acting autonomously. Today, many individuals are comfortable interacting with machines that can sense autonomously, collecting information (e.g., about the weather) and conveying it back to us.[25]

At least thirty nations currently employ supervised autonomous weapons systems, often in a defensive capacity. And Scharre posits that in the future, states may fight utilizing swarm warfare, in which swarms of tiny machines can act in sequence to deny an enemy access to a resource like an airfield. States might also deploy unmanned autonomous vehicles in a situation like a pandemic or other national emergency, utilizing machines to get help to humans who are in distress without risking additional human lives to do so.

However, many are not yet ready for a world in which machines can make decisions and implement them autonomously.

Levels of Autonomy and the Problem of Responsibility

Indeed, there are legal, political, and ethical issues associated with artificial intelligence and autonomy that have caused planners to move cautiously. The issue of what limits should thus be placed upon the actions of autonomous actors has arisen in recent years, particularly in relation to questions about the use of autonomous soldiers in combat operations.

As a result, engineers have defined levels of autonomy, which range from systems that are fully autonomous (including learning and making planning decisions on their own) to those that still require levels of human input—from limited input, such as turning the machine on and setting it in motion, to a more involved human input, such as having a human sign off on decisions made by the robot or making decisions on the robot's behalf.

This distinction between levels of autonomy is particularly important for military planners as they often must apply preexisting ethical and legal frameworks regarding the laws of war to consider how automatic, autonomous, and semiautonomous weapons may be used in warfare. Currently, many of our weapons are **semiautonomous**; a semiautonomous robot possesses some level of independence but ultimately is not self-directed. That is, such a machine does not possess decision-making capabilities and may require human participation. (The MQ-1 Predator drone is an example of an automated weapons system. It is unmanned in that it does not carry a human operator. Instead, it is remotely controlled by a human pilot on the ground. However, it is not fully autonomous because it still has a human controller.)[26]

That is, they allow for a **human in the loop** or a decision-making sequence. For example, whereas an unmanned autonomous vehicle (UAV, or drone) is capable of firing on a target without seeking human permission to do so, military decision makers have chosen to put a human into the decision-making process so that a human will have both legal and moral responsibility for any mistakes that may occur (such as the death of a civilian). Human Rights Watch distinguishes among three levels of autonomy: Human in the loop weapons are those that are capable of targeting and striking solely as a result of a human directive. Human on the loop weapons are those that are capable of independently targeting and delivering force while under the supervision of a human operator who can override the robot if necessary. Finally, human out of the loop machines can select targets and deliver force without any human input or interaction.

All can have the effect of removing the human from the battlefield and thus have the ability to reduce warfighter casualties. However, not all remove humans from the decision-making process regarding when and under what circumstances these weapons should utilize deadly force.

Legal scholars utilize the term *distributed responsibility* to refer to a system in which human and autonomous agents might share responsibility (ethically, legally, and morally) for outcomes.[27] However, although this idea is attractive in the abstract, it may be difficult to implement in practice. Legal experts still have not worked out how such legal matters might be resolved, as whether an artificial intelligence system might bear responsibility: For example, could an artificial intelligence system that makes medical diagnostic or treatment decisions be sued for malpractice if a problem occurs? Could an artificial intelligence system be held criminally liable for certain actions (like vehicular manslaughter), and could it be held liable for breach of warranty? A related problem occurs when we begin to conceptualize future situations in which an artificial intelligence agent might be said to be legally and ethically responsible for the consequences of a decision that it has made or an action that it has either undertaken or that has been undertaken on its behalf or at its behest. Here, legal experts warn of the emergence of a gray area in which seemingly no one is responsible for a decision that occurs—a human may claim that he or she has outsourced the taking of an action to an intelligent agent, whereas the intelligent agent may not be legally responsible for the outcome of a decision in the real world.[28]

Ethicists, in contrast, often advocate for the creation of a system of what they term *meaningful human control* (MHC). MHC is a more broad-ranging concept than the narrow human in the loop principles advocated by military planners. Ethicists argue that for a human to be meaningfully involved in making decisions about how to deploy a robot, the human must have significant amounts of contextual information about the decision being made and must also be able to decide upon what grounds the decision will be made. They argue that designers of such weapons, thus, need to think about the problem of human control from the earliest stages of conceptualizing and designing these tools rather than merely asking (after a weapon or tool is created), "Now how can we graft on some mechanisms that would allow for humans to be involved in the decision-making process regarding how we deploy this machine?"[29]

Here, some critics of the widespread adoption of artificial intelligence have suggested that our societal reliance on machines allows us to "outsource" some of the ethical and legal responsibility that we might otherwise feel as a

SHOULD THE UNITED NATIONS BAN AUTONOMOUS WEAPONS?

Today, the use of UAVs is commonplace but still controversial. At least eleven countries are using fifty-six different types of UAVs.[30] But despite the widespread use of drones worldwide, opposition to their acquisition and deployment is widespread. Arguments have been made at the national and international levels, and anti-drone initiatives have been presented to the European Commission and the United Nations.

Weapons and Bans: A Short History

Presently, there is no specific legal treaty among nations governing the use or nonuse of autonomous weapons. However, the notion that certain types of weapons are simply too terrible to be used is not new. Indeed, within international law, there is a strong precedent for declaring an international ban on research, development, and deployment of certain classes of weapons.

In the 20h century, nations implemented international weapons bans, including the 1977 Additional Protocol to the Geneva Convention of August 1949.[31] The Protocol also led eventually to the adoption of two international treaties banning the development, production, stockpiling, transfer, or use of chemical and biological weapons.

The ethical justification for banning both biological and chemical weapons is that their use constitutes deliberate cruelty. In addition, both types of weapons are said to violate the principle of proportionality (codified in the LOAC), which says that states should use only enough force to conclude hostilities so that peace can then be restored. In contrast, a weapon that seeks deliberately to maim or blind an individual thus seeks to prolong the suffering of one's opponents beyond the battlefield, an effect that constitutes a disproportionate response. In addition, chemical and biological weapons have been banned due to the inability of those who deploy them to ensure that only combatants would be harmed by these weapons. They are not clearly steerable and can easily drift into civilian areas, harming noncombatants.

Should We Ban Autonomous Weapons?

Recently, activists have begun to call for a ban on autonomous weapons. These efforts have been led by Human Rights Watch and Harvard Law School's

International Human Rights Clinic.[32] Although the arguments for banning autonomous weapons share some common ground with the earlier bans on chemical and biological weapons, there are also differences.[33]

Proponents of a ban are concerned with ethical issues resulting from a scenario in which individuals could be "exterminated by a machine" (or fully autonomous drone) with no human either aware of their deaths or responsible for the decision.[34] Such a scenario is seen to violate the principles of chivalry, which have existed since the Middle Ages. Ethicists claim that the honor associated with warfare derives from the notion that it is a "principle of reciprocal injury" in which both sides put their lives on the line. In contrast, some have described a scenario in which some individuals are on a battlefield, whereas others fight from the safety of a computer, behind their own lines, as cowardly.[35]

Other analysts suggest that drone warfare represents a type of covert activity in which a leader could undertake unpopular strikes against enemy regimes without notifying or involving his or her constituents about this decision. They worry that in the future, a president might decide to fight wars secretly, rather than openly, and to do so unilaterally, rather than engaging in public debate with Congress first.[36]

Reasons against a Ban

In contrast to those who would seek to ban autonomous weapons, those who support their use and deployment often have a military background. These individuals argue that these weapons can be deployed in a variety of settings, including humanitarian settings, as well as in emergency management settings.

Drone proponents also argue that it is too soon to ban these weapons as we are not yet fully aware of all of their potential uses. They also regard it as premature to say at this stage that they cannot be regulated or that legal regulations cannot be created.

Indeed, some proponents of drone use argue that because these weapons can be targeted more precisely, they are actually likely to cause less unnecessary suffering and are less likely to injure civilians. Ideally, then, combat could be more efficient and thus shorter.

In his work, Carafano suggests that what look like ethical discussions are actually military-strategical technical discussions about the capabilities of weapons. Thus, based on his arguments, military decision makers could and should challenge the assumption that technology makes people do things or choose things—such as compelling decision makers to reach a certain conclusion about

(Continued)

(Continued)

how to deploy these weapons. Instead, decision makers need to point out that individuals and states have the ability to choose how to use technologies.[37]

Similarly, David Fischler wrote the following about nuclear weapons: "Possession of nuclear weapons, then, is not inherently immoral. Possession may facilitate the demonstration of the user's immorality, but in and of themselves nuclear weapons are nothing more than mechanisms for the expression of human ideas and emotions."[38]

Thus, those who oppose a ban may believe that the ethical decisions regarding drone use rest not on the ethics of the weapons themselves but on the ethics of those who wield them.

Sources

Bartels, H. "Drones Simply Aren't the Height of Technology." *IP Journal* (August 1, 2014). http://www.hans-peter-bartels.de/drones-simply-aren't-the-height-of-technology.

Carafano, J. "Future Technology and Ethics in War." *Utah Law Review* 5 (2013): 1263–1269.

Fischler, D. "Nuclear Weapons in the Ethics of Reinhold Niebuhr." *Perspectives in Religious Studies* 12, no. 2 (1985): 72.

Human Rights Watch. "Q and A on Fully Autonomous Weapons." Last modified October 21, 2012. https://www.hrw.org/news/2013/10/21/qa-fully-autonomous-weapons.

Manjikian, M. *A Typology of Arguments about Drone Ethics* (Carlisle, PA: Strategic Studies Institute, US Army War College, 2017). https://ssi.armywarcollege.edu/pubs/display.cfm?pubID=1367ary.

Manjikian, M. "Becoming Unmanned: The Gendering of Lethal Autonomous Warfare Technology." *International Feminist Journal of Politics* 16, no. 1 (2014). https://www.tandfonline.com/doi/abs/10.1080/14616742.2012.746429?scroll=top&needAccess=true&journalCode=rfjp20

Rogers, S. "Drones by Country: Who Has all the UAVs?" *The Guardian* (August 3, 2012).

Sandoz, Y. "Turning Principles into Practice: The Challenge for International Conventions and Institutions." In Maresca, L. and Masen, S., eds. *The Banning of Anti-Personnel Landmines: The Legal Contribution of the International Committee of the Red Cross* (Cambridge, UK: Cambridge University Press, 2008).

Sparrow, R. "Killer Robots." *Journal of Applied Philosophy* 24, no. 1 (2007): 62–77.

result of our actions. The idea that complicated legal and ethical decisions that were previously taken by thoughtful humans might today be taken by machines running algorithms again raises this question of uniqueness. In Chapter 7, on crime, we asked if criminal activities undertaken in cyberspace were the same as or different from the types of crimes that might take place in real space. In the same way, ethicists, and lawyers, today struggle to understand what rules and regulations might be applied to analyzing and evaluating the effects of activities like the carrying out of air strikes against terrorists by fully autonomous weapons systems or the carrying out of censorship activities on Facebook by fully autonomous content management systems.

Currently, policy makers struggle with whether the existing LOAC and International Humanitarian Law (IHL) can be applied to regulating wartime activities carried out by autonomous warfighting weapons and perhaps someday autonomous warfighting soldiers. Here, analysts are particularly concerned about the fact that it appears that there is no one—or no human—who can be said to be ethically, legally, and morally responsible for the decision to kill another human being. In situations where mistakes are made, such as the killing of civilians due to improper information or improper targeting, it is difficult for investigators to decide who is legally responsible and who must bear the costs of this wrongdoing.

Limitations of Artificial Intelligence

In thinking about how computers learn more new knowledge, however, analysts are concerned about the fact that these programs may unconsciously "learn" things about the world that we would rather that they not learn. Here, computer scientists sometimes use the phrase "garbage in, garbage out" to describe the ways in which computations are only as good as the inputs provided. In the case of social learning, the bots may end up mimicking the same biases that exist in larger society.

In particular, analysts worry about the ways in which artificially intelligent agents are "learning" stereotypes and biases about human behavior based on the sources that they are accessing. For example, if you look at a source like Google Images and type in a term like *nurse*, you will see that most of the images are female, whereas Googling a term like *doctor* brings up mostly male images. As a result, artificially intelligent bots have "learned" social "facts" about the world such as that men are doctors, whereas women are nurses.[39] And in 2016, Microsoft was forced to shut down an artificially intelligent chatbot known as Tay, which had been granted its own Twitter account. Tay "learned" from other Twitter users, and as a result, it began tweeting a series of offensive messages. Among other things, Tay suggested that feminism was a cancer upon society and that the Holocaust did not happen.[40] The chatbot was only online for sixteen hours before Microsoft revoked its privileges.

In addition, ethicists have raised issues associated with a move toward complete autonomy for these machines. They ask what it means to say that a computer "knows" things. In response to this question, philosopher John Searle famously proposed the "Chinese box" thought experiment. In his thought experiment, he asks us to suppose that an individual is taught to recognize certain Chinese letter symbols and to make connections among them. When one card containing a symbol is presented to you, then you would know through practice and observation which card to hand to your partner so that the cards match. However, you would not know what actual words the cards corresponded to. In this way, you would appear to be engaging in conversation in the same way that other humans do. However, you could not actually be said to "speak Chinese." In the same way, then, a computer might be taught to respond, "I am so sorry for your loss," when informed that a relative of yours has died. However, the computer would not genuinely feel sorry, nor could it comprehend the fact that you were sad because you had lost a fellow human being with whom you had a relationship. It would merely be mimicking what humans do in these interactions but would not be engaged in a meaningful interaction as one might have with a human.[41]

Other researchers worry today about situations in which autonomous agents—or those that operate without human oversight or control—would have to react in a new and novel or complex situation that they had not encountered before. Here, ethicists consider, for example, the possibility that a self-driving car might need to independently make a planning decision, such as deciding how best to avoid harming people if it knows that it is about to have an accident. Some analysts, like Arkin, suggest that a computer can be taught to calculate the probabilities of outcomes related to actions it might take, and that in this way a computer could be taught to implement the solution that would generate the least harm. Such a computer would thus be said to be applying utilitarian ethics in searching for the best outcome in the situation. Other analysts, however, counter Arkin's assertions, suggesting that it is meaningless to talk about artificially intelligent agents as actual moral actors largely because a robot would never be fully capable of comprehending the emotional and moral import of its actions due to its limited abilities to perceive and experience the real world.

Despite these limitations, however, in recent years, computer scientists have created artificially intelligent agents that are able to perform tasks such as writing poetry, writing academic reports, and generating legal contracts. This raises the question as to whether at some point in the future, humans might become dependent upon the actions of artificially intelligent agents to carry out many of the tasks that humans carry out today. In the future, an artificially intelligent agent might review a medical scan, analyze lab results, and ultimately make recommendations to humans about their medical care. The fear that we may become too dependent upon the machines that carry out so many of our tasks today is magnified by the fact that as these machines become faster and more complex, humans risk finding themselves in a situation where they truly do not understand how these machines "think" or reason because the processes themselves are opaque rather than transparent.

In his work, Matsuzaki refers to the **hidden layer**. This phrase refers to the middle layer of the neural networks in the deep learning algorithm. He notes that this layer includes millions of parameters that are optimized by automatic calculation. However, he warns that it is difficult to know exactly how all of the calculations work and how they might interact with each other. (Here, a complex system refers to one in which multiple systems interact with each other. In this scenario, it is not always possible to predict all of the ways in which one system may affect another, particularly if something malfunctions or fails to perform as expected.)

Technology specialists refer to a problem known as "the black box" to describe situations in which a computer appears to arrive at the right answer, but we are not sure how it got there.[42] Wissner-Gross, a "Wall street whiz" financial analyst, has identified behaviors that appear when highly complex financial algorithms are used to carry out stock trades on Wall Street. He argues that in some extremely high-speed trading environments, the algorithms appear to be signaling each other, interacting in ways we don't understand.[43] Barrett, an artificial intelligence pessimist, points out that we don't actually know what they're doing—and yet our financial system depends on these algorithms.

Collins, an engineer, notes that the advent of artificial intelligence raises fundamental existential questions for those who create artificial agents as well as for those who interact with them. Here the most crucial question is simply this: What does it mean to know something? Can a machine be said to "know" about the world around it, and what is the quality of that knowledge? Is a machine's knowledge more accurate than the knowledge that we possess as humans? As Collins notes, a machine's calculations may be more accurate and more precise. For example, we might describe a neighbor as being about 6 feet tall, whereas a robot might use a highly precise laser measurement tool to measure the neighbor as 6.0012 feet tall. But machines are not infallible. Just as humans might misinterpret data, a machine is sometimes unable to understand a new situation, a new phrase, or the inputs of a user. (Think of an artificial agent whom you might encounter when you phone the bank. When it asks about the nature of your problem, it expects answers like "fraud" or "lost bank card" and not an anecdote about how your nephew threw your wallet overboard when you went out on the fishing boat last week.)[44]

In addition, knowledge is socially bounded, created, and existing within a community. Thus, a computer might not be conversant with the latest slang, is notoriously bad at recognizing sarcasm, and will likely require updates to its knowledge programs and system or new inputs as society changes and the computer's knowledge of that society thus becomes stale and outdated. That is, computers are not social isolates but rather something that exists within society. Thus, communities develop relationships with these thinking or knowing machines, and these relationships change over time.

In addition, the artificially intelligent agents we are using today and will continue to use in the future are highly complex systems. Here, Collins notes that many complex systems are prone to accidents because of a cascade of effects. When multiple systems are combined, we may not know how a failure of one subsystem will affect other subsystems. He writes that "we have produced designs so complicated that we cannot possibly anticipate all the possible interactions of the inevitable failures."[45] Here again, technological developments seem to be outpacing the ability of states and international organizations to predict what policy issues will arise or to create new structures to govern these events when they do occur. Some states have begun to adopt specific legislation and national strategies that respond to questions like "Should an artificially intelligent bot be treated as having similar rights and responsibilities as a human?"[46] and "How should a state best prepare to prevent and respond to threats posed by the increased reliance on artificial intelligence in all aspects of social, political, and economic life?" That is, states are struggling to define regulatory regimes for the use of artificial intelligence as well as deciding whether rules and regulations related to the use of artificial intelligence in cyberspace should be decided on at the state, regional, or international level.

The Danger of Rule by Algorithm

Given the flaws we have thus identified in artificial intelligence in its current incarnations, policy makers have begun voicing concerns about the ways in which societies may be becoming too dependent upon what they term *rule by algorithm*.[47]

These analysts worry that users may be initially wooed by the short-term benefits that artificial intelligence offers, such as the ability to carry out tasks more cheaply and to identify efficiencies in our existing processes and institutions. However, they worry that citizens will cede too much personal control to inanimate entities without understanding the long-run implications of this decision. By the time users realize what they have done, they argue, it may be too late for humans to wrest back this control from the machines. Here, they point to the ways in which artificial intelligence might generate predictive analytics that could be used by governments to act proactively to prevent certain outcomes. The authors ask if children could be taken from their parents by a social service agency in the future because the data suggests that they are likely to abuse their children, even if in point of fact they have not yet done so.

We may not always completely understand how artificial intelligence works, and it is likely that this problem may become worse in the future. Traditionally, in a democracy, citizens have expected and even demanded that their governments be both accountable to the citizens and transparent in their decision-making. That is, policy makers are expected to provide citizens with complete information regarding how decisions that affect their lives have been made. Indeed, the European Union's General Data Protection Requirement (GDPR) laws state that citizens have the right to obtain "meaningful information about the logic involved" even in automated decisions.[48] However, because of the opaqueness of the decision-making mechanisms utilized by artificially intelligent agents in some situations, it is difficult to see how these criteria of accountability and transparency will be met.

One example of an automated decision-making process that has recently been the subject of controversy is the use of sentencing software by judges. Currently, even without artificial intelligence, a judge might use an algorithm to decide how long to sentence an individual as punishment for a crime he or she has committed. Many judges utilize the Correctional Offender Management Profiling for Alternative Sanctions system (COMPAS), which provides a risk score that gives the likelihood that an offender will re-offend based on the person's characteristics (such as age, gender, and race). COMPAS has been criticized for being opaque, and indeed, its creators argue that it should be used merely as guidance for a judge, not as a device that makes decisions on their behalf. (That is, judges should not trust the software but instead should consult MHC in enacting its directives.) COMPAS has also been accused of being biased against black defendants, thereby depriving citizens of their due process rights to be sentenced individually, without bias.[49]

In France, Parliament recently acted to remove data analytics and algorithms from criminal sentencing, enacting laws that forbid France's citizens from creating databases that include the calculation of sentencing rates for judges within France's system. The fear was that lawyers could "game the system" through figuring out in advance which judges were likely to be lenient in which cases and then requesting these judges.[50] However, there currently exist multiple companies whose sole mission is to calculate "litigation analytics," and it is likely that as technology gets better at predicting and aggregating multiple data sources, this industry will likely grow and not shrink.

SMART CITIES

What is a smart city? A smart city is defined as "a new concept and a new model, which applies the new generation of ICT to facilitate the planning, construction, management and smart services of cities."[51]

The adjective "smart" describes the fact that many different infrastructure attributes can be brought into communication with one another, including transportation, public utilities, security and policing, communications and wireless technology, electronics, and software. In a smart city, parts of the city "talk" to one another, either through the facilitation of a computer programmer or city planner or, in some instances, independently or autonomously, with programs sharing data with one another. For example, a traffic algorithm might alter traffic patterns in the smart city in response to data it receives about a weather event causing flooding in certain areas of the city or a sports event causing increased traffic.

Data about citizen activities can be aggregated and shared across platforms (as well as stored), allowing sectors to cooperate to plan activities more efficiently, share resources with less waste, and also plan for future activities and preempt harmful consequences of some citizen activities.[52]

A smart city is envisioned as one in which all parts of the city are enabled with internet connectivity or Wi-Fi, which is often provided for free, as a public utility by the city. In addition, cities are smart in that citizens can carry out many of the functions of interfacing with their city through utilizing e-governance services. Smart cities also feature open spaces and sustainable transportation. Smart cities often also rely on a smart power grid, which tracks where power is being used and enables one household's unused power to be used by someone else within the network, thus saving resources and lowering costs. Smart cities also contain smart devices that allow users to program services like computer updates to be carried out at times when the electrical load is low and costs are cheaper.

A smart city thus relies on the internet of things, defined as "a technical concept and a paradigm that provides Internet connective between diverse things (devices) utilizing network technology, so that intelligence services can be created utilizing those things."[53]

Building Smart Cities

Smart cities use best practices to improve environmental sustainability and economic efficiency. Although planners have been talking about smart cities

(Continued)

CRITICAL ISSUES

(Continued)

since the 1990s, only recently have technological advances proceeded far enough to make a smart city a reality.

Some analysts describe smart cities as naturally evolving as more and more devices go online, and the devices are linked up so that data can be shared. However, more often, smart cities are built and managed by existing governments. Smart city plans also depend on PPPs among construction companies, the federal government, and ISPs and other technology actors to create a "fully integrated cyber environment."[54] Currently, planners have more than $3 trillion invested in the concept of a smart city,[55] and a variety of players, including Google, are involved in creating smart cities.

Smart city projects are ongoing in many places, including Tampere, Finland; Geneva, Switzerland; Bandong, South Korea; Vienna, Austria; Washington, DC, and New York City in the United States; and in Melbourne, Australia.

Are Smart Cities a Utopian Fantasy?

Although smart cities present clear advantages over existing cities in theory, in practice, there are many critics of the smart city. Some critics question whether environmental sustainability can be achieved. Others worry about the growth of a surveillance state, suggesting that the state's major objectives are to deploy watchers to reduce crime and to preempt social disruption and crime through deploying resources preemptively.

Others believe that the goals of smart cities are simply unachievable. Here, analysts suggest that thus far the internet of things has resulted in "silos" of information, applications, and services but that these services are far from fully integrated.[56]

Finally, critics are concerned about the lack of a clear regulatory structure and set of standards for governing smart cities. Questions raised by their advent include: Who would own data generated by citizens operating in a smart environment? To whom would that data be available and for what purposes? And are citizens endangering themselves by allowing this sort of data to be created about each of them? Could citizens opt out of participating in these governance regimes in their smart city if they were concerned about the consequences of these procedures?

Regulating the Smart City

At present, several US national and international bodies have been involved in drafting regulations and standards pursuant to smart cities. These bodies include the International Standards Organization (ISO), the International

Telecommunications Union (ITU), the International Electrotechnical Commission (IEC), the American National Standards Institute (ANSI), the European Standards Organization (CEN), and the British Standards Institute (BSI). However, these organizations have been predominantly concerned with addressing the technical specifications problems presented by the rise of smart cities rather than the underlying legal and ethical questions that the growth of these cities presents.[57]

Smart Cities and Surveillance

A particular concern with the development of smart cities concerns their reliance on ambient intelligence. **Ambient intelligence** is defined as

> a new world where computing devices are spread everywhere, allowing the human being to interact in physical world environments in an intelligent and unobtrusive way. These environments should be aware of the needs of people, customizing requirements and forecasting behaviors.[58]

Citizens and users do not always realize when they are in an ambient intelligence environment because such processes run in the background on many programs. An example of ambient intelligence might be a situation where you go to a nearby grocery store and your smartphone, which has a GPS tracking device, is aware that you are in a grocery store. This information is relayed to the site for the grocery store, which then texts you to remind you of a store special on some of your favorite products, which the site knows from your previous purchasing history that it has stored. Although some individuals appreciate the guidance as they carry out their weekly shopping, others worry about the fact that they are being watched or being surveilled, often without their knowledge, as they go about their daily activities.

In 2018, such questions were raised publicly after several individuals contracted to work on a Canadian smart city project organized by a Google subsidiary, Sidewalk Labs, resigned due to surveillance concerns. Former Ontario Privacy Commissioner Ana Cavoukian stated that "I imagined us creating a Smart City of Privacy, as opposed to a Smart City of Surveillance." And Blackberry's former chief executive officer referred to it as "a colonizing experiment in surveillance capitalism."[59]

Going forward, some nations may struggle to reconcile their desire to deploy resources efficiently with their existing legislation regarding citizen privacy. Currently, the European Union has a strict set of privacy guidelines, codified in the GDPR of 2016. These guidelines allow Europe's citizens to be made aware of when

(Continued)

(Continued)

their data is being collected and to have the option of opting out of data collection practices. In Great Britain, regulations require that citizens be informed when they are in neighborhoods or areas where their activities are being tracked via CCTV. Many of the seamless functions of data collection using ambient intelligence may be in conflict with such practices.

Why Do Authoritarian Regimes Like Smart Cities?

However, other nations do not have the same strict data protection guidelines as Europe does. And ambient intelligence within the smart city may be of particular utility to authoritarian nations that wish to preempt political organizing by opposition forces within, for example, a one-party state.

China has taken a leading role in funding and encouraging the growth of technologies associated with smart cities. Indeed, China is pioneering the use of facial recognition technologies and biometric identification to track the activities of citizens in smart cities. For example, Chinese cities may include technology that can identify those who are on police watch lists to provide increased surveillance of these individuals.[60]

Human rights activists, however, have criticized China's use of these surveillance technologies, even though they are ostensibly being utilized to confront and preempt serious security threats to the city, such as terrorism. They have accused China of engaging in differential surveillance, whereby certain types of individuals are more likely to be the subject of monitoring than others. (In the United States, differential surveillance might mean that citizens who are African American or Hispanic are followed more closely by law enforcement agencies in public settings or that they are stopped more often while driving.) In China, those who are members of China's ethnic minorities are likely to be the subject of increased surveillance. To these critics, ambient intelligence practices do not represent the way forward toward creating a more responsive, efficient city. Instead, they point out, China may be weaponizing artificial intelligence through utilizing the internet of things for purposes of social management.[61]

In response, China's leaders have pointed out that the increased number of rural migrants coming to China's urban areas has placed a strain on many urban resources. Planners in China's major cities struggle to provide enough affordable housing or an efficient transportation infrastructure, and they also struggle with the environmental challenges produced by a rapid increase in urban populations. For this reason, China's Ministry of Housing and Urban and Rural Development (MOHURD) has worked with the China Development Bank to create a $16 billion investment in the development of 193 smart cities across China. They hope that having better data collection and more responsive social and infrastructure services will lead to increased foreign investment in these regions.[62]

In international relations, smart city technologies could provide a solution to the growing security problems associated with the growth of so-called megacities. Megacities are defined as urban population centers with more than 10 million inhabitants, which are characterized by extremely dense population patterns.[63] The world's megacities pose new types of human security problems as they are often associated with high levels of pollution and disease as well as containing large numbers of displaced persons including refugees, homeless individuals, and undocumented workers. In some parts of the developing world, these cities can spread out and join together, creating an urban corridor.

Such spaces can be difficult to govern using conventional means. Smart cities may be useful in allowing planners to track activities like health information and migration flows. Planners will also be able to reduce pollution and facilitate better uses of resources like water. In addition, planners can carry out traffic management activities, including reducing bottlenecks and traffic jams, which can be severe in the developing world.

Security Concerns with Smart Cities

Other critics of the smart city approach are concerned not with surveillance issues but rather with issues of security. Some are concerned that it may be difficult to protect all of the critical infrastructure in the smart city, particularly given the interconnections among utilities. They note that it is possible that a well-timed and targeted attack by a state or nonstate adversary could shut down the smart city, causing social chaos. Others are concerned that citizen data could be stolen by hackers, if a city is aggregating and storing that data.

Some critics believe that national-level plans for securing the cybersecurity of internet of things networks need to be implemented, with internet of things networks designed as critical infrastructure. Others argue that smart cities are safer than their traditional urban counterparts. They argue that a smart city is too complex for a run-of-the-mill hacker to target. Therefore, if smart cities are targeted at all, they are likely to be targeted by other states. Kim et al. thus argue that creating a highly complex system thus advantages a state but also creates a new and unique source of threat.[64]

(Continued)

(Continued)

Sources

Anthopoulos, L. "Smart Utopia vs. Smart Reality: Learning by Experience from 10 Smart City Cases." *Cities* 63 (2017): 128–148.

IGI Global. "Ambient Intelligence Environments." https://www.igi-global.com/dictionary/ambient-intelligence-environments/1062.

Johnson, D. "Smart City Development in China." *China Business Review* (June 17, 2014). https://www.chinabusinessreview.com/smart-city-development-in-china/.

Kim, K., I. Kim, and J. Lim. "National Cyber Security Enhancement Scheme for Intelligence Surveillance Capacity with Public IoT Environment." *Journal of Supercomputing* 73 (2016): 1140–1151.

Robert, J., S. Kubler, N. Kolbe, A. Cerioni, E. Gastaud, and K. Framling. "Open IoT Ecosystem for Enhanced Interoperability in Smart Cities—Example of Metropole De Lyon." *Sensors* 17 (2017): 2838–2850. http://sylvainkubler.fr/wp-content/themes/biopic/images/publications/documents/Sensors_2017.pdf.

Telegraph. "Privacy Expert Resigns from Google—Backed Smart City over Surveillance Concerns." Last modified October 24, 2018. https://www.telegraph.co.uk/technology/2018/10/24/privacy-expert-resigns-google-backed-smart-city-surveillance/.

Velghe, P. "Reading China." *China Perspectives* 1 (2019): 85–89. https://journals.openedition.org/chinaperspectives/8874.

Whittaker, Z. "Security Lapse Exposed a Chinese Smart System." Tech Crunch. Last modified May 3, 2019. https://techcrunch.com/2019/05/03/china-smart-city-exposed/.

World Atlas. "What Is a Megacity?" https://www.worldatlas.com/articles/what-is-a-megacity.html.

The Issue of Trust

Today, as society becomes more dependent upon artificial intelligence programs and agents in a number of spheres, policy makers are asking questions about whether humans should trust artificial intelligence and if there are instances in which doing so might be a mistake. But what does it mean to trust someone or something? Taddeo offers an operational definition, stating that trust means being able to delegate a task to another without feeling compelled to supervise that activity based on a certain level of assurance that it will be understood and performed properly.[65]

Today, we can identify more and more situations in which humans are asked to trust autonomous agents. We are asked to trust that they will do their jobs—carrying out active cyberdefense, monitoring credit, and shutting down credit and banking systems if a problem occurs or even in the future perhaps carrying out autonomous drone strikes independent of human monitoring.

Today, individual users frequently must decide if they trust artificial intelligence. We make decisions about whether to use online banking, whether to order products online, and whether to follow the instructions of a national emergency management app that is telling our families to evacuate due to an incoming hurricane. In deciding to evacuate, we would need to believe that the information the app had compiled was somehow more accurate and trustworthy than any sort of local knowledge that our neighbors might be able to provide, even if they had lived in the area for many years and been through similar hurricanes. We would also need to believe that the app had not been hacked by an outside user who had reason to harm us by providing us with false information.

Policy makers worry about two scenarios: one in which users "undertrust" (i.e., they don't trust any information provided by artificial intelligence, leading them to disregard information like vital safety warnings) and one in which users "overtrust," even accepting false information if they believe that the artificial intelligence is competent and that the information is true. (For example, during a hurricane, users might drive into a flooded area, believing that it is safe due to information provided by an app.)

As noted earlier in Chapter 9, the information that users procure—even in a disaster—is increasingly likely to be provided by a third-party source, including private actors, such as the designers and owners of an app, rather than directly from the government itself. Thus, it has been difficult for the government to steer or control the ways in which private actors practice quality control in checking and verifying the trustworthiness of the information that their artificial intelligence and their apps provide.

Governments Respond to the Problem of Artificial Intelligence

In Chapter 2 of this textbook, we learned about technological determinism and the ways in which a new technology may appear to be leading humans inexorably to behave in certain ways. The agency, it may seem, belongs to the technology.

However, in recent years, governments have been considering how planners can speak back to this technology. In addressing the issues raised here—overtrust and undertrust, the problem of algorithmic bias, and the legal and ethical issues associated with responsibility—planners have suggested three ways states might respond to the rapid growth of artificial intelligence.

Relinquishment

The most extreme strategy would be for states to decide to ban further research into the technologies of artificial intelligence. Pessimists suggest that perhaps citizens and policy makers should simply give up on utilizing artificial intelligence because the risks it poses are simply too great. Indeed, some writers advocate a strategy of relinquishment. They point out that there have previously been technological developments (such as the discovery of forms of biological and chemical warfare) where states have decided not to invest further resources into research and development and where states have implemented strict regulations, placing limits on further development of these technologies. We can tie this strategy into the precautionary principle, which states that "if the consequences of an action are unknown but judged by some scientists to have even a small risk of being profoundly negative, it's better to not carry out the action than risk negative consequences."[66]

However, critics of the relinquishment approach argue that relinquishment is immoral because it would deprive us of profound benefits. Furthermore, they believe that it would be impossible to enforce the precautionary principle in the field of artificial intelligence.[67] Furthermore, as Goertzel has argued, we're only going to find out how to make ethical artificial intelligence systems by building them, not concluding from afar that they're bound to be dangerous.

Limitation and Regulation

A second approach to regulating artificial intelligence would be to place clear limits on the ways in which humans (and states) should and should not use it. Kaplan, for example, suggests that artificial intelligence can help answer empirical queries but not those that have a normative component. A tool like Amazon's Alexa, thus, could be used by a person to find out information like the weather report for tomorrow but probably should not be asked to make decisions regarding who you should marry. Thus, some policy makers have proposed limiting the use of artificial intelligence—focusing predominantly on the development of so-called **weak AI** or **narrow AI**, in which artificial intelligence is used for performing basic tasks (like carrying out a Google search).[68] And the ethical limitations described here—the possibility that artificial intelligence will learn offensive stereotypes and encapsulate the worst forms of human bias as well as philosophical doubts about the nature of artificial intelligence's own consciousness—have led many policy makers today to advocate for the implementation of only limited forms of autonomous agents rather than allowing agents to become fully autonomous.

In a widely discussed article published in 2019, Paul Nimitz, an employee of the European Commission, described the danger he feels artificial intelligence poses to the "trinity" of human rights, democracy, and rule of law, qualities that he considers to be the hallmarks of constitutional democracy.[69] Thus, he proposes drafting rules that would require designers to bear all three of these values in mind as they create new types of artificial intelligence and new ways of deploying it. Here, he echoes the design view, suggesting that those who create new tools will have a significant role in shaping what the tools become and, further, what society will become as a result. He also calls for the use of impact assessments to attempt to predict what effects a new technology might have. (Such procedures would be similar to an environmental impact assessment being carried out before a new residential development is approved.)

Nimitz argues that artificial intelligence policy in particular needs to be developed consciously by states within an international community rather than piecemeal as a reaction to individual business decisions made by corporations. He argues that "there is a long history of technology regulation by law." For example, architects are routinely regulated and automobiles are regulated. He concludes that "over and over society has confirmed the experience that law, and not the absence of law, related to critical technology serves the interests of the general public."

Augmentation

A final, somewhat controversial stance in regard to technology regulation has been proposed by technology designer Ray Kurzweil. He argues on behalf of what he terms *intelligence augmentation*. He argues that the greatest risks from artificial intelligence may come in situations where an artificially intelligent agent perceives humans as the enemy. Thus, he argues, ideally artificial intelligence would be "married with" humans through implanting technology within the human body. He states that through embedding this technology within our bodies and brains, it will reflect our values and drives because it will be us.[70]

CONCLUSION

As we conclude this textbook and perhaps this course, it is useful to form some general conclusions. As this text has shown, technologies' impacts are often unpredictable, difficult to regulate, and initially misunderstood by policy makers and users alike. Nations with different cultures may understand technologies differently and may seek to use them in different ways.

In addition, we have seen how regulatory procedures and the development of law and ethics often lag behind the speed at which technologies themselves develop. Nowhere is this truer than in the field of artificial intelligence.

Yet as we have shown throughout this text, many of the issues policy makers face today are not unique. Inventors have in the past created technologies and tools that have had military implications. Governments have sought to marshal technologies toward certain ends, and activists have spoken out against new and rapidly evolving technologies. Societies have adjusted to new ways of thinking about ownership, privacy, and user agency in the past, and our societies will adjust in the future. Today's students have a role to play in this process—as legislators, lawyers, engineers, and as consumers. Hopefully this course has prepared you to better understand and advocate for your positions on these issues.

QUESTIONS FOR DISCUSSION

1. In *Artificial Intelligence: What Everyone Needs to Know*, Jerry Kaplan proposes a number of possible future ethical scenarios involving artificial intelligence.[71] What is your response to the following scenarios that he proposes?
   a. Should robots be treated as independent agents or "citizens" with the right to own property? To testify (perhaps against you) in court? To vote in national elections?
   b. Should robots be treated as wholly responsible for their actions in, for example, being tried for manslaughter if they cause an auto accident or the death of a pedestrian, or does there need to be an individual who exerts MHC over the robot?

2. Some experts suggest that artificially intelligent agents should never be allowed to become fully autonomous. They suggest that there are degrees of autonomous behavior, and that artificially intelligent bots and agents should never be allowed to escape from MHC in which some of the decisions, including planning, still have a human in the loop. This is the best way, they argue, to reduce the legal and safety risks that might result from fully autonomous artificial intelligence.

   However, in writing about the utopian possibilities of artificial intelligence, many journalists suggested that driverless cars could provide independence to elderly people who could no longer drive. Such vehicles might also reduce drunk driving incidents if people who were inebriated could opt to ride in a self-driving vehicle. The disabled might also have more independence if they could ride in self-driving vehicles.

   These two views are at odds: People who suffer from cognitive or physical impairments are not actually able to provide MHC over the robots who would drive the cars. Placing such restrictions on the use of autonomous vehicles thus threatens to exclude these users from the goods produced by technological progress.

   a. In your opinion, whose interests should prevail—the interests of individuals who might have cognitive and physical deficits whose lives would be improved by having access to autonomous vehicles or the needs of society to have a risk-free and safe driving experience, even if it means excluding some users from accessing this technology?

3. Watch the following short talk: Sam Harris: 15-minute YouTube TED Talk—*Can We Build AI without Losing Control over It* (https://www.youtube.com/watch?v=8nt3edWLgIg).

   a. After watching the video, describe whether you are optimistic or pessimistic about the promise of artificial intelligence. Do you advocate governments setting limits on the use of artificial intelligence or even banning it altogether?

KEY TERMS

FOR FURTHER READING

Bakhai, A., I. Parsa, and N. Peters. *AI in Healthcare: The Great Debate*. Digital Health. https://digitalhealth.london/ai-healthcare-great-debate/. (This link is to a thirty-minute video discussion about the use of artificial intelligence in health care, including issues of public policy like patients' rights.)

Barrat, J. *Our Final Invention: Artificial Intelligence and the End of the Human Era* (New York, NY: St. Martin's Books, 2013).

Dutton, T. "An Overview of National AI Strategies." Medium. Last modified June 28, 2018. https://medium.com/politics-ai/an-overview-of-national-ai-strategies-2a70ec6edfd.

Kaplan, J. *Artificial Intelligence: What Everyone Needs to Know*? (New York, NY: Oxford University Press, 2016).

Nemitz, Paul. "Constitutional Democracy and Technology in the Age of Artificial Intelligence." In *Philosophical Transactions of the Royal Society A: Mathematical, Physical and Engineering Sciences*, 376. http://doi.org/10.1098/rsta.2018.0089.

GLOSSARY

Active cyber defense: Strategic and tactical measures used in cybersecurity that integrate cyber intelligence, cyber protection, and cyber analytics technologies to predict and respond proactively to cyberattacks and to protect data.

Active measures: Actions taken by Soviet and later Russian intelligence organizations aimed at both influencing world events and influencing how these events were perceived. Includes the deployment of propaganda, disinformation, and the establishment of front organizations that may appear to be independent but are actually state backed.

Advanced persistent threat (APT): Designation for classes of high targeted cyber-weapons that are perceived to be too complex technologically for most actors to create. Generally, refers to weapons created by states, particularly China.

Affordances: The factors and conditions affecting how and under what conditions a technology may be used. May include factors like cost, bandwidth, or interoperability conditions in relation to other associated technologies.

AI governance: The idea that nations and specialists in particular should cooperate to create an international legal and ethical framework for guiding the development of artificial intelligence technologies and systems. Goals may include fairness and the building in of values like respect for privacy and humanity.

Algorithm: A set of rules used by a computer in making decisions or carrying out operations.

Ambient intelligence: Environments in which technology is seamlessly integrated into the surroundings—often without humans being aware of its activities. Technology is responding to human actions in the space and also collecting and storing data about human actions in the space. Related to ubiquitous surveillance.

Antitrust: Laws designed to protect trade and commerce by preventing situations that would establish unfair competition or restrict companies' ability to engage in free and open competition.

Architecture: The organization of technology and information processing services, including descriptions of technologies available, the rules governing them, and the data and information collected and organized by them.

Artificial intelligence: The capacity of a computer to act as an expert system, engaging learning, decision-making, and the carrying out of actions through performing cognitive and sensory operations similar to those performed by people.

Asymmetric cryptography: A type of encryption that uses a separate key for decrypting and encrypting the information. This type of encryption is more secure and requires a computer to set up.

Asymmetric warfare: War in which there is no inherent advantage given to the larger or more professional combatant in situations where two or more adversaries may experience a significant difference in relative military power or in strategy or tactics. Most often refers to wars between professional armies and insurgencies that are not legally recognized as combatants.

Attribution problem: The difficulty that law enforcement may encounter in identifying the source of a cyberattack or cybercrime due to the anonymous, networked nature of the internet.

Backbone: A physical attribute of the internet, a high-speed data transmission route between core routers (ISPs) on the internet.

Big data: The large volumes of data produced daily by individuals and groups interacting online, requiring new methodologies for analysis, aggregation, and storage.

Blockchain: A growing list of records, called blocks, that are linked using cryptography. Each block contains a cryptographic hash of the previous block, a timestamp, and transaction data. Can be used to track the transmission of physical and electronic goods and services, including e-currencies.

Botnet: A number of internet-connected devices, each of which is running one or more bots. Botnets can be used to carry out acts of cyber warfare, including DDOS attacks, spam attacks, and botnet takeovers of systems.

Bulletproof hosting: Practices by web hosting services where operators may be lenient about the sorts of materials allowed on their servers. Such servers may host pornography or criminal material. Often located in states where laws regarding content hosting are quite lenient and supervision and accountability practices are poor.

Cloud computing: The delivery of different services (including data access, data manipulation, and data storage) through the internet, utilizing platforms that are not based on a company's own servers but may be located remotely anywhere in the world. A cloud can be public or private.

Computer forensic investigation: The investigation of computer systems to gather and preserve evidence related to crimes, including cybercrimes.

Computer network attack (CNA): Operations to disrupt, deny, degrade, or destroy information resident in computers and computer networks or the computers and networks themselves.

Computer network exploitation (CNE): A technique that uses computer networks to infiltrate target computers' networks to extract sensitive or confidential data that are typically not shared with the general public.

Constructivism: A stance within international relations theory that assumes that ideas and identities form the main building blocks of the international system. This stance assumes that change is possible within the international system and that narratives and language are important elements of building our international system.

Critical infrastructure: The body of systems, networks, and assets that are so essential that their continued operation is required to ensure the security of a given nation, its economy, and the public's health and/or safety.

Cryptocurrency: A digital currency that uses encryption techniques to regulate currency generation and to verify the transfer of funds. Cryptocurrencies operate independently of a central bank and are tracked through distributed ledger technology utilizing peer-to-peer networking.

Cryptography: The science of creating (either manually or through the use of technology) codes that allow information to be encrypted or kept secret.

Cybersecurity: Both immediate and longer-term measures taken by both civilian and military operators to provide for the defense of a computer or computer system against unauthorized attacks or access.

Cyberweapons: Devices or programs (including viruses and worms) which can be used to permanently or temporarily damage or disrupt individual computers or computer systems, often including those acting as critical infrastructure within a state.

Cyber enabled economic warfare (CEEW): A hostile strategy involving attacks against a nation using cyber technology with the intent to weaken its economy and thereby reduce its political and military cyber power.

Cyber forensic investigation: The carrying out of civil criminal or military investigative techniques aimed at verifying the source of a cyberattack as well as the gathering of evidence regarding cyberattacks or cyberactivities that can be used in legal proceedings against a perpetrator or perpetrators.

Cyber industrial complex: An informal alliance between the military and government cyberdefense contractors. Some believe that cyber contractors are invested in exaggerating the scope of the cyberthreat to create a market for cybersecurity services.

Cyber power: The ability of a state or other nonstate actor to use the cyber domain to compel and coerce other actors. Cyber power includes four components: a state's capital strength or physical resources, its cyber workforce technical skills, its intelligence capabilities, and its ability to think strategically about activities in cyberspace.

Cyber sovereignty: The idea that individual states should be the deciding factors regarding the shape, ideology, and legal climate governing the internet that their citizens encounter.

Cyber threat intelligence program (C-TIP): Structures created by both private organizations and some government agencies aimed at organizing, collecting, and analyzing information about current and potential attacks upon an organization's cyber infrastructure.

Dark web: That part of the internet that is not readily available to the general public but instead requires specific software, configurations, or authorization to access.

Deep fake: A technology based on artificial intelligence that can be used to alter or produce new video content to present events, including speeches and quotes, as though they occurred when in fact they did not.

Deep learning: A subset of machine learning in which a computer imitates the workings of a human brain in processing data and developing decision-making algorithms.

Deep web: The hidden part of the internet that is not generally accessible to internet users through, for example, a web search engine like Google.

Digital economy: A broad range of economic activities, usually occurring within a state, that use digitized information and knowledge as key factors of production. The internet, cloud computing, big data, fintech, and other new digital technologies are used to collect, store, analyze, and share information digitally and transform social interactions.

Digital Geneva Convention: Ongoing initiatives to create an international legal framework committing governments to comply with and implement norms to protect civilians on the internet during peacetime.

Digital identification system: Government-sponsored initiatives, particularly in China, to create an online or networked identity management system for individuals, organizations, and electronic devices operating in cyberspace. Such a system would remove the anonymous browsing characteristic of today's internet in favor of a managed, real-world identification-browsing system.

Digital sovereignty: The question of owning the personal data of users, collected by different company websites on the internet with or without the consent of the users. Sovereignty may be individual or belong to a state or another entity like the European Union.

Digital superpower: A state possessing excessive or superior power in relation to its neighbors or others within the international system, in this case possessing a preponderance of power in the digital sphere.

Disinformation: A technique, originally developed in Russia, for spreading false information, often covertly, to influence public opinion or obscure the truth about an event or person.

Distributed denial of service (DDOS) attack: An attempt to make an online service unavailable by overwhelming it with traffic from multiple sources.

Distributed ledger technology (DLT): A technology for keeping records of transactions or digital interactions through achieving consensus among replicated, shared, and synchronized digital data geographically spread across and stored upon multiple sites, countries, and/or institutions.

Domain Name System (DNS): Translates internet domain and host names to IP addresses and vice versa. On the internet, DNS automatically converts between the names we type in our web browser address bars to the IP addresses of web servers hosting those sites. Larger corporations also use DNS to manage their own company intranet.

Doxing: A technique of tracing and identifying someone or gathering information about an individual using sources on the internet.

Dual use: A technology that can be used for the achievement of multiple related but separate ends (e.g., military and civilian use).

Duopoly: A market situation in which two companies own all or nearly all of the market for a product or service.

Emerging technology: A new technology that has the ability to create wide-ranging social, economic, political, and legal issues when it is introduced into society.

Fifth domain: A military term for the cyber environment. Fifth domain operations are those that incorporate the three dimensions of land, sea, and aerospace operations—along with temporal and cyber dimensions of warfare.

First-mover advantage: The notion that the first business to establish a position in a market niche has an advantage in being able to dictate the terms and set expectations for how such a business will operate.

Free good: A good with zero opportunity cost that can be consumed in as much quantity as needed without reducing its availability to others. That is, just like one individual's breathing of air does not create a shortage that would affect other humans who breathe air, one individual or group's use of the internet does not create a shortage that would deprive others of their ability to use the internet. Free goods are also social goods that are owned in common and available to all potential users.

Function creep: The notion that a technology or tool introduced for the fulfillment of one purpose may gradually be deployed for multiple additional purposes.

Grafting: The adding on of multiple, related functions to an office or function originally created to serve one function.

Gray areas: Specific legal and ethical questions for which there are not yet clearly defined rules and regulations due to the newness and novelty of these questions.

Hacktivist: An individual or group that engages in computer hacking for the achievement of political or social ends.

Hidden layer: That layer of an artificial neural network in which engineers simulate the types of activity that go on in the human brain.

Human in the loop: Those autonomous computing systems in which total control or autonomy is not ceded to the machine but rather a human must input permission for certain actions to occur. The machine's ability to decide and to act autonomously is limited.

Information warfare: The use and management of information technology to achieve a competitive advantage over one's adversaries in both a physical and an online battlespace. Includes providing false information as well as denying an opponent the ability to access or utilize information to manipulate or control decision-making.

Infosphere: A term developed by cybersecurity ethics professionals to describe the built environment of the information space broadly defined as well as the information and communication flows that occur within it.

Intellectual property: Products of individual or group creativity, including intangible assets such as music, literature, or ideas and processes, that can be patented and registered.

Internet kill switch: The concept that a state, individual, or group could utilize a single shut-off mechanism to cut off citizen access and use of the internet within a defined space in response to a threat to the system or in the face of social or political disruption.

Internet Protocol (IP) address: A unique address identifying a computer or other device on a computer network.

Internet service provider (ISP): A company providing its members with access to the internet.

Landing station: The point at which a computer cable carrying data, such as across the sea, is located. From there data is routed on to additional networks.

Legal tender: Any currency that serves as a legally recognized or official means of payment. In most countries the national currency is legal tender, but in most of Europe, the euro is legal tender. In both cases, the currency is issued by an official body, such as a national bank or the European Central Bank.

Machine learning: An artificial intelligence discipline that allows computers to formulate new knowledge and create new algorithms for knowledge development through analysis, training on existing data, and self-training.

Malware: Any type of computer program that is intended to harm a user's computer. A general term that encompasses viruses, Trojans, and spyware.

Maskirovka: A Russian intelligence and information warfare technique in which deceptive means, including false identities, are utilized in online communication interactions to spread false information or extract information concessions from targets.

Mature information society: A period in the future in which individuals and groups will be able to depend upon and work with the information environment without questioning its quality or availability.

Narrow AI: An ethical standpoint within the machine learning community that stresses that the ways and means by which artificial intelligence may be deployed should be carried out within strictly defined parameters. For example, AI could be used to analyze data but not to make judgment calls or give advice to humans in ambiguous situations.

Natural Monopoly: A market situation in which one company naturally has the majority of shares in an industry due to built-in factors that are difficult to correct without unduly influencing a free market economy.

Net neutrality: The notion that all information available online should be carried at the same speed without discrimination based on the content of communications.

Neural network: A series of algorithms that are deployed to identify and analyze relationships in a data set through a process that mimics the way the human brain operates.

Oligopoly: A market situation in which there are only a few participants.

Online piracy: The theft or unauthorized misuse of intellectual property, such as music or video performances, through internet transmission and copying or cloning.

Open information viewpoint: A stance taken by some early internet architects that stated that information should flow freely across the internet, unimpeded by national, technical, or financial barriers.

Open source software: Software programs that are available for sharing among users and that are not subject to copyright laws.

Passive cyber defense: Measures taken to reduce the probability and minimize the effects of damage caused by hostile actions within or enabled by the cyber environment—without the intention of taking the initiative. Generally taken to mean a situation in which one responds to an identified cyberthreat rather than acting preemptively to neutralize the threat.

Path dependence: The notion that design decisions made at an earlier stage of a technology's development may have long-lasting repercussions on the evolution and limits of the technology.

Peer-to-peer network: A network of computers configured to allow certain files and folders to be shared with everyone or with selected users.

Penetration rate: The percentage of a nation's citizens who are considered to have access to the internet either at home, at work, at school, or in a commercial setting

Platform: The basic hardware (computer) and software (operating system) on which software applications can be run. Taken to refer to applications that host activities related to the exchange of goods and services without actually providing goods and services themselves.

Psychological operations (PSYOPS): A military term for planned operations aimed at influencing both military and civilian adversaries' perceptions and actions through influencing their emotions, reasoning, and behavior. May include deception and propaganda (e.g., manipulating an election outcome through convincing a nation's voters not to turn out to vote because it is unlikely that their candidate would win).

Quantum computing: A new model of computing in which data are handled differently because it is not treated as binary. Quantum computing will be much faster and able to handle far greater volumes of data than current systems can.

Quantum superiority: The potential of quantum computing devices to solve problems that current computers cannot due to advances in computing speed created by quantum methods of data handling.

Ransomware: A type of computer network attack in which the attacker maintains control over information or data files, threatening to delete or destroy them if conditions, usually monetary, are not met.

Referent object of security: Used by constructivists within international relations theory and refers to the thing or object that is being protected through a state's national security and defense postures. A state may seek to defend its borders, belief systems, economy, or way of life.

Reinforced learning: A system for training algorithms through using a system of reward and punishment.

Resilience: The ability of an organization to continue to carry out operations after an attack takes place on the system.

Rootkit: A collection of computer software, typically malicious, designed to enable access to a computer or an area of its software that is not otherwise allowed (e.g., to an unauthorized user) and often masks its existence or the existence of other software.

Semiautonomous: Automation that can make decisions and perform actions without direction. Refers to technologies that can handle real-world conditions that are unpredictable and dynamic.

Social construction of technology: The notion that a technology's function and meaning rests on decisions made by users in society rather than the designers or developers or the technology.

Social credit system: A national reputation system being developed by China's government that would give each citizen a reputation score similar to a credit rating.

Social engineering: The use of nontechnical means to gain the trust of users to "con" them into providing confidential information.

Sovereignty gap: The gap between a state's capacity to carry out the activities of a sovereign state within an international system (such as policing its borders and providing a strong infrastructure) and its actual ability to do so.

Spoofing: A computer network hacking technique in which attackers utilize deception to establish the perception that they are a legitimate member of the system to extract information or concessions from others within the network.

Stablecoin: Cryptocurrencies designed to minimize the volatility of the price of the stablecoin, relative to some "stable" asset or basket of assets. A stablecoin can be pegged to a currency or to exchange traded commodities (such as precious metals or industrial metals). Stablecoins redeemable in commodities are said to be backed, whereas those leveraging fiat money or other cryptocurrencies are referred to as unbacked.

Standards war: A competition for market dominance between two or more producers of a particular type of technology (i.e., Android and Apple).

Strategic stability: The development of an equilibrium between states in which neither side has a strong incentive to engage in the first use of nuclear or cyber weapons.

Subversion: A systematic attempt to overthrow or undermine a government or political system, often by the use of disinformation and deception.

Supervisory control and data acquisition (SCADA): A category of software application programs for process control, that is, the gathering of data in real time from remote locations to control equipment and conditions. Used in power plants as well as in oil and gas refining, telecommunications, transportation, and water and waste control.

Surface web: That part of the web that is immediately and easily accessible to users, such as through a Google search.

SWIFT (Society for the Worldwide Interbank Financial Telecommunication) code: An internationally recognized identification code for banks around the world. Most commonly used for international transactions.

Technological closure: The stage at which the meaning and function of a technology has been decided and stabilized, being no longer in flux.

Trojan horse: A computer network hacking technique in which malware may be attached to or secreted within a legitimate communication or file transfer.

Unsupervised learning: A technique for training an artificially intelligent algorithm through providing it with information that is not classified or labeled and allowing the algorithm to act on that information without guidance.

Virtual currency: Currencies stored and transferred electronically. Any money based in 1s and 0s meets this definition; dollars stored in a bank account are supposed to be a representation of dollars actually held somewhere, whereas physical Bitcoins are a representation of their digital counterparts.

Virtual private network (VPN): A network constructed using a public network to connect to a private server (often abroad or remote) associated with a company or other enterprise. Once on the private server, users can browse free of public surveillance, access prohibited websites, or send messages using encryption.

Virus: A piece of malignant computer code that is capable of replicating either on its own or in response to commands sent, allowing it to reproduce itself across or among computer networks.

Wassenaar Arrangement: A multilateral export control regime (MECR) with forty-two participating states aimed at reducing arms proliferation, particularly in the areas of biological and chemical weapons.

Weak AI: An approach to artificial intelligence research and development that acknowledges the limitations inherent in artificial intelligence and in particular the ways in which it many simulate human consciousness but is not actually conscious.

Weapons of mass disruption: Information warfare weapons whose primary intent is to instill fear and confusion in a society, including the incitement of financial, political, or social panic.

White hat hackers: Individuals who engage in hacking activities without malign intent and who may often share information about vulnerabilities found with their targets for the purposes of improving information security.

Whole of government approach: Refers to activities performed jointly by a number of different public agencies and organizations to solve a problem common to all. In cybersecurity, it refers to the cooperation among the private sector, Department of Homeland Security, Department of Defense, and related agencies to prepare for and respond to cyberattacks.

Worm: Self-replicating malware that duplicates itself to spread to uninfected computers. Often uses parts of an operating system that are automatic and invisible to the user.

Zero day exploit (ZDE): An adversary activity that occurs on the same day a weakness is discovered in software before a fix is made available.

Zero sum: In a contest between two actors, the only solution set is one in which one side's gain is the other's loss. In any conflict, there is no solution set in which both sides can win. Instead, there must be one winner and one loser.

NOTES

Chapter 1

1. Miniwatts Marketing Group, *Internet Usage Statistics: The Internet Big Picture: World Internet Users and 2018 Population Stats*, last modified 2018, https://www.internetworldstats.com/stats.htm.

2. Lindner, M., "E-Commerce Is Expected to Grow to 17 Percent of US Retail Sales by 2022," Digitalcommerce360.com, last modified August 9, 2017, https://www.digitalcommerce360.com/2017/08/09/e-commerce-grow-17-us-retail-sales-2022/.

3. Klimburg, A., *The Darkening Web: The War for Cyberspace* (New York, NY: Penguin Books, 2018), 5.

4. Michael Hayden. 2017. Playing to the Edge: American Intelligence in an Age of Terror. (New York: Penguin), p. 132

5. Hayden, M. V., *Playing to the Edge: American Intelligence in the Age of Terror* (New York, NY: Penguin Books, 2016).

6. History.com Editors, *What Hath God Wrought?*, last modified 2018, https://www.history.com/this-day-in-history/what-hath-god-wrought.

7. Mitchell, B., "How Packet Switching Works on Computer Networks," *Lifewire*, last modified 2018, https://www.lifewire.com/packet-switching-on-computer-networks-817938.

8. MacAskill, E., "Putin Calls the Internet a 'CIA Project' Renewing Fears of Web Breakup," *The Guardian* (April 24, 2014), https://www.theguardian.com/world/2014/apr/24/vladimir-putin-web-breakup-internet-cia.

9. Lord, Nat, "What Is Social Engineering? Defining and Avoiding Common Social Engineering Threats," *Data Insider*, last modified September 11, 2018, https://digitalguardian.com/blog/what-social-engineering-defining-and-avoiding-common-social-engineering-threats.

10. Kaplan, F., "'Wargames' and Cybersecurity's Debt to a Hollywood Hack," *The New York Times* (February 19, 2016), https://www.nytimes.com/2016/02/21/movies/wargames-and-cybersecuritys-debt-to-a-hollywood-hack.html.

11. Manjikian, M., "The Social Construction of Technology: How Objects Acquire Meaning in Society," in *Technology and World Politics: An Introduction* (Taylor & Francis Group, 2017), 25–41, http://ebookcentral.proquest.com/lib/umanitoba/detail.action?docID=4912808.

12. Agentura.ru, "SORM-2," last modified 2000, http://agentura.ru/timeline/1998/sorm/.

13. Manjikian, M., "The Social Construction of Technology: How Objects Acquire Meaning in Society," in *Technology and World Politics: An Introduction* (Routledge, 2017), 17–37.

14. Drezner, D., "Globalization and Policy Convergence," *International Studies Review* 3 (2001): 53–78, https://www.jstor.org/stable/3186512?seq=1#metadata_info_tab_contents.

15. Fukuyama, F., *The End of History and the Last Man* (New York, NY: Free Press, 2006).

16. Drezner, D., "Globalization and Policy Convergence," *International Studies Review* 3 (2001): 53.

17. Gore, A., *Remarks by Vice President Al Gore: Digital Divide Event*, last modified 1998, https://clintonwhitehouse2.archives.gov/WH/EOP/OVP/speeches/edtech.html.

18. Manjikian, M., "From Global Village to Virtual Battlespace: The Colonizing of the Internet and the Extension of Realpolitik," *International Studies Quarterly* 54 (2010), 381–401, https://doi.org/10.1111/j.1468-2478.2010.00592.x.

19. Soldatov, A., and I. Borogan, *The Red Web: The Struggle between Russia's Digital Dictators and the New Online Revolutionaries* (New York, NY: PublicAffairs, 2015).

20. McKnight, D. H., V. Choudhury, and C. Kacmar, "Developing and Validating Trust Measures for E-Commerce: An Integrative Technology," *Information Systems Research* 13 (2002): 334–359, https://www.jstor.org/stable/23015741?seq=1#metadata_info_tab_contents.

21. Nadler, J., "Electronically-Mediated Dispute Resolution and E-Commerce," *Negotiation Journal* 17 (2001): 333–347, https://doi.org/10.1023/A:1014534707294.

22. Wang, S., H. Cavasoglu, and Z. Deng, "Early Mover Advantage in E-Commerce Platforms with Low Entry Barriers: The Role of Customer Relationship Management Capabilities," *Information and Management* 53 (2016): 197–206, https://doi.org/10.1016/j.im.2015.09.011.

23. Broome, P. A., "Conceptualizing the Foundations of a Regional E-Commerce Strategy: Open Networks or Closed Regimes? The Case of CARICOM," *Cogent Business & Management* 3 (2016): 1–32, https://www.tandfonline.com/doi/full/10.1080/23311975.2016.1139441#aHR0cHM6Ly93d3cudGFuZGZvbmxpbmUuY29tL2RvaS9mdWxsLzEwLjEwODAvMjMzMTE5NzUuMjAxNi4xMTM5NDQxLjEyExMzk0NDE/bmVlZEFjY2Vzcz10cnVlQEBAMA==.

24. Kwak, J., Y. Zhang, and J. Yu, "Legitimacy Building and E-Commerce Platform Development in China: The Experience of Alibaba," *Technological Forecasting and Social Change* (2018): 1–10, https://doi.org/10.1016/j.techfore.2018.06.038.

25. Russell, J., "Alibaba Gets Serious in Southeast Asia in Preparation for Battle with Amazon," *Tech Crunch*, last modified 2016, https://techcrunch.com/2017/03/24/alibaba-gets-serious-in-southeast-asia/.

26. Outsource2India, *The Outsourcing History of India*, https://www.outsource2india.com/why_india/articles/outsourcing_history.asp.

27. Palley, T., "The Economics of Outsourcing: How Should Policy Respond?" *Review of Social Economy* 66 (2008): 279–295, https://doi.org/10.1080/00346760701821896.

28. Bauer, J. M., "The Internet and Income Inequality: Socio-Economic Challenges in a Hyper-Connected Society," *Telecommunications Policy* 42 (2018): 333–343, https://doi.org/10.1016/j.telpol.2017.05.009.

29. Business Insider, "Facebook Investors Boasting $3 Billion in Shares Want to Topple 'Robber Baron' Mark Zuckerberg," *The Economic Times* (June 27, 2018), https://

economictimes.indiatimes.com/news/international/business/facebook-investors-boasting-3-billion-in-shares-want-to-topple-robber-baron-mark-zuckerberg/articleshow/64759195.cms.

30. The History of SEO, *Short History of Early Search Engines*, http://www.thehistoryofseo.com/The-Industry/Short_History_of_Early_Search_Engines.aspx.

31. Zook, M. A., and M. Graham, "The Creative Reconstruction of the Internet: Google and the Privatization of Cyberspace and Digiplace," *Geoforum* 38 (2007): 1322–1343, https://doi.org/10.1016/j.geoforum.2007.05.004.

32. Manjikian, M., "From Global Village to Virtual Battlespace: The Colonization of the Internet and the Extension of Realpolitik," *International Studies Quarterly* 54 (2010): 381–401, https://www.jstor.org/stable/40664172.

33. McKay, A., "The Problem with 'Great Schools,'" *Medium*, last modified May 28, 2018, https://medium.com/s/story/the-problem-with-great-schools-69b4ef4f5079/.

34. Shah, R. C., and J. F. Kezan, "The Privatization of the Internet's Backbone Network," *Journal of Broadcasting & Electronic Media* 51 (2007): 93–109, https://doi.org/10.1080/08838150701308077.

35. Information Infrastructure Task Force, *The National Information Infrastructure: Agenda for Action* (Washington, DC: Executive Office of the President, 1993).

36. Committee on the Judiciary, United States Senate. One Hundred Fourth Congress, First Session. Congress of the United States. "Cyberporn and Children: The Scope of the Problem, the State of the Technology, and the Need for Congressional Action." Hearing on S.892, a Bill to Amend Section 1464 of Title 18, United States Code, to Punish Transmission by Computer of Indecent Material to Minors. Washington, DC, Senate Committee on the Judiciary, last modified July 24, 1995, https://files.eric.ed.gov/fulltext/ED400779.pdf.

37. White House, *The Cost of Malicious Cyber Activity to the US Economy* (Washington, DC: Executive Office of the President, February 2018), https://www.whitehouse.gov/wp-content/uploads/2018/02/The-Cost-of-Malicious-Cyber-Activity-to-the-U.S.-Economy.pdf.

38. Manjikian, M., "From Global Village to Virtual Battlespace: The Colonization of the Internet and the Extension of Realpolitik," *International Studies Quarterly* 54 (2010): 381–401, https://www.jstor.org/stable/40664172.

39. Campen, A., D. Dearth, and T. R. Godden, eds., *Cyberwar: Security, Strategy, and Conflict in the Information Age* (Washington, DC: Afcea International Press, 1996), 1.

40. Campen, Dearth, and Godden.

41. Sageman, M., *Understanding Terrorist Networks* (Philadelphia: University of Pennsylvania Press, 2004).

42. Metz, S., and D. V. Johnson II, "Asymmetry and US Military Strategy: Definition, Background, and Strategic Concepts," Strategic Studies Institute, last modified 2001, http://ssi.armywarcollege.edu/pdffiles/pub223.pdf.

43. Spannon, C., "Can the Internet Be Saved?" *Le Monde Diplomatique* (April 7, 2018).

44. Manjikian, M., *Cybersecurity Ethics: An Introduction* (New York, NY: Routledge, 2017), 213.

45. Ems, L., "Twitter's Place in the Tussle: How Old Power Struggles Play Out on a New Stage" *Media, Culture and Society* 36, no. 5 (2014): 720–731.

46. Richtel, M., "Egypt Cuts off Most Internet and Cell Service," *New York Times* (January 28, 2011), https://www.nytimes.com/2011/01/29/technology/internet/29cutoff.html.

47. Web Designer Depot Staff, "A Brief History of Blogging," last modified March 14, 2011, https://www.webdesignerdepot.com/2011/03/a-brief-history-of-blogging/.

48. Porter, E., "Anti-Social Media?" *Chronicle of Higher Education* (April 23, 2017).

49. Sunstein, C., *Republic.com 2.0* (Princeton, NJ: Princeton University Press, 2007).

50. People Press, *"Understanding the Partisan Divide over American Values,"* last modified June 4, 2012, http://www.people-press.org/2012/06/04/section-1-understanding-the-partisan-divide-over-american-values/.

51. Dirzauskaite, G., and N. Ilinca, Understanding Hegemony in International Relations Theories (Aalborg, Sweden: Aalborg University, 2017), https://projekter.aau.dk/projekter/files/260247380/Understanding__Hegemony__in_International_Relations_Theories.pdf.

52. Kligiene, quoted in Manjikian, 212.

53. Manjikian, 216.

54. Lyon, D., "Surveillance, Snowden and Big Data: Capacities, Consequences, Critique," *Big Data and Society* 1, no. 1 (2015): 1–13.

55. Boyd, D., and K. Crawford, "Critical Questions for Big Data: Provocations for a Cultural, Technological and Scholarly Phenomenon," *Information, Communication and Society* 15, no. 5 (2012): 662–679.

56. Kaplan, J., *Artificial Intelligence: What Everyone Needs to Know* (New York, NY: Oxford University Press, 2016).

57. ACM US Public Policy Council, "Statement of Algorithmic Transparency and Accountability," last modified May 25, 2017, https://www.acm.org/binaries/content/assets/public-policy/2017_usacm_statement_algorithms.pdf.

Chapter 2

1. Reporters without Borders, "Our Values," https://rsf.org/en/our-values.

2. Warner, Charles, "Information Wants to Be Free," *Huffington Post* (May 25, 2011), accessed August 10, 2019, https://www.huffpost.com/entry/information-wants-to-be-f_b_87649.

3. Negroponte, quoted in Kenny, C., *Overselling the Web? Development and the Internet* (Boulder, CO: Lynne Reiner, 2006), 218. Cairnes, quoted in Goldsmith, J. and T. Wu, *Who Controls the Internet? Illusions of a borderless World* (New York: Oxford University Press, 2006), 141.

4. Manjikian, M., "From Global Village to Virtual Battlespace: The Colonizing of the Internet and the Extension of Realpolitik," *International Studies Quarterly* 54, no. 3 (2010), 381.

5. Wheeler, T., "In Cyberwar There Are No Rules," *Foreign Policy* (September 12, 2018), https://foreignpolicy.com/2018/09/12/in-cyberwar-there-are-no-rules-cybersecurity-war-defense/.

6. Klimburg, A., *The Darkening Web: The War for Cyberspace* (New York, NY: Penguin Books, 2017).

7. Morozov, E., *The Net Delusion: The Dark Side of Internet Freedom* (New York, NY: Public Affairs, 2012).

8. Winner, L., "Do Artifacts Have Politics?" *Daedalus* 109, no. 1 (1980), 121–136.

9. Berman, M., "Pfizer Says It Is Tightening Restrictions on Its Drugs to Keep Them from Being Used in Lethal Injections," *New York Times* (May 13, 2016), https://www.washingtonpost.com/news/post-nation/wp/2016/05/13/pfizer-says-it-is-tightening-restrictions-on-its-drugs-to-keep-them-from-being-used-in-lethal-injections/?noredirect=on.

10. Ems, L., "Twitter's Place in the Tussle: How Old Power Struggles Play Out on a New Stage," *Media, Culture & Society* 36, no. 5 (2014): 720–731.

11. Quoted in Manjikian, 381.

12. "Net Neutrality Explained: What It Means (and Why It Matters)," *Fortune* (November 23, 2017), http://fortune.com/2017/11/23/net-neutrality-explained-what-it-means-and-why-it-matters/.

13. Reporters without Borders, "List of the 13 Internet Enemies," last modified January 25, 2016, https://rsf.org/en/news/list-13-internet-enemies.

14. Reporters without Borders.

15. Cohn, C., "Foreword," in *The End of Trust* (Toronto, Canada: McSweeneys, 2018), 1–24.

16. Cohn, 23.

17. Singer, P. W., and E. Brooking, *Likewar: The Weaponization of Social Media* (New York, NY: Houghton and Mifflin, 2018), 3.

18. Lessig, L., *Code: and Other Laws of Cyberspace, Version 2.0* (New York, NY: Basic Books, 2006), 54.

19. Ivgi, N., "Rough Consensus and Running Code and the Internet-OSI Standards War," *IEEE Annals of the History of Computing* 28, no. 3 (2017): 48–61.

20. Zhang, J., and P. Nyiri, "'Walled' Activism: Transnational Social Movements and the Politics of Chinese Cyber-Public Space," *International Development Planning Review* 36, no. 1 (2014): 111–132.

21. Yuen, S., "Becoming a Cyber Power: China's Cybersecurity Upgrade and Its Consequences," *China Perspectives* 2, no. 102 (2015): 53.

22. Yakupitiyage, T., "Africa: America First or America Alone?" Allafrica, last modified June 21, 2018, http://allafrica.com/stories/201806220456.html.

23. NBC News, "Does the World Wide Web Need a Bill of Rights?," last modified March 12, 2014, http://NBCNews.com/tech/internet/does-world-wide-web-need-bill-rights-n50841.

24. Internet Encyclopedia of Philosophy, "Philosophy of Technology," https://www.iep.utm.edu/technolo/.

25. Halaweh, M., "Emerging Technology: What Is It?" *Journal of Technology Management & Innovation* 8, no. 3 (2013): 108–115, doi:https://doi.org/10.4067/S0718-27242013000400010.

26. Ramzy, A., "Architect of China's 'Great Firewall' Bumps into It," *New York Times* (April 6, 2016), https://www.nytimes.com/2016/04/07/world/asia/china-internet-great-firewall-fang-binxing.html.

27. Tiezzi, S., "VPNs: The China–US Proxy War," *The Diplomat* (January 29, 2015), article is no longer available.

28. Mozur, P., "US Adds China's Internet Controls to List of Trade Barriers," *New York Times* (April 7, 2016), https://www.nytimes.com/2016/04/08/business/international/china-internet-controls-us.html.

29. BBC News, "Google Censors Itself for China," last modified January 25, 2006, http://news.bbc.co.uk/2/hi/technology/4645596.stm.

30. Rauhala, E., "Holes Close in China's 'Great Firewall' as Apple and Amazon Snub Apps to Bypass Censors," *Los Angeles Times* (August 2, 2017), https://www.latimes.com/business/technology/la-fi-tn-amazon-china-vpn-20170802-story.html.

31. Jin, M., and S. Dei, "Behind the Great Firewall. China's Internet Is Thriving Even in Rural Areas," *South China Morning Post* (February 3, 2018), https://search-proquest-com.ezproxy.regent.edu/docview/1993581153?pq-origsite=summon.

32. Tavani, H., "The Uniqueness Debate in Computer Ethics: What Exactly Is at Issue and Why Does It Matter?" *Ethics and Information Technology* 4 (2002): 37–54.

33. Cammaerts, B., "Networked Resistance: The Case of WikiLeaks," *Journal of Computer-Mediated Communication* 18, no. 4 (2013), 420–436.

34. Hinduja, S., and J. Patchin, "Bullying, Cyberbullying and Suicide," *Archives of Suicide Research* 14 (2010): 201–221.

35. Manjikian, 338.

36. Rosenblatt, Seth, "Uncertain Future for Wassenaar 'Cyberweapons' Agreement under Trump," *The Parallax* (March 2, 2017), https://the-parallax.com/2017/03/02/future-wassenaar-trump./.

37. Article19.org, "#InternetofRights: Creating the Universal Declaration of Digital Rights," last modified March 24, 2017, https://www.article19.org/blog/resources/internetofrights-creating-the-universal-declaration-of-digital-rights/.

38. Garrett, B. N., "Taming the Wild Wild Web: Twenty-First Century Prize Law and Privateers as a Solution to Combating Cyber-Attacks," *University of Cincinnati Law Review* 81, no. 2 (2013): 683–708.

39. Sales, N. A., "Regulating Cyber Security" *Northwestern University Law Review* 107, no. 4 (2013): 1503–1546.

Chapter 3

1. Sahl, S., "Researching Customary International Law, State Practice and the Pronouncements of States Regarding International Law," *GlobaLex*, last modified 2007, http://www.nyulawglobal.org/globalex/Customary_International_Law.html.

2. Hobbes, T., *Leviathan* or *The Matter, Forme, and Power of a Commonwealth, Ecclesiastical and Civil* (Adelaide, Australia: University of Adelaide), http://ebooks.adelaide.edu/au/hobbes/thomas/h681/Chapter13.html.

3. Morgenthau, H., *Politics Among Nations: The Struggle for Power and Peace* (New York, NY: Knopf, 1948), 10–17.

4. Rattray, G., *Strategic Warfare in Cyberspace* (Cambridge, MA: MIT Press, 2001).

5. Posen, B., "Command of the Commons: The Military Foundations of US Hegemony," *International Security* 28 (2003): 5–46, https://doi.org/10.1162/016228803322427965.

6. Cho, Y., and J. Chung, "Bring the State Back In: Conflict and Cooperation among States in Cybersecurity," *Pacific Focus* 32 (2017), https://onlinelibrary-wiley-com.ezproxy.regent.edu/doi/full/10.1111/pafo.12096.

7. Sheldon, J. B., "Geopolitics and Cyber Power: Why Geography Still Matters," *American Foreign Policy Interests* 36 (2014): 286–293, https://johnbsheldon.files.wordpress.com/2014/11/108039202e20142e969174.pdf.

8. Venables, A., S. Shaikh, and J. Shuttleworth, "The Projection and Measurement of Cyber Power," *Security Journal* 30 (2015): 1000–1011, https://link.springer.com/article/10.1057%2Fsj.2015.35.

9. Nye, J., *The Future of Power* (New York, NY: Hachette, 2011), 300.

10. Peter, A., "Cyber Resilience Preparedness of Africa's Top-12 Emerging Economies," *International Journal of Critical Infrastructure Protection* 17 (2017): 49–59.

11. Karabacak, B., S. O. Yildirim, and N. Baykal, "A Vulnerability-Driven Cyber Security Maturity Model for Measuring National Critical Infrastructure Protection Preparedness," *International Journal of Critical Infrastructure Protection* 15 (2016): 47–59.

12. Lehto, M., and J. Limnell, eds., "Cyber Security Capability and the Case of Finland," proceedings from ECCW, Munich, Germany, 2016.

13. Rowland, J., M. Rice, and S. Shenoi, "The Anatomy of a Cyber Power," *International Journal of Critical Infrastructure Protection* 7 (2014): 3–11, https://ac.els-cdn.com/S187454821400002X/1-s2.0-S187454821400002X-main.pdf?_tid=4c4508fc-6550-4e38-b07b-5e7abc1cd3a3&acdnat=1545161037_f13fc50bae24d5cca3ce51e7bc6ce30f.

14. Moteff, J., "Critical Infrastructure Resilience: The Evolution of Policy and Programs and Issues for Congress," Congressional Research Service, last modified August 23, 2012, http://fas.org/sgp/crs/homesec/R42683.pdf.

15. Kern, S., "Expanding Combat Power through Military Cyber Power Theory," *Joint Forces Quarterly* 79 (2015): 88–95, https://ndupress.ndu.edu/Portals/68/Documents/jfq/jfq-79/jfq-79_88-95_Kern.pdf.

16. Evans, M., "Australia and the Revolution in Military Affairs," *Land Warfare Studies Center* 115 (2001), https://www.army.gov.au/sites/g/files/net1846/f/wp115-australia_and_the_revolution_in_military_affairs_michael_evans.pdf.

17. Klimburg, A., "The Whole of Nation in Cyber Power," *Georgetown Journal of International Affairs* (2011): 171–179, https://www.jstor.org/stable/pdf/43133826.pdf?refreqid=excelsior%3A76a84e45ce1ae5ce3507a0eea771e4c6.

18. Veracode.com. "What Is a Rootkit?" accessed June 4, 2019, https://www.veracode.com/security/rootkit.

19. Zetter, K., "Hacker Lexicon: What Are CNE and CNA?" *Wired Magazine* (July 6, 2016), https://www.wired.com/2016/07/hacker-lexicon-cne-cna/.

20. Gostev, A., "The Flame: Questions and Answers," Securelist.com, last modified May 28, 2012, no longer available.

21. Zetter, K., "Meet 'Flame' the Massive Spy Malware Infiltrating Iranian Computers," Wired.com, last modified May 28, 2012, no longer available.

22. Zetter, "Hacker Lexicon."

23. Kuo, M., "Cyber-Enabled Economic Warfare: Assessing US Strategy," *Extreme Hacking* (blog), last modified March 23, 2018, https://www.fdd.org/analysis/2018/03/23/cyber-enabled-economic-warfare-assessing-us-strategy/.

24. Kuo.

25. Carberry, S., "How to Define Cyber-Enabled Economic Warfare," FCW.com, last modified February 23, 2017, https://fcw.com/articles/2017/02/23/critical-ceew-cyber-carbery.aspx.

26. Venables, A., S. Shaikh, and J. Shuttleworth, "The Projection and Measurement of Cyber Power," *Security Journal* 30 (2015): 1000–1011, https://link.springer.com/article/10.1057%2Fsj.2015.35.

27. Sanger, D. E., *The Perfect Weapon: War, Sabotage, and Fear in the Cyber Age* (New York, NY: Crown, 2018).

28. Nye. 300.

29. Holsti, O., P. T. Hopmann, and J. D. Sullivan, *Unity and Disintegration in International Alliances: Comparative Studies* (New York, NY: John Wiley and Sons, 1973).

30. Bergmann, Stefan. "The Concept of Military Alliance," accessed December 5, 2018, http://www.bildungundberuf.atwww.bundesheer.at/pdf_pool/publikationen/05_small_states_04.pdf.

31. Hathaway, O. A., et al., "The Law of Cyber-Attack." *California Law Review* 100 (2012): 817–886, https://digitalcommons.law.yale.edu/cgi/viewcontent.cgi?article=4844&context=fss_papers.

32. India Today, "What Is Shanghai Cooperation Organisation and Why Is Its Membership Crucial for India?" last modified June 10, 2018, https://www.indiatoday.in/education-today/gk-current-affairs/story/what-is-shanghai-cooperation-organisation-and-why-does-its-membership-matter-for-india-1256624-2018-06-10.

33. Deibert, R., "Cyberspace under Siege," *Journal of Democracy* 26, no. 3 (2015): 64–78, https://doi.org/10.1353/jod.2015.0051.

34. Sigh, S., "India-ASEAN Cooperation on Cybercrime," *International Journal of Advanced Research in Computer Science* 7, no. 6 (2016): 273–275, file:///C:/Users/Brian/Downloads/2779-5533-1-SM.pdf.

35. Sanger.

36. DeVore, M. R., and S. Lee, "APT (Advanced Persistent Threat)s and Influence: Cyber Weapons and the Changing Calculus of Conflict." *The Journal of East Asian Affairs* 31, no. 1 (2017): 39–64,https://www.jstor.org/stable/pdf/44321272.pdf.

37. Foltz, A., "Stuxnet, Schmitt Analysis and the Cyber 'Use-of-Force' Debate," *Joint Forces Quarterly* 67, no. 4 (2012): 40–48.

38. Deibert, R. J., R. Rohozinski, and M. Crete-Nishihata, "Cyclones in Cyberspace: Information Shaping and Denial in the 2008 Russia-Georgia War," *Security Dialogue* 43, no. 1 (2012): 3–24, https://doi.org/10.1177%2F0967010611431079.

39. Gamreklidze, E., "Cybersecurity in Developing Countries: A Digital Divide Issue," *The Journal of International Communications* 20, no. 2 (2014): 200–217, https://doi.org/10.1080/13216597.2014.954593.

Chapter 4

1. Mulligan, D., and F. Schneider, "Doctrine for Cybersecurity," http://www.cs.cornell.edu/fbs/publications/publicCybersecDaed.pdf.

2. Floridi, L., *The Fourth Revolution: How the Infosphere Is Reshaping Human Reality* (New York, NY: Oxford University Press, 2014).

3. Techopedia, "Digital Economy," accessed January 14, 2019, https://www.techopedia.com/definition/32989/digital-economy.

4. Techopedia.

5. Lawton, T., and S. McGuire, "Governing the Electronic Market Space: Appraising the Apparent Global Consensus on E-Commerce Self-Regulation," *MIR: Management International Review* 43, no. 1 (2003), 51–71.

6. Miller, W., and D. Stokes, "Constituency of Influence in Congress." *American Political Science Review* 42, no. 1 (1963): 45–56.

7. Koremonos, B., "Contracting around International Uncertainty," *American Political Science Review* 90, no. 4 (2005): 549–562.

8. Koremonos.

9. Krasner, S., "Introduction," in Krasner, S., ed. *International Regimes*. (Ithaca, NY: Cornell University Press, 1983).

10. For more on this point, see Bauer, J., and M. van Eeten, "Cybersecurity: Stakeholder Incentives, Externalities, and Policy Options," *Telecommunications Policy* 33 (2009): 706–719.

11. Heinl, C., "Moving toward a Resilient ASEAN Cybersecurity Regime," *Asia Policy* 18 (2014), https://www.nbr.org/publication/regional-cybersecurity-moving-toward-a-resilient-asean-cybersecurity-regime/.

12. Hund, M., "From 'Neighborhood Watch Group' to Community?" *Australian Journal of International Affairs* 56, no. 1 (2002): 99–122.

13. Chou, M. H., M. Howlett, and K. Koga, "Image and Substance Failures in Regional Organizations: Causes, Consequences, Learning and Change?" *Politics and Governance* 4, no. 3 (2016): 50–61.

14. Sand, P., "Sovereignty Bounded: Public Trusteeship for Common Pool Resources?" *Global Environmental Politics* 4, no. 1 (2004): 47–71.

15. Disparte, D., "A Cyber Federal Deposit Insurance Corporation? Achieving Enhanced National Security," *Prism* 7, no. 2 (2017): 53–64.

16. Nielsen, S., "Pursuing Security in Cyberspace: Strategic and Organizational Challenges," *Orbis* 56, no. 3 (2012): 345.

17. Wall, J., "Russia: Vladimir Putin Outlines Development of Digital Economy as a Priority," Investinblockchain, last modified March 15, 2019, https://www.investinblockchain.com/russia-vladimir-putin-outlines-development-digital-economy-priority/.

18. Reuters, "Privacy Coin Monero Offers Near Total Anonymity." *New York Times* (June 11, 2019), https://www.nytimes.com/reuters/2019/06/11/business/11reuters-crypto-currencies-altcoins-explainer.html.

19. Investopedia, "Cryptocurrency," https://www.investopedia.com/terms/c/cryptocurrency.asp.

20. Kall, J., "Blockchain Control," *Law Critique* 29 (2018): 133–140.

21. Xie, R., "Why China Had to 'Ban' Cryptocurrency but the US Did Not: A Comparative Analysis of Regulations on Crypto-Markets between the US and China," *Washington University Global Studies Law Review* 18, no. 2 (2019): 467.

22. Xie, 472.

23. Xie.

24. Brainard, L., "Cryptocurrencies, Digital Currencies and Distributed Ledger Technologies: What Are We Learning?" Remarks at the Decoding Digital Currency Conference, May 15, 2018, https://www.federalreserve.gov/newsevents/speech/brainard20180515a.htm.

25. Xie, 457.

26. Masterthecrypto, "Guide to How to Value a Cryptocurrency," https://masterthecrypto .com/guide-how-to-value-a-cryptocurrency/.

27. Allen, D., C. Berg, and M. Novak, "Blockchain: An Entangled Political Economy Approach," *Journal of Public Finance and Public Choice* 33, no. 2 (2018): 105–123.

28. O'Keefe, D., "US Federal Reserve Bank Recognizes Cryptocurrency," Cryptodisrupt, last modified June 25, 2018, https://cryptodisrupt.com/ us-federal-reserve-bank-recognizes-cryptocurrency/.

29. Sharov, L., "Global Cryptocurrency as Prospects for the World Monetary System," *Journal of the European Economy* 17, no. 1 (2018): 116–128.

30. DeVries, Peter, "An Analysis of Cryptocurrency, Bitcoin and the Future," *International Journal of Business Management and Commerce* 1, no. 2 (2018): 5.

31. Dale, B., "Project Libra: Everything We Know about Facebook's Cryptocurrency," Blockchain 101, last modified May 29, 2019, https://finance.yahoo.com/news/project-libra-everything-know-facebook-160006170.html.

32. Popper, N., and M. Isaac, "Facebook and Telegram Are Hoping to Succeed Where Bitcoin Failed," *New York Times* (February 26, 2019), https://www.nytimes .com/2019/02/28/technology/cryptocurrency-facebook-telegram.html.

33. Chan, S. P., "Facebook Plans to Launch 'Globalcoin' Currency in 2020," BBC News, last modified May 24, 2019, https://www.bbc.com/news/business-48383460.

34. Lepecq, G., "Cash Is Critical: Personal and National Security Would Be Imperiled by a Cashless Society," *US News and World Report* (April 7, 2016), https:// www.usnews.com/opinion/economic-intelligence/articles/2016-04-07/ cashless-society-would-be-dangerous-for-financial-and-national-security.

35. Deniston, G., *The Global Transition Away from the Dollar and the American Military Implications* (Newport, RI: Naval War College, 2018).

36. Bordo, M., and A. Levin, "Central Bank Digital Currency and the Future of Monetary Policy," Hoover Institution, last modified May 2017, https://www.hoover.org/sites/ default/files/bordo-levin_bullets_for_hoover_may2017.pdf.

37. Hall, M., "Weaponizing an Economy: The Cryptoruble and Russia's Dystopian Future," Mad Scientist Laboratory, last modified November 5, 2018, https:// madsciblog.tradoc.army.mil/tag/distributed-ledger-technology/.

38. De Almeida, P., P. Fazendeiro, and P. Inacio, "Societal Risks of the End of Physical Cash," *Futures* 104 (2018): 48.

39. DeVries, 1–9.

40. Veritas, R., "State of Global Cryptocurrency Regulation in 2018: Where the World Stands Right Now," Robertveritas, last modified February 18, 2018, https:// robertveritas.wordpress.com/2018/02/18/state-of-global-cryptocurrency-regulation-in-2018-where-the-world-stands-right-now/.

41. Veritas.

42. Xie, 457–489.

43. Xie, 475.

44. Clark, C., and L. Chen, "This Is How China Is Stifling Bitcoin and Cryptocurrencies," Bloomberg, last modified January 17, 2018, https://www.bloomberg.com/news/articles/2018-01-09/how-china-s-stifling-bitcoin-and-cryptocurrencies-quicktake-q-a.

45. Bauer and Van Eeten.

46. Bauer and Van Eeten, 707.

47. Techtarget, "SWIFT (Society for the Worldwide Interbank Financial Telecommunication)," https://searchcio.techtarget.com/definition/SWIFT.

48. Schwartz, M., "Bangladesh Bank Attackers Hacked SWIFT Software," Bank Info Security, last modified April 25, 2016, http://www.bankinfosecurity.com.

49. Gilderdale, S., "SWIFT's Customer Security Programme: Preventing, Detecting and Responding to the Growing Cyber Threat," *Journal of Securities Operations and Custody* 9, no. 1 (2017), 198–205.

50. Das, K., and J. Spicer, "The SWIFT Hack: How the New York Fed Fumbled over the Bangladesh Bank Cyber-Heist," *Reuters* (July 21, 2016), https://www.reuters.com

51. Groll, E., "NSA Official Suggests North Korea Was the Culprit in Bangladesh Bank Heist," *Foreign Policy* (March 21, 2017), https://foreignpolicy.com/2017/03/21/nsa-official-suggests-north-korea-was-culprit-in-bangladesh-bank-heist/.

52. Lee, M., "Revising the 'Google in China' Question from a Political Economic Perspective," *China Media Research* 6, no. 2 (2010): 15–32.

53. Lindskold, L., "Google as a Political Subject: The Right to Be Forgotten Debate, 2014–2016," *Online Information Review* 42, no. 6 (2017): 768–783.

54. Iansiti, M., and K. Lakhani, "Managing Our Hub Economy: Strategy, Ethics and Network Competition in an Age of Digital Superpowers," *Harvard Business Review* (2017): 88–91.

55. Statista, "United States 2019," https://www.statista.com/study/48356/united-states/.

56. Facebook, "Number of Monthly Active Facebook Users Worldwide as of 2nd Quarter 2019 (in Millions)," Statista, last modified July 24, 2019, https://www.statista.com/statistics/264810/number-of-monthly-active-facebook-users-worldwide/.

57. Facebook, "Facebook's Annual Revenue from 2009 to 2018 (in Million U.S. Dollars)," Statista, last modified February 1, 2019, https://www.statista.com/statistics/268604/annual-revenue-of-facebook/.

58. Facebook, "Number of Full-Time Facebook Employees from 2004 to 2018," Statista, last modified February 1, 2019, https://www.statista.com/statistics/273563/number-of-facebook-employees/.

59. Clements, J., "Google—Statistics & Facts," Statista, last modified February 8, 2019, https://www.statista.com/topics/1001/google/.

60. Clements.

61. Alphabet. "Number of Full-Time Alphabet Employees from 2007 to 2018, Statista, last modified February 6, 2019, https://www.statista.com/statistics/273744/number-of-full-time-google-employees/.

62. All Belgium statistics are from: Plecher, H., "Belgium—Statistics & Facts," Statista, last modified February 14, 2019, https://www.statista.com/topics/2384/belgium/.

63. All France statistics are from: Plecher, H., "France—Statistics & Facts," Statista, last modified December 1, 2019, https://www.statista.com/topics/2497/france/.

64. All Russia statistics are from: Plecher, H., "Russia—Statistics & Facts," Statista, last modified December 7, 2017, https://www.statista.com/topics/2675/russia/.

65. Smith, Craig. "120 Amazing Ali Baba Statistics, Facts and History (2019)," last modified August 5, 2019, https://expandedramblings.com/index.php/alibaba-statistics/.

66. Smith, August 5, 2019.

67. Alibaba, "Number of Full-Time Employees at Alibaba from 2012 to 2019," Statista, last modified May 15, 2019, https://www.statista.com/statistics/226794/number-of-employees-at-alibabacom/.

68. Smith, Craig, "90 Amazing Baidu Statistics, Facts and History (2019),"last modified July 30, 2019, https://expandedramblings.com/index.php/baidu-stats/.

69. Smith, July 30, 2019.

70. Baidu, "Number of Employees at Baidu from 2009 to 2018," Statista, last modified March 15, 2019, https://www.statista.com/statistics/253173/number-of-employees-at-baidu/.

71. Smith, Craig, "150 Amazing Amazon Statistics, Facts and History (2019)," last modified August 3, 2019, https://expandedramblings.com/index.php/amazon-statistics/.

72. Smith, August 3, 2019.

73. Amazon, "Number of Amazon.com Employees from 2007 to 2018," Statista, last modified January 30, 2019, https://www.statista.com/statistics/234488/number-of-amazon-employees/.

Chapter 5

1. Ferdinand, P., "Westward Ho—the China Dream and 'One Belt, One Road': Chinese Foreign Policy under XI Jinping," *International Affairs* 92, no. 4 (2016): 949–950.

2. Ferdinand, 941–957.

3. Wong, E., L. Chi, S. Tsui, and W. Tiejun, "One Belt, One Road China's Strategy for a New Global Financial Order," *Monthly Review* (January 1, 2017), https://monthlyreview.org/2017/01/01/one-belt-one-road/.

4. Wong et al., 36.

5. Abi, M., "China's 'Belt and Road' Plan in Pakistan Takes a Military Turn," *The Toronto Star (Online)* (December 19, 2018), https://www.thestar.com/?redirect=true.

6. Virmani, A., "OBOR: Economic, Diplomatic and Strategic Directions," *Dialogue with Virmani* (blog), last modified June 5, 2016, https://dravirmani.blogspot.com/2016/06/obor-economic-diplomatic-and-strategic.html.

7. Abi.

8. Abi.

9. Barker, P., "Undersea Cables and the Challenges of Protecting Seabed Lines of Communication," Fortunascorner, last modified March 15, 2018, https://fortunascorner.com/2018/03/19/undersea-cables-challenge-protecting-seabed-lines-communication/.

10. Deutsche Welt, "Belt and Road Forum: Will China's 'Digital Silk Road' Lead to an Authoritarian future?" accessed May 29, 2019, https://www.dw.com/en/belt-and-road-forum-will-chinas-digital-silk-road-lead-to-an-authoritarian-future/a-48497082.

11. Ferdinand, 952.

12. Shen, H., "Building the Digital Silk Road? Situating the Internet in China's Belt and Road Initiative," *International Journal of Communication* 12 (2018): 2683–2701.

13. Kohlenberg, P., and N. Godehardt, "China's Global Connectivity Politics: On Confidently Dealing with Chinese Initiative's," *Center for Security Studies* (blog), last modified April 2018, https://isnblog.ethz.ch/international-relations/chinas-global-connectivity-politics-on-confidently-dealing-with-chinese-initiatives.

14. Zeng, J., "Does Europe Matter? The Role of Europe in Chinese Narratives of 'One Belt, One Road' and 'New Type of Great Power Relations," *Journal of Common Market Studies* 55, no. 5 (2017): 1162–1176.

15. Deutsche Welte.

16. Wolf, S., " 'New Silk Road' and China's Hegemonic Ambitions," Deutsche Welt, https://www.dw.com/en/new-silk-road-and-chinas-hegemonic-ambitions/a-38843212.

17. Singer, P. W., and A. Friedman, *Cybersecurity and Cyberwar: What Everyone Needs to Know* (New York, NY: Oxford University Press, 2014), 14.

18. Wendt, A., *A Social Theory of International Politics* (Cambridge, UK: Cambridge University Press, 1999).

19. Fierke, K. M., "Breaking the Silence: Language and Method in International Relations," N. F. Debrix, ed., *Language, Agency, and Politics in a Constructed World* (Armonk, NY: Sharpe, 2003): 66–86.

20. Betz, D., and T. Stevens, "Analogical Reasoning and Cybersecurity." *Security Dialogue* 44, no. 2 (2013): 147–163, https://doi.org/10.1177%2F0967010613478323.

21. Gromov, G., "Al Gore's Pileup on the Information Superhighway," Netvalley, last modified 2019, http://www.netvalley.com/silicon_valley/Al_Gore_Pileup_on_the_Information_Superhighway.html.

22. Betz and Stevens.

23. Gray, A., "This Map Shows How Undersea Cables Move Internet Traffic around the World." World Economic Forum, last modified November 24, 2016, https://www.weforum.org/agenda/2016/11/this-map-shows-how-undersea-cables-move-internet-traffic-around-the-world/.

24. Burrington, I., "The Strange Geopolitics of the International Cloud," *The Atlantic* (November 17, 2015), https://www.theatlantic.com/technology/archive/2015/11/the-strange-geopolitics-of-the-international-cloud/416370/.

25. Manjikian, M., "But My Hands Are Clean: The Ethics of Intelligence Sharing and the Problem of Complicity," *International Journal of Intelligence and Counter Intelligence* 28 (2015): 692–709, https://doi.org/10.1080/08850607.2015.1051411.

26. Kaspersky, "What Is Cyber-Security?" Kaspersky Lab, https://www.kaspersky.com/resource-center/definitions/what-is-cyber-security.

27. International Telecommunications Union, "Definition of Cybersecurity," *International Telecommunications Union*, last modified 2018, https://www.itu.int/en/ITU-T/studygroups/com17/Pages/cybersecurity.aspx.

28. Kaspersky.

29. Anderson, R., and A. Hearn, *An Exploration of Cyberspace Security R&D Investment Strategies for DARPA: "The Day After . . . in Cyberspace II"* (Arlington, VA: The Rand Corporation, 1996), https://www.rand.org/pubs/monograph_reports/MR797.html.

30. US Department of Defense, "DOD Dictionary of Military and Associated Terms, last modified May 2019, http://www.jcs.mil/Portals/36/Documents/Doctrine/pubs/dictionary.pdf.

31. Cho, Y., and J. Chung, "Bring the State Back In: Conflict and Cooperation among States in Cybersecurity," *Pacific Focus* 32, no. 2 (2017): 290–314, https://doi.org/10.1111/pafo.12096.

32. Hensen, L., and H. Nissenbaum, "Digital Disaster, Cybersecurity, and the Copenhagen School," *International Studies Quarterly* 53 (2009): 1155–1175, https://doi.org/10.1111/j.1468-2478.2009.00572.x.

33. Nielsen, S., "Pursuing Security in Cyberspace: Strategic and Organizational Challenges," *Orbis* 56, no. 3 (2012): 336–356, http://dx.doi.org/10.1016/j.orbis.2012.05.004.

34. Sageman, M., *Leaderless Jihad: Terror Networks in the Twenty-First Century* (Philadelphia: University of Pennsylvania Press, 2008).

35. O'Connell, J., "Google Joins the Fight against ISIS," Hacked, last modified January 22, 2016, https://hacked.com/google-joins-fight-isis/.

36. US Department of Justice, "USA Patriot Act: Preserving Life and Liberty," https://www.justice.gov/archive/ll/highlights.htm.

37. Department of Homeland Security, "The Physical Protection of Critical Infrastructures and Key Assets, last modified 2003, http://www.dhs.gov/xlibrary/assets/Physical_Strategy.pdf.

38. Inductive Automation, "What Is SCADA?" accessed November 29, 2018, https://inductiveautomation.com/what-is-scada.

39. PC Magazine, "Critical Infrastructure," accessed November 29, 2018, https://www.pcmag.com/encyclopedia/term/40480/critical-infrastructure.

40. Obama, B., "Remarks by the President on Securing Our Nation's Critical Infrastructure," The White House Office of the Press Secretary, last modified May 29, 2009, http://whitehouse.gov/the-press-office/remarks-president-securing-our-nations-cyber-infrastructure.

41. Quoted in Futter, A., "War Games Redux? Cyber Threats, US-Russian Strategic Stability and New Challenges for Nuclear Security and Arms Control," European Security 25, no. 2 (2015): 163–180, https://doi.org/10.1080/09662839.2015.1112276.

42. Quigley, K., C. Burns, and K. Stalard, "'Cyber Gurus': A Rhetorical Analysis of the Language of Cybersecurity Specialists and the Implications for Security Policy and Critical Infrastructure Protection," Government Information Quarterly 32 (2015): 108–117, https://ac.els-cdn.com/S0740624X15000209/1-s2.0-S0740624X15000209-main.pdf?_tid=d956b2b2-e608-4107-a018-076cfaa115a4&acdnat=1545162772_e883f2228e7b1393bf94b22c2ea18ad6.

43. Emerson, R. G., "Limits to a Cyber-Threat," Contemporary Politics 22, no. 2 (2016): 178–196, https://doi.org/10.1080/13569775.2016.1153284.

44. Halbert, D., "IP Theft and National Security: Agendas and Assumptions," The Information Society 32, no. 4 (2016): 256–268, https://doi.org/10.1080/01972243.2016.1177762.

45. Coalson, R., "New Kremlin Information-Security Doctrine Calls for 'Managing' Internet in Russia," Radio Free Europe Radio Liberty, last modified December 6, 2016, https://www.rferl.org/a/russia-informaiton-security-internet-freedome-concerns/28159130.html.

46. Epstein, D., M. Roth, and E. Baumer, "It's the Definition, Stupid! The Framing of Online Privacy in the Internet Governance Forum Debates," Journal of Information Policy 4 (2014): 146–147.

Chapter 6

1. Burke, R., Decolonization and the Evolution of International Human Rights (Philadelphia, PA: Pennsylvania Studies in Human Rights, 2013).

2. Sahl, S., "Researching Customary International Law, State Practice and the Pronouncements of States regarding International Law," GlobaLex, last modified 2007, http://www.nyulawglobal.org/globalex/Customary_International_Law.html.

3. Jepperson, Ronald L., Alexander Wendt, and Peter J. Katzenstein. "Norms, Identity, and Culture in National Security," in Peter Joachim Katzenstein, ed., The Culture of National Security: Norms and Identity in World Politics (New York: Columbia University Press, 1996), 33.

4. Barnett, M., "The UN and Global Security: The Norm Is Mightier than the Sword," *Ethics and International Affairs* 9 (1993): 49–50.

5. Mowbray, S., "IUCN, UN, Global NGOs, Likely to See Major Budget Cuts under Trump," Mongabay, last modified January 8, 2018, https://news.mongabay .com/2018/01/iucn-other-global-ngos-un-likely-to-see-major-budget-cuts-under-trump/.

6. Baumann, M. O., "Forever North–South? The Political Challenges of Reforming the UN Development System," *Third World Quarterly* 39, no. 4 (2018): 626–641.

7. Human Rights Watch, "Traditional Values a Potent Weapon against LGBT Rights," Human Rights Watch, last modified November 6, 2017, https://www.hrw.org/ news/2017/11/06/traditional-values-potent-weapon-against-lgbt-rights.

8. Peacewomen, "Security Council's Open Debate on Children and Armed Conflict, last modified July 2018, https://www.peacewomen.org/security-council/ security-council-open-debate-children-and-armed-conflict-july-2018.

9. Clark, H., "The United Nations Is Failing to Give Its Leader Real Power to Act," *The Guardian* (September 13, 2017), https://www.theguardian.com/global-development/2017/ sep/13/the-un-united-nations-is-failing-give-its-leader-real-power-to-act-helen-clark.

10. PIR Center, "Global Internet Governance and Cybersecurity as Viewed by Russian Experts," PIR Center Library, last modified 2017, http://www.pircenter.org/en/static/ global-internet-governance-and-cyber-security-as-viewed-by-russian-experts.

11. Halbert, D., "IP Theft and Nat Sec: Agendas and Assumptions," *The Information Society* 32, no. 4 (2016): 256–268.

12. Grauer, Y., "Government Internet Kill Switches Violate Human Rights, but Telecom Companies Can Fight Back," *Forbes* (October 26, 2015), https://www.forbes.com/ sites/ygrauer/2015/10/26/internet-kill-switch/#2c808fb42fa2.

13. Catalin C., "Russia to Disconnect from the Internet as Part of a Planned Test," Zero Day, last modified February 11, 2019, zdnet.com/article/.

14. Joint Chiefs of Staff, "Cyberbrief: Joint Publication 3-12," last modified June 27, 2018. https://nsarchive.gwu.edu/news/cybervault/2018-06-27/ cyber-brief-joint-publication-3-12.

15. Department of Homeland Security, "Critical Infrastructure Sectors," https://www .dhs.gov/critical-infrastructure-sectors.

16. Ward, T., *The Ethics of Destruction: Norms and Force in International Relations* (Ithaca, NY: Cornell University Press, 2001), 7.

17. TASS Russian News Agency, "Russia to Roll Out Digital IDs in 2024," Science and Space, last modified February 11, 2019, http://tass.com/science/1044074.

18. Demchak, C., and P. Dombrowski, "Cyber Westphalia: Asserting State Prerogatives in Cyberspace," *Georgetown Journal of International Affairs* (2013): 29–38.

19. Demchak and Dombrowski, 32.

20. Cho, Y., and J. Chung, "Bring the State Back in Conflict and Cooperation among States in Cybersecurity," *Pacific Focus: Inha Journal of International Studies* XXXII, no. 2 (August 2017): 290–314.

21. Schmit, Michael, Tallinn Manual 2.0 on the International Law Applicable to Cyber Operations (Cambridge, UK: Cambridge University Press, NATO Cooperative Cyber Defence Centre of Excellence, 2017).

22. Rowland, J., M. Rice, and S. Shenoi, "Whither Cyberpower?" *International Journal of Critical Infrastructure Protection* 7 (2014): 124–137, doi:10.1016/j.ijcip.2014.04.001.

23. Hsueh, R., "Nations or Sectors in the Age of Globalization: China's Policy towards Foreign Direct Investment in Telecommunications," *Review of Policy Research* 32, no. 6 (2015): 627–648.

24. Sunstein, C., "Sunstein on the Internet and Political Polarization," The University of Chicago Law School, last modified December 14, 2007, https://www.law.uchicago.edu/news/sunstein-internet-and-political-polarization.

25. Cavelty, M., "Breaking the Cyber-Security Dilemma: Aligning Security Needs and Removing Vulnerabilities," *Science and Engineering Ethics* 20 (2014): 701–715.

26. Berman, P., "Cyberspace and the State Action Debate: The Cultural Value of Applying Constitutional Norms to 'Private' Regulation," *Law and Technology* 42, no 3 (2009): 20–49.

27. Zajko, M., "Telecommunications Regulation: Internet Governance, Surveillance and New Roles for Intermediaries," *Canadian Journal of Communications* 41, no. 1 (2016): 75–93.

28. Shoigu, S., "Russia: European Cyber Operations Center—US Help?" Polygraph, last modified July 31, 2018, https://www.polygraph.info/a/cyber-centers-europe-russia/29401693.html.

29. Lewis, J. A., "Cognitive Effect and State Conflict in Cyberspace," Center for Strategic and International Studies, last modified September 2018, https://csis-prod.s3.amazonaws.com/s3fs-public/publication/180924_Cognitive_Effect_Cyberspace.pdf?R6FPUdDaOystuUCWsMCXUhKTBg.4CW.D.

30. Galloway, T., and H. Baogang, "China and Technical Global Internet Governance: Beijing's Approach to Multi-Stakeholder Governance within ICANN, WSIS and the IGF," *China: An International Journal* 12, no. 3 (2014): 79.

31. UN General Assembly, "Group of Governmental Experts on Developments in the Field of Information and Telecommunications in the Context of International Security," United Nations General Assembly, 68th Session, June 24, 2013, http://www.unidir.org/files/medias/pdfs/developments-in-the-field-of-information-and-telecommunications-in-the-context-of-international-security-2012-2013-a-68-98-eng-0-518.pdf.

32. Cuihong, C., "China and Global Cyber Governance: Main Principles and Debates," *Asian Perspective* 42 (2018): 649.

33. Nye, Joseph S., Jr., *Cyber Power* (Cambridge, MA: Belfer Center for International Affairs, 2010), https://www.belfercenter.org/sites/default/files/legacy/files/cyber-power.pdf.

34. Brezhnev, D., N. Ryan, and R. Bradbury, "Modelling Hegemonic Power Transition in Cyberspace," Complexity, last modified 2018, https://www.hindawi.com/journals/complexity/2018/9306128/cta/.

35. Halbert, D., "Intellectual Property Theft and National Security: Agendas and Assumptions," *The Information Society* 32, no. 4 (2016): 256–268.

36. Liaropoulos, A., "Exploring the Complexity of Cyberspace Governance: State Sovereignty, Multi-Stakeholders, and Power Politics," *Journal of Information Warfare* 15, no. 4 (2016): 14–26.

37. Hoffman, J., C. Katzenbach, and K. Gollatz, "Between Coordination and Regulation: Finding the Governance in Internet Governance," *New Media and Society* 19, no. 9, 1411.

38. Singer, P. W., and A. Friedman, *Cybersecurity and Cyberwar: What Everyone Needs to Know* (Oxford, UK: Oxford University Press, 2014), 45.

39. Hoffman, J., C. Katzenbach, and K. Gollatz, "Between Coordination and Regulation: Finding the Governance in Internet Governance," *New Media and Society* 19, no. 9 (2017): 1423.

40. Global Forum on Cyber Expertise, "Budapest Convention on Cybercrime," TheGCFE, last modified July 12, 2016, https://www.thegfce.com/news/news/2016/12/07/budapest-convention-on-cybercrime.

41. Singer and Friedman, 14.

42. Take, I., "Regulating the Internet infrastructure: A Comparative Appraisal of the Legitimacy of ICANN, ITU, and the WSIS," *Regulation and Governance* 6 (2012): 499–523.

43. World Summit on the Information Society, "Declaration of Principles: Building the Information Society: A Global Challenge in the New Millenium," Document WSIS-03/GENEVA/DOC/4-E, last modified December 12, 2003, http://www.itu.int/net/wsis/docs/geneva/official/dopp.html\.

44. Michl, W., "Paradigms of Internet Regulation in the European Union and China," *Frontiers of Law in China* 13, no. 3 (2018): 428–453.

45. Schiller, D., (2013, February). "Masters of the Internet," Le Monde Diplomatique, last modified February 2013, https://mondediplo.com/2013/02/15internet.

46. See, for example, Chimni, B., (2004). "International Institutions Today; an Imperial Global State in the Making," *European Journal of International Law* 15, no. 1 (2004), 1–37.

47. Chakraverty, P., "Who Speaks for the Governed? World Summit on Information Society, Civil Society and the Limits of 'Multistakeholderisms,'" *Economic and Political Weekly* (January 21, 2006): 250–257.

48. Quoted in Masters, Johnathan, "What Is Internet Governance?" New York: Council on Foreign Relations, last modified April 23, 2014, https://www.cfr.org/backgrounder/what-internet-governance.

49. Satell, G., "How the NSA Uses Social Network Analysis to Map Terrorist Networks," *Digital Tonto*, last modified June 12, 2013, https://www.digitaltonto.com/2013/how-the-nsa-uses-social-network-analysis-to-map-terrorist-networks/.

50. Schmitz, S., "Facebook's Real Name Policy: Bye-Bye, Max Mustermann?" *Journal of Information Policy and Information Technology of the European Community* 1 (2013): 90, https://www.jipitec.eu/issues/jipitec-4-3-2013/3844/citation.

51. Freedom House, "Internet Freedom," last modified 2019, https://freedomhouse.org/issues/internet-freedom.

52. Milanovic, M., "The Extraterritorial Application of Human Rights Treaties," United Nations, last modified 2018, http://legal.un.org/avl/ls/Milanovic_HR.html.

Chapter 7

1. Farrell, G., and D. Birks, "Did Cybercrime Cause the Crime Drop?" *Crime Science* 7, no. 8 (2018): 1–4.

2. Fruhlinger, J., "Top Cybersecurity Facts, Figures and Statistics for 2018," CSO, last modified 2018, https://www.csoonline.com/article/3153707/top-cybersecurity-facts-figures-and-statistics.html.

3. Essential Ecommerce Statistics for 2018, eCommerce Platforms, last modified September 17, 2018, https://ecommerce-platforms.com/articles/ecommerce-statistics.

4. Donalds, C., and K. Osei-Bryson, "Toward a Cybercrime Classification Ontology: A Knowledge-Based Approach," *Computers in Human Behavior* 92 (2019): 403–418.

5. Ghosh, A., "Wannacry: List of Major Companies and Networks Hit by Deadly Ransomware around the Global," *International Business Times* (May 16, 2017), https://www.ibtimes.co.uk/wannacry-list-major-companies-networks-hit-by-deadly-ransomware-around-globe-1621587.

6. Holto, T. J., "Regulating Cybercrime through Law Enforcement and Industry Mechanisms," *Annals of the AAPSS* 679 (2018): 140–157.

7. Johnson, B. G., "Tolerating and Managing Extreme Speech on Social Media," *Internet Research* 28, no. 5 (2018): 1275–1291.

8. National Institutes of Health, "Severe Acute Respiratory Syndrome (SARS)," Medline Plus, http://medlineplus.gov/ency/article/007192.htm.

9. Broadhurst, R., "Developments in the Global Law Enforcement of Cybercrime," *Policing: An International Journal of Police Strategies and Management* 29, no. 3 (2004): 408–433.

10. Goodman, M., *Future Crime* (New York, NY: Doubleday, 2015).

11. Finnemore, M., and D. Hollis, "Constructing Norms for Global Cybersecurity," *American Journal of International Law* 110, no. 3 (2016): 425–479.

12. Currie, R., "Cross-Border Evidence Gathering in Transnational Criminal Investigation: Is the Microsoft Ireland Case the 'Next Frontier'?" *Canadian Yearbook of International Law* 54 (2016): 69.

13. Currie, 71.

14. Currie, 89.

15. US Senate, Committee on the Judiciary, Subcommittee on Crime and Terrorism, Taking down Botnets: Public and Private Efforts to Disrupt and Dismantle Cyber-criminal Networks [Video recording], last modified July 15, 2014,https://www.judiciary.senate.gov/meetings/taking-down-botnets_public-and-private-efforts-to-disrupt-and-dismantle-cybercriminal-networks.

16. World Intellectual Property Organization, "What Is Intellectual Property?" https://wipo.int/about-ip/en/.

17. For more on both of these issues, see Manjikian, M., *Cybersecurity Ethics: An Introduction* (New York, NY: Routledge, 2018), chap. 6 on intellectual property.

18. Shirk, S., B. Allen-Ebrahimian, and E. Parker, "It's Official: Washington Thinks Chinese Internet Censorship Is a 'Trade Barrier,'" *Foreign Policy* (April 14, 2016). https://foreignpolicy.com/2016/04/14/chinese-censorship-trade-barrier-great-firewall-ustr-business-trade-internet/.

19. Mason, G., and Czapski, N. (2017). "Regulating Cyber-Racism," Melbourne University Law Journal 41(1). Available at www.questia.com/library/journal/1G1-517878500/regulating-cyber-racism

20. Twitter CEO Jack Dorsey Criticized for "Tone Deaf" Myanmar Tweets, BBC News, last modified December 9, 2018,https://www.bbc.com/news/world-us-canada-46498876.

21. Wikipedia, "Christopher Lamprecht," last modified February 10, 2019, https://en.wikipedia.org/wiki/Chris_Lamprecht.

22. GVZH Advocates, "Malta: Can Internet Use Be Banned?" *Mondaq* (October 26, 2015), http://www.mondaq.com/x/437770/Social+Media/Can+Internet+Use+Be+Banned.

23. The Harvard Law Review Association, "Criminal Law—Supervised Released—Third Circuit Approves Decade-Long Internet Ban for Sex Offender," *Harvard Law Review* 123, no. 3 (2010), 776–783.

24. Masnick, M., "Supreme Court Says You Can't Ban People from the Internet, No Matter What They've Done," *Techdirt* (June 20, 2017), https://www.techdirt.com/articles/20170620/10455137631/supreme-court-says-you-cant-ban-people-internet-no-matter-what-theyve-done.shtml.

25. Howland, C., and D. M. West, "The Internet as a Human Right," Brookings Institute, last modified November 7, 2016, https://www.brookings.edu/blog/techtank/2016/11/07/the-internet-as-a-human-right/.

26. Broadhurst, R., "Developments in the Global Law Enforcement of Cyber-Crime," *Policing: An International Journal of Police Strategies and Management* 29, no. 2 (2006): 408–433.

27. Broadhurst, 409.

28. Mittal, S., and P. Sharma, "A Review of International Legal Framework to Combat Cybercrime," *International Journal of Advanced Research in Computer Science* 8, no. 5 (2017): 1372–1376.

29. Bacchus, James, "How the World Trade Organization Can Curb China's Intellectual Property Transgressions," CATO at Liberty, last modified March 22, 2018, https://phillipsphiles.blogspot.com/2018/04/how-world-trade-organization-can-curb.html.

30. Donalds and Osei-Bryson.

31. Finnemore, M., and B. D. Hollis, "Constructing Norms for Global Cybersecurity," *The American Journal of International Law* 110, no. 3 (2016): 425–479.

32. Usnick, W., and L. Usnick, "A Fortress Made of Clouds: Copyright Law, the Computer Fraud and Abuse Act, and Cloud Computing," *Southern Law Journal* 26, no. 2 (2016): 191–232.

33. McLean, S., "Beware the Botnets: Cyber Security Is a Board Level Issue," *Intellectual Property and Technology Law Journal* 25, no. 12 (2013): 22–27.

34. US Senate Select Committee on Intelligence, Assessing Russian Activities and Intentions in Recent US Elections (Washington, DC: US Senate Publications, Senate Select Committee on Intelligence Review of Intelligence Community Assessment, last modified July 3, 2018, https://www.intelligence.senate.gov/publications/assessing-russian-activities-and-intentions-recent-us-elections.

35. Sheptycki, James, "High Policing in the Security Control Society," *Policing: A Journal of Policy and Practice* 1, no. 1 (2007): 70–79.

36. US Department of Defense, *Department of Defense Dictionary of Military and Associated Terms* [DOD Joint Publication 1-02] (Washington, DC: US Government Printing Office, 2016).

37. Brown, G., "Spying and Fighting in Cyberspace: Which Is Which?" *Journal of National Security Law and Policy* 8 (2016): 621–635.

38. Coles-Kemp, L., Ashenden, D., and K. O'Hara, "Why Should I? Cybersecurity, the Security of the State and the Insecurity of the Citizen," *Politics and Governance* 6, no. 2 (2018): 41–48.

39. Weitzner, D., "Promoting Economic Prosperity in Cyberspace," *Ethics and International Affairs* 32, no. 4 (2018): 425–439.

40. Lawson, T., and S. McGuire, "Governing E-Commerce," *MIR* 43 (2003): 55.

41. Jamal, K., M. Maier, and S. Sunder, "Enforced Standards versus Evolution by General Acceptance: A Comparative Study of E-Commerce Privacy Disclosure and Practice in the United States and the United Kingdom," *Journal of Accounting Research* 43, no. 1 (2005): 73–96.

42. Graff, G. M., "How a Dorm Room Minecraft Scam Brought down the Internet," *Wired* (December 13, 2017), https://www.wired.com/story/mirai-botnet-minecraft-scam-brought-down-the-internet/.

43. Associated Press, "Symantec Assists FBI-Led Takedown of the 3ve Ad-Fraud Botnet," AP News, last modified November 28, 2018, https://www.apnews.com/28d07d0895d04995a173002635e264bf.

44. Kitten, T., "Botnet Takedown: A Lasting Impact?" Bank Info Security, last modified June 3, 2014, https://www.bankinfosecurity.com/malware-takedown-lasting-impact-a-6903.

45. World Economic Forum, "Botnet Disruption," *Cyber Resilience*, http://reports.weforum.org/cyber-resilience/botnet-disruption/.

46. Kitten.

47. Sanders, C., and J. Sheptycki, "Policing, Crime and 'Big Data': Towards a Critique of the Moral Economy of Stochastic Governance," *Criminal Law and Social Change* 68 (2017): 1–15.

48. Du, L., and A. Maki, "These Cameras Can Spot Shoplifters Even before They Steal," *Blomberg* (March 4, 2019), https://www.bloomberg.com/news/articles/2019-03-04/the-ai-cameras-that-can-spot-shoplifters-even-before-they-steal.

49. Braman, S., *Change of State: Information, Policy and Power* (Cambridge, MA: MIT Press, 2009), 142.

50. Harris, S., and L. Castelao, "The Social Laboratory," *Foreign Policy* 207 (2014): 64–71.

51. Technopedia, "Data Mining," https://www.techopedia.com/definition/1181/data-mining.

52. Leese, Matthias, "The New Profiling: Algorithms, Black Boxes and the Failure of Anti-Discriminatory Safeguards in the European Union," *Security Dialogue* 45, no. 5 (2014): 494–511.

53. Leese, 494–511.

54. Castronovo, Russ, "State Secrets: Ben Franklin and WikiLeaks," *Critical Inquiry* 39, no. 3 (2013): 429.

55. Technopedia, "Definition—What Does Data Mining Mean?" https://www.technologyreview.com/s/421949/everything-you-need-to-know-about-wikileaks//.

56. Snowden, Edward, "You can despise WikiLeaks and everything it stands for. You can think Assange is an evil spirit reanimated by Putin himself. But you cannot support the prosecution of a publisher for publishing without narrowing the basic rights every newspaper relies on," November 16, 2018, https://twitter.com/snowden/status/1063520583789539328?lang=en.

Chapter 8

1. Keck, M., and K. Sikkink, "Transnational Advocacy Networks in International and Regional Politics," *International Social Science Journal* 51 no. 159 (2002): 89.

2. Eichensehr, K., "Public-Private Cybersecurity," *Texas Law Review* 995, no. 3 (2017): 467–538.

3. Finnemore, M., and D. Hollis, "Constructing Norms for Global Cybersecurity," *American Journal of International Law* 110, no. 3 (2016): 425–479, doi:10.1017/S0002930000016894.

4. Osnos, E., "Can Mark Zuckerberg Fix Facebook before It Breaks Democracy?" *The New Yorker* (September 17, 2018), https://www.newyorker.com/magazine/2018/09/17/can-mark-zuckerberg-fix-facebook-before-it-breaks-democracy.

5. Osnos.

6. Osnos.

7. Osnos.

8. Taddeo, M., and L. Floridi, "The Debate on the Moral Responsibilities of Online Service Providers," *Science and Engineering Ethics* 22 (2016): 1575–1603.

9. Osnos.

10. Herder, J., "The Power of Platforms: How Biopolitical Companies Threaten Democracy," PublicSeminar.org, last modified January 25, 2019, http://www.publicseminar.org/2019/01/the-power-of-platforms/.

11. Hatmaker, T., "Facebook Bans the Proud Boys," Techcrunch, https://techcrunch.com/2018/10/30/facebook-proud-boys-mcinnes-kicked-off/.

12. Taddeo and Floridi, 1578.

13. Herder.

14. Quoted in Osnos.

15. Fisher, M., "Inside Facebook's Secret Rulebook for Global Political Speech," *New York Times* (December 28, 2018), https://www.nytimes.com/2018/12/27/world/facebook-moderators.html.

16. Pagallo, U., "ISPs and Rowdy Web Sites before the Law: Should We Change Today's Safe Harbor Clauses," *Philosophy and Technology* 24, no. 4 (2011): 419–436.

17. Article13, "Trialogue Talks on Copyright Directive Postponed," last modified January 19, 2019, https://www.article13.org/blog/trialogue.

18. Nynonen, K., "No More Mere Conduit? Abandoning Net Neutrality and Its Possible Consequences on Internet Service Providers Content Liability," *The Journal of World Intellectual Property* 16, no. 1–2 (2013): 72–86.

19. Taddeo and Floridi.

20. Geiger, B., and V. Cuzzocrea, "Corporate Social Responsibility and Conflicts of Interest in the Alcohol and Gambling Industries: A Post-Political Discourse," *The British Journal of Sociology* 68, no. 2 (2017): 254–270.

21. Renouard, C., "Corporate Social Responsibility (CSR), Utilitarianism and the Capabilities Approach," *Journal of Business Ethics* 98, no. 1 (2011): 85–97.

22. Ethics Sage, "What Are Corporate Social Responsibilities?" last modified January 4, 2018, https://www.ethicssage.com/2018/01/what-are-corporate-social-responsibilities.html.

23. Beilinski, T., "Competition between Chinese and US Companies in the Internet Market," *International Studies, Interdisciplinary Political and Cultural Journal* 22, no. 1 (2018): 137–152.

24. Chen, T., and Y. Ku, "Rent-Seeking and Entrepreneurship: Internet Startups in China," *Cato Journal* 36, no. 3 (2016): 659–678.

25. Shim, Y., and D. Shin, "Analyzing China's Fintech Industry from the Perspective of Actor-Network Theory," *Telecommunications Policy* 40 (2015): 168–181.

26. Gough, N., "Tops in E-Commerce, Alibaba Is Now Taking on China's Banks," *New York Times* (September 18, 2014), https://dealbook.nytimes.com/2014/09/18/tops-in-e-commerce-alibaba-is-now-taking-on-chinas-banks/.

27. Beilinski.

28. Chen and Ku, 672.

29. Zachs Equity Research, "Zacks Investment Research: Alibaba (BABA) to Expand in Asia with 2 New Data Facilities," *Newstex Finance and Accounting* (blogs), last modified June 12, 2017, https://www.zacks.com/stock/news/263881/alibaba-baba-to-expand-in-asia-with-2-new-data-facilities.

30. Sender, H., "China Fears Threaten the Bullish Case for Tencent and Alibaba," *Financial Times* (June 16, 2017), https://www.ft.com/content/ac7d1120-51ba-11e7-a1f2-db19572361bb.

31. Dudovskiy, J., "Google Corporate Social Responsibility," Research Methodology, last modified June 8, 2017, https://research-methodology.net/google-corporate-social-responsibility-csr/.

32. Quoted in Maak, T., "The Cosmopolitical Corporation," *Journal of Business Ethics* 84 (2009): 361–372.

33. Taddeo and Floridi.

34. Nussbaum, M., *Creating Capabilities: The Human Development Approach* (Cambridge, MA: Harvard University Press, 2013), 213.

35. Geiger and Cuzzocrea.

36. France 24, "Saudi Arabia Eases Travel Restrictions on Women," last modified August 21, 2019, https://www.france24.com.

37. Human Rights Watch, "Saudi Arabia's Absher App: Controlling Women's Travel while Offering Government Services," last modified May 6, 2109, https://www.hrw.org/news/2019/05/06/saudi-arabias-absher-app-controlling-womens-travel-while-offering-government.

38. Human Rights Watch.

39. Ingram, M., "Google, Apple and the Saudi Wife-Tracking App," *Columbia Journalism Review* (May 9, 2019), https://www.cjr.org/analysis/google-saudi-wife-tracking-app.php.

40. Brenkert, G. "Google, Human Rights and Moral Compromise," *Journal of Business Ethics* 85 (2009): 453–478.

41. Tan, J., and A. Tan, "Business under Threat, Technology under Attack, Ethics under Fire: The Experience of Google in China," *Journal of Business Ethics* 110 (2012): 469–479.

42. New York Times, "Condemned to Repeat the History of Bank Failures?" (March 20, 2017), https://www.nytimes.com/2019/03/20/opinion/trump-bank-regulation.html.

43. Banton, C., "Duopoly," Investopedia, last modified April 13, 2019, https://www.investopedia.com/terms/d/duopoly.asp.

44. Forden, S., "FTC's Timothy Wu Says Dominant Internet Firms Should Not Add Monopolies," *Bloomberg News* (April 21, 2011), https://www.bloomberg.com/news/articles/2011-04-21/ftc-s-wu-says-dominant-internet-companies-can-t-have-multiple-monopolies.

45. Epstein, M., "Google and Facebook Worsen Media Bias: Silicon Valley's Advertising Monopoly Translates into Editorial Influence," *Wall Street Journal* (February 10, 2019), https://www.wsj.com/articles/google-and-facebook-worsen-media-bias-11549829040.

46. Wu, T., *The Master Switch: The Rise and Fall of Information Empires* (New York, NY: Vintage, 2011).

47. Reed, B., "Does the AT and T Breakup Still Matter 25 Years On?" Networkworld, last modified December 19, 2008, https://www.networkworld.com/article/2271010/does-the-at-t-breakup-still-matter-25-years-on-.html.

48. Ducci, F., *Competition Law and Policy Issues in the Sharing Economy* (Ottawa, Canada: University of Ottawa Press, 2018).

49. Business Outlook, "Airbnb Challenging Monopoly of Hotels in Africa," Africa Business Pages, https://news.africa-business.com/post/airbnb-challenging-monopoly-of-hotels-in-africa.

50. Khan, L., "Amazon's Antitrust Paradox," *Yale Law Journal* 126, no. 3 (2017), https://www.yalelawjournal.org/note/amazons-antitrust-paradox.

51. Sifry, M., "In Facebook We Antitrust," *The Nation* (October 12, 2017), https://www.thenation.com/article/in-facebook-we-antitrust/.

52. Chander, A., *The Electronic Silk Road: How the Web Binds the World Together in Commerce* (New Haven, CT: Yale University Press, 2013), 121.

53. Chander, 121.

54. Chander.

55. Sifry, M., "In Facebook We Antitrust," *The Nation* (October 12, 2017), https://www.thenation.com/article/in-facebook-we-antitrust/.

Chapter 9

1. McCarthy, D., "Privatizing Political Authority: Cybersecurity, Public-Private Partnerships, and the Reproduction of Liberal Political Order," *Politics and Governance* 8, no. 2 (2018): 5–12.

2. Segal, A., "Bridging the Cyberspace Gap: Washington and Silicon Valley," *Prism* 7, no. 2 (2017): 67–73.

3. Kovacevic, B., "*Americko Javno-Privatno partnerstvo I cyber sigurnost*," *Politicka Misao* 51, no. 3 (2014): 76–100.

4. Collier, J., "Cyber Security Assemblages: A Framework for Understanding the Dynamic and Contested Nature of Security Provision," *Politics and Governance* 6, no. 2, https://www.cogitatiopress.com/politicsandgovernance/article/view/1324.

5. Stainer, Alexia, "Sovereignty Gap," Irenees, last modified July 2010, http://www
.irenees.net/bdf_fiche-notions-226_en.html.

6. Sassen, Saskia, "The Impact of the Internet on Sovereignty: Real and Unfounded
Worries," Global Disclosure Project Information Technology and Tools, last modified December 10, 1999, https://nautilus.org/information-technology-and-tools/
the-impact-of-the-iternet-on-sovereignty-real-and-unfounded-worries./.

7. Eichensehr, K., "Public-Private Cybersecurity," *Texas Law Review* 95, no. 3 (2017):
467–538.

8. Klimburg, A., "The Whole of Nation in Cyber Power," *Georgetown Journal of International Affairs* (2011): 171–179, https://www.jstor.org/stable/pdf/43133826.pdf?refreq
id=excelsior%3A76a84e45ce1ae5ce3507a0eea771e4c6.

9. Unver, H. A., "Challenges to Democracy: Politics of Automation, Attention and
Engagement," *Journal of International Affairs* 71, no. 10 (2017): 127–146.

10. Klimburg.

11. Carr, M., "Public-Private Partnerships in National Cyber-Security Strategies.
International Affairs 92, no. 1 (2016): 43–62.

12. Macak, Kubo, "From Cyber Norms to Cyber Rule: Re-Engaging States as Law
Makers," *Leiden Journal of International Law* 30 (2017): 877–899.

13. Center for Strategic and International Studies, "Reference Note on Russian Communications Surveillance," last modified April 18, 2014, http://csis.org/analysis/
reference-note-russian-communications-surveillance.

14. Carr.

15. Zajko, M. (2016). "Telecommunications Regulation: Internet GOvernance, Surveillance and New Roles for Intermediaries," *Canadian Journal of Communications* 41(1),
75–93.

16. Unver.

17. van Erp, J., "New Governance of Corporate Cybersecurity: A Case Study of the
Petrochemical Industry in the Port of Rotterdam," *Crime Law and Social Change* 68
(2017): 75–93.

18. Webster, S., "Senator Wyden: CISPA Creates a 'Cyber Industrial Complex' to Feed
on Private Data," last modified May 22, 2012, https://www.rawstory.com/2012/05/
sen-wyden-cispa-creates-cyber-industrial-complex-to-feed-on-private-data/.

19. Harkins, M., "The Rise of the Cyber Industrial Complex," Threatvector, last modified
February 20, 2019, https://threatvector.cylance.com/en_us/home/the-rise-of-the-
cyber-industrial-complex.html.

20. Talbot, D., "The Cyber Security Industrial Complex," *MIT Technology
Review* (December 6, 2011), https://www.technologyreview.com/s/426285/
the-cyber-security-industrial-complex/.

21. Segal.

22. Lecher, C., "Elizabeth Warren Says She Wants to Break Up Amazon, Google and Facebook: A Proposal to Unwind Big Tech," *The Verge* (March 8, 2019), https://www.theverge.com/2019/3/8/18256032/elizabeth-warren-antitrust-google-amazon-facebook-break-up.

23. Greiman, V. A., "To Catch a Thief in the Cloud: A Paradigm for Law Enforcement," *The Journal of Information Warfare* 13, no. 3 (2014), first published in the proceedings, International Conference on Cyber Warfare and Security, Purdue University, Lafayette, Indiana, March 24–25.

24. Directorate-General for Communications Networks, Content and Technology (European Commission), Clarification of applicable legal framework for full, co or self-regulatory actions in the cloud computing sector, Brussels, Belgium: Council of Europe, September 20, 2017, https://publications.europa.eu/en/publication-detail/-/publication/3bd74f8f-9f47-11e7-b92d-01aa75ed71a1/language-en.

25. Harkins.

26. Electronic Frontier Foundation, "Responsibility Deflected, the CLOUD Act Passes," last modified March 20, 2018, https://www.eff.org/deeplinks/2018/03/responsibility-deflected-cloud-act-passes.

27. Aitchison, S., "Privacy in the Cloud: The Fourth Amendment Fog," Handle, last modified June 2018, http://hdl.handle.net/1773.1/1811.

28. Smith, B., "A Call for Principle-Based International Agreements to Govern Law Enforcement Access to Data," *Microsoft on the Issues* (blog), last modified September 11, 2018, https://blogs.microsoft.com/on-the-issues/2018/09/11/a-call-for-principle-based-international-agreements-to-govern-law-enforcement-access-to-data/.

29. Greiman.

30. Keohane, Robert O., and Joseph S. Nye, *Power and Interdependence Revisited* (New York, NY: Longman Classics in Political Science, 2011), 58.

31. Perryer, S., "Huawei Denies Claims It Is Owned by the Chinese Government," *New Economy Magazine* (April 26, 2019), https://www.theneweconomy.com/business/huawei-denies-claims-it-is-owned-by-chinese-government.

32. Financial Times, "Huawei Pulls Back the Curtain on Ownership Details," (February 27, 2014), https://www.ft.com/content/469bde20-9eaf-11e3-8663-00144feab7de.

33. Hardy, E., "US Government Bans Employees from Using Risky Chinese Phones," Cultofmac, last modified August 14, 2018, https://www.cultofmac.com/570331/us-government-bans-lte-huawei-chinese-smartphones/.

34. Office of Public Affairs, "Department of Commerce Announces the Addition of Huawei Technologies CO. Ltd to the Entity List," Washington, DC: United States Department of Commerce, last modified May 15, 2019, https://www.commerce.gov/news/press-releases/2019/05/department-commerce-announces-addition-huawei-technologies-co-ltd.

35. Segan, S., "What Is 5G?" *PC Magazine*, last modified April 16, 2019, https://www.pcmag.com/article/345387/what-is-5g.

36. Kuo, L., and J. Borger, "US Ban on Huawei a 'Cynically Timed' Blow in Escalating Trade War,' says firm," *The Guardian* (May 20, 2019), https://www.theguardian.com/technology/2019/may/20/trump-us-ban-huawei-google-trade-war.

37. Kuo and Borger.

38. Roff, H., "The Frame Problem: The AI 'Arms Race' Isn't One," *Bulletin of the Atomic Scientists: Special Issue: The Global Competition for AI Dominance (2019)*, https://thebulletin.org/2019/05/special-issue-the-global-competition-for-ai-dominance/.

39. Quoted in Patrikarakos, D., *War in 140 Characters: How Social Media Is Reshaping Conflict in the 21st Century* (New York, NY: Basic Books, 2017).

Chapter 10

1. Hurley, J., "The Evolving Demands of a Data-Driven Society: The New Cyber Challenge," unpublished conference paper presented at the 14th annual International Conference on Cyberwarfare, University of Stellenbosch, South Africa, March 1, 2019.

2. Roto, D., D. Hicks, and B. Martin, "What Is an Emerging Technology?" *Research Policy* 44, no. 10 (2015): 1827–1843.

3. See, for example, materials found at the website for the International Committee for Robot Arts Control (ICRAC): https://www.icrac.net/tag/killer-robots/.

4. Beard, M., J. Galliot, and S. Lynch, "Soldier Enhancement: Ethical Risks and Opportunities," *Australian Army Journal* XII, no. 1 (2016): 5–20.

5. Salna, K., "'It's Not Cricket': Indonesia's Spy Anger," *The Guardian* (November 1, 2013), https://www.theguardian.com/world/2013/nov/01/indonesia-says-australia-spying-unacceptable.

6. Elliott, D., "Anonymity for Rape Victims," *FineLine: The Newsletter on Journalism Ethics* 1, no. 3 *(1989): 1–2*, https://sites.mediaschool.indiana.edu/ethics-case-studies/anonymity-for-rape-victims/.

7. Manjikian, M., *Cybersecurity Ethics: An Introduction* (New York, NY: Routledge, 2017).

8. Grodzinsky, F., and H. Tavani, "Cyberstalking, Personal Privacy, and Moral Responsibility," *Ethics and Information Technology* 4, no 2 (2002): 123–132.

9. Ormand, D., "Intelligence Ethics: Not an Oxymoron," Center for Research and Evidence on Security Threats (CREST), last modified April 4, 2018, https://crestresearch.ac.uk/comment/intelligence-ethics-not-an-oxymoron/.

10. Selgelid, M., "Governance of Dual-Use Research, an Ethical Dilemma," Bulletin of the World Health Organization, last modified June 30, 2009, who.int/bulletin/volumes/87/9/08-051383/en/.

11. Microsoft Corporation, "Microsoft's Journey to Compliance," last modified 2018, https://resources.office.com/ww-landing-M365E-GDPR-microsoft-journey-to-compliance-ebook.html.

12. Gaskarth, J., "The Virtues in International Society," *European Journal of International Relations* 18, no. 3 (2012), 431–453, https://doi.org/10.1177/1354066110389833.

13. Bull, H., *The Anarchical Society: A Study of Order in World Politics* (New York, NY: MacMillan, 1977).

14. Cohen-Almagor, R., "Responsibility of and Trust in ISPs," *Knowledge, Technology and Policy* 23, no. 3–4 (2010): 381–397.

15. Floridi, L., *The Fourth Revolution: How the Infosphere Is Reshaping Reality* (Oxford, UK: Oxford University Press, 2014).

16. Floridi, L., "Mature Information Societies: A Matter of Expectations," *Philosophy of Technology* 29, no. 1 (2016): 1–4.

17. Bok, S., *Secrets: On the Ethics of Concealment and Revelation* (New York, NY: Vintage Books, 1989).

18. Valeriano, B., and R. Maness, "The Dynamics of Cyber Conflict between Rival Antagonists, 2001–2011," *Journal of Peace Research* 51, no. 3 (2014): 366.

19. Bok, S., *Lying: Moral Choice in Public and Private Life* (New York, NY: Pantheon Books, 1978).

20. Bagge, D., *Unmasking Maskirovka: Russia's Cyber Influence Operations* (Washington, DC, Defense Press, 2018), 43.

21. Pasentshev, E., "Destabilization of Unstable Dynamic Social Equilibriums through High-Tech Strategic Psychological Warfare," unpublished conference paper presented at the 14th annual International Conference on Cyberwarfare, University of Stellenbosch, South Africa, February 28, 2019.

22. Hardin, R., *Trust* (New York, NY: Polity, 2006).

23. Carigliano, M., "Why China's Real Name Internet Policy Doesn't Work," *The Atlantic* (March 26, 2013), https://www.theatlantic.com/china/archive/2013/03/why-chinas-real-name-internet-policy-doesnt-work/274373/.

24. Thomas, W., *The Ethics of Destruction: Norms and Force in International Relations* (Ithaca, NY: Cornell University Press, 2001).

25. Acharya, A., "How Ideas Spread: Whose Norms Matter? Norm Localization and Institutional Change in Asian Regionalism," *International Organization* 58 (2004): 239–275.

26. Jinnah and Lindsay describe the actions of front-runner states—including the United States, Canada, and the European Union—in establishing norms in the fields of environmental protection. See Jinnah, S. and A. Lindsay, "Navigating NAFTA's Environmental Provisions: The Role of the Secretariat," in Peter Stoett and Owen Temby, eds., *Trilateral Ecopolitics: Continuity and Change in Canadian-American-Mexican Environmental Relations* (Albany: SUNY Press, 2017).

27. Marks, J., "US Makes New Push for Global Rules in Cyberspace," *Politico* (May 5, 2015), https://www.politico.com/story/2015/05/us-makes-new-push-for-global-rules-in-cyberspace-117632.

28. Maznec, B., *The Evolution of Cyber War: International Norms for Emerging-Technology Weapons* (Washington, DC: Potomac Books, 2015).

29. Hurwitz, Roger, "A New Normal? The Cultivation of Global Norms as Part of a Cyber Security Strategy," in A. Panayotis and A. Lowther, eds., *Conflict and Cooperation in Cyberspace: The Challenge to National Security* (Boca Raton, FL: CRC Press, 2013).

30. Smith-Spark, L., "Germany's Angela Merkel: Relations with U.S. 'Severely Shaken' over Spying Claims," CNN, last modified October 24, 2013, https://edition.cnn.com/2013/10/24/world/europe/europe-summit-nsa-surveillance/index.html.

31. Acharya.

32. Austin, G., "International Legal Norms in Cyberspace; Evolution of China's National Security Motivations," in A. Osula and H. Roigas, eds., *International Cyber Norms: Legal, Policy and Industry Perspective* (Tallinn, Estonia: NATO CCD COE Publications, 2016).

33. Yuen, S., "Becoming a Cyber Power: China's Cybersecurity Upgrade and Its Consequences," *China Perspectives* 2, no. 102 (2019): 53–58.

34. Pannier, B., and A. Kuncina, "Reporters without Borders Names Enemies of the Internet," Radio Free Europe Radio Liberty, last modified March 12, 2014, https://www.rferl.org/a/media-internet-report-rsf/25294297.html.

35. Chasi, Colin, "Ubuntu and Freedom of Expression," *Ethics and Behavior* 24, no. 16 (2014), 495–509.

36. Feldman, Steven, "The Ethics of Intellectual Property in China," *China Business Review* (October 24, 2013), https://www.chinabusinessreview.com/the-ethics-of-intellectual-property-in-china/.

37. Levy, Steven, *Hackers: Heroes of the Computer Revolution* (New York: Doubleday, 1984).

38. Martin, Jennifer A., "Encryption Backdoors: A Discussion of Feasibility, Ethics, and the Future of Cryptography," Honors Projects, last modified 2014, https://digitalcommons.spu.edu/honorsprojects/69.

39. Goldschmidt, Pierre, "Exposing Nuclear Non-Compliance," *Survival* 51 (2009): 1143–1164.

40. Schmitt, M., and L. Vihul, "The Nature of International Law Cyber Norms," in A. Osula and H. Roigas, eds., *International Cyber Norms: Legal, Policy and Industry Perspectives* (Tallinn, Estonia: NATO CCD COE Publications, 2016), 42.

41. Wu, Tim, *The Master Switch: The Rise and Fall of Information Empires* (New York, NY: Basic Books, 2010).

Chapter 11

1. Keegan, J., *A History of Warfare* (New York, NY: Alfred A. Knopf, 1993).

2. Brey, P., "Ethical Aspects of Information Security and Privacy," in M. Petkovic and W. Jonker, eds., *Security, Privacy, and Trust in Modern Data Management* (Berlin, Germany: Springer, 2007), 22.

3. Hansen, L., and H. Nissenbaum, "Digital Disaster, Cyber Security, and the Copenhagen School," *International Studies Quarterly* 53 (2009): 26, https://nissenbaum.tech.cornell.edu/papers/digital%20disaster.pdf.

4. Klimburg, A., "Mobilizing Cyber Power," *Survival* 53, no. 1 (2011): 41–60.

5. Brey.

6. Rouse, E., "Psychological Operations/Warfare," http://www.psywarrior.com/mybio.html.

7. Buchanan, B., and M. Sulmeyer, "Russia and Cyber Operations: Challenges and Opportunities for the Next U.S. Administration," Carnegie Endowment for International Peace, last modified December 13, 2016, https://carnegieendowment.org/2016/12/13/russia-and-cyber-operations-challenges-and-opportunities-for-next-u.s.-administration-pub-66433.

8. Gvosdev, N., "The Ethics of Cyberweapons," Ethics and International Affairs, last modified January 2014, https://www.ethicsandinternationalaffairs.org/2014/the-ethics-of-cyberweapons/.

9. Tavani, H., *Ethics and Technology: Ethical Issues in an Age of Information and Communication Technology* (New York, NY: Wiley, 2004).

10. Klimburg, A., *The Darkening Web: The War for Cyberspace* (London, UK: Penguin Press, 2017), 14.

11. Manjikian, M., "From Global Village to Virtual Battlespace: The Colonizing of the Internet and the Extension of Realpolitik," *International Studies Quarterly* 54, no. 2 (2010): 381–401.

12. Danyuk, Y., T. Maliarchuk, and C. Briggs, "Hybrid War: High-Tech, Information and Cyber Conflicts," *Connections: The Quarterly Journal* 16, no. 2 (2017): 5–24.

13. Connell, M., and S. Vogler, "Russia's Approach to Cyber Warfare," CAN: Analysis & Solutions, last modified 2017, https://www.cna.org/cna_files/pdf/DOP-2016-U-014231-1Rev.pdf.

14. Williams, B. D., "How Russia Adapted KGB 'Active Measures' to Cyber Operations, Part II," Fifth Domain, last modified March 19, 2017, https://www.fifthdomain.com/home/2017/03/19/how-russia-adapted-kgb-active-measures-to-cyber-operations-part-i/.

15. Pasentshev, E., "Destabilization of Unstable Dynamic Social Equilibriums through High-Tech Strategic Psychological Warfare," paper presented at the 14th Annual International Conference on Cyberwarfare, Stellenbosch, South África, 2019.

16. Connell and Vogler.

17. Sabbagh, Karim Michel, "Satellite—a Critical Infrastructure for Defense and Security," SES News, last modified November 19, 2015, https://www.ses.com/blog/satellite-critical-infrastructure-defence-and-security.

18. Federal Aviation Administration, "Airspace Classification," https://aspmhelp.faa.gov/index.php/Airspace_Classification.

19 de Selding, Peter B. "ITU Grapples with Small-Satellite Regulatory Challenge," SpaceNews, last modified March 13, 2015, https://spacenews.com/itu-grapples-with-small-satellite-regulatory-challenge/.

20. Cilluffo, Frank, *Trends in Technology and Digital Security: Space Satellites and Critical Infrastructure* (Washington, DC: George Washington University Center for Cyber and Homeland Security, 2017), 2, https://cchs.gwu.edu/sites/g/files/zaxdzs2371/f/downloads/DT%20panel%203%20issue%20brief%20final.pdf.

21. Cilluffo, 3.

22. Livingstone, David, and Patricia Lewis, *Space, the Final Frontier for Cybersecurity?* (London, UK: Chatham House Publications, 2016), https://www.chathamhouse.org/publication/space-final-frontier-cybersecurity.

23. Livingstone and Lewis.

24. Cited in Livingston and Lewis, 34, "Critical Foundations: Protecting America's Infrastructures," Presidents' Commission on Critical Infrastructure Protection, 1997.

25. Livingstone and Lewis.

26. Livingstone and Lewis.

27. Legal Information Institute, "18 U.S. Code Article 2331. Definitions," https://www.law.cornell.edu/uscode/text/18/2331.

28. Devore, M. R., and Sangho, Lee "APT (Advanced Persistent Threats) and Influence: Cyber Weapons and the Changing Calculus of Conflict," *The Journal of East Asian Affairs* 31, no. 1 (2017): 39–64.

29. Taddeo, Mariarosaria, and Luciano Floridi, "Regulate Artificial Intelligence to Avert Cyber Arms Race," *Nature* 556, no. 7701 (2018).

30. Scharre, Paul, "The Real Dangers of an AI Arms Race," *Foreign Affairs* (May/June 2019): 135, https://www.foreignaffairs.com/articles/2019-04-16/killer-apps.

31. Craig, Anthony, and Brandon Valeriano, "Conceptualizing Cyber Arms Races," proceedings from the 8th International Conference on Cyber Conflict, Tallinn, Estonia, 2016.

32. Mead, Rob, "10 Tech Breakthroughs to Thank the Space Race For," World of Tech, last modifed July 20, 2009, https://www.techradar.com/news/world-of-tech/10-tech-breakthroughs-to-thank-the-space-race-for-617847.

33. Scharre.

34. Taddeo and Floridi.

35. Department of Defense, "Summary: Department of Defense Cyber Strategy," last modified 2018, https://media.defense.gov/2018/Sep/18/2002041658/-1/-1/1/CYBER_STRATEGY_SUMMARY_FINAL.PDF.

36. Quoted in Gilli, Andrea and Mauro Gilli, "Why China Has Not Caught up Yet: Military-Technological Superiority and the Limits of Imitation, Reverse Engineering and Cyber Espionage," *International Security* 43, no. 3 (2019): 141–189.

37. Segal, Adam, "When China Rules the Web: Technology in Service of the State," *Foreign Affairs* 97, no. 5 (2018): 10–18.

38. Gan, Nectar, "Cyberspace Controls Set to Strengthen under China's New Internet Boss," *South China Morning Post* (September 20, 2018), https://www.scmp.com/news/china/politics/article/2164923/cyberspace-controls-set-strengthen-under-chinas-new-internet.

39. Scharre, 140.

40. Darnell, Casey, "Concern over Facial Recognition Technology Unites Progressive and Conservatives in Congress," Yahoo News, last modified May 22, 2019, https://

news.yahoo.com/concern-over-facial-recognition-technology-unites-progressives-and-conservatives-in-congress-234327186.html.

41. Gilli and Gilli.

42. Jervis, Robert, *Perception and Misperception in International Politics* (Princeton, NJ: Princeton University Press, 1976).

43. Dupont, Benoit, "Bots, Cops, and Corporations: On the Limits of Enforcement and the Promise of Polycentric Regulation as a Way to Control Large-Scale Cybercrime, *Crime Law Social Change* 67 (2017): 97–116, https://doi.org/10.1007/s10611-016-9649-z.

44. Lee, R., "The Active Cyber Defense Cycle: A Strategy to Ensure Oil and Gas Infrastructure Cyber Security," Control Engineering, last modified February 25, 2015, https://www.controleng.com/articles/the-active-cyber-defense-cycle-a-strategy-to-ensure-oil-and-gas-infrastructure-cyber-security/.

45. Wong, T. P., *Active Cyber Defense: Enhancing National Cyber Defense*, master's thesis, Naval Postgraduate School, Monterey, CA, 2011, http://hdl.handle.net/10945/10713.

46. Wong, 22–23.

47. Connell and Vogler.

48. Solis, G. D., "Cyber Warfare," *Military Law Review* 219 (2014): 1–52.

49. Kieffer, H., "Can Intelligence Preparation of the Battlefield/Battlespace Be Used to Attribute a Cyber-Attack on an Actor?" *The Cyber Defense Review* 2, no. 3 (2016), https://cyberdefensereview.army.mil/CDR-Content/Articles/Article-View/Article/1136067/can-intelligence-preparation-of-the-battlefieldbattlespace-be-used-to-attribute/.

50. Gartzke, E., and J. Lindsay, "Weaving Tangled Webs: Offense, Defense and Deception in Cyberspace," *Security Studies* 24 (2015): 316–348.

51. Valeriano, B., and R. Maness, "The Dynamics of Cyber Conflict between Rival Antagonists, 2001–2011," *Journal of Peace Research* 51, no. 3 (2014): 366.

52. Schmitt, M., "International Law in Cyberspace: The Koh Speech and the Tallin Manual Juxtaposed," *Harvard International Law Journal* 54 (2012), https://harvardilj.org/wp-content/uploads/sites/15/2012/12/HILJ-Online_54_Schmitt.pdf.

53. Schmitt.

54. Hofmann, J., C. Katzenbach, and K. Gollatz, "Between Coordination and Regulation: Finding the Governance in Internet Governance," *New Media and Society* 19, no. 9 (2017): 411.

55. Hollis, D. B., and J. D. Ohlin, "What If Cyberspace Were Fighting?" *Ethics and International Affairs* 32, no. 4 (2018): 441–456.

56. Devore and Lee.

57. Devore and Lee.

58. Harvey, F., "The Future of Strategic Stability and Nuclear Deterrence," *International Journal* 58, no. 2 (2003): 321–346.

59. Futter, A., "*War Games* Redux? Cyberthreats, US-Russian Strategic Stability, and New Challenges for Nuclear Security and Arms Control," *European Security* 25, no. 2 (2016): 163–180.

60. Axelrod, R., and R. Iliev, "Timing of Cyber Conflict," *Proceedings of National Academy of Sciences* 111, no. 4 (2014): 1298–1303.

61. Andres, R., "Cyber Gray Space Deterrence," *Prism* 7, no. 2 (2017): 91–98.

62. Andres.

63. Devore and Lee, 63.

64. Libicki, M., "The Nature of Strategic Instability in Cyberspace," *Brown Journal of World Affairs* 18, no. 1 (2011): 71.

65. Geist, E., "Deterrence Stability in the Cyber Age," *Strategic Studies Quarterly* 9, no. 4 (2015), 44–61.

66. Geist.

67. Bracken, P. "The Cyber Threat to Nuclear Stability," *Orbis* 60, no. 2 (2016): 188–203.

68. Futter.

69. Futter, 166.

70. Hilali, A. Z., "Confidence and Security Building Measures for India and Pakistan," *Alternatives: Global, Local, Political* 30 (2005): 191–222.

71. Futter, 173.

72. Denning, D. E., and B. J. Strawser, "Active Cyber Defense: Applying Air Defense to the Cyber Domain," in E. Goldman and J. Arquilla, eds., *Cyber Analogies* (Monterey, CA: Naval Postgraduate School, 2014), 72, http://hdl.handle.net/10945/40037.

73. Eilstrup-Sangiovanni, M., "Why the World Needs an International Cyberwar Convention," *Philosophy and Technology* 31, no. 3 (2018): 379–407.

74. Iasello, Emilio, "Complacency in Cyberspace May Be our Biggest Vulnerability," last modified December 2, 2015, https://fabiusmaximus.com/2016/03/13/is-offense-best-defense-in-cybersecurity-94550/.

75. Litwak, R., and M. King, "Arms Control in Cyberspace?" Wilson Center: Digital Futures Project, last modified November 2, 2015, https://www.wilsoncenter.org/publication/arms-control-cyberspace.

Chapter 12

1. Barratt, J., *Our Final Invention: Artificial Intelligence and the End of the Human Era* (New York, NY: St. Martin's Books, 2013).

2. Roto, D., D. Hicks, and B. Martin, "What Is an Emerging Technology?" *Research Policy* 44, no. 10 (2015): 1827.

3. Klein, B., "This Wonderful Lengthening of Lifespan," Fight Aging, last modified January 2003, https://www.fightaging.org/archives/2003/01/this-wonderful-lengthening-of-lifespan/.

4. Philipson, C., "The Political Economy of Longevity: Developing New Forms of Solidarity for Later Life," *The Sociological Quarterly* 5 (2015): 80–100.

5. Morgan, J., "What Is the Fourth Industrial Revolution?" *Forbes* (February 19, 2016), https://www.forbes.com/sites/jacobmorgan/2016/02/19/what-is-the-4th-industrial-revolution/.

6. Lyon, D., "Surveillance, Snowden and Big Data: Capacities, Consequences, Critique," Big Data and Society (July–December 2014): 1–13. doi:10.1177/2053951714541861.

7. Lyon, 5.

8. Lyon.

9. Kerr, O., "When Does a Carpenter Search Start—and When Does It Stop?" *Lawfare* (blog), last modified July 6, 2018, https://www.lawfareblog.com/when-does-carpenter-search-start-and-when-does-it-stop.

10. Tardi, C., "Moore's Law." Investopedia, Last modified April 20, 2019, https://www.investopedia.com/terms/m/mooreslaw.asp.

11. Diamandis, P., "Massive Disruption Is Coming with Quantum Computing," Singularity Hub, last modified October 10, 2016, https://singularityhub.com/2016/10/10/massive-disruption-quantum-computing/.

12. Marr, B., "Six Practical Examples of How Quantum Computing Will Change Our World," *Forbes* (July 10, 2017), https://www.forbes.com/sites/bernardmarr/2017/07/10/6-practical-examples-of-how-quantum-computing-will-change-our-world/#1191e82380c1.

13. Tech Target, "Encryption," accessed June 5, 2019, https://searchsecurity.techtarget.com/definition/encryption.

14. Giles, M., "The US and China Are in a Quantum Arms Race That Will Transform Warfare," MIT Technology Review (January 3, 2019), https://www.technologyreview.com/s/612421/us-china-quantum-arms-race/.

15. Giles.

16. Marr, B., "The Key Definitions of AI That Explains Its Importance," *Forbes* (February 14, 2018), https://www.forbes.com/sites/bernardmarr/2018/02/14/the-key-definitions-of-artificial-intelligence-ai-that-explain-its-importance/#d832e74f5d8a.

17. Expert System, "What Is Machine Learning? An Explanation," http://info.expertsystem.com/w3-hp-eng.

18. Matsuzaki, T., "Ethical Issues of Artificial Intelligence in Medicine," *California Western Law Review* 55, no. 1 (2018): 4, https://scholarlycommons.law.cwsl.edu/cwlr/vol55/iss1/7.

19. Zendesk, "A Simple Way to Understand Machine Learning vs. Deep Learning," (July 18, 2018), https://www.zendesk.com/blog/machine-learning-and-deep-learning/.

20. DeMuro, J., "What Is a Neural Network?" Tech Radar, last modified August 11, 2018, https://www.techradar.com/news/what-is-a-neural-network.

21. Reese, H., "Google DeepMind: A Cheat Sheet," Tech Republic, last modified August 3, 2016, https://www.techrepublic.com/article/google-deepmind-the-smart-persons-guide/.

22. Chollet, F., "The Limitations of Deep Learning," *The Keras* (blog), last modified July 17, 2017, https://blog.keras.io/the-limitations-of-deep-learning.html.

23. Sandberg, A., "Ethics for Neural Networks," Aleph, last modified 2019, http://aleph.se/andart2/ethics/ethics-for-neural-networks/.

24. Quoted in Conn, Ariel. "The Problem of Defining Autonomous Weapons," (November 30, 2016), https://futureoflife.org/2016/11/30/problem-defining-autonomous-weapons/.

25. Scharre, P., *Army of None* (New York, NY: W.W. Norton, 2018): 29.

26. Bradan, T., "Autonomous Weapon Systems: The Anatomy of Autonomy and the Legality of Lethality," *Houston Journal of International Law* 37, no. 1 (2015), https://www.questia.com/library/journal/1G1-401380004/autonomous-weapon-systems-the-anatomy-of-autonomy.

27. Schulzke, M., "Autonomous Weapons and Distributed Responsibility," *Philosophy of Technology* 26 (2013): 203–219.

28. Matsuzaki.

29. De Sio, F., and J. van den Hoven, "Meaningful Human Control over Autonomous Systems: A Philosophical Account," *Frontiers in Robotics and AI* 5 (2018): 1–20.

30. Rogers, S., "Drones by Country: Who Has All the UAVs?" *The Guardian* (August 3, 2012), https://www.theguardian.com/news/datablog/2012/aug/03/drone-stocks-by-country.

31. Sandoz, Y., "Turning Principles into Practice: The Challenge for International Conventions and Institutions," in L. Maresca and S. Masen, eds., *The Banning of Anti-Personnel Landmines: The Legal Contribution of the International Committee of the Red Cross* (Cambridge, UK: Cambridge University Press, 2008).

32. Human Rights Watch, "Q and A on Fully Autonomous Weapons," last modified October 21, 2013, https://www.hrw.org/news/2013/10/21/qa-fully-autonomous-weapons.

33. Bartels, H., "Drones Simply Aren't the Height of Technology," *IP Journal* (August 1, 2014), http://www.hans-peter-bartels.de/drones-simply-aren't-the-height-of-technology.

34. Sparrow, R., "Killer Robots," *Journal of Applied Philosophy* 24, no. 1 (2007): 62–77.

35. Manjikian, M., "Becoming Unmanned: The Gendering of Lethal Autonomous Warfare Technology," *International Feminist Journal of Politics* 16, no. 1 (2014): 48–65.

36. Manjikian, M., *A Typology of Arguments about Drone Ethics* (Carlisle, PA: US Army War College, Strategic Studies Institute, 2017), https://ssi.armywarcollege.edu/pubs/display.cfm?pubID=1367ary.

37. Carafano, J., "Future Technology and Ethics in War," *Utah Law Review* 5 (2013): 1263–1269.

38. Fischler, D., "Nuclear Weapons in the Ethics of Reinhold Niebuhr," *Perspectives in Religious Studies* 12, no. 2 (1985): 72.

39. Manjikian, M., *Cybersecurity Ethics: An Introduction* (New York, NY: Routledge, 2017).

40. The Guardian, "Microsoft 'Deeply Sorry' for Racist and Sexist Tweets by AI Chatbot," (March 26, 2016), https://www.theguardian.com/technology/2016/mar/26/microsoft-deeply-sorry-for-offensive-tweets-by-ai-chatbot.

41. Searle, J., *Minds, Brains and Science* (Cambridge, MA: Harvard University Press, 1984).

42. Matsuzaki, 268.

43. Barrett, J. (2013) *Our Final Invention: Artificial Intelligence and the End of the Human Era*. New York: St. Martin's Books.

44. Collins, H. M., *Artificial Experts: Social Knowledge and Intelligent Machines* (Cambridge, MA: MIT Press, 1991).

45. Collins.

46. Bugeja, C., "An Open Letter to Silvio Schembri," Times of Malta, last modified November 4, 2018, https://www.timesofmalta.com/articles/view/20181125/opinion/an-open-letter-to-silvio-schembri-christopher-bugeja-and-others.695079.

47. Mchangama, J., and H. Liu, "The Welfare State Is Committing Suicide by AI," Foreign Policy, last modified December 25, 2018, https://foreignpolicy.com/2018/12/25/the-welfare-state-is-committing-suicide-by-artificial-intelligence/.

48. Matsuzaki.

49. Mbadiwe, T., "Algorithmic Injustice," *The New Atlantis* (2018), https://www.thenewatlantis.com/publications/algorithmic-injustice.

50. Artificial Lawyer, "France Bans Judge Analytics, 5 Years in Prison for Rule Breakers," last modified June 4, 2019, https://www.artificiallawyer.com/2019/06/04/france-bans-judge-analytics-5-years-in-prison-for-rule-breakers/.

51. Kim, K., I. Kim, and J. Lim, "National Cyber Security Enhancement Scheme for Intelligence Surveillance Capacity with Public IoT Environment," *Journal of Supercomputing* 73 (2016): 1140–1151.

52. Kim et al.

53. Kim et al.

54. Anthopoulos, L., "Smart Utopia vs. Smart Reality: Learning by Experience from 10 Smart City Cases," *Cities* 63 (2017): 128–148.

55. Anthopoulos.

56. Robert, J., S. Kubler, N. Kolbe, A. Cerioni, E. Gastaud, and K. Framling, "Open IoT Ecosystem for Enhanced Interoperability I Smart Cities—Example of Metropole De Lyon," *Sensors* 17 (2017): 2838–2850, http://sylvainkubler.fr/wp-content/themes/biopic/images/publications/documents/Sensors_2017.pdf.

57. Anthopoulos.

58. IGI Global, "Ambient Intelligence Environments," https://www.igi-global.com/dictionary/ambient-intelligence-environments/1062.

59. Telegraph, "Privacy Expert Resigns from Google—Backed Smart City over Surveillance Concerns," last modified October 24, 2018, https://www.telegraph.co.uk/technology/2018/10/24/privacy-expert-resigns-google-backed-smart-city-surveillance/.

60. Whittaker, Z., "Security Lapse Exposed a Chinese Smart System," Tech Crunch, last modified May 3, 2019, https://techcrunch.com/2019/05/03/china-smart-city-exposed/.

61. Velghe, P., "Reading China," *China Perspectives* 1 (2019): 85–89, https://journals.openedition.org/chinaperspectives/8874.

62. Johnson, D., "Smart City Development in China," *China Business Review* (June 17, 2014), https://www.chinabusinessreview.com/smart-city-development-in-china/.

63. World Atlas, "What Is a Megacity?" https://www.worldatlas.com/articles/what-is-a-megacity.html.

64. Kim et al., 1146.

65. Taddeo, M., "Trusting Digital Technologies Correctly," *Minds and Machines* 27, no. 4 (2017), 565–568.

66. Barrett, 151.

67. Barrett, 151.

68. Barrett.

69. Nemitz, Paul, "Constitutional Democracy and Technology in the Age of Artificial Intelligence," in *Philosophical Transactions of the Royal Society A: Mathematical, Physical and Engineering Sciences*, 376, http://doi.org/10.1098/rsta.2018.0089.

70. Barrett, 156.

71. Kaplan, J., *Artificial Intelligence: What Everyone Needs to Know* (New York, NY: Oxford University Press, 2016), xiii.

INDEX

BAT, 204–208
as cashless economy, 101
China Cybersecurity Law, 142
constructivist approach to regulating
cryptocurrencies, 101–102
cyber espionage by, 78, 131
cyber sovereignty and, 144
Cyberspace Administration of China
(CAC), 285
DDOS attacks by, 184
development of cyberweapons, 282
digital human rights in, 43
Digital Silk Road, 112–119, 285
Document 9, 41, 265
extension of internet into, 107
freedom of speech and, 171–172
Google in, 159, 223
Great Firewall of China, 40, 46–47, 171
hardware and, 112–119, 239–240, 285
as hegemon, 116
Hua Wei, 113, 237–241, 287
ICANN and, 150
Law on People's Bank of China, 94
Ministry of Housing and Urban
and Rural Development
(MOHURD), 328–329
"misuse" of internet technology,
40–41
online identities and, 157, 158, 262
quantum computing and, 311
regulatory measures in, 53
reliance upon local ISPs, 92
Shanghai Cooperation Organization
(SCO), 76–77, 150–151
smart cities and, 328
social credit system, 41
state-sponsored hacks and, 168
strategy aimed at creating Chinese
internet, 208
surveillance and, 41, 157, 328
Trump administration and, 178
use of CEEW, 73
Cho, Y., 144
Chollet, F., 314
Chung, J., 144
City-states, 60
Civilian use of internet, 4, 7
Civil rights, protecting, 158

Clapper, James, 298
Clarifying Lawful Use of Overseas Data
(CLOUD) Act, 234–235
Clearnet, 52
Clinton, Bill, 12
Clinton, Hillary, 245
Clinton administration, 107, 127
CLOUD Act, 234–235
Cloud computing, 232–236, 247
international legal challenges in,
236–241
norms regarding, 235–236
CNAs (computer network attacks), 72
CNE (computer network exploitation),
70–71, 72
Code, 15. *See also* Infrastructure,
internet
Cohen, Jared, 128
Cohn, Cindy, 38
Colangelo, 169
Cold War, 12, 74, 114, 241, 296–297
Collective good
free riders and, 103
internet as, 92
Collins, H. M., 323
Collusion, 216
Colonialism, 9, 156
Commission on Critical Infrastructure
Protection, 127
Commons, internet as, 135
Commonwealth of Independent States
(CIS), 12, 13. *See also* Russia
Communications Assistance for Law
Enforcement Act, 39
Communications Decency Act, 202
Complex interdependence, 238
Complicity, 211, 231
Computer attacks, 70–71. *See also*
Cyberattacks; Hacking
Computer crimes, 179. *See also*
Cybercrime
Computer emergency response team
(CERT), 8, 65, 71, 89, 149, 170
Computer-enhanced crimes, 178–179
Computer forensic investigation, 71
Computer Fraud and Abuse Act (CFAA),
179–180
Computer network attacks (CNAs), 72

control over, 308
ownership of, 144
passenger name records (PNRs), 187
as resource, 308
sharing of among states, 187
as vital resource, 28
Data breaches, 21. *See also* Cyberattacks
Data privacy, 252
Data retention, 158
Data Retention Directive (DRD), 158
Data sovereignty/data governance, 26,
    125–126, 230
Data storage, 125–126, 277, 308–309
"Day After . . . in Cyberspace, The"
    (Rand Corporation), 127
DDOS (distributed denial of service)
    attacks, 79, 184, 290
Deception, 259–262, 273, 292
"Declaration of the Independence of
    Cyberspace, A" (Barlow), 37
Deep Ecology, 255
Deep fakes, 257
Deep learning, 312, 313–315, 322
DeepMind Project, 314
Deep web, 52
Defense Advanced Research Projects
    Agency (DARPA), 6, 187
Deibert, R., 77, 79
Demchak, C., 145
Democracy
    power and, 67
    threats to, 195–196. *See also* Election
        hacking
    transparency in, 257
Democratic National Committee, 245
Democratization, 39
Denning, D. E., 300
Deontological ethics, 260–261
Department of Commerce, 121, 239
Department of Defense, 6, 63, 141,
    143, 293
    critical infrastructure and, 129
    on cyber domain, 143
    cyber sovereignty position and, 141
    Cyber Strategy, 263, 284
    Dictionary of Critical Terms, 127
    Directive Number 3000.09, 315
    intranet, 7

Space Command, 277
    See also Military
Department of Defense information
    networks (DODIN), 22, 63
Department of Education, 284
Department of Homeland Security, 141,
    157, 284
    critical infrastructure and, 128, 129
    cybersecurity branch, 127
    cyber sovereignty and, 141
Deprivation of liberty, 174
Design perspective, 36–40, 48 (figure)
Deterrence, 296–297
Deutsch, Karl, 3
Developing nations
    cybercrime and, 177
    development of technology
        community in, 8, 268
    ethical responsibility and, 210
    global policy making and, 156
    intellectual property and, 171
    internet growth in, 8
    normative compliance and, 268
Devries, Peter, 99
Digital Bill of Rights, 43
Digital economy. *See* Cryptocurrency;
    E-commerce; Economy, digital
Digital Freedom Fund, 43
Digital Geneva Convention, 231
Digital identification systems, 144
Digital Millennium Copyright Act, 202
Digital Millennium Copyright Law, 17
Digital Silk Road, 112–119, 285
Digital space
    compared to terrestrial space, 49–52,
        50 (figure)
    See also Cyberspace; Uniqueness
        debate
Directive on Privacy and Electronic
    Communications (E-Privacy
    Directive), 29
Discourse power, 118
Disinformation, 276
Distributed denial of service (DDOS)
    attacks, 79, 184, 290
Distributed ledger technology (DLT),
    93, 96, 97, 99
Distributed responsibility, 317

Global governance, 140, 152–158
Globalization, 11, 12, 15
  of crime, 165
  inclusive, 118
Global Navigation Satellite System
  (GNSS) data, 277, 279, 280
Global positioning system (GPS)
  technology, 278, 311
Global Threat Intelligence Network, 185
Global village/global commons, 12
Global Zero Commission on Nuclear
  Risk Reduction, 130
GNSS (Global Navigation Satellite
  System) data, 277, 279, 280
Godehardt, N., 117, 118
Goertzel, Benjamin, 332
Google, 15–16, 197
  China and, 107, 159, 213–214, 223
  corporate social responsibility of, 209
  DeepMind Project, 314
  influence on information seen, 15–16
  as monopoly, 216
  policy influence of, 2
  quantum computing and, 311
  See also Internet companies; Nonstate
    actors; Search engines;
    Technology actors
Google Earth, 16
Google Ideas, 128
Gorbachev, Mikhail, 241
Gore, Al, 12, 123
Governance, 135–161
  cloud-based environment and, 233–234
  creating structures of, 138–139
  defined, 153
  disagreement about, 3–4, 136–137
  global governance view, 140, 152–158
  growth of, 4, 20–23, 23–25 (figure)
  international organizations developed
    for, 20
  issues in, 139–140
  multilateral governance, 151
  multistakeholder model of, 54, 140,
    151, 155–157, 195, 232
  nonstate actors in, 154, 155
  norms/values and, 139–140
  privacy/anonymity and, 157–158

sovereignty model of, 141–148, 157,
    158, 159–160, 195
  United Nations and, 155
  See also Cyber sovereignty
GPS (global positioning system)
  technology, 278, 311
Grafting, 54
Gray areas, 246–247
Great Firewall of China, 40, 46–47, 171
Greiman, V. A., 234
Group of Governmental Experts (GGE)
  for cybersecurity, 145
Gulf War, 273

Hackers
  Certified Ethical Hacker (CEH),
    253, 254, 264
  ethics and, 253, 254, 264, 266
  Lamprecht, 174
  Lazarus Group, 104
  tools of, 67–74
Hacking
  as act of war, 281
  birth of, 7–8
  social engineering and, 7
  state-sponsored, 168, 281. *See also*
    Election hacking
  See also Computer attacks;
    Cyberattacks
Hacktivists, 167–168
Halbert, D., 131–132, 152
Hall, M., 99
Hardin, Russell, 261
Hard power, 117
Hardware, 15, 66
  bypassing United States, 230
  China and, 239–240
  physicality of, 62
  See also Backbone of internet;
    Infrastructure, internet
Harms, 4. *See also* Risks; Threats
Harvard Information Infrastructure
  Project, 152
Harvard Law School International
  Human Rights Clinic, 318–319
Harvey, Frank, 296
Hate speech, 172–173, 197

Hayden, Michael, 6, 8, 46
Health Insurance Portability and
	Accountability Act (HIPAA), 251
Hegemons
	China as, 116
	digital superpowers as, 109
	rising, US response to, 152
	US as, 27. *See also* American nature of
		internet; First-mover advantage
Herder, J, 198
Hidden layer, 322
High crimes, 180–181
High policing, 181
History of internet, 1–32
	advent of e-commerce, 13–14
	American nature of internet and,
		2–3, 8–9
	birth of hacking, 7–8
	civilian control of internet, 7
	era of surveillance and big data,
		4, 25–29, 29–30 (figure)
	foreign suspicion of internet and, 6–7
	growth, top-down, 8
	growth of and early regulation, 4, 5,
		11–19, 18–19 (figure)
	growth of internet governance, 4, 20,
		23–25 (figure)
	growth of internet threats,
		18–19 (figure)
	growth of off-shoring, 14–15
	infancy of internet, 4, 5–10
	intellectual property and, 16–18
	key milestones in, 9–10 (figure)
	major policy issues, 3–4
	path dependence and, 5, 8, 75, 117
	phases of, 4–5
	privatization, 15–16
	rise of social media analytics, 29–30
	securitization and militarization of
		cyberspace, 4, 20–23, 23–25 (figure)
Hobbes, Thomas, 61
Hofmann, J., 153, 154
Hollis, D., 294
Hosting, bulletproof, 126, 184
Howland, C., 174
Hua Wei, 113, 237–241, 287
Hubs, 117
Human in the loop weapons, 316–317

Human out of the loop machines, 317
Human rights, 38, 39, 54, 136
	applied to cyberspace, 160
	CLOUD Act and, 235
	corporate social responsibility and,
		211, 212–214
	cyber sovereignty and, 147
	digital, 42–44, 43–44 (figure)
	internet access and, 146
	surveillance technologies and, 328
	Universal Declaration of Human
		Rights, 42, 54, 60, 136, 174,
		210, 213
Human Rights Watch, 212, 213, 235,
	317, 318
Hund, M., 90
Hybrid warfare, 275–276. *See also*
	Cyberwarfare

Iansiti, M., 107
ICANN (Internet Corporation for
	Assigned Names and Numbers),
	9, 18, 121, 145, 149–150
Ideas, 119–120, 122. *See also* Intellectual
	property
Identity theft, 167. *See also* Cybercrime
Iliev, R., 297
India, 142, 299
Indonesia, 250
Information
	curating, 27, 147
	influence on, 15–16
Information security
	Russian view of, 149
	See also Security
Information superhighway, 123
Information warfare, 22, 272–273.
	See also Cyberwarfare
Infosphere, 85
Infosphere ethics, 255, 261
Infrastructure, internet, 15, 16, 66
	physicality of, 62
	private, 166
	protection of, 63
	See also Backbone of internet; Cables;
		Critical infrastructure

Initial coin offerings (ICOs), 102
Innocence, presumption of, 309
Intellectual property, 16–18, 167
  culture and, 266
  disagreement about, 171
  See also Cybercrime
Intelligence augmentation, 333
Intelligence Community Assessment
    Report of Russian Activities
    and Intentions in Recent
    US Elections, 180
Intelligence-led policing, 185–186
International Atomic Energy Agency
    (IAEA), 236
International Civil Aviation
    Organization (ICAO), 236
International Cloud Policy Center for
    Law Enforcement (ICPCLE), 236
International Convention on the
    Prohibition of the Development,
    Production and Stockpiling of
    Bacteriological (Biological) and
    Toxin Weapons and on Their
    Destruction, 248
International Humanitarian Law
    (IHL), 321
International Human Rights
    Clinic, 319
Internationalization, 118. *See also*
    Globalization
International law, 72
  according to *Tallinn Manual*, 293–294.
    *See also Tallinn Manual on the
    International Law Applicable to
    Cyber Warfare*
  acts of war under, 72
  conflict and, 54
  customary, 60, 136
  cyberwarfare and, 181
  election hacking and, 72
  espionage and, 181
International Monetary Fund, 97
International monetary systems, 104.
    See also Economy; Financial
    governance
International organizations, 226. *See also
    Individual organizations*

International relations of cyberspace,
    paradigms for understanding.
    See Constructivism; Liberal
    internationalist paradigm; Realist
    paradigm
International society paradigm, 254–255
International Strategy for Operating in
    Cyberspace, 293
International system, 136
  as anarchic, 58–59. *See also* Realist
    paradigm
  changed by internet, 169
  conflict in, 84
  constructivist view of, 111. *See also*
    Constructivism
  emergence of, 136
  ethics and, 253
  Morgenthau on, 61
  possibility of peace in, 84
  stances toward. *See* Constructivism;
    Liberal internationalist
    paradigm; Realist paradigm
  state sovereignty and, 60
International Telecommunications
    Union (ITU), 65, 91, 121, 124, 277
Internet, 6
  access to. *See* Access to internet
  as built environment, 49
  effects of expansion of, 2
  as free good, 37
  growth of, 106
  history of, 1–32. *See also* History of
    internet
  international character of, 17, 41
  as international territory, 135
  original hopes for, 33
  as public good, 85
  as theater of war/conflict, 59
  ubiquity of, 1–2
  See also Cyberspace
Internet architects
  design perspective, 36–40
  technological determinists, 34–36
Internet Architecture Board (IAB), 153
Internet companies
  accountability of, 26, 194
  clashes with Chinese authorities, 47
  as monopoly corporations, 97

smart cities and, 326
threats and, 226
Putin, Vladimir, 7

Quantum computing, 309–311
Quantum superiority, 311
Questions for Discussion, 220–221
Brief History of the Internet, A, 31–32
Constructivism and the Creation of
Cybersecurity, 132–133
Cyber Conflict, 302–303
Cybercrime, 189–190
Ethics, Norms, and Rules, 269–270
Governing the Internet, 161–162
Internet, Technology Studies, and
International Relations, Tha, 56
Liberal Internationalism,
Cooperation, and Regimes, 110
Looking Toward the Future, 333–334
Realist View of Cyberspace, A, 81
States and Private Actors Cooperating
in Cyberspace, 242–243
Quigley, K., 131

Rand Corporation study, 127
Ransomware, 68–69, 164, 165
Rattray, Gregory, 62
Reagan, Ronald, 8, 131
Realist paradigm, 58, 84, 136, 141, 148
alliances in cyberspace and, 75–78
balance of power in cyberspace and,
74–75
beginning of cyberwar and, 78–79
cryptocurrencies and, 98–99
cyber arms control treaties and, 301
cyber arms race and, 286–287
cybercrime and, 165, 167
cyber sovereignty and, 141, 145–146
Digital Silk Road and, 114–116
Hua Wei dispute and, 239–240
view of cyberthreat and, 61–75
Real space. See Terrestrial space
Reconnaissance, engaging in, 71
Redundancies, 216–217
Referent object of security, 132
Reform Government Surveillance (RGS)
group, 203
Regimes, 76, 77, 88–90

definition of, 154
Regulation
approaches to, 54
borrowing, 55
in China, 53
of cryptocurrency, 96–97
disagreement over, 3
lag time of, 16
in Russia, 13, 53
uniqueness debate and, 53–55
See also Governance
Reinforced learning, 313
Rent seeking, 198
Ren Zhenfei, 237
Reporters without Borders, 33, 38,
213, 265
Resilience, 65, 67, 127
Restraint, 249–250, 253, 257–258
Rid, Thomas, 292–293
Rights, conferred by state, 43
Rights, positive, 42
Risks, 88
constructivism and, 132
cooperating to reduce, 86–88
of monopolies, 216–217
perception of, 130–131
See also Cyberattacks; Cyberthreats;
Security; Threats
Ristolainen, Mari, 149
Rivest, Shamir, and Adelman (RSA)
algorithm, 7
Roff, H., 241
Rolland, Nadege, 118
Rona, Thomas, 22
Rootkit, 68
Rules, 138. See also Ethics; Governance;
Norms/values
Russia, 99, 139, 142, 144
administration of cyberspace in, 146
alliances for cybersecurity, 150–151.
See also Shanghai Cooperation
Organization (SCO)
cyber sovereignty and, 144
cyberwarfare against Estonia, 78, 290
cyberwarfare against Georgia, 78–79
cyberwarfare against Ukraine, 72
cyberwarfare by, 291
DDOS attacks by, 184

Sun Tzu, 273
Superpowers, digital, 107–109,
 108 (figure)
Supervisory control and data acquisition
 (SCADA) systems, 88, 129, 179
Surface web, 52
Surveillance, 4, 5, 21, 25–29,
 29–30 (figure), 186, 245, 249
 big data and, 308–309
 in China, 41
 cyber sovereignty and, 147–148
 design and, 39
 digital-only economy and, 99
 ethics and, 249–250, 253, 255
 facial recognition technology, 286
 freedom from, 54
 growth of, 186–187
 internet service providers (ISPs)
  and, 157
 by NSA, 228–229. *See also* National
  Security Agency; Snowden
  revelations
 in Russia, 11
 smart cities and, 327–328
 state-sanctioned, 159. *See also*
  National Security Agency;
  Snowden revelations
 See also National Security Agency;
  Privacy; Snowden revelations
Swarm warfare, 316
SWIFT codes, 103–104
Symantec Corporation, 170, 185
Syntactic layer, 66
System for Operative Investigative
 Activities (SORM), 227
Taddeo, M., 194, 197, 202, 210, 330
Take, I., 155, 156
*Tallinn Manual on the International Law
 Applicable to Cyber Warfare*, 54, 143,
 145, 226, 263, 293–294
Tan, A., 214
Tan, J., 214
Taobao, 205
Tay (chatbot), 321
Technological closure, 45
Technological determinism, 34–36,
 39, 48 (figure), 106, 123

Technology
 fear of, 34
 imbuing with meaning, 34–48
Technology actors, 194–195, 223
 Chinese, 204–208
 complicity and, 231
 corporate social responsibility and,
  196–197, 203–204, 209–214, 232
 ethical liability of, 199–203
 ethical vs. legal responsibilities
  of, 201
 gatekeeping and, 196–197, 231–232
 legal responsibilities of, 201–203
 as platforms, 198–199
 policy priorities of, 223
 power of, 195
 as regulators, 206–207
 relation with states, 195–196
 responsibilities of, 196, 199–203
 See also Internet companies; Nonstate
  actors; Platforms; Public-private
  partnerships (PPP)
Tencent, 204–208
Terrestrial space
 compared to digital space, 49–52,
  50 (figure), 136. *See also*
  Uniqueness debate
 internet as part of, 13, 41
 See also Nonterritoriality of internet;
  Uniqueness debate
Terrorism, 22, 128, 276
 San Bernardino, California,
  attack, 192
 See also 9/11; Security
Thielemann, United States v., 174
Thirty Years War, 60, 145
Threats, 8, 124
 biological analogies for, 124
 PPPs and, 226
 See also Cyberattacks; Cyberthreats;
  Risks; Security
Tomlinson, Ray, 7
ToneLoc software, 174
Tools of the Trade, 67–74
Top-level domain, 120
TOR, 20, 52, 53
Total Information Awareness (TIA), 187